IMAGINING SHAKESPEARE'S WIFE

What has been the appeal of Anne Hathaway, both globally and temporally, over the past four hundred years? Why does she continue to be reinterpreted and reshaped? *Imagining Shakespeare's Wife* examines representations of Anne Hathaway, from the earliest depictions and details in the eighteenth century to contemporary portrayals in theatre, biographies, and novels. Residing in the nexus between Shakespeare's life and works, Anne Hathaway has been constructed to explain the women *in* the plays but also composed *from* the material in the plays. Presenting the very first cultural history of Anne Hathaway, Katherine West Scheil offers a richly original study that uncovers how the material circumstances of history affect the later reconstruction of lives.

Katherine West Scheil is Professor of English at the University of Minnesota. Her previous works have focused on the reception history of Shakespeare, and include *The Taste of the Town: Shakespearian Comedy and the Early Eighteenth-Century Theater* (2003), *Shakespeare/Adaptation/Modern Drama*, co-edited with Randall Martin (2011), and *She Hath Been Reading: Women and Shakespeare Clubs in America* (2012).

IMAGINING SHAKESPEARE'S WIFE

The Afterlife of Anne Hathaway

KATHERINE WEST SCHEIL

University of Minnesota

CAMBRIDGE
UNIVERSITY PRESS

University Printing House, Cambridge CB2 8BS, United Kingdom

One Liberty Plaza, 20th Floor, New York, NY 10006, USA

477 Williamstown Road, Port Melbourne, VIC 3207, Australia

314–321, 3rd Floor, Plot 3, Splendor Forum, Jasola District Centre, New Delhi – 110025, India

79 Anson Road, #06–04/06, Singapore 079906

Cambridge University Press is part of the University of Cambridge.

It furthers the University's mission by disseminating knowledge in the pursuit of education, learning, and research at the highest international levels of excellence.

www.cambridge.org
Information on this title: www.cambridge.org/9781108416696
DOI: 10.1017/9781108241724

First published 2018

Printed in the United Kingdom by TJ International Ltd. Padstow Cornwall

A catalogue record for this publication is available from the British Library.

Library of Congress Cataloging-in-Publication Data
NAMES: Scheil, Katherine West, 1966– author.
TITLE: Imagining Shakespeare's wife : the afterlife of Anne Hathaway / Katherine West Scheil, University of Minnesota.
DESCRIPTION: Cambridge ; New York, NY : Cambridge University Press, 2018. | Includes bibliographical references and index.
IDENTIFIERS: LCCN 2017061801 | ISBN 9781108416696 (alk. paper)
SUBJECTS: LCSH: Hathaway, Anne, 1556?–1623. | Authors' spouses – England – Biography. | Shakespeare, William, 1564–1616 – Marriage. | Shakespeare, William, 1564–1616 – Relations with women. | Hathaway, Anne, 1556?–1623 – In literature.
CLASSIFICATION: LCC PR2906 .S34 2018 | DDC 822.3/3–dc23
LC record available at https://lccn.loc.gov/2017061801

ISBN 978-1-108-41669-6 Hardback
ISBN 978-1-108-40406-8 Paperback

CONTENTS

ILLUSTRATIONS

ACKNOWLEDGMENTS

Many colleagues and friends have been encouraging and influential in this book's fruition, and I am grateful for their support: Clara Calvo, Christy Desmet, Michael Dobson, Frances Dolan, Andy Elfenbein, Paul Franssen, Shirley Nelson Garner, Ton Hoenselaars, Graham Holderness, Peter Holland, Doug Lanier, Jill Levenson, Randall Martin, Nabil Matar, Ellen Messer-Davidow, Andrew Murphy, Lena Cowen Orlin, Julie Sanders, Robert Sawyer, J. B. Shank, Jim Shapiro, Monika Smialkowska, John Watkins, Nicola Watson, and Stanley Wells. I am especially grateful to Paul Edmondson, who has done so much to bring the world of Shakespeare's Stratford to life, and who has been an advocate and supporter for my work on Anne from the start. Ewan Fernie has offered encouragement and advice on multiple aspects of the project. This book has benefitted from the specific expertise of Robert Bearman on the Shakespeare family graves; Amanda Bevan on Shakespeare's will; Jacqueline Green on Anne Hathaway's Cottage; Jeffrey Kahan on the Irelands; Michael Lackey on biofiction; Marek Oziewicz on young adult literature; Peter Seary on Lewis Theobald's travels; Tom Reedy on William Dugdale; and Kate Rumbold on Garrick's Jubilee. M. J. Kidnie shares my enthusiasm for Carol Ann Duffy's poem about Anne Hathaway, among other mutual interests. My early modern graduate students at the University of Minnesota continue to inspire me – Amy Bolis, Ashley Campbell, Clara Biesel, Melissa Johnson, Marc Juberg, Jenna Lester, Caitlin McHugh, David Moberly, Katie Sisneros, and Amanda Taylor. Gale Mason-Chagil, Jackie Smith, and Tobi Tanzer have kept me grounded in the real world (and on the running path), and offered crucial advice on the cover.

The anonymous readers from Cambridge University Press made this a much better book than it was before their thoughtful feedback. I have also benefitted from the wisdom of two editors at Cambridge, Sarah Stanton and Emily Hockley, both of whom provided enthusiasm and guidance for the project. Tim Mason has been invaluable for keeping track of multiple details and illustrations, and Sarah Lambert kept the production process moving forward on time.

Thanks to Ella Marchment from the Helios Collective for the photo from the production of *Hathaway*, and to Bea and Leah Koch of the Ripped Bodice bookstore for advice on women readers of historical fiction. Phillip Watson (phillip.g.watson@me.com) generously provided his beautiful illustration of New Place for me to use in Chapter 1.

I owe a special gratitude to the staff at the Shakespeare Birthplace Trust library – especially Maddie Cox, Mareike Doleschal, Hazel Gatford, Amy Hurst, and Julia Nottingham – who have tracked down countless documents and texts related to Anne Hathaway, and have answered too many queries to count. The Folger Shakespeare Library, The National Archives at Kew, and the British Library have provided exquisite spaces to work in and generous access to crucial materials. Wilson Library at the University of Minnesota, especially the Interlibrary Loan staff, supplied copious materials related to Anne from near and far.

Much of this book was written in the interstices of my two sons' lives, amid sports practices and games, school runs, and homework. The many youth baseball fields across small-town Minnesota, in between innings, provided green space to edit and contemplate issues related to this early modern woman who made her life on the other side of the world.

My husband Andy has made the journey from Stratford to Shottery with me more times than I can count, and still maintains enthusiasm about Anne Hathaway. I am grateful to him for his encouragement, his critical reading of the entire book, his ability to endure multiple conversations about Anne, and his unending confidence in me. My two sons, William and David, have grown up as this book was being written, and their sense of humor, their kindness, and their contagious energy make motherhood a complete joy for me. My parents, Bob and Jan West, and brother Jim West and family, have always been dedicated supporters of all of my endeavors, and I am so thankful for their love and encouragement. My in-laws, George and Jeanne Scheil, have likewise been caring and supportive.

This book benefited from much support at the University of Minnesota, including the Grant-in-Aid program, the Single Semester Leave program, the Institute for Advanced Study, and the Scholar of the College Award. Earlier versions of some material have been published in *The Shakespeare Circle: An Alternative Biography*, ed. Paul Edmondson and Stanley Wells (Cambridge University Press, 2015); in *Celebrating Shakespeare: Commemoration and Cultural Memory*, ed. Coppélia Kahn and Clara Calvo (Cambridge University Press,

2015); as "The Shakespeare Courtship in the Millennium," in *Critical Survey: Special Issue on Shakespeare and Biography*, edited by Paul Edmondson and Paul Franssen 25.1 (2013), 6–18; "Filling in the 'Wife-Shaped Void': The Contemporary Afterlife of Anne Hathaway," in *Shakespeare Survey* 63 (2010), 225–236; and "The Second Best Bed and the Legacy of Anne Hathaway," in *Critical Survey* 21.3 (2009), 41–53.

The epitaph on Anne Hathaway's grave in Holy Trinity Church, likely written by her daughter Susanna, immortalizes her as "so great a gift." I can't think of a better phrase to describe my own mother Janet West, to whom this book is dedicated, in honor of her steadfast loyalty, her warm friendship, and her supreme companionship.

PREFACE

Bill Cain's 2014 play *Equivocation* centers on the idea of Shakespeare writing a play about the 1605 Gunpowder Plot to blow up the Houses of Parliament and King James I. In the process of writing the play, Shakespeare discovers another side to the famous plot, and must decide whether he will tell the truth or not. The play takes place in London, and although Shakespeare's wife Anne Hathaway never appears, she is referred to several times. Early on, Shag (short for the alternate spelling of "Shagspeare") asks his daughter Judith how things are at home:

SHAG: (*Offstage.*) How's your mother?
JUDITH: An embarrassment. Like my father.
SHAG: (*Offstage.*) What's she up to these days?
JUDITH: Seducing nineteen-year-olds.
SHAG: (*Offstage.*) She sees it as her civic duty.

Later in the scene, when Shag gets irritated with Judith, he chastises her, "You're just like your mother. Why must you take up what others throw away?" Further on in the same scene, Shag asks Judith if she is interested in Sharpe, a member of his acting company. "You like him?" Shag asks. "Well, he hasn't slept with my mother. It's a start," responds Judith. Anne comes up one more time in a confrontation with Sir Robert Cecil, who threatens Shakespeare, "If, in the future, you wish to make people laugh, I suggest you leave my family alone and write a comedy about your dead son, your foolish father and your endlessly rutting wife."[1] In a play where Shakespeare's wife Anne Hathaway does not appear and has no bearing on the plot, she nevertheless hovers in the margins as a predatory and promiscuous woman, with an "endless" sexual appetite for young men.

Equivocation was developed as part of the New Works Festival and the Ojai Playwrights Conference at TheatreWorks in Palo Alto, California, produced

at the Oregon Shakespeare Festival, subsequently widely performed, and
generally well received. Charles Isherwood's review in the *New York Times*
points out that Cain, who founded his own Shakespeare company in Boston,
"brings a scholarly dedication and an impish humor to his portrait of history's
most famous playwright at work."[2] The review in the *Washington Post* by
Peter Marks notes that "Those with abundant passion for all things Bard-
tastic may find much here to nod and chuckle over," and calls the play
"catnip for iambic pentameter-parsers."[3] When the play was performed in
Chicago, it was similarly praised for its "theatre nerd-friendly laughs" and
"gags that will make Shakespearean experts and theater insiders feel as if their
membership in that sophisticated club is being fully appreciated."[4]
The *Chicago Tribune* reviewer observes that Cain "quite cleverly works
Shakespeare's biography (such as it is) into his yarn." Not a single reviewer
commented on the disparaging remarks about Shakespeare's wife – indeed, as
only a point of reference and not a fully realized character, this Anne would
not ordinarily merit attention in a review. Yet Cain's persistent off-hand
derogatory comments about her are in some ways even more disturbing,
since his play has been passed off as a work designed with "scholarly dedication" for "Shakespearean experts," and praised for its incorporation of
Shakespeare biography. What would compel a contemporary playwright to
create this version of Anne, and what needs does Cain's promiscuous Anne
serve?

Cain's 2014 play, like the texts discussed throughout this book, raises
questions about the long history of imagining Shakespeare's wife. Because
a full archive does not survive for Anne (or even a modest archive), is she fair
game, to be manipulated and exploited in order to create a particular
Shakespeare? Given the fact that there is no way to retrieve an "original"
or "real" Anne Hathaway, is there a responsibility to acknowledge the
possible "Annes," or is her only purpose to shed light on her famous
husband? Michael Lackey poses just such a question in his study of biographical novels: "Given that authors use the life of an actual historical figure in
order to project their own vision, what kind of liberties can writers ethically
take with their subject?"[5]

Imagining Shakespeare's Wife examines these representations of Anne
Hathaway, from the earliest depictions and details in the eighteenth century,
to contemporary portrayals in biographies of Shakespeare and in imaginative
literature. Throughout this book, we will meet a widely divergent cast of
characters, from an eighteenth-century teenager forging documents to please
his father, to a twentieth-century young adult novelist writing primarily for
young women, from Ivy League biographers to World War II soldiers.

No one Anne emerges from this mix, but instead, we will encounter a multitude of Annes, in conjunction with their equally fictive Shakespeares. Together, these Annes represent the many attempts to find the key to "unlock Shakespeare's heart," to paraphrase Wordsworth; to bring him into alignment with various social, political, and personal agendas; and to transform him from a Genius to a man.

As the following chapters will show, Anne's afterlife is interwoven with the history of the Hathaway family, the survival and disappearance of physical spaces to represent stages in Shakespeare's biography, and the desire for particular stories about Shakespeare. The afterlife of Anne Hathaway would not be the same if she had been allocated something else in her husband's will instead of the famous "second best bed," such as the "broad silver gilt bowl" that daughter Judith receives in Shakespeare's will. Similarly, Anne might have been constructed differently if the Hathaway cottage had not survived, or had been purchased by a private individual instead of by the Shakespeare Birthplace Trust in 1892. These hypothetical scenarios explore a central tenet of this book – that the material circumstances of history (like beds, wills, and houses) affect the later reconstruction of lives. Most important, if not for her marriage to Shakespeare, Anne Hathaway would have suffered the same fate as her sisters, inheriting a sheep or a small dowry from her father, but not the second-best bed in one of the most famous wills in history.

The Annes that have been constructed over the last several hundred years are not just efforts to reconstruct the past; they are also commentaries on the present, and on how the past is filtered through contemporary mindsets and attitudes. As Alexa Alice Joubin and Elizabeth Rivlin point out, "the ethics of appropriation have a transformational force for the participating texts and textual agents."[6] With regards to Anne, the fact that she is linked to Shakespeare, and to his cultural power, offers unusual opportunities for her to give voice to various positions; she has the potential to unleash, authorize, endorse, and promote a wide variety of conceptions of women, mother-hood, and marriage. Some of the ways that Anne's afterlife has taken shape have given credence to regressive views of shrewish controlling wives, lusty calculating paramours, or passive devotees who yearn for the return of Shakespeare to give their lives meaning. Indeed, many of the Annes discussed in this book are trapped forever in subservient roles, outshone by the glory of a famous husband, doomed to an afterlife of fantasy scenes in a picturesque English cottage, or cast in the role of angry wife. Others, though, take on Shakespeare, commandeering his plays, his genius, and even his fan base. Always constructed in relation to her famous husband and his canon of plays and poems, this most famous of literary wives provides a case study of how

ideas about women, wives, marriage, artistic inspiration, domesticity, and
sexuality have shifted over the last few centuries.

***

Henry James's story *The Birthplace* (1903) tells the story of the Gedges, who are
brought from a "grey town-library" to take over as caretakers of Shakespeare's
Birthplace in Stratford. As they are getting adjusted to life in the Birthplace, the
Gedges experience "the wonder of fairly being housed with Him, of
treading day and night in the footsteps He had worn, of touching the objects,
or at all events the surfaces, the substances, over which His hands had played,
which his arms, his shoulders had rubbed, of breathing the air – or something
not too unlike it – in which His voice had sounded."[7] Breathing the same air,
treading the same floors, touching the same objects – all characterize the desire
to commune with Shakespeare, to locate his absent presence, to participate in
what Brian Cummings calls "the cult of the past" by getting closer to
Shakespeare.[8]

Over the last several centuries, many readers have mourned the absence of
personal biographical details about Shakespeare. Nineteenth-century biographer James Orchard Halliwell-Phillipps lamented that "the general desire
to penetrate the mystery which surrounds the personal history of Shakespeare
cannot be wholly gratified."[9] A similar yearning for "Shakespeare the man"
animates the major twentieth-century archival discovery of Shakespeare's
London life. Not long after James's story was published, American Charles
William Wallace, along with his wife Hulda, uncovered Shakespeare's
deposition in the Bellott–Mountjoy case in the Public Record Office, linking Shakespeare to the Huguenot Mountjoy family's rented London lodgings. After searching through countless documents, the Wallaces
announced their discovery in 1910 not so much as factual details about
Shakespeare's London life, but rather as an unearthing of "Shakespeare as
a man among men. He is here as unmythical as the face that speaks living
language to you across the table or up out of the jostling street. He is as real
and as human as you and I who answer with word or touch or look." Wallace
proclaimed his excitement to discover a Shakespeare "as the world would
gladly know him, an unpretentious, sympathetic, thoroughly human Man."
For Wallace, these documents have "lifted the veil for a moment and shown
us a man among men, whom we call poet and seer and know as friend."[10]
To know Shakespeare as a "man among men," to call him a "friend," and to
see him in "the play of Everyday Life" necessitates a personal story – a life.

In the ongoing quest to discover a private side to Shakespeare, to make
him a "man among men," Anne Hathaway offers a particular mode of access,

connected to sexual intimacy, reproduction, domesticity, and maternal power. Through imagining Shakespeare's relationship with his wife, he becomes more human, mortal, even fallible – a husband with a wife and children – the opposite of the celebrated immortal bard and genius that eighteenth-century actor-manager David Garrick envisioned. Likewise, Anne counteracts Goethe's 1796 description of Shakespeare as a "celestial genius, descending among men."[11] Anne works against this sanctioned version of Shakespeare the immortal poet, and as the mother of his children, she provides a personal story for him. These accoutrements of his private life, however, do not always blend with the agendas of biographers and other writers of Shakespeare's life. The presence of Anne Hathaway, Shakespeare's wife, interferes with the theory that Shakespeare's vigorous urban sex life was connected to, and even inspired his literary output. There is rarely a place for Anne in such narratives. She either needs to be consigned to a "disastrous mistake" which Shakespeare must escape, as in Stephen Greenblatt's biography *Will in the World* (2004), or cast as the shrewish nagging wife who makes Shakespeare miserable, as she is in the film and stage play *Shakespeare in Love* (1999; 2014). It is thus no surprise that Anne has not always been recognized, celebrated, and esteemed. Shakespeare's Stratford wife can humanize Shakespeare as a mortal man, but she can also make him conventional rather than subversive, and the domestic, maternal, familial associations that Anne represents have been both embraced and suppressed.

This study will show that as the desire to know Shakespeare developed, and especially to know more about his private life, so too did the body of literature featuring Anne Hathaway. And, because of the survival of Anne Hathaway's Cottage (discussed in Chapter 3) and the fact that she spent her life in Stratford, she is the closest link to Warwickshire, and thus to ideas of heritage, Englishness, homes, and haunts. One reaction to Grace Carlton's play *The Wooing of Anne Hathaway* (1938) evokes just such a sentiment. The reviewer in the *Poetry Review* notes that Carlton's "construction of the speculative life of Shakespeare is a very satisfying one," because she shows him as "an impetuous man of noble and tender impulses, driven into days of despair and recklessness by the blow of little Hamlet's [sic] death and returning to the harbour of wife and home and ambition of re-building New Place in the end. Anne is not the shrew but the patient loyal wife."[12]

Nineteenth-century writers and tourists created even more Annes who complemented romantic and domestic Shakespeares. One 1896 writer thought that by connecting Anne to William, "the man who is to move the whole world with his words," one could connect with a writer who "compresses the fervor of his soul into the story of his love."[13] In other words, if one could get closer to Shakespeare's "love," it might offer access to his "soul."[14] Thomas De Quincey similarly described (in 1838–41) Shakespeare as one of "the great poets who have made themselves necessary to the human heart."[15] The history of Anne's afterlife is linked to the history of Shakespeare's changing reputation – as a national poet, godlike and ethereal; a boy husband; a writer "necessary to the human heart"; or a "bloke."[16]

In biographies of Shakespeare, Anne is an inescapable component, yet she has proven difficult to integrate into Shakespeare's life story. With no evidence that she ever spent time outside of Stratford, her position in the London phases of Shakespeare's life is unclear, but Shakespeare's presence in Stratford at the end of his life necessitates that biographers construct a narrative to explain the Shakespeare marriage. The story of Shakespeare the happily married man is often incompatible with the image of Shakespeare as the child of nature, the national poet, or the artist inspired by a robust London sex life. Overcoming, explaining, or obscuring Shakespeare's Shottery wife in order to produce a particular "Shakespeare" has been a long-standing enterprise. Anne's position as a touchstone for readers and audiences to connect with Shakespeare has given her a crucial part in the "involvement and affection and fidelity," as Deidre Shauna Lynch puts it, of literary love, particularly for Shakespeare.[17]

As part of what early biographer Nicholas Rowe called Shakespeare's "personal story," Anne Hathaway inhabits the space between Shakespeare's life and his works, constructed to explain the women *in* the plays but also frequently composed *from* the material in the plays as well. Creating an Anne out of Shakespeare's oeuvre, however, can be a very questionable enterprise. It is a truism that there are few happily married couples in his canon of plays; as one critic puts it, marriage in Shakespeare "isn't always a happy ending; sometimes it's an unhappy beginning."[18] The shortage of favorable wives in Shakespeare's works complicates the possible ways Anne is imagined; she is often cast in the role of a shrew or domineering, manipulative wife, like Kate or Lady Macbeth, but also has been fashioned as a strong-willed, independent-minded woman like Rosalind or Beatrice. Andrew Hadfield cautions against "anchor[ing] the works in the life, because not enough facts remain for us to be able to do this: we must use the works to explain the life, so that the two exist in a problematic symbiotic relationship."[19] However, we can never be certain which works, if any, Shakespeare wrote in reaction to, or inspired by, his wife. The Anne Hathaway narrator in Carol Ann Duffy's 1999 poem about Anne reflects that "Some nights, I dreamed he'd written me," and in a sense, Shakespeare *has* written her into existence, or at least, he has inspired the construction and memorialization of multiple Annes.[20]

Imagining Shakespeare's Wife outlines how readers, audiences, critics, biographers, novelists, and others who have been "drawn, moth-like, to the Shakespearean flame" (to use Samuel Schoenbaum's phrase) have invented an "Anne Hathaway" to suit their own needs and desires, moving from speculation to certainty in pinning down various details about her life in their quest to invent a private life, a marriage and a wife for Shakespeare. These Annes often reflect the inadequacy of facts to address cultural needs and desires. As Andrew Hadfield puts it, Shakespeare "has had an eventful life invented for him," and Anne Hathaway has often played a major role in these imagined life stories.[21] The central argument of this book is that the afterlife of Anne Hathaway is connected more with developments in literary criticism, in literary forms, and in ideological aims over the last three centuries, than with an accumulation of newly discovered factual evidence that eventually coalesces into a fully formed, definitive result. Although factual information has been available about Anne since the seventeenth century, she has been wildly exaggerated, outrageously degraded, enthusiastically embellished, and completely ignored. Throughout this book, I interrogate these various Annes, within their own historical contexts but also as texts that contribute to a collective sense of the possibilities for how Anne can be constructed. Organized chronologically, this book explores how and why Anne Hathaway has remained a significant figure of worldwide fascination and global obsession, analyzing why various populations and individuals have invested in, reimagined, reshaped, and even disregarded her for over three centuries.

Anne has not always had a place in Shakespeare's biography, and the first part of this book, *Establishing Anne*, chronicles her emergence to a position in his life story. While I set out the basic details about her life in Chapter 1, the remaining chapters examine how these points emerged to provide a collective and at times selective portrait of her. As the first three chapters in this book will show, the circumstances that produced Anne Hathaway are entwined with the history of property, the history of families in Stratford, the increase in tourism, and the development of literary biography. Although I cover representative works about Anne Hathaway throughout this book, it would be impossible to include discussion of every work; readers are encouraged to consult the Appendices, where I provide a full list of imaginative works together with the documentary evidence about Anne.

In the century following Anne's death, she was virtually absent from narratives about Shakespeare, in part because she had no place in conceptions of Shakespeare as a poetic genius or as the national poet. Many of the earliest travelers to Stratford literally stood on Anne's grave in order to get a better view of her husband's monument in Holy Trinity Church, without acknowledging her existence, and some illustrators have even erased the personal epitaph on her grave in favor of enlarging Shakespeare's. Likewise, actor David Garrick deliberately suppressed knowledge of Anne for his Stratford Jubilee of 1769, choosing to emphasize Shakespeare's Warwickshire influences in the countryside itself but ignoring his country wife. Only in the marginal forms of William Henry Ireland's forgeries, and Charles Dibdin's incidental music, did Anne receive any extended treatment in the eighteenth century. Chapter 2 chronicles the emergence of Anne, from her overlooked grave of little interest, to a full-fledged character in stories of Shakespeare's courtship at the end of the nineteenth century, commanding her own three-volume novel to preserve the beauty and significance of her family home and its nationalistic resonances. As the most prominent woman in Shakespeare's life story, Anne's afterlife developed alongside women's investment in Shakespeare. It is no coincidence that interest in Anne increased in the second half of the nineteenth century, in large part due to the enthusiasm of Victorian women. "Shakespeare is both known and made known by the Victorian period and its women," as Gail Marshall notes.[22]

Literary tourism, combined with the efforts of the surviving Hathaway family members at Anne Hathaway's Cottage, promoted and circulated a pastoral, domestic version of Anne that invited personal involvement and intimacy for guests to her family's Shottery property as well as for a developing audience of women. Chapter 3 shows how the Hathaway family capitalized on the Cottage's place as a commemorative space, memorializing a romantic courtship, and later serving as an enduring symbol of British perseverance and stability in times of global turmoil.

The second part of this book, *Imagining Anne*, traces how Anne is constructed in various forms of fiction and biography, from the eighteenth century to the present. This section opens with a brief interlude where I discuss the relationship between literary biography and fiction. This nexus, in fact, is where this book began, with a classroom discussion about Stephen Greenblatt's biography *Will in the World* and Grace Tiffany's novel *Will*, both published in 2004. My students were surprised that a biographer would engage in just as much speculation as a novelist; I was intrigued by the conflicting portrayals of Anne in both works. In some ways, this book is the answer to our initial questions about why, how, and for whom Anne could be constructed in such divergent ways.

Chapter 4 looks at the vastly diverse and contradictory Annes in Shakespeare biographies from the eighteenth century until the end of World War II. The expanding fields of Shakespeare biography and Shakespeare biofiction in the second half of the twentieth century comprise Chapter 5, where Anne is given a major role well beyond her documented presence. In Chapter 6, I examine the millennial texts written largely by and for women readers and audiences, where Anne plays a major part in bringing Shakespeare into alignment with feminism and with a more general female readership, as part of the long-standing interest in Anne by women. While many of these works extend past the bounds of believability, they are crucial for keeping interpretive possibilities about Anne in play.

★★★

It has been nearly fifty years since the publication of *Shakespeare's Lives* (1970; 1994), Samuel Schoenbaum's magisterial study of the people and processes behind the stories of Shakespeare's life. Inspired by Schoenbaum's work, I take up a narrower but no less important topic, looking at the lives of the woman closest to Shakespeare, and the only woman intimately linked to him for which there is documentary evidence – his own wife.

Imagining Shakespeare's Wife owes a debt to the growing field of Shakespeare's cultural afterlife, including such mainstays as Gary Taylor's *Reinventing Shakespeare* (1989); Michael Dobson's *The Making of the National Poet* (1992); Jonathan Bate's *The Genius of Shakespeare* (1997); and Jack Lynch's *Becoming Shakespeare* (2007). Other works that explore the cultural, literary, and historical genealogy of Stratford have influenced this study, including Julia Thomas's *Shakespeare's Shrine: The Bard's Birthplace and the Invention of Stratford upon Avon* (2012); Paul Edmondson's *Finding Shakespeare's New Place: An Archaeological Biography* (2016); and Paul Edmondson and Stanley Wells's collection *The Shakespeare Circle: An Alternative Biography* (2015). Germaine Greer's biography of Anne Hathaway, *Shakespeare's Wife* (2007), came out early on in my work on Anne Hathaway. While Greer does not deal with Anne's afterlife, her concern to redeem Anne from the "traditional disparagement of the wife of the Man of the Millennium" was a consistent inspiration in the face of the frequently disturbing portrayals of Anne over the last several centuries.[23] Lena Cowen Orlin's essay "Shakespeare's Marriage" (2016) shares a commitment to reconsidering the vexing narratives about Shakespeare's marriage that have been "stubbornly resistant to change," especially in the twenty-first century.[24]

The other important historical woman in Shakespeare's life, Queen Elizabeth I, inspired several works that have been important to this book.

Helen Hackett's *Shakespeare and Elizabeth: The Meeting of Two Myths* (2009)
provides an exemplary analysis for tracing the representation of literary and
cultural myths through different periods, genres, and historical contexts.
Similarly, Michael Dobson and Nicola J. Watson's *England's Elizabeth:
An Afterlife in Fame and Fantasy* (2002) served as a model for this book,
notably in their serious analysis of a wide variety of both scholarly and
popular texts and in their appreciation of the complexities and complications
of afterlives. Paul Franssen's excellent *Shakespeare's Literary Lives* (2016)
demonstrates the wealth of rich analyses possible for Shakespeare's afterlife.
Franssen observes that "constructions of Shakespeare's relations with Anne
Hathaway" merit their own study, and *Imagining Shakespeare's Wife* fills this
gap.[25] Ewan Fernie's inspiring *Shakespeare for Freedom* (2017) shares a conviction that Shakespeare matters in the contemporary world.

Consider two diametrically opposing views of Anne Hathaway. In one
rendition, she is a loving, devoted wife who ran the Shakespeare household
at New Place, embarked on a project to see her husband's plays gathered
together in his memory in 1623 (the year of her death), and was immortalized
in her epitaph as a caring mother. In another version, she is a disastrous
mistake Shakespeare made in the heat of teenage lust, a woman he gladly left
behind for a more glamorous life in London, who experienced a slow decline
until her death in 1623, illiterate and unaware of her husband's literary
output.[26] We have no way of knowing which of these versions is the closest
to the historical Anne Hathaway. However, each time an Anne Hathaway is
constructed, her creator makes a series of choices that have implications for
the final product, and that reveal the current desires of readers, critics, and
audiences for a version of Shakespeare's private life. Throughout *Imagining
Shakespeare's Wife*, I am not making a case for a "correct" interpretation of
Anne, or about the "true" Anne – such a claim, while tempting, would be
impossible – but I *am* arguing that there needs to be more responsibility in
how this malleable early modern woman has been made to serve various
constructions of her famous husband with little regard for what's at stake.
We can never recover the real Anne, but we should examine the motivations
behind the ways she has been fashioned, and the implications of these
aesthetic and historical choices.

When American clergyman Henry Ward Beecher visited Anne
Hathaway's Cottage in 1887, he lamented that Anne "has left not a single
record of herself, [but] she and her home are immortal, because hither came
the lad Shakespeare, and she became his wife." He then declared, "This is my
Anne Hathaway. Whether it was Shakespeare's, I find nothing in this cottage
and these trees and verdant hedges to tell me."[27] Readers of this book may

notice the recurrence of the terms "likely," "probable," and "desirable," all of which animate this study. Having spent a great deal of time immersed in the plethora of Annes that I chronicle in this book, I am acutely aware of my own desires about Anne – "my Anne Hathaway," as Beecher puts it – to represent her fairly, to uncover the myths and misconceptions about her, and to bring to light the diverse Annes that have resonated with real lives for over three hundred years, even if they are at times unpalatable and unsettling. In the absence of a definitive (and unattainable) Anne, the more Anne is adapted, reshaped, and reworked, the better, for keeping alive the multifarious possible Annes and not allowing one narrow account to dominate. In Frank McGuinness's play *Mutabilitie* (1997) the character of Shakespeare comments, "I do exist but not as you imagined."[28] Likewise, we can never know what the historical Anne Hathaway was really like, but we can imagine – that's what this book is about.

PART I

Establishing Anne

I

ORIGINS

ANNE HATHAWAY COULD SOLVE MANY MYSTERIES ABOUT SHAKESPEARE. She could tell us how he got his start as a playwright, how he negotiated work and family, how he grieved for the death of his only son, how he died, and whether or not he was a closet Catholic. She could reveal where he wrote his plays, if he was a family man dutifully traveling back to Stratford, or if he heartlessly abandoned his wife and children to seek fame and fortune. She could also tell us why her name is on their marriage bond, while the name "Anne Whateley" is on the marriage license. She could divulge what the term "second best bed" in Shakespeare's will really meant – whether she was devastated to learn that this was her only bequest, as she is in Vern Thiessen's play *Shakespeare's Will* (2005), or if it was a term of endearment, a private shared sign of intimacy preserved forever. Likewise, Anne Hathaway could disclose what the woman was like who was married for 34 years to the man who became the world's most famous poet – was she witty, quiet, affectionate, angry, supportive, vengeful, inspirational, or forgettable?

The questions that remain about Shakespeare's famous and elusive wife highlight the biographical problems that have accumulated about Shakespeare over the last several centuries. In turn, the answers that biographers, novelists, critics, playwrights, and others have put forward to answer those questions uncover much about the persons involved, and about the "Shakespeare" that they seek to construct through depictions of his wife.

Even though there are hundreds of portrayals of Anne Hathaway, details of her life are fragmentary and elusive. Many are less certain than one might think, and these openings have led to assumptions about Shakespeare's wife that fit with the desires of readers, audiences, and tourists for particular Shakespeares, but that obscure other equally plausible narratives. Gaps in the historical record have opened up opportunities for imaginative portrayals and reconstructions of Shakespeare's wife, as readers and audiences have filled in the absences in order to create various Annes that can reflect particular conceptions of Shakespeare – a faithful married man, a libertine, a philanderer who abandoned his wife and children for another life in London, or a sham who exists only as a front for his wife's literary achievements.

This chapter sets out factual evidence about Anne's life, which the remainder of the book explores, to show how these details have been reshaped, reanimated, selectively neglected, and embellished to produce imaginative constructions of her for centuries. The few facts that survive about Anne – her age, family home, bequest in Shakespeare's will, children, etc. – have been manipulated to construct a relationship between Shakespeare and his wife, about which there is otherwise little documentation. Likewise, evidence about Anne has been read back into Shakespeare's literary works to appease the insatiable desire to discover what Shakespeare *really* felt about women, based on the one intimate relationship we *know* he had with a *real* woman: his wife. Through Anne Hathaway, dozens of authors and readers have created an imaginary through-line to the poet's supposed innermost thoughts, desires, habits, and actions, in hopes of unlocking the secrets of his literary achievements. As a result, in the nearly 400 years since her death, Anne Hathaway has enjoyed a vigorous afterlife in the imaginations of authors and readers worldwide.

Family

The information that survives about the Hathaway family is surprisingly extensive. Anne Hathaway came from a family of long-standing residents, both before and after Shakespeare's time, of the village of Shottery just outside Stratford-upon-Avon, and her life was circumscribed by local history and events. Anne Hathaway's Cottage (discussed in Chapter 3), one of the centerpiece Shakespeare Birthplace Trust properties, still exists in much the same manner as it did in her lifetime. It was previously known as Hewlands, the Hathaway family farm dating back to the sixteenth century, estimated at between fifty and ninety acres.[1] Anne's grandfather John Hathaway was a tenant of Hewlands Farm as early as 1543, and held a number of leadership roles in the community.[2]

While the Hathaway family name is the one that has endured, in numerous historical records it appears as "Hathaway alias Gardner," or even just "Gardner," probably denoting their occupation or profession. Anne's father and several of her siblings were listed as "Hathaway alias

Gardner" in parish records, and it is likely that the family would have been identified as Gardners just as much as Hathaways until the end of the sixteenth century.[3]

Anne's father Richard (d. 1581) was a tenant on Hewlands, and the property was not owned by the Hathaways until Anne's brother Bartholomew purchased it in 1610. It is likely that Anne lived at Hewlands until her marriage to Shakespeare in 1582, but no surviving evidence confirms this. Richard Hathaway was a Shottery yeoman farmer who seemed well-connected in his community, as the relationship between the Hathaways and the neighboring Burman family attests. Burman's Farm was next to the Hathaway family farm in Shottery and would much later be developed into an auxiliary attraction for visiting tourists in the 1930s.[4] Stephen Burman was executor of Richard Hathaway's will (along with Fulk Sandells, whose name appears on Shakespeare's marriage bond), and Richard Burman served as a witness to the will. An early nineteenth-century account of the inscriptions on the floor of Holy Trinity Church in Stratford lists numerous Hathaways and Burmans in the eighteenth century, buried together in the same section, which may suggest a close, long-term relationship.[5] Other members of the Burman family had connections with both the Hathaways and the Shakespeares; Stephen Burman was executor to Anne's brother Bartholomew Hathaway's will, along with Shakespeare's son-in-law John Hall. A later Richard Burman owed money to Thomas Nash, the husband of Elizabeth, Shakespeare's granddaughter. The impressive memorial tablet in Holy Trinity Church attests to the influence that the Burman family had in Stratford and Shottery for over 300 years, and their many links to the Hathaways and to the Shakespeares suggest that all three families were closely knit and were influential in the larger community of Stratford.[6]

The connections between the Hathaways and the Shakespeares both before and after the marriage of their two famous family members underline the fact that the union of Anne and William was a match between two families with long-standing relationships. According to C. J. Sisson, "there is a marked tendency, especially among the more imaginative writers upon Shakespeare's life, to represent Anne as a yokel daughter of a peasant father, and the marriage as a *mésalliance* for the son of a prominent Stratford burgess," but Sisson points out that Richard Hathaway's "influence was potent in local affairs at Shottery" and he was "a man of substance" in the community.[7] John Shakespeare paid some of Richard Hathaway's debts as early as 1566, and they likely were close friends; the marriage of Anne and William in 1582 may have even been arranged before Richard Hathaway died the year before.[8]

Anne was one of ten children, born in 1555 or 1556, if the inscription on her grave is correct (it says she died at the age of 67 years in August of 1623). There is some speculation that Richard Hathaway may have married twice, though if so, the name of a first wife does not survive.[9] His wife Joan, named in his will, outlived him by fifteen years, dying in 1599. No details remain about Joan's relationship with Anne, although it is likely that Anne lived with her at Hewlands until her marriage in 1582.[10] Though no evidence survives about Anne's relationship with her father, (step)mother, or siblings, knowing Anne's family situation at the time she met William Shakespeare might determine whether she was desperate, reluctant, or eager to marry.

Little information survives about most of Anne's siblings, except for her brother Bartholomew, who purchased Hewlands in 1610; Shakespeare's lawyer Francis Collins drew up the deed.[11] In Richard Hathaway's will, he instructs his son Bartholomew to "be a guyde to my saide wife in hir husbandrie" and "also a Comforte vnto his Bretherne and Systers to his power."[12] Like his sister Anne, Bartholomew also married in November of 1582, and both marriages had an uncanny similarity in their timing. His wife Isabella Hancocks of Treadington died in 1617, the year after Shakespeare. Bartholomew and Isabella had five children: a daughter (coincidentally?) named Anne in 1584, an unnamed infant who died in 1588, and three sons: Richard (1583–1636), John (born 1586) and Edmund (1590–1648).[13] Though he farmed for a year or so in nearby Tysoe in the 1580s, Bartholomew later remained active in Stratford civic life (serving as a churchwarden for Holy Trinity Church from 1605–1609, for example), until his death in 1624, a year after his sister.

Bartholomew and Isabella's eldest son Richard was the one most likely to be close to the Shakespeares in Stratford, since he became a baker at the Crown in Bridge Street, just around the corner from William and Anne's final home of New Place, and he held several positions in Stratford civic life.[14] In 1623, he supplied bread for seven communions, including one on 3 August that year, just a few days before his aunt Anne died.[15] Anne's brother William may have had a more complicated relationship with her family. In 1619 he was involved in an anti-Puritan riot over removal of a maypole in Stratford, sanctioned by the new Puritan vicar Thomas Wilson.[16] Though Wilson was not well liked, his "most passionate adherent" was Susanna Shakespeare's husband John Hall, which may have caused conflict with Susanna's uncle William Hathaway, who protested the new vicar's practices.[17]

Further links between the Hathaways and the Shakespeares extended well into the eighteenth century. Shakespeare's son-in-law John Hall was the executor of Shakespeare's will as well as Bartholomew Hathaway's will in 1624.[18] Hall was also a trustee in the marriage settlement of Bartholomew Hathaway's granddaughter Isabel in 1625, daughter of Richard Hathaway of Bridge Street.[19] Richard Hathaway and his cousin Susanna (John Hall's wife) were both born in 1583, so the fact that Susanna's husband had a role in the marriage of Richard's daughter comes as no surprise.

In 1647, Anne's cousin Thomas Hathaway owned the house at No. 20 Chapel Street, just a few doors away from New Place (No. 23 Chapel Street).[20] That same year, members of the Hathaway family appear in a 1647 resettlement, undertaken by Elizabeth Nash and her mother Susanna Hall to prevent Thomas Nash's estate from going to his kinsman Edward. Two cousins of Anne, William Hathaway of Weston-upon-Avon, yeoman, and Thomas Hathaway of Stratford-upon-Avon, joiner, were parties to the resettlement; both signed and sealed the document as well.[21] In her will, Anne's granddaughter Elizabeth Nash Barnard also mentions the Hathaway family cousins, giving "Judith Hathaway, one of the daughters of my kinsman Thomas Hathaway late of Stratford aforesaid," £5 twice a year, and £50 to Joan Hathaway Kent, wife of Edward Kent, as well as £40 to the three other daughters of Thomas Hathaway (Rose, Elizabeth, and Susanna).[22] A later Hathaway cousin, Edmund Hathaway, relied on Shakespeare Hart, a grandson of William Shakespeare's sister Joan, as a trustee for his will in 1729.[23]

The long-running associations between the Shakespeares and the Hathaways were further enriched as the tourist trade developed in Stratford. When Samuel Ireland visited Shottery in 1793, he commented that the Hathaway cottage "is still occupied by the descendants of her family, who are poor and numerous." The Harts were apparently in similar dire financial straits in the eighteenth century.[24] Ireland was referred to the "humble" cottage by a "Mr. Harte, of Stratford," who suggested that an oak chair and purse in his possession had been "handed down from [Shakespeare] to his grand-daughter Lady Barnard, and from her through the Hathaway family to those of the present day." This would have been Thomas Hart (c. 1729–1794), son of George Hart, a descendant of Shakespeare's sister Joan, who lived in the Birthplace on Henley Street. Even several generations after the death of Anne in 1623, descendants of both families collaborated to take advantage of the tourism income from their famous relatives, as the next chapters will show. Thomas Hart certainly capitalized on the fame of the family; he was "known to have sold numerous chairs" as relics of Shakespeare.[25] In sum, the historical Anne Hathaway and her family had a long association with the Shakespeares, and their marriage was part of the well-established relationship between two families.

One additional surviving document related to Anne, the will of Hathaway family shepherd Thomas Whittington, confirms several facts about her. First, while more than one Hathaway family lived in Shottery around the time of Anne, Whittington makes clear that Anne was descended from the family of Richard Hathaway, since Anne's father Richard mentions Whittington in his will. In turn, Whittington's 1602 will leaves money to the poor, which he entrusted "in the hand of Anne Shax^spere, wyf unto Mr Wyllyam Shaxspere."[26] The fact that the Hathaway family shepherd singled out Anne as the recipient of his funds, rather than another family member like her brother Bartholomew, suggests that she was an esteemed and respected member of her family, and one who could be responsible for the financial bequests of others.

Marriage

Although Shakespeare's marriage to Anne Hathaway was not only typical for his day, but was also a good match for the poet, the inconsistencies in the historical records have inspired much speculation.[27] In November of 1582 the marriage license obtained from the Bishop of Worcester, "inter Willelmum Shaxpere et Annam Whateley de Temple gratfon," gave permission for William and Anne to wed with only one asking of the banns instead of the customary three. The marriage bond for £40 from 28 November was backed by family friends Fulk Sandells and John Richardson, for a marriage between "William Shagspere" and "Anne hathwey of Stratford in the Dioces of Worcester maiden." No one knows why two different names appear on these documents (Anna Whateley and Anne Hathaway), or why two different locations are mentioned (Temple Grafton and Stratford). It is possible that Anne was then living at Temple Grafton, though records of that village do not survive. Most likely, as Samuel Schoenbaum puts it, the Worcester clerk was "fairly incompetent – careless at least – for he got a number of names wrong in the Register."[28] Both Fulk Sandells and John Richardson were Shottery husbandmen; Sandells was described as a "trustie friend and neighbor" in Richard Hathaway's will, and he also was a supervisor of the will.[29] After their marriage, the Shakespeares would likely have lived with William's family in the house on Henley Street, though no evidence confirms this.

William and Anne were the parents of three children, but the nature of their family life remains a mystery. The birth of Susanna Shakespeare in May of 1583, a mere six months after their marriage and thus conceived before-hand, and the subsequent birth of twins Hamnet and Judith two years later, are the clearest testament to Anne's legacy as a mother, memorialized in the epitaph on her grave (discussed later in this chapter). It is unclear why the Shakespeares did not have additional children after the twins, perhaps due to Anne's physical condition after the birth of twins, or due to the long-distance relationship between the Shakespeares.[30] Other women of the Shakespeare family were not especially prolific either; Susanna Shakespeare Hall, who by all accounts lived with her husband in Stratford for all of their married life (as opposed to her mother's situation), only had one daughter, Elizabeth, who even though she was married twice, never had any children. Daughter Judith Shakespeare Quiney had three sons, but none lived to adulthood. According to Jeanne Jones's study of Stratford residents, "the favoured family sizes were three, four or six," making the Shakespeares well within the norm.[31] As subsequent sections of this book will show (particularly Chapter 5), the fact that daughter Susanna was conceived out of wedlock, sometime in the late summer/early fall of 1582 but well before their November wedding, has incited substantial speculation about the possible circumstances and scenarios.

Home

In 1597, Shakespeare purchased New Place, the second largest house in Stratford, and this would have remained Anne's home until the end of her life in 1623. George Vertue describes New Place in 1737 as "where [Shakespeare] livd and dyed with his wife after him 1623."[32] The community at New Place, likely with Anne in a prominent role, may have influenced Shakespeare's works in ways that have yet to be explored. "New Place was his writer's base, as well as his gentleman's family home," write Paul Edmondson, Kevin Colls, and William Mitchell.[33]

Exactly who lived at New Place during Anne's life is uncertain, though the size of the house, with ten chimneys and twenty to thirty rooms, suggests a large household. The Shakespeare family home on Henley Street may have been damaged by fire in 1594–1595, and there is evidence that by April of 1602 it had already become a tavern. Robert Bearman attests that Shakespeare's "shrewd and opportunistic" purchase of New Place in 1597, shortly after the fires in Stratford of 1594–1595, may have been "an effort by a man conscious of family obligations to provide a suitable home for his dependents in the wake of misfortune."[34] Shakespeare's father John could have lived at New Place from 1597 until his death in 1601; his mother Mary

Arden until her death in 1608; and Shakespeare's brothers Gilbert and Richard until their deaths in 1612 and 1613, respectively.[35] Hall's Croft was not built before 1613, so it is likely that Susanna and John Hall lived in New Place from their marriage in 1607, during daughter Elizabeth's birth in 1608, and probably from 1616 onward, after Shakespeare's death. Judith Shakespeare may have lived there until her marriage to Thomas Quiney in 1616. Thus, there could have been a relatively large Shakespeare circle at New Place from the start of Shakespeare's ownership. In addition to the extended Shakespeare family, New Place was also the home for Stratford town clerk Thomas Greene and his wife Lettice, at least in 1609 but probably longer, and possibly as early as 1603.[36]

The area around New Place included an extensive female community during Anne's lifetime. In addition to several neighbor widows, Shakespeare's sister Joan Hart had also become a widow in 1616, a few weeks before Anne.[37] No details survive about their relationship, but Shakespeare makes a point to provide for Joan in his will, which suggests a close connection between the siblings.[38] Daughter Susanna Hall may have even taken on a supervisory role there, since she and her husband John Hall were the executors to Shakespeare's will. In 1614, a visiting clergyman was entertained at New Place, and was provided with "one quart of sack and one quart of clarett winne given to a preacher at the Newe Place."[39] After the death of John Hall in 1635, Susanna lived in New Place with her daughter Elizabeth and son-in-law Thomas Nash, so there may have been something of a family tradition of mothers and daughters at New Place.[40]

There is no evidence that any members of the extended Hathaway family lived in New Place, though the families must have remained close, since Susanna's husband John Hall was involved with the Hathaways until his death in 1635. As a physician, it is likely that Hall treated members of the Hathaway family, as he often traveled to Shottery, though no references to family members (other than his wife and daughter) survive in his casebook. Hall was known for treating extended family members, particularly women, but he may not have felt that the Hathaway family cases were medically significant enough to document.[41]

It is unclear what role Shakespeare himself played in the New Place household and its activities, though Paul Edmondson has argued that "New Place was too fine a house for Shakespeare to have been most of his time away from it."[42] Archaeological discoveries at New Place corroborate the affluent lifestyle of the occupants during Shakespeare's lifetime: pig bones from animals slaughtered before maturity probably derive from suckling pig prepared for a special feast; and venison was associated with the well-off.

Julian Bowsher and Pat Miller also note that deer were a "high-status food species."[43] Pottery remains that date from Shakespeare's time also confirm a well-to-do status, and remains of Rhenish stoneware indicate "prosperous bourgeois living."[44]

Life at New Place, where Anne lived for 26 years, first as a single mother and later as a widow, likely included a large circle of family members and friends, but it was also the site of cottage industries that she probably managed, as part of what Paul Edmonson describes as "her lucrative, working-day world as manager of New Place."[45] Based on archaeological finds, the most likely crafts involve "bone-working (offcuts, buttons) and the production and mainte- nance of textile."[46] Shakespeare's brother Gilbert was a haberdasher, dealing in the clothing trade, so it is possible he was involved in this type of cottage industry at New Place until his death in 1612.[47] The discovery of "an oval pit, possible oven/kiln, brick storage pit and possible quarry pit" prove that "the back plots were being used for more than just gardens over an extended period of time," and these activities may have involved Anne.[48]

Some sort of brewing business at New Place is feasible, since Stratford was well known for its brewing industry. According to one statistic, in 1598, roughly a third "of the more substantial householders in the borough, had stores of malt on their premises; and in two later historical documents,

Figure 1.1. Drawing of New Place by Phillip Watson. Used by permission of Phillip Watson.

maltsters were the most common occupations."[49] A 1598 "Note on Corn and Malt" shows Shakespeare hoarding malt at New Place, which suggests a malt brewing business.[50] Paul Edmondson remarks that "It was Anne Shakespeare, rather than her husband, who would have been in charge of the malt supplies" in 1598.[51] Shakespeare also paid for a load of stone that same year, likely for repairs or renovations to New Place; given that in 1598 Shakespeare was likely in London most of the time, both the repairs of New Place and the brewing business may have been carried out by Anne.[52] Whether Shakespeare regularly spent time at New Place and did not "retire," or whether the cottage industries there operated without him, Anne Hathaway would have had a major role in either scenario.

Remembrance

Of all the surviving documents related to Anne Hathaway, the twelve enigmatic words in Shakespeare's will have received the most conjecture and fantasy, well beyond their proportion in the will, producing multiple fictions and myths about Shakespeare's final years of life, and about his personal relationships. Even a documentary historian such as B. Roland Lewis, for example, fantasizes that the will "more than any other one thing epitomizes the spirit of the man and mirrors his personality . . . the essential spirit of William Shakespeare is to be found in his will."[53] Anne appears only once, on the third and last page, in an interlineated line most likely reading "Unto my wyf I gyve my second best bed with the furniture." The fact that Anne is not mentioned by name (only as "wyf") in an interlineated line has been fodder for much speculation, yet closer inspection of the will should urge greater caution in assigning this line and its position in the will a single interpretive meaning, or even one directly connected to Shakespeare. It is worth setting out the history of this particular detail related to Anne, since nearly all interpretations of her rely on her place in the will.

The three pages of the will are in different stages of finality. Multi-spectral analysis carried out by the National Archives shows that the same ink was likely used to correct the date from January to March on page one, to add the bequests of mourning rings to actor friends, and to add the second-best bed to Anne on page three.[54] Given that the interlineated line on page three of the will referring to the "second best bed" is the only alteration on that page, it may not necessarily date from the same time as the other changes, even if it looks like the same ink. Moreover, all the changes to Shakespeare's will may derive from different causes at different times; the three sheets of paper that comprise the will are all composed on different makes of paper as well.[55]

Some changes may be attributed to clerical error, while others may be due to personal circumstances, but there is no necessary connection between the status of each of the three pages.

Further, the origin of this interlineation is uncertain. Did Shakespeare himself realize that he forgot to include his wife, and only added her at the last minute? Eighteenth-century editor Edmond Malone advanced this argument, later endorsed and expanded by biographer Stephen Greenblatt, among others. Yet the interlineation might have had nothing to do with Shakespeare, and could be a result of the copier of the will having been interrupted and having missed his place. In Shakespeare's playtexts, scholars allow for a variety of accidental omissions in the printing process and in the transmission of texts that have nothing to do with Shakespeare, but are a result of secondary circumstances; the same possibilities may obtain for the composition of a will. Francis Collins, Shakespeare's lawyer, was known for producing imperfect and uncorrected wills, and Shakespeare's was most likely written by Collins's clerk.[56] The question of whether the "second best bed" interlineation is an insult, a term of endearment, or something else, has been dealt with elsewhere, but it is worth underlining the uncertainty of interpretation that still remains. In her study of Stratford residents during Shakespeare's time, Jeanne Jones argues that "the most important items of furniture are the beds,"[57] so even the bequest of a bed is not a definitive insult or compliment. Stanley Wells points out that the will of Thomas Combe from 1608 also includes a bequest of a second-best bed to his wife: "Clearly the bequest of bedsteads, including the second-best, to his wife is made entirely without acrimony."[58]

Nevertheless, the ambiguous position of Shakespeare's wife in his will has inspired a plethora of attempts at explanation, and an equally abundant number of imaginary scenarios about Shakespeare's personal life. Nineteenth-century scholar James Orchard Halliwell-Phillipps claimed that the will included "testimonies we may cherish of his last faltering accents to the world he was leaving." Joyce Rogers similarly argues that "the interlineations ... represent the intimated gestures of the dying man." Stephen Greenblatt contends that "when Shakespeare lay dying, he tried to forget his wife and then remembered her with the second-best bed."[59] We do not know that these were Shakespeare's last words, or that they were added in rather than accidentally omitted in the transcription process. Or, if the second-best bed bequest is some sort of insult to Anne, what prompted it.

While Anne Hathaway's position in Shakespeare's will may be a result of his wishes, it is just as likely that Shakespeare had nothing to do with the

interlineated line, and fully intended his wife to have her rightful and legal
share in his estate upon his death. Legal historians have confirmed that Anne
would have had rights to a third of Shakespeare's lands (dower rights) or
income from his lands (jointure).[60] In the end, we cannot know one way or
another whether Anne Hathaway's reference in Shakespeare's will is a term
of endearment or of dismissal.

The drastically different and contradictory possibilities behind the origin
and meaning of the interlineated line underpin an overabundance of imaginary scenarios that took place behind these twelve words. Germaine Greer
points out that Anne may have been the one who encouraged Shakespeare to
make his will in the first place, since the Hathaways had more of a tradition of
making wills than did the Shakespeares. John, Mary, Gilbert, Richard, and
Joan Shakespeare did not leave wills that survive, whereas many of the
Hathaways did.[61] Ascribing the details in the will to Shakespeare himself
rather than to a clerical error, is a way to give him opinions about those
around him, especially his wife, but the specter of a deathbed Shakespeare
doling out vindictive bequests necessitates suppressing the possibility of
alternative equally plausible scenarios.

Death and Burial

Anne Hathaway died in August of 1623, according to the parish register at
Holy Trinity Church, and was buried there on 8 August, just to the left of her
husband, between his grave and his monument. Seventeenth-century lawyer
John Dowdall, in a 1693 manuscript, attested that Shakespeare's "wife and
daughters did earnestly desire to be layd in the same grave with him," though
this was attributed to a church clerk who was "above 80 years old."[62]

The Shakespeare family occupies five gravesites near the altar of the
church; burial in Holy Trinity was "prestigious but by no means exclusive,"
and depended on one's ability to pay for the burial space. William Dugdale
records the engravings of all of the family graves in 1656, so unless they were
moved sometime between Susanna's death in 1649 and Dugdale's *Antiquities
of Warwickshire* (1656), their present place is their original location.[63] Of the
Shakespeare family graves, only three have epitaphs in Latin – Anne, granddaughter Elizabeth's husband Thomas Nash, and son-in-law John Hall. Both
Shakespeare's own epitaph and daughter Susanna's are in English (his daughter Judith is buried outside the church in an unmarked spot in the churchyard). Shakespeare's epitaph is notable for its absence of his name and date of
death, and for its famous curse, "Good friend for Jesus sake forebare, / To dig

Figure 1.2. Shakespeare family graves, Holy Trinity Church. Photo courtesy of David Scheil.

the dust encloased heare. / Bleste be the man that spares thes stones, / And curst be he that moves my bones."[64]

Anne's is the only grave in the Shakespeare family plot with an epitaph on a brass marker, which is the most reliable piece of evidence that survives about her (Figure 1.3). The epitaph itself can be dated as early as 1634, since Dugdale reproduces it in his manuscript notes from that year.[65] Thus, it dates from the time of Susanna Hall, who must have had some role in its creation.[66] The epitaph reads:

> Here lyeth interred the body of Anne wife of William Shakespeare, who departed this life the 6 day of August 1623 being of the age of 67 yeares.
>
> Ubera, tu mater, tu lac vitamque dedisti;
> Vae mihi, pro tanto munere saxa dabo
> Quam mallem amoveat lapidem, bonus angelus ore
> Exeat, ut Christi corpus, imago tua,

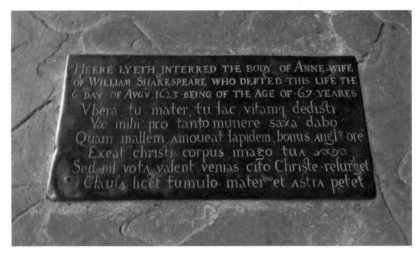

Figure 1.3. Grave of Anne Hathaway, Holy Trinity Church. Photo courtesy of David Scheil.

Sed nil vota valent venias cito Christe resurget
Clausa licet tumulo mater et astra petet
[Mother, you gave me the breast, you gave me milk and life;
Woe is me, that for so great a gift my return will be but a tomb
Would that the good angel would roll away the stone from its mouth!
And that your form, like the body of Christ, would come forth!
Yet my prayers are of no avail; come quickly, Christ!
That my mother, though shut in the tomb, may rise again and seek the stars.][67]

The most frequently suggested authors for the epitaph are John Hall (written for his wife Susanna), or Susanna herself, since the epitaph is written from a child to a mother. A third option is family friend Thomas Greene, who probably lived at New Place until 1611, and according to Edgar I. Fripp, next to Shakespeare and John Hall, was "the ablest man in the town" and was "something of a poet who wrote Latin verses in his diary." Bearman points out that Greene had moved to St. Mary's, a house next to the Stratford churchyard, in 1611 with his family. Greene and Shakespeare "clearly knew each other well," and "more evidence exists to document Shakespeare's dealings with Greene than with any other of his contemporaries." Yet the likelihood that Greene left Stratford in 1617 due to debt makes him an unlikely candidate.[68]

The epitaph is the only source of Anne Hathaway's age, and is a substantial piece of evidence about her as a mother figure, as well as about her maternal practices, particularly breastfeeding (if taken literally). In her study of breast-feeding in early modern England, Marylynn Salmon remarks that "a nursing mother represented selfless devotion to early modern men and women, for in feeding her child she gave, quite literally, of herself." Phyllis Rackin notes that "maternal breastfeeding was regarded as an extraordinary sign of devo-tion, worthy to be commemorated on a tombstone."[69] The use of breast-feeding as a particularly Puritan image of the grace of God and of divine love may suggest another likely author of Anne's epitaph, Puritan vicar Thomas Wilson, who was a close associate of John Hall, and who probably had both the Oxford education and the motivation to compose an epitaph for the mother-in-law of one of his ardent supporters.[70] In fact, Charlotte Carmichael Stopes argues that Wilson "is almost sure to have officiated at the funeral of Mrs. Anne Shakespeare."[71]

Wilson had been appointed vicar of Stratford in 1619, replacing John Rogers, but his appointment was accompanied by great unrest due to his stringent Puritan beliefs. Rioters, including Anne Hathaway's brother William, set up maypoles as a form of protest. Wilson served until 1640, making him ideally poised to compose the epitaph for the mother-in-law of his supporter John Hall. Before his stint as vicar in Stratford, Wilson lived in Evesham, and according to Ann Hughes, "would have been well-known to several of the aldermen and burgesses" in Stratford.[72] It is possible that Wilson was the visiting clergyman entertained at New Place in 1614 (discussed earlier in this chapter), and later composed the epitaph for his hostess Anne on behalf of her daughter Susanna. Regardless of the identity of its author, the fact that Anne's grave is intentionally marked with a brass plate engraved with a eulogy to her as a mother "remembered with intense affection" testifies to her important role in her family.[73] Further, the obvious references to Christian resurrection suggest a pious and devout quality to Anne, and something that surviving family members thought appropriate to immorta-lize on her grave.

Readers may have observed my use of the word "likely" in this chapter, to signal the interpretation of Anne's life that most closely matches historical documents and circumstances for women of her day. However, the most "likely" versions are not necessarily the most prominent ones in the history of Anne's afterlife, and ideological appeal has often held sway over factual sense. As the rest of this book will show, the surviving historical documents about Anne Hathaway discussed in this chapter have been stitched together, selectively recombined, neglected, and embellished, to create various narra-tives and to construct a wife for Shakespeare, but often without acknowl-edging what is missing, or what other narratives may be possible from those same historical scraps. Other Annes have been fabricated from literary characters selectively conscripted from Shakespeare's plays in order to produce a shrewish or overbearing wife who can then be dismissed; or imagined as a desirable, independent woman unlikely to resemble any historical early modern woman. The material objects connected to Anne that do remain, both legitimate and forged – love letters, a bed, a house, an epitaph, a carved casket – have been made to stand in for the haunting sense of absence in the archives about this enigmatic woman. The remainder of this book explores the reasons behind the immense variety of Annes that subsequent generations have created for their Shakespeares.

2

FORGING THE SHAKESPEARE MARRIAGE
Anne Hathaway in the Eighteenth and Nineteenth Centuries

A NYONE INTERESTED IN THE DETAILS OF SHAKESPEARE'S private life throughout the seventeenth century might well have thought of him as a promiscuous womanizer, and for good reason. Until Nicholas Rowe's biography of 1709, Anne Hathaway's name did not appear in print, nor did accounts of Shakespeare's private life include details about a wife and children. Today it is common knowledge that Shakespeare married an older woman who resided in a picturesque cottage in the nearby village of Shottery, just outside of Stratford. However, these details slowly accumulated over the last few centuries. Anne Hathaway and her family home did not become standard components of Shakespeare's life story until the nineteenth century. As we shall see, in a bizarre twist of history, prior to the imaginative forgeries of teenaged William Henry Ireland in the 1790s, Anne Hathaway remained in the margins of Shakespeare's biography, and at times she was deliberately excluded from his life story.

Not long after Shakespeare's death, travelers to Stratford sought out his grave at Holy Trinity Church. As early as the First Folio of 1623, Stratford was identified as Shakespeare's burial place; Leonard Digges's elegy alludes to "thy *Stratford* Monument," and Stratford was described in 1630 as "a Towne most remarkable for the birth of famous William Shakespeare," by a writer who was "walking in the Church to doe his devotion."[1] Val Horsler points out that Holy Trinity was "the main focus of Shakespeare pilgrims" in the seventeenth and eighteenth centuries and was "usually the first port of call."[2] Any visitor to Shakespeare's grave from at least 1634 onward (but probably earlier) would have encountered Anne Hathaway's grave and laudatory epitaph, located between her husband's grave and his monument, since antiquarian William Dugdale's transcription in his manuscript notes that year confirms the epitaph's existence.[3]

Figure 2.1. George Vertue's sketch of the Shakespeare monument, 1737. © The British Library Board. MS Portland Loan 29/246, p. 17.

Many seventeenth-century travelers lingered over Shakespeare's grave and copied down the famous curse (discussed in the previous chapter), but no visitor to Holy Trinity Church other than Dugdale commented on Anne's.[4] Both John Dowdall in 1693 and William Hall in 1694 copied Shakespeare's epitaph, but make no reference to Anne's epitaph. Further, both Dowdall and Hall remark on Shakespeare's monument, and they would have had to stand on Anne's grave in order to see it from the best angle, given that until the middle of the nineteenth century, the altar rail was behind, not in front of, the Shakespeare family graves, and visitors could walk over the stones (Figure 2.1).[5] Neither mentioned Shakespeare's wife, even though details about her literally lay at their feet.

Shakespeare the Libertine

The existence of Shakespeare's wife was largely unnoticed in the seventeenth century, in favor of long-lived anecdotal stories about Shakespeare's private life, in which he was represented as a libertine and ladies' man.[6] The longevity of "anti-Annes," that is, women (and men) proposed as substitute love interests, betrays the appeal of an imaginary love life for Shakespeare, involving rich women, courtesans, boy actors, and noblemen, among others. These alternatives have proven attractive in order to tell a salacious story about a sexually active, promiscuous Shakespeare, rather than the faithful, loyal husband of a steadfast wife, though that latter scenario exists in plenty of versions as well.

The myth of a libertine Shakespeare began before the existence of Anne Hathaway was documented in print, and its origins are unclear. The first such depiction dates from Shakespeare's own lifetime, where law student John Manningham records in his diary of 13 March 1602 the anecdote that when Richard Burbage played Richard III, a woman in the audience arranged to call for him at night under the name of Richard III. Manningham writes that "Shakespeare, overhearing their conclusion, went before, was entertained, and at his game ere Burbage came. The message being brought that Richard III was at the door, Shakespeare caused return to be made that William the Conqueror was before Richard III."[7] While it is impossible to know if there is any truth to Manningham's anecdote, it is significant that it originated during Shakespeare's lifetime, and that similar stories have endured for over 400 years.[8]

The appeal of a libertine Shakespeare continued throughout the long eighteenth century. Restoration playwright Sir William Davenant located Shakespeare's amorous advances in Oxford, and connected them to Davenant's own mother. Likely because of his desire to link his name to

Shakespeare's and increase his literary reputation, Davenant circulated the story that he was the illegitimate son of Shakespeare. Davenant's father was the landlord of the Crown Inn in Oxford, between Stratford and London, and versions of this story involve Shakespeare's seduction of Davenant's supposedly attractive mother. Kate Bennett notes that Shakespeare "would have been a personal guest of the Davenant family as taverns, unlike inns, did not offer lodging to the public."[9] John Aubrey, in his search for material to include in *Brief Lives*, first documented this tale of an affair between Davenant's mother and Shakespeare, possibly as early as the 1640s, though not circulated until much later.[10] According to Aubrey's notes, Shakespeare "was wont to goe into Warwickshire once a yeare, and did commonly in his journey lye at this house in Oxon: where he was exceedingly respected."[11] When Davenant had too much wine, he would brag that "he writt with the very spirit that Shakespeare [did], and seemd contented enough to be thought his Son. he would tell [his most intimate friends] the story as above. (in which way his mother had a very light report, whereby she was called a whore)."[12] Davenant's biographer Mary Edmond contends that there likely was a personal relationship between Davenant's father and Shakespeare, and that Davenant may have been the godson of Shakespeare, since Aubrey's fellow historian Anthony Wood records in 1691–1692 that Davenant's father was "an admirer and lover of plays and play-makers, especially Shakespeare."[13] Regardless of the truth, this anecdote persisted throughout the late seventeenth century and well into the eighteenth century, with no new evidence to support it.

Aubrey includes this version of Davenant's parentage in his life of Davenant, but omits it from his life of Shakespeare, even though elsewhere in his entry on Shakespeare, Aubrey uses material from his Davenant life.[14] He mentions that Shakespeare visited "his native country" once a year and left some money to a sister, but does not include the salacious story of Shakespeare fathering Davenant. Other than Shakespeare's sister, Aubrey does not mention any other family members, despite his claim that he received his information about Shakespeare from his neighbors, and from Davenant and Thomas Shadwell. Further, Aubrey visited Holy Trinity Church and noted his observations about Shakespeare's monument, perhaps as early as the 1640s, where he would have encountered Anne Hathaway's grave with its epitaph, but he makes no mention of it.[15] Aubrey described his manuscript as a "booke of Secrets and reflections concerning so many great persons still alive," and hoped to preserve his work for posterity.[16] While Aubrey was the first to document this oral tradition of a libertine Shakespeare, his work existed only in manuscript form until the end of the nineteenth century, and Aubrey himself felt some material in his manuscript was "too sensitive for print."[17] It is possible that associating Shakespeare with a bastard son was undesirable for a life of Shakespeare, whereas linking Davenant's parentage to Shakespeare was acceptable; thus Aubrey includes the bastard anecdote in notes on Davenant's life but not Shakespeare's.

Numerous other seventeenth-century writers propagated the link between Shakespeare and Davenant's mother. Anthony Wood, who collaborated with Aubrey and had access to Aubrey's materials, noted in his Oxford history *Athenae Oxonienses* (1691–1692) that Davenant's mother was "a very beautiful woman, of a good wit and conversation," and (as we saw earlier) that Davenant's father was "an admirer and lover of plays and play-makers, especially Shakespeare, who frequented his house in his journies between Warwickshire and London."[18] Wood does not link Davenant's parentage with Shakespeare, and neither does Charles Gildon, who attested in 1698 that Davenant's father "*Iohn D'avenant, Vintner* of *Oxford*, [resided] in that very House that has now the Sign of the Crown near *Carfax*; a House much frequented by *Shakespear* in his frequent Iourneys to *Warwick-shire*; whither for the Beautiful Mistress of the House, or the good Wine, I shall not determine."[19] Giles Jacob, in *The Poetical Register* (1719), records a similar story that Davenant's "Father's House being frequented by the famous Shakespear, in his Journeys to Warwickshire, his Poetical Genius, in his Youth, was by that means very much encourag'd; and some will have it, that the handsome Landlady, as well as the good Wine, invited the Tragedian to those Quarters."[20] This version of Shakespeare the ladies' man was kept alive and later recycled, albeit with no new added evidence.

Perhaps in his desire to build on anecdotes about a promiscuous Shakespeare, Oxford antiquarian Thomas Hearne enhanced the story in 1709, noting that "Twas reported from tradition in Oxford" that Shakespeare "us'd to pass from London to Stratford upon Avon, where he lived and now lies buried, always spent some time in the Crowne Tavern in Oxford." Unlike Wood, Gildon, and Jacob, Thomas Hearne spelled out the implications of this story, asserting that "in all probability [Shakespeare] got him," i.e. fathered Davenant.[21] The combination of a traveling poet, an Oxford tavern, and an attractive woman, proved irresistible to many writers seeking personal details about Shakespeare's life.

The tale of a philandering Shakespeare was "well known in literary circles," especially via word of mouth, and appealed to numerous seventeenth- and eighteenth-century collectors of lore about Shakespeare.[22] Antiquarian William Oldys relayed a version told to him by Alexander Pope around

1740: "Shakespeare often baited at the Crown Inn or Tavern in Oxford, in his journey to and from London. The landlady was a woman of great beauty and sprightly wit; and her husband, Mr. John Davenant ... a grave melancholy man, who as well as his wife used much to delight in Shakespeare's company." Oldys prefaced his anecdote with the phrase, "If tradition may be trusted," which testifies to the longevity of this tale, which was "endlessly repeated" throughout the eighteenth century.[23] In Oldys's copy of Langbaine's *Account of the English Dramatic Poets* (1691), he admits to knowledge of Shakespeare's wife, noting that sonnets 92–95 seem "to be written to his beautiful wife under some Rumour of Inconstancy,"[24] but Oldys never connects Shakespeare's Stratford family with his supposed activities en route to visit them.

By the mid-eighteenth century, stories of Shakespeare's philandering were deep-rooted, in both written and oral accounts, and the tale of Shakespeare fathering Davenant was now accepted as truth. Alexander Pope wrote to Joseph Spence in 1742–1743 that the "notion of Sir William [Davenant]'s being more than a poetical child only of Shakespeare, was common in town ... and Sir William himself seemed fond of having it taken for truth."[25] Drury Lane prompter William Chetwood carried on the story, remarking in 1749 that "Sir *William Davenant* was, by many, supposed the natural Son of Shakespear."[26] The Manningham anecdote resurfaced in print in 1785, and in the early nineteenth century, the Davenant story even appeared in a fictional work. Sir Walter Scott's novel *Woodstock* (1826) includes a character who, upon hearing that Davenant's mother was "a good-looking, laughing, buxom mistress of an inn between Stratford and London, at which Will Shakspeare often quartered as he went down to his native town," chastises Davenant for "purchas[ing] the reputation of descending from poet, or from prince, at the expense of his mother's good fame."[27] The myth of the sexualized "buxom mistress" who attracted Shakespeare had a long life.

As late as 1892, the American journal *Shakespeariana*, designed for a broad general readership, published an essay on "Shakespeare at Oxford," noting that the story of Shakespeare's sexual dalliances in Oxford "was put upon paper so many times."[28] Regardless of the factual basis of this story, it is significant that the model of a licentious and clandestine Shakespeare whose sexual energy inspired his literary output eclipsed available information about Shakespeare the married man until nearly a hundred years after his death, and held appeal to a wide variety of audiences. These anecdotes depend on Shakespeare traveling between London and Stratford, but they do not address the reason for his trek to Stratford – to visit his family. A wife undercuts a narrative of a lusty, sexually active urban Shakespeare, turning him into an adulterer rather than an impassioned Romeo. The citified, passionate, libertine Shakespeare still holds appeal today, though as the end of this chapter will show, the image of Shakespeare the dutiful father and family man became a viable alternative in the early nineteenth century.

Anne Hathaway's Debut in Shakespeare Biography

The epitaph on Anne Hathaway's grave was printed in Dugdale's *Antiquities of Warwickshire* in 1656 (and appeared in his manuscript notes from 1634), but it wasn't until Nicholas Rowe's 1709 biography (prefixed to his edition of Shakespeare's works) that the first two sentences about Anne Hathaway as Shakespeare's wife appeared in print. Rowe writes that "in order to settle in the World after a Family manner, [Shakespeare] thought fit to marry while he was yet very Young. His Wife was the Daughter of one *Hathaway*, said to have been a substantial Yeoman in the Neighbourhood of *Stratford*."

The source of Rowe's information was retired actor Thomas Betterton, who reportedly traveled to Stratford, went to Holy Trinity Church, and looked at the parish records. Rowe observes,

> I must own a particular Obligation to him, for the most considerable part of the Passages relating to his Life, which I have here transmitted to the Publick; his Veneration for the Memory of *Shakespear* having engag'd him to make a Journey into *Warwickshire*, on purpose to gather up what Remains he could of a Name for which he had so great a Value.[29]

It is unclear what information Betterton actually gathered about Anne Hathaway, since no surviving parish records from Holy Trinity provide evidence of her parentage, birth, or marriage. In fact, the only parish record is of her burial; according to her gravestone, she was born before parish records began in Stratford, and her marriage is absent from any Stratford record. Perhaps Betterton's information came from oral tradition rather than parish records, hence Rowe's phrase "said to have been," unless he saw parish documents that no longer survive. Such a scenario is plausible, given that, later in the eighteenth century, Edmond Malone had the Stratford Parish Register sent to him by Birmingham coach for use in completing his biography of Shakespeare. He returned the Register almost two months later after having it bound, but Malone was notorious for his careless habits, losing manuscripts and even cutting out pages for his own use.[30] Even so, if Betterton did visit Holy Trinity Church in Stratford, he likely would have stood on Anne's grave in order to get the best view of the Shakespeare monument (mentioned in Rowe's biography). Rowe's biography contains no information that Betterton could have gleaned from Anne's grave, and he omits her birth and death dates in favor of verbal lore.

Rowe's "Account" remained the standard biography of Shakespeare throughout the eighteenth century, and was reprinted in most editions of Shakespeare.[31] Although Alexander Pope made many changes to Rowe's biography in his 1725 edition, he did not change the material about Anne Hathaway.[32] Lewis Theobald, in 1733, was the first biographer to add facts about Anne derived from her grave. Theobald writes:

> [Shakespeare] married the Daughter of one *Hathaway*, a substantial Yeoman in his Neighbourhood, and She had the Start of him in Age no less than 8 years. She surviv'd him, notwithstanding, seven Seasons, and dy'd that very Year in which the *Players* publish'd the first Edition of his Works in *Folio*, Anno Dom. 1623, at the age of 67 Years, as we likewise learn from her Monument in *Stratford*-Church.[33]

No details survive about Theobald's travels, though his reference to "learn[ing] from her Monument in *Stratford*-Church" suggests that he made an excursion to Stratford at some point. Theobald makes no mention of her Latin epitaph, but he was the first to take note of the age difference between husband and wife, and to hint at a possible relationship between Anne Hathaway and the printing of Shakespeare's works.[34]

Four years after Theobald's 1733 biography, another traveler to Stratford, engraver and antiquarian George Vertue, sketched Shakespeare's monument and grave in 1737, including a figure standing on Anne's grave to get the best view of the monument (Figure 2.1). In the margin of the illustration, Vertue writes, "his wifes grave stone. anne . . . wife of Shakespeare dyd aug. 6. 1623," but he does not copy down her laudatory epitaph.[35] Instead, the epitaph praising her as a faithful mother is replaced with the word "wife" under the figure's foot, as he gazes admiringly up at the Shakespeare monument. Given the relative neglect of the most reliable piece of evidence about Anne, few in this period would have remembered her as the devoted mother and wife immortalized on her epitaph, even if she was slowly gaining a place in accounts of Shakespeare's life.[36]

Missing Anne Hathaway: David Garrick's 1769 Jubilee

One of the more intentional and carefully calculated exclusions of Anne Hathaway occurs with the most well-known Shakespeare event of the eighteenth century, David Garrick's 1769 Stratford Jubilee. Described by Nicola J. Watson as an occasion that "established Stratford, together with the surrounding countryside of Warwickshire as [the] ... location of a Shakespeare cult,"[37] it is surprising that Garrick did not incorporate the Hathaway home, or even references to Shakespeare's wife, in any of his festivities, especially since he was engaged in what Watson has called "theatricalizing real locations" in and around Stratford as part of his "general invocation of the Bard as a local."[38]

Garrick's omission of Anne Hathaway from the Jubilee is all the more striking, given the fact that he had visited her family home several years earlier in search of relics. In the 1740s, Garrick, his brother George, and fellow actors Charles Macklin and Denis Delane traveled to Stratford and were the first recorded visitors to Anne Hathaway's Cottage. According to Edmond Malone, they visited Stratford in May of 1742, where they were "hospitably entertained under Shakespeare's mulberry-tree" by Sir Hugh Clopton.[39] When Garrick visited the Hathaway homestead, it would still have been occupied by the Hathaway family, as it was until the end of the nineteenth century.[40]

David Garrick's brother George, who had visited Anne Hathaway's Cottage and purchased relics (an inkstand and gloves) from her family there, stayed behind in Stratford to work on local arrangements before the start of the Jubilee, though he spent much time "entertaining his Stratford cronies by reading aloud the letters which arrived each day from Garrick in London, exhorting George to further activity."[41] He could have set up an event in nearby Shottery to incorporate this stage of Shakespeare's life into the festivities, offering a parallel experience to the Birthplace. Garrick clearly knew about the existence of Shakespeare's wife, and it would have been logical for him to incorporate the Hathaway family home into the Jubilee plans, since he included the Henley Street Birthplace as part of the Jubilee. Garrick's friend Thomas Becket even sold books and pamphlets from the Jubilee there to capitalize on the event.[42]

Garrick did not ignore Shottery altogether, though he never linked it to Anne Hathaway. A horserace connected to the Jubilee was held on Shottery Meadows on the Friday of the event. The blurb in *The Public Advertiser* for 28 August 1769 described the area as a "delightful Meadow (allowed to be one of the finest in the Kingdom)" which "has been altered and made greatly more convenient and agreeable both for Horses and Spectators; indeed there was very little Occasion for Art, where Nature has done so much; the Stream of the surrounding Avon, the verdant lawns, and the rising Hills and Woods, form a most agreeable Scene." Lodging in Stratford was at a premium, and even neighboring towns accommodated visitors. According to one account, "some people had taken houses for a month so as to be able to entertain during the festive days. Towns and estates for miles around bulged with humanity. Tradesmen of all sorts came to ply their trades, to see what could be seen in the streets by day and to sit up all night watching the great comet." *The Public Advertiser* for 1 September 1769 carried a notice for lodgings and "Abundance of Room for Servants, Horses and Carriages" in nearby villages, including Shottery, but made no mention of the Hathaway family home.[43]

Rather than constructing a "Shakespeare" based on the historical details of his life and family in Stratford, Garrick wanted to present Shakespeare as a "sacred being," appropriate as the national poet, through a series of pageants and songs that were "deemed objects for consumption by fashionable metropolitan visitors," as Kate Rumbold puts it.[44] He deliberately omitted any reference to Anne Hathaway in order to produce a particular conception of Shakespeare, a poet bred from nature and unfettered by the mundane realities of domestic life symbolized by his wife. Garrick's Shakespeare needed to be set free from a local Stratford girl (Anne Hathaway), to make him available as the "darling boy" of nature and the "sweet swan" of the Avon.[45] One of the featured songs from the Jubilee highlights Shakespeare's youth and death in Stratford, skipping over his family life entirely, and instead praising the Avon where "by thy silver stream / Of things more than mortal sweet Shakespeare would dream" and later where "the turf ever hallowed that pillowed his head." As Michael Dobson notes, the version of Shakespeare as the national poet "seems to require the suppression of any actual historical details of his physical life."[46]

Garrick located the genesis of Shakespeare's writing in the heart of England and branded him as the "Warwickshire Will" of his famous song, but he showed no interest in establishing biographical information about the poet and linking him to the daughter of a local yeoman, one of the "Country People of Stratford" Garrick complained about in his letters, who bilked tourists but were indifferent to the Jubilee festivities.[47] Michael Dobson remarks that Garrick "sought to link Shakespeare's creativity even more directly with his local roots," but he did not want to link him to his local wife.[48] In order for the "god of our idolatry," as Garrick's *Ode* described him, to remain "ethereal, abstract and elevated," he could not be associated with someone from the area of "lowly Stratford."[49] Thus, it would have been difficult, if not impossible, to incorporate Anne Hathaway's Cottage into the Jubilee festivities without also invoking Shakespeare's domestic and married life.

Relics and Early Visitors to Anne Hathaway's Cottage

Even though David Garrick omitted Anne Hathaway from his tribute to Shakespeare, other visitors to the Jubilee began to take interest in Shakespeare's wife. When James Boswell was in Stratford for the Jubilee, he visited Holy Trinity Church, where he "viewed calmly and solemnly the tomb of Shakespeare." Boswell took note of Anne Hathaway's grave, and remarked that "His wife lies buried beside him. I observed with pleasure that she was seven years older than he, for it has been objected that my valuable spouse is a little older than I am."[50] Boswell felt a camaraderie with Shakespeare through the fact that they both married older women, and his comment shows the seeds of increasing interest in Anne Hathaway as a window into Shakespeare's personal life.

David Garrick himself never showed an interest in Anne Hathaway's Cottage except as a possible repository of Shakespeare relics. The Hathaway family, however, saw the potential in linking the Cottage to Garrick as a way to establish its legitimacy by promoting stories of the famous actor-manager's visit and of the relics he purchased there, primarily the legendary Shakespeare family gloves.[51] During the Shakespeare Jubilee, according to engraver Samuel Ireland, David Garrick's brother George bought a pair of Shakespeare's gloves and an inkstand at the Shottery home. When Ireland later visited the Cottage in the 1790s in search of relics, he recorded that "an old woman upwards of seventy" told him that "at the time of the Jubilee, the late George Garrick obtained from her a small inkstand, and a pair of fringed gloves, said to have been worn by Shakespeare."[52] The Hathaway family was clearly using Garrick's name as a way to link their home to the tourist traffic encouraged by his Jubilee. Paradoxically, Garrick's emphasis on Shakespeare's Warwickshire context focused interest on the very thing that he sought to suppress in the Jubilee – namely, Shakespeare's wife.

The shifting emphases on the material items promoted at the Hathaway Cottage can serve as a measure of Anne's developing significance in Shakespeare's life story. The initial relics offered at the Hathaway family home represent not the romantic courtship, the focus of most later tourist mementos, but, rather, evoke the figure of Shakespeare the author. The gloves and the inkstand that Garrick's brother purchased are not domestic or romantic items (like the courting chair, discussed later in this chapter), but are traces of Shakespeare the writer and gentleman, one a relic of authorship and writing, the other of Shakespeare's family trade and of gentrification. The initial attraction of the Hathaway home was thus connected to Shakespeare as an author, but by the end of the eighteenth century, the material objects promoted at the Cottage were linked to stories of Shakespeare's romantic life – the courting settle, courting chair, and a family bed. In the subsequent two centuries, these two spheres would be combined, as the Cottage gained prominence as a mythical space where William not only courted Anne, but also where he was inspired to craft some of his most famous characters and plots.

One visitor to the Cottage in 1817, Nathan Drake, was enticed by just such a sales pitch about Shakespeare relics. His story reveals that by the early nineteenth century, mementos associated with a romantic courtship between William and Anne (mainly the famous courting chair, Figures 2.2 and 2.3) were becoming part of the narrative promoted by the Cottage. Drake notes that he was "referred" to the Cottage by "the late Mr. Harte, of Stratford," who told him that Shakespeare's courting chair and a purse were still there. Wanting to "obtain the smallest trifle appertaining to our Shakespeare," Drake "became a purchaser of these relics." He also noted a bed and other furniture, but "the proprietor of this furniture, an old woman upwards of seventy, had slept in the bed from her childhood," and was always told it had been there since the house was built. Her "absolute refusal to part with this bed at any price" prevented him from purchasing it. Drake was also regaled with stories about Garrick's now famous visit, and he reprints Ireland's description of the inkstand and the "pair of fringed gloves, said to have been worn by Shakespeare."[53]

Drake, like the Irelands two decades earlier, was interested in Shakespeare's courtship of Anne, and he clearly expected to find some written remnants of their love. He lamented, "It is to be regretted, and it is indeed somewhat extraordinary, that not a fragment of the bard's poetry, addressed to his Warwickshire beauty, has been rescued from oblivion."[54] The absence of a documented relationship between William and Anne – no letters, poems, or the like – was increasingly a space to be filled with imaginary accounts of their courtship and nuptials, set amid the picturesque Warwickshire backdrop. In his *Shakspeare and His Times: Including the Biography of the Poet* (1817), Drake did his part to remedy the absence of details about Anne by including the Hathaway family history from the Stratford Parish Register, as well as the year of Anne's death from her gravestone, which he reprints from Robert Bell Wheler's *History and Antiquities of Stratford-upon-Avon* (1806).

Later nineteenth-century histories of Warwickshire promoted the connection between the Garricks, the relics related to the courtship of William and Anne, and the Hathaway Cottage. William West notes in his *The History,*

Topography, and Directory of Warwickshire (1830) that Anne Hathaway's Cottage was "a few years back, provided with several articles, affirmed to have belonged to the great poet."[55] Connecting the Cottage to the famous actor-manager helped establish its legitimacy on the burgeoning nineteenth-century tourist trail. By 1843, Charles Knight reported that "tradition . . . has associated for many years the cottage of the Hathaways at Shottery with the wife of Shakespere. Garrick purchased relics out of it at the time of the Stratford Jubilee; Samuel Ireland afterwards carried off what was called Shakespere's courting-chair; and there is still in the house a very ancient carved bedstead, which has been handed down from descendant to descendant as an heirloom."[56]

As the next chapter will discuss in greater detail, by the second half of the nineteenth century, the relics that enthralled Garrick, Ireland, and others contributed to the Cottage's status as a tourist site, shepherded and enhanced by descendants of the Hathaway family. The last Hathaway relative, Mary Baker, relied on these relics as a central component of her spiel. According to James Hain Friswell's 1864 account: "In addition to the bedstead, which might have been the 'second best bedstead' left by Shakespeare in his will to his wife, [Baker] exhibits one or two relics, and some old bed-linen and pillow-cases beautifully hand-made, and of the finest linen, with open worked seams, which, she relates, were only used in the family at the birth and death of a member of it."[57] In the latter half of the nineteenth century, the material objects on display at the Hathaway family home shifted from objects of Shakespeare's authorship, family trade, and status (an inkstand and gloves) to domestic and romantic goods (a bed, chair, linens, and a courting settle), eventually adding a family Bible, tea, and flowers of remembrance, engineered largely by Mary Baker herself, as Chapter 3 will show. Anne Hathaway's Cottage emerged as a physical space where visitors were encouraged to link William's courtship of Anne with his status as a poet, inspiring many accounts of the possible roles Anne could have played in her husband's literary career. The intersection of a burgeoning tourist trade in Stratford, active members of the Shakespeare and Hathaway families involved in promoting this traffic, and growing interest in the private lives of authors, including their homes and personal details, all combined to promote Anne to an important position in accounts of Shakespeare's life.

Shakespeare's Will

Like the details on Anne Hathaway's grave that existed with little notice for nearly a century, Shakespeare's will remained sequestered in the hands of the

Hart family for just as long. The growth of eighteenth-century antiquarian interest in Shakespeare eventually led to the rediscovery and circulation of the will, adding the "second best bed" detail to the accumulated knowledge about Anne. Reconciling the possible negative connotations of her mention in the will with the alternative view of Shakespeare as a devoted wooer and husband has been a long-standing challenge.

When engraver George Vertue sketched Shakespeare's Stratford monument and grave in October of 1737, he also crossed paths with Shakespeare Hart, the owner of the Birthplace and a descendant of Shakespeare's sister Joan. Hart informed Vertue that he possessed a copy of Shakespeare's will, which was actually a "transcript of a copy of the original in Somerset House," now in the National Archives, undated but probably from the first half of the seventeenth century.[58] According to Levi Fox, the copy that Hart owned was likely made between 1635 and 1639, after the death of Shakespeare's son-in-law John Hall in 1635.[59]

Vertue was not the only one interested in Shakespeare's will. Around the same time, in order to satisfy increasing antiquarian interest in Shakespeare, Reverend Joseph Greene, vicar and headmaster of Stratford Grammar School, apparently made two copies of Hart's copy of the will, at two different times, at some point before 1747.[60] Greene shared his passion for Shakespeare with his friend and patron, the lawyer James West, who lived just outside of Stratford, at Alscot, Preston-on-Stour. Greene cataloged West's library, made a number of transcriptions for him, and offered him one of his copies of Shakespeare's will.[61] West was keen to get his hands on a version of this document; Greene wrote to West on 17 September 1747, "I have been extremely concern'd I shou'd disappoint you in your expectation of seeing Shakespear's will: As soon as you left me I made a diligent search, and at length had ye luck to meet with it, and hope for the time to come I shall have more prudence than to promise what I cannot readily perform." Realizing the potential growing interest in the will, Greene notes, "I have now transcrib'd it a second time."

When he wrote to West, Greene pointed out that he did not think Shakespeare's will would live up to his expectations, and that West would likely be disappointed in its contents: "I am pretty certain the thing itself will not come up to the Idea you may have entertain'd of it, as it bears the name of Shakespear's will," though "the manner of introducing" the legacies and bequests is "so dull and irregular, so absolutely void of ye least particle of that spirit which animated our great Poet; that it must lessen his Character as a Writer, to imagine ye least sentence of it his production."[62] According to Greene, the will lacks the "spirit which animated our great Poet," which suggests that Greene was hoping to find clues to Shakespeare's private life, especially his true feelings about his wife and about others close to him.

Regardless of its disappointing "dull and irregular" content, soon after Greene sent his copy of the will to West, interest in Shakespeare's will began to increase, as did the availability of the will to a broader audience, and it was not long before the meaning of Shakespeare's bequest to his wife became a topic of widespread speculation. Editor Lewis Theobald printed Shakespeare's will for the first time, in the posthumous third edition of his *Works of Shakespeare* in 1752. This first mass reproduction of the will entailed two important changes. Theobald reproduced the bequest to Anne in the body of the will (standard printing practice of the time), not as an interlineation, camouflaging the possibility that this line was an afterthought. More importantly, the line reads: "*Item*, I give unto my Wife my brown best Bed with the Furniture."[63] By changing "second best bed" to "brown best bed," it is unclear whether Theobald wanted to soften the bequest to Shakespeare's wife, or whether he was rectifying what he thought was an error in transcription. Either way, Theobald's version offered an alternative reading of the will, which perhaps sought to reconcile Anne's mention in the will with the Anne of the picturesque Shottery cottage, mythologized in a growing number of romantic stories of the Shakespeares' young love.

Theobald's more positive presentation of the will in 1752, and concurrently of the relationship between the Shakespeares, was soon challenged. Editor Edmond Malone went to see Shakespeare's will in 1776, and was the first to advance a negative interpretation of Shakespeare's wife, grounded in his interpretation of this twelve-word passage. As Chapter 4 will show in greater detail, Malone had long planned his own biography of Shakespeare, but it never materialized.[64] What material Malone did compile about Shakespeare's life appears in his 1780 *Supplement* to the Johnson–Steevens 1778 edition of Shakespeare's works, where he used the will as an opportunity to excise Anne from Shakespeare's life story and demote her from any possible position of affection: "His wife had not wholly escaped his memory; he had forgot her, – he had recollected her, – but so recollected her, as more strongly to mark how little he esteemed her; he had already (as it is vulgarly expressed) cut her off, not indeed with a shilling, but with an old bed."[65] Malone's interpretation of this bequest helped him make a case for a marriage doomed from the start, and is the cornerstone of his large-scale denunciation of Anne.

Malone's impassioned attempt to construct a vengeful, malicious Shakespeare was countered by other readers of the will, who sought to advance the opposite view by neutralizing the type of bed Anne received, following

Theobald's lead in calling it a "brown best bed" rather than a "second best bed." A transcribed copy of the will from the register in the Prerogative Court of Canterbury was first printed in *Biographia Britannica* (1763), where the bequest to Anne appeared as "I give unto my wife my brown best bed, with the furniture."[66] Several subsequent works repeated the same phrase, including that of Samuel Johnson, who in 1765 "happily averted" the "impassioned debate" over this bequest. The author of *The Modern Universal British Traveller* (1779), perhaps influenced by Johnson, contended that Shakespeare "lived very happy" as a married man, and brought his wife to London as soon as he had enough money.[67] In 1788 George Steevens sought further evidence to defend Anne Hathaway, reprinting the epitaph that describes her as a loyal mother. Steevens also commented that Shakespeare would have valued "the love of his wife who had already brought him two children."[68]

The circulation of details from Shakespeare's will in the later eighteenth century brought to light the possibility of multiple interpretations of Anne Hathaway and of the Shakespeare marriage, discussed further in Chapter 4. Now, in addition to being the devoted mother described on her epitaph, she is also the inheritor of a piece of furniture that is either a sign of an intimate relationship with Shakespeare, or of a deep animosity between them. At the end of the eighteenth century, interpretations of Anne Hathaway began to proliferate, in tandem with antiquarianism, tourism, bibliography, and biography, all of which encouraged additional interest in Shakespeare's private life. The indisputable existence of a wife, as evidenced by the physical space of her family home, her grave next to Shakespeare's, her reference in the will, and by the increasing number of imaginative works about her, made Anne a battleground for competing interpretations of Shakespeare the man. By the end of the eighteenth century, authors seeking to imagine a romantic life for Shakespeare had to either involve Anne, or excise her by setting Shakespeare's amorous adventures in London, and in the process forsaking the potential of the Warwickshire countryside as a prime romantic setting.

Imagining the Shakespeare Courtship

The first imaginative version of Shakespeare's relationship with his wife comes not from a novelist, poet, or dramatist, but rather from a teenaged boy, motivated by the chance to appease his father's failed relic-seeking trip to Stratford. William Ireland was eighteen when he traveled to Stratford with his father, engraver and artist Samuel Ireland. William Ireland has been derided as a "calculating criminal,"[69] but he had a knack for discerning what was missing from the landscape of Shakespeariana, and for identifying the related desires of audiences and readers. One of Ireland's most famous forgeries was aimed at the absence of documentation about the intimate relationship between Shakespeare and his wife. The initial success of Ireland's initiative is a testament to the intense desire to know more about Shakespeare's private life, and to the need to create a "Shakespeare" who is a lover and a poet. This "man of flesh and blood," as Paul Franssen calls him, embodies the shift from an eighteenth-century Shakespeare who is "the abstract semi-divine authority" to the more humanized Shakespeare of the nineteenth century.[70]

In 1793, the Irelands journeyed to Stratford in search of any relics or papers connected to Shakespeare. The Irelands were part of a growing number of pilgrims coming to Stratford, from the mid-eighteenth century onward. Roger Pringle explains that between 1726 and 1754, "the roads into Stratford from Birmingham, Banbury, Oxford/Shipston, Bromsgrove/Alcester, and Warwick were turnpiked, helping to boost the town's prosperity from trade and visitors."[71] Local Stratfordian and Shakespeare aficionado John Jordan catered to this increased tourist traffic, and he took the Irelands around in search of clues to the poet's personal life. Jordan promoted a connection between Anne and the lost details of Shakespeare's life. He reminisces, "Perhaps the reader will be surprised that his wife should only have a legacy of a bed; but we must naturally suppose that she was provided either by a marriage settlement, or what is more probable, possessed an estate at Shottery, which she obtained as sole heiress to her father Mr. Hathaway, and which she, either herself alone or jointly with Mr. Shakespeare, conveyed to her daughter Judith in fee, after her own decease."[72] Jordan's comments hint at the mystique of lost materials related to Shakespeare that inspired such relic hunters.

It will come as no surprise that Jordan took the Irelands to the Hathaway family home, which was still occupied by members of the Hathaway family, where Ireland bought a bugle purse and what he thought was Shakespeare's "courting chair" (Figure 2.2).[73] The initials " W.A.S." for William and Anne Shakespeare (Figure 2.3) may have been added later by William Ireland to further enhance the chair's significance, part of what Ellen MacKay describes as an attempt to "[manufacture] an archive that is plainly the wish-fulfillment of his bardolatrous age."[74] It is worth pointing out that this relic of the Shakespeares' courtship has come full circle; it disappeared after Ireland's purchase, and was returned to the Hathaway Cottage after it was purchased by the Shakespeare Birthplace Trust at an auction in 2002; it continues to serve as a physical testament to the idea of Shakespeare's courtship.

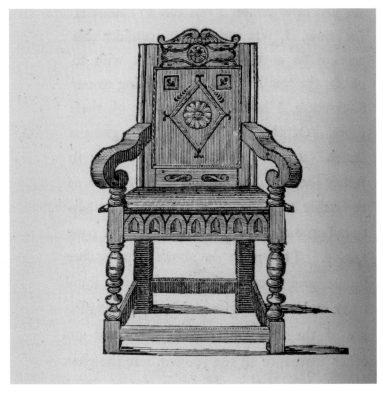

Figure 2.2. The courting chair, from Samuel Ireland, *Picturesque Views on the Upper, or Warwickshire Avon*, 1795.

Samuel Ireland was not only interested in the relics at Anne Hathaway's Cottage, he was also apparently captivated by the actual place where Shakespeare's wife spent part of her life, and perhaps where the poet courted her. Ireland sketched the Cottage to include in his *Picturesque Views* of 1795, which was the first of a long line of illustrations of the Cottage, with the caption "House at Shotery, in which Ann Hathaway the wife of Shakspere resided," immortalizing the Cottage's connection to Shakespeare (see Chapter 3, Figure 3.1). Ireland's interest in Anne Hathaway's family home had little to do with the woman herself, and more to do with his desire to acquire any existing relics or items that might have a connection to Shakespeare. Ireland was also not above embellishing and even misrepresenting the scenes he illustrated, in order to foreground his interests. When he reproduces Shakespeare's monument and grave from Holy Trinity Church (Figure 2.4), not only does he omit Anne's grave and epitaph, which

Figure 2.3. The courting chair, Anne Hathaway's Cottage. Image courtesy of the Shakespeare Birthplace Trust.

occupied the space between Shakespeare's grave and the monument, he also replaces her grave with an enlarged version of the famous curse on Shakespeare's grave. Readers of Ireland's *Picturesque Views* would thus have no idea that Shakespeare's wife was buried next to him, with a prominent brass plaque commemorating her as a devoted mother.

Samuel Ireland's teenaged son William saw the potential for creating fake relics to fabricate a romantic relationship between William and Anne, and the

Figure 2.4. "Shakspeare's Monument," from Samuel Ireland, *Picturesque Views on the Upper, or Warwickshire Avon*, 1795. Image courtesy of the Folger Shakespeare Library.

extensive popularity of these forgeries speaks to a widespread desire to give Shakespeare a personal life. Robert Bell Wheler remarked in his 1814 *A Guide to Stratford-upon-Avon* that John Jordan may have given Ireland "his first information on which he created his visionary falsehood."[75] After their largely unsuccessful trip to Stratford, in order to appease his disappointed father, William Ireland announced that a "Mr. H" had given him a trunk of Shakespeare-related documents, including a profession of Shakespeare's Protestant faith, a letter from Queen Elizabeth to Shakespeare, playhouse documents, and a love letter and love poem from Shakespeare to Anne Hathaway, complete with a lock of Shakespeare's hair (Figure 2.5).[76]

The love letter implores Anne to "perfume this my poor lock with thy balmy kisses for then indeed shall kings themselves bow and pay homage to it," assuring her that "no rude hand that knotted it thy Willys alone hath done the work." Shakespeare boldly proclaims his love for her, exclaiming, "O Anna do I love do I cherish thee in my heart for thou art as a tall Cedar stretching forth its branches and succoring the smaller plants from nipping Winneterre or the boysterouse Windes." The love letter is accompanied by a love poem of several stanzas, including the following:

> Is there inne heavenne aught more rare
> Thanne thou sweete Nymphe of Avon fayre
> Is there onne Earthe a Manne more trewe
> Thanne Willy Shakspeare is toe you.

In spite of the poor quality of the verse, William Ireland was the first to document a romantic life for William and Anne, certified with a bodily remembrance from William himself. Ireland may have drawn part of his inspiration from Mary Hornby, caretaker of the Birthplace when the Irelands visited Stratford. According to W. T. Moncrieff's 1824 *Excursion to Warwick*, Hornby "used to point out a small deep cupboard, in a dark corner of the room where Shakespeare was born, in which, she stated, a letter was found some years since, addressed by Shakespeare to his wife, from the play-house in London, which she used to exhibit, but which was stolen by some visitors."[77] Hornby never produced such a letter, but it is likely that her claim may have motivated Ireland to create a similar document.

Building on the interest in the love letter between the Shakespeares, William Ireland undertook a related project in June of 1795 to further supplement this romance. Ireland claimed to have found a version of Shakespeare's will, dated 11 February 1611, which included a substantial bequest to "mye deare Wife" of an impressive £180, a "gray velvet suit edged with silver, three rings, and a silver case containing a small portrait for

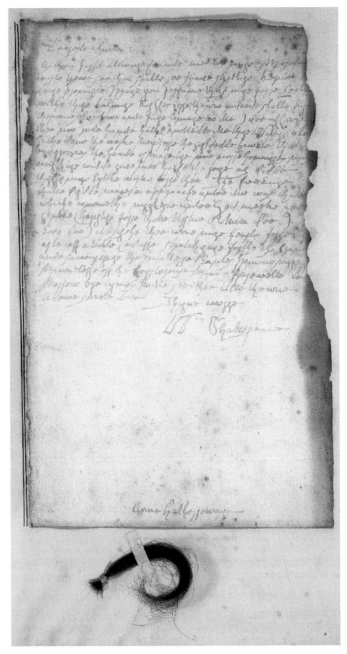

Figure 2.5. William Henry Ireland, forged letter to Anne Hathaway, 1805. Image courtesy of the Folger Shakespeare Library.

her to remember him by," along with seven love letters from their courtship, with the proviso, "these I doe beg herr toe keepe safe if everr she dydd love me."[78] Giving Anne money, a portrait, and love letters was a substantial improvement over what she was given in the original will – only a bed – and Ireland's version offered multiple affirmations of Shakespeare's tender regard for his "deare Wife."

William Ireland was not the only one interested in details of Shakespeare's intimate relationship with his wife. In 1795 the Irelands set up a public viewing of their cache, where several visitors affirmed the proof of what one called "the Stamp of [Shakespeare's] soul." Here the "milk of human kindness flows as readily from his Pen . . . Here we see the Man, as well as the Poet," wrote Frances Webb, secretary at the College of Heralds. James Boswell, who noted his connection to Shakespeare through Anne when he was at the Stratford Jubilee of 1769, was particularly moved by these affectionate testimonies, and proclaimed, "I shall now die contented . . . I now kiss the invaluable relics of our bard: and thanks to God that I have lived to see them."[79] James Boaden, editor of the newspaper *The Oracle*, also exclaimed a particular "tremor of purest delight" at the love letter between the Shakespeares for its "utmost delicacy of passion and poetical spirit."[80] Clearly, William Ireland had identified a topic of growing obsession in the life of Shakespeare the man – his love, passion, soul, and human elements, particularly in relation to his wife. Jonathan Bate aptly describes the appeal of the Ireland forgeries: "When you want something badly enough, it is easy to close your eyes."[81]

The excitement in London over the Ireland papers was so intense that Samuel Ireland began to charge a fee and set up a timed entrance system in order to handle the demand. For anyone unable to get to the Ireland residence and view the documents in person, Ireland published in late 1795 his *Miscellaneous Papers and Legal Instruments under the Hand and Seal of William Shakespeare . . . From the Original Mss. In the Possession of Samuel Ireland of Norfolk Street*, including the love letter and poem to Anne Hathaway.[82] In his prospectus, Samuel Ireland described the love letter as "the expression and feeling of his very soul upon a subject the most momentous that can occupy the thoughts of mortal man."[83] The appeal of the Anne-related forgeries was their ability to testify to Shakespeare's innermost feelings, particularly love, and to certify the poet's amorous sentiments.

One of the many visitors to the Ireland papers was editor Edmond Malone, who was at work on his never-completed biography of Shakespeare. As soon as he obtained his own copy of Ireland's *Miscellaneous Papers*, Malone famously exposed the documents as forgeries in March of 1796.[84] It must have been satisfying for Malone to be able to invalidate the love letters and annul the new wife-friendly will, since these documents worked against his crusade for an unhappily married Shakespeare. Nevertheless, the fact that one of the central and most valued texts in the Ireland cache was a love letter from Shakespeare to his wife gives credence to the growing desire for evidence of Shakespeare's romantic life. As James Shapiro observes, the Ireland forgeries "perfectly matched what people hoped to discover about Shakespeare."[85] Even after the Ireland papers had been exposed as forgeries, over twenty copies of the love letter circulated; eagerness for clues about Shakespeare's "personal story," as Rowe put it, outweighed authenticity.[86]

Shakespeare the Domestic Moralist

Two major Shakespeare events of the eighteenth century, the 1769 Jubilee and the Ireland forgeries, came together to inspire another early reimagining of Anne Hathaway. The composer Charles Dibdin, who helped David Garrick organize the Jubilee and wrote some of the music, also composed a song about Anne Hathaway, which may have originated from his time in Stratford, but was not performed at the Jubilee.[87] In the third volume of Dibdin's novel *Hannah Hewit; or, The Female Crusoe* (the first volume was published in 1792, and the third in 1796), Dibdin's central character pens a song as evidence of her ability to craft a fake document in imitation of Ireland's efforts. In this account, Anne Hathaway is a charming, angelic, and godly woman:

> But were it to my fancy given
> To rate her charms, I'd call them heaven;
> For though a mortal made of clay,
> Angels must love Ann Hathaway;
> She hath a way so to control,
> To rapture the imprisoned soul,
> And sweetest heaven on earth display,
> That to be heaven Ann hath a way;
> She hath a way,
> Ann Hathaway, –
> To be heaven's self Ann hath a way.

First published with the full title "A Love Dittie, Addressed to the idole of mine harte, and the delyghte of mine eyes, the faireste among the most faire,

Anne Hatheawaye," Dibdin's piece was such a convincing tribute that it was frequently attributed to Shakespeare. Sir Sidney Lee points out that Henry Longfellow "rashly accepting a persistent popular fallacy," accepted the poem as authentic, reprinting it in his *Poems of Places*, 1877.[88]

Dibdin's song remained popular throughout the nineteenth century. In 1796 he included the song in his entertainment *The General Election*, and it subsequently appeared under the title "BALLAD" in his four-volume auto-biography *The Professional Life of Mr. Dibdin* in 1803.[89] It was later reprinted in 1842, and again in 1848 with the music in *Dibdin's Songs*.[90] Audiences throughout the nineteenth century were quick to see the link between Dibdin's work and the Ireland forgeries. One 1886 critic described Dibdin's song as an attempt "to emulate the skill of Chatterton and Ireland in forging poems by ancient writers."[91] Later printings of Dibdin's song include Samuel Ireland's engraving of Anne Hathaway's Cottage, which gave readers a visual representation of the domestic space mentioned in the song, and it was even sold at the Cottage. Dibdin's laudatory song of praise had a wide circulation throughout the next hundred years, likely because he constructed a version of Anne as a chaste, domestic woman, but also made Shakespeare the adoring admirer of such a woman – in essence, a moral Shakespeare.[92] Dibdin's Anne was aligned with works such as Elizabeth Griffith's *The Morality of Shakespeare's Drama Illustrated* (1775), part of what Fiona Ritchie describes as "a burgeoning tradition of women critics of Shakespeare."[93] Griffith's work also contributed to a growing crusade to show Shakespeare as a moralist as well as a poet, and Anne was ideally suited to contribute to this Shakespeare.

The emerging view of Anne as a virtuous, domestic heroine helped to create a Shakespeare steeped in the Warwickshire countryside, communing with nature in a blissful domestic scene. Further, this version of Shakespeare underlines David Ellis's point that Anne as "a pregnant bride was troubling to many commentators in the nineteenth century" because it was unsuitable to have the "National Bard indulging in pre-marital sex."[94] Far from the libertine womanizer of the earlier eighteenth century, this redeemed Shakespeare was one ready to serve as a moral authority. As Kate Rumbold argues, Shakespeare's moral authority was commodified "as new, lucrative markets for Shakespeare's virtuous wisdom (school; home; women; the young) began to emerge."[95] After all, if Shakespeare were to serve as a moral authority, he needed to be moral himself.

In order to set Shakespeare up as a moral expert on love, a tale of courtship had to be fashioned for him. Whether or not such a courtship actually took place is beside the point; this Shakespeare needed to have "personal experi-ence of romantic love" in order to "authoriz[e] his insights."[96] The growing

Figure 2.6. Glass relic probably from New Place, reproduced in F. W. Fairholt, *The Home of Shakspere*, 1848.

popularity of Anne in the early nineteenth century can be ascribed not so much to an increase in knowledge about her, but rather to the role she could play in creating a Shakespeare that fit the moral image of the poet. Anne's popularity was also part of what Julia Thomas describes as the "crucial shift in the construction of Shakespeare from divine to domestic" between Garrick's Jubilee and the Tercentenary, and a related "shift in the proper location of his commemoration from London to Stratford."[97]

Desire for physical evidence of the Shakespeares' romantic life spawned numerous material items in the nineteenth century. Clara Fisher's intriguing "Shakespearean Cabinet" from 1830 memorialized the Shakespeare relationship in twenty miniature carvings, including one entitled "Remains of the Church Where Shakespeare and Anne Hathaway Were Married."[98] A few years later in 1848, F. W. Fairholt claimed that a leaded glass window was a surviving relic from New Place, with the letters "W.A.S." for William and Anne, entwined in a lover's knot, with the date of 1615 (Figure 2.6).[99] Presumably, this window would have proclaimed William's love for Anne in the last years of his life, perhaps working against the negative connotations

Figure 2.7. Casket, carved in an Elizabethan style, 1866. Image courtesy of the Folger Shakespeare Library.

suggested by Malone in the bequest to his wife of the "second best bed" in Shakespeare's will. The origins and authenticity of this window are unclear, but its sentiment is obvious – to testify to Shakespeare's immortal love for his wife at the end of his life, in contrast to the possible implications of his will.

Other material items, including some specially commissioned, affirmed the Shakespeares' love, and corroborated the link between Shakespeare's passion for his wife and his creative output. William Perry, Queen Victoria's wood carver, fashioned a wooden casket in 1866 from a souvenir piece of Herne's Oak in Windsor, at the request of heiress Angela Georgina Burdett-Coutts. The casket, now held by the Folger Shakespeare Library, includes spaces for the First Folio and for Shakespeare's poems, along with a portrait of Shakespeare from the Droeshout engraving, and the monograms AH and WS on the sides (Figure 2.7). The commemoration of Shakespeare's works alongside his passion for his wife is a substantial shift in depictions of Anne Hathaway, whose initials are now entwined with her husband's, a mere 200 years after visitors to Holy Trinity Church stood on her grave only to get a better view of her husband's monument.

As we shall see in Chapter 4, the potential for Anne Hathaway to supply a personal life for her husband became even more important and desirable. Increasing interest in Shakespeare as an authority on love, women, morality, and emotional life spawned further fascination with Shakespeare the man, who needed a full-scale biography. Many Victorian writers had already identified Shakespeare's female characters as models for emulation, and in the second half of the nineteenth century, Anne Hathaway began to be treated as a literary character, sometimes created in the image of one of Shakespeare's heroines (usually Portia, Rosalind, or Juliet), and capable of providing a unique link between Shakespeare's women and his personal life. Further, as Anne became part of the growing body of works about Shakespeare, in fiction, biography, and tourism, she also was part of what Gail Marshall describes as a movement by women to "radicalize" Shakespeare by "making him speak explicitly to their own time, to their specific historical conditions, through which process he is himself realized as historically situated, rather than simply the purveyor of timelessness." The imaginative works that employ Anne to create a relationship between Shakespeare and women are thus part of the ways that Shakespeare can remain current for subsequent generations, by giving him "a language in which to speak to nineteenth-century women."[100]

The shift from Shakespeare the libertine in the early eighteenth century, to Shakespeare the family man at the end of the nineteenth, encouraged a number of women to identify with Shakespeare as a "girl's friend" (in Mary Cowden Clarke's phrase). It is no accident that the period that inspired such women-centered works as Mary Cowden Clarke's *The Girlhood of Shakespeare's Heroines* (1850) and Anna Jameson's *Shakespeare's Heroines: Characteristics of Women: Moral, Poetical, and Historical* (1832) also produced imaginative retellings of Shakespeare's courtship and marriage. Cowden Clarke described Shakespeare as offering "vital precepts and models [which] render him essentially a helping friend" for girls, who should model themselves "by carefully observing the women drawn by Shakespeare." Just as his works offer examples for women, according to Cowden Clarke, so too did Shakespeare's own life, as a poet who could "discern with sympathy the innermost core of woman's heart."[101]

Through the creation of lengthy poems and literary works, and the cultivation of Anne Hathaway's Cottage as a tourist destination, Shakespeare's wife and her origins in the Warwickshire countryside became crucial elements in the campaign to craft Shakespeare as a "man among men," as one admirer put it, who can also speak to women. Interest in Anne thus increased not in order to discover more about her as an early modern woman in her own right, but rather for the role she could play in creating a Shakespeare with a romantic courtship in the pastoral setting of her family home. Shakespeare's emerging status not only as the national poet, but also as an authority on the natural world, on love, and on the range of human emotions, fueled desire for ways to tell his own personal story, and to locate his personal investment in the "heart of England."[102]

As the next chapter will show, Anne Hathaway's Cottage was perfectly poised to supply visitors with physical evidence of this mythology. Attracted to the model of Shakespeare as a family man and an authority on love in the nineteenth century, women would continue in the twentieth century to craft some of the most subversive and unconventional works about Shakespeare's wife, as we will see in Chapter 6. In the second half of the nineteenth century, a number of imaginative works explored the possibilities of creating a romantic version of Shakespeare, often alongside an idealized portrait of a worthy and virtuous Anne Hathaway. Due to the intersection of growing interest in antiquarianism, tourism, and biography, Anne Hathaway developed from a gap in Shakespeare's life story in the seventeenth century, whose grave and descriptive epitaph remained unnoticed, to a full-fledged imaginary creation by the middle of the nineteenth century, and an essential component in establishing a private romantic life for Shakespeare.

3

THE LEGACY OF ANNE HATHAWAY'S COTTAGE

All readers of Shakespeare know that he married when only nineteen, and that his wife, Ann Hathaway, was eight years his senior. There is certainly something rather romantic in this boy-lover episode in the life of the poet, and one naturally feels a desire to visit the scenes connected with it before he can realize to himself the fact that he who held all the passions of the human breast in his control could have allowed one of them – the gentlest of his subjects – to conquer and tyrannise over himself.[1]

THIS DESCRIPTION IN THE PROGRAM FOR THE 1864 TERCENTENARY OF Shakespeare's birth endorses Anne Hathaway's Cottage for its ability to conjure a "romantic" vision of Shakespeare as a "boy-lover," enraptured by his emotions for an enchanting woman. The Tercentenary program recommends the village of Shottery as "the very spot on which the boy lover, with all the ardour of a Romeo, pleaded his cause with Ann Hathaway, and her cottage still remains reverentially preserved on account of its literary associations." Further, the program locates the source of Shakespeare's love poetry in the Cottage, observing that "All the purity, freshness, and ardour of love, so beautifully described in the lines quoted above, were here felt and experienced by the poet himself." Even Romeo and Juliet's "Verona pales in comparison with Shottery" of William and Anne. As this chapter will show, the evolution of the Shottery Hathaway family home into Anne Hathaway's Cottage was a result of several factors that coalesced toward the end of the nineteenth century. Increasing fascination with the private lives of authors, and with Shakespeare's romantic life in particular; interest in the homes and haunts of authors; literary tourism; and the efforts of the Hathaway family all combined to solidify the Cottage's important place in the afterlife of Shakespeare and especially of his wife.

Anne Hathaway's Cottage has become the central visual image of Shakespeare's wife, in part because no likeness of her survives, and the association of Anne with the Cottage has immortalized her as Anne Hathaway rather than Anne Shakespeare. As part of the network of Shakespeare Birthplace Trust properties, the Cottage is entwined with these other physical spaces to present a series of stages in Shakespeare's life story – origins (the Birthplace on Henley Street), parentage (his mother Mary Arden's house), children (daughter Susanna's home at Hall's Croft), romantic love (Anne Hathaway's Cottage) and prosperous maturity (New Place). The Hathaway home represents a particularly desirable "Shakespeare" in this biographical network because it anchors Shakespeare's life in the Warwickshire countryside, and authenticates a physical setting for his courtship of Anne Hathaway. As James Walter remarked in 1890, "Shakespeare's biography is handed down to us through the rural scenes around Stratford."[2]

Unlike adaptations of Shakespeare's plays, which are connected with a text that is then reworked and reshaped, Anne Hathaway's Cottage is bound by three nontextual factors that determine how it has been given meaning – its rural locale, its association with the Hathaway family from the time of Shakespeare until the end of the nineteenth century, and its adaptability to facilitate romantic narratives about Shakespeare as a wooer, lover, and native English son. When the Hathaway family home in Shottery came up for sale in 1892, an essay published that year in *All the Year Round* captured the significance of this space for inspiring desirable stories about Shakespeare's life: "If Stratford speaks to us of the poet's birth and education, of his years as a prosperous man of business, of the material side, which is yet so necessary a side even to the man of genius, Shottery speaks to us of the ideal side, of the time of youth's opening love, and of manhood's sweet communing with the peaceful sights and sounds of country life."[3] Because it involved a physical journey for travelers from Stratford to Shottery, Anne Hathaway's Cottage also tapped into the late nineteenth-century vogue for perambulatory experiences, and part of its appeal was its suitability for the "homes and haunts" connected with nineteenth-century literary tourism.[4] Nicola J. Watson describes this process of uniting a space with an author's biography and literary works as "superimposing [a] narrative upon a surviving house."[5] Had Shakespeare married a woman from the heart of the market town of Stratford, whose family lived on Sheep Street, for example, this narrative would not be as feasible. As Harald Hendrix points out, "the existence of a house facilitates the rise of a cult and favors its subsistence," but this only happens "if the interpretation of what the house expresses agrees with the dominant opinions on what their dwellers and their literary works stand for."[6]

The fact that Anne Hathaway's Cottage has survived virtually intact in relatively the same configuration as it had in Shakespeare's day has further secured its position.[7] The Cottage "remained a working farm throughout the nineteenth century," combining growing tourist traffic with ongoing domestic activities, supported by the longevity of the Hathaway family, particularly the last caretaker, Mary Baker.[8] Over the last 100 years, items of Shakespeariana in the form of relics, stories, and material objects, have been added to the Cottage to create a tangible, physical memorial to an idea of romantic love located in the picturesque Warwickshire countryside, but one for which minimal evidence survives. The current state of Anne Hathaway's Cottage, replete with a sculpture garden paying homage to Shakespeare's plays, a "willow cabin" where visitors can listen to famous actors reciting Shakespeare's sonnets, and tour guides repeating the story of a courtship between William and Anne, memorializes and perpetuates a myth of idealized romance.

As this chapter will show, however, this story builds on several centuries of family members, tourists, and Shakespeare industry promoters who saw the potential in creating a romantically charged space where visitors could immerse themselves in an imaginary love story between Shakespeare and Anne Hathaway, deep in the heart of Shakespeare-land.[9] To further extend these associations internationally, Anne Hathaway Cottages have been recreated in Asheville, North Carolina; Ashland, Oregon; Green Lake, Wisconsin; Perth, Australia; Victoria, British Columbia; Staunton, Virginia; and Wessington Springs, South Dakota. The 1893 World's Fair in Chicago even featured a full replica of the Cottage, which was then transported to the Midwinter International Exposition in San Francisco in January of 1894. While some Cottages (like the one in Asheville, North Carolina) connected Shakespeare's family story to a larger political canvas, others have promoted what Barbara Hodgdon calls "myths of contact and presence," well beyond the borders of the original Shottery property.[10]

First Visitors and Early Relics

As we saw in the previous chapter, some of the earliest tourists to visit Stratford were David Garrick and his brother George, who traveled to Anne Hathaway's Cottage in 1742 to collect Shakespeare relics, nearly thirty years before the famous Jubilee. David Garrick's brother George obtained the first relics, an ink stand and pair of gloves that, according to Samuel Ireland, were owned by Shakespeare himself. The ink stand is a clear attempt to link Shakespeare the writer to the Cottage, and the pair of gloves connects the Cottage to Shakespeare's family business (John Shakespeare's glove-making) as well as to gentlemanly fashions of the period. The second group of relics from the Cottage, procured by Samuel Ireland fifty years later in the 1790s, consisted of an oak chair supposed to be Shakespeare's courting chair, and bugle purse. The courting chair (also discussed in the previous chapter) is the first piece of physical evidence of the poet's courtship. The bugle purse, "said to have been a present from our great poet to the object of his choice," suggests perhaps a love interest. Shakespeare's courting chair, "wherein it was stated our bard was used to sit, during his courtship with his Anne upon his knee," is now owned by the Shakespeare Birthplace Trust and displayed in Anne Hathaway's Cottage.[11] The shift of these relics from associations of authorship to romantic love reveals the Cottage's role in the developing tourist circuit. As Nicola J. Watson points out, the Cottage helped fill in a notable absence of romantic love in the documentary record of Shakespeare's biography, offering "an idealized pastoral love of the sort that is conspicuously absent" from Shakespeare's texts.[12]

The Ireland family visit to Stratford in the 1790s inspired the well-known forgeries detailed in the previous chapter, and while there, Samuel Ireland made the first illustration of Anne Hathaway's Cottage, under the title "House at Shotery [sic], in which Ann Hathaway the wife of Shakspere resided" (Figure 3.1), included in his *Picturesque Views on the Upper, or Warwickshire Avon* of 1795. The Irelands were partly responsible for the shift from the "House at Shotery" to what is now known as Anne Hathaway's Cottage, and with the construction of a romantic, rural, pastoral love story between Shakespeare and Anne Hathaway. Ireland's sketch even includes a female figure at the door of the cottage, signifying its long tradition of feminine associations, and foreshadowing the popularity of Victorian homes and haunts that give a "prominent role to women."[13] One visitor in 1908 attested that at Anne Hathaway's Cottage, she "felt the spell of the eternally feminine."[14] As Cecilia Morgan explains, tourists "brought their own needs, fantasies, and desires to bear on the meanings that they attributed" to attractions such as Anne Hathaway's Cottage.[15]

American critic William Winter epitomizes this vision in his popular work *Shakespeare's England* (initially printed in 1886 but reprinted numerous times), where he sought to "reflect the gentle sentiment of English landscape and the romantic character of English rural life," for American travelers who "might be attracted to roam among the shrines of the mother-land."[16] Drawing on his visits in 1877 and 1882, Winter imagines Shakespeare "as the lover, strolling through the green lanes of Shottery, hand in hand with the darling of his first love, while round them the honeysuckle breathed out its

Figure 3.1. "House at Shotery, in which Ann Hathaway the wife of Shakspere resided," from Samuel Ireland, *Picturesque Views on the Upper, or Warwickshire Avon,* 1795. Image courtesy of the Folger Shakespeare Library.

fragrant heart upon the winds of night, and overhead the moonlight, stream-ing through rifts of elm and poplar, fell on their pathway in showers of shimmering silver."[17] Winter fittingly affirms that his book "depicts not so much the England of fact as the England created and hallowed by the spirit of her poetry, of which Shakespeare is the soul."[18]

For pilgrims like Winter, the sensual overload of being in a space where William *may* have expressed his own overflowing emotions to Anne is almost too much to handle: "It is a homely, humble place, but the sight of it makes the heart thrill with a strange and incommunicable awe. You cannot wish to speak when you are standing there. You are scarcely conscious of the low rustling of the leaves outside, the far-off sleepy murmur of the brook, or the faint fragrance of woodbine and maiden's blush that is wafted in at the open casement and that swathes in nature's incense a memory sweeter than itself."[19] The ability to share a physical space with the specter of Shakespeare allows the past and present to come together, and Winter yearns for the "memory" of Shakespeare, evoked by the continuity of nature at the Cottage.

Such perambulations, though, required an infrastructure to facilitate travel, as well as a population interested in and able to undertake this type of expedition.

Roger Pringle has detailed the development of travel for pleasure and intellectual fulfillment, beginning in the later eighteenth century and continuing through the nineteenth, involving an affluent population of "well-educated, middle-class visitors" whose travels were made possible by increased accessibility due to turnpike trusts and other facilities. Pringle observes that for Stratford in particular, roads into the city were turnpiked between 1726 and 1754, and coaching inns such as the White Lion offered lodging for travelers. Pringle remarks that the White Lion "became one of the best regarded hostelries in the midlands," and that Stratford's location "in the centre of England made it an important staging point within a nationwide network." He notes that by 1817, two dozen coaches passed through the town, and the development of "a national transport system" to bring tourists to Stratford, available lodgings, and guide books helped propel Shakespeare's home town to the status of a highly sought after destination.[20] Simultaneous developments at the Hathaway family home resonated with both availability of and desire for particular types of experiences related to Shakespeare. Anne Hathaway's Cottage functioned as what Aaron Santesso describes as an "imaginative meeting place where the reader might engage with the author."[21] By the time the London–Birmingham railway opened in 1826, and the railway was established in Stratford in 1864, the Hathaway home was ideally poised for growing numbers of travelers and their pursuits.

Early Tourists

Increased access to Stratford for tourists brought more travelers to Anne Hathaway's Cottage, as demonstrated by the growing number of references to the Cottage in guidebooks to the area. Robert B. Wheler's 1806 *History and Antiquities of Stratford-upon-Avon* did not include a section on Anne Hathaway's Cottage, and Washington Irving, in his 1815 trip to Stratford, visited the Birthplace, Holy Trinity Church, and Charlecote, but did not visit or even mention Anne Hathaway's Cottage.[22] In 1817, Nathan Drake casually remarked in his biography of Shakespeare that "the cottage at Shottery, in which Anne and her parents dwelt, is said to be yet standing, and is still pointed out to strangers as a subject of curiosity."[23] Within a decade or so of the 1826 opening of the London–Birmingham railway, however, Anne Hathaway's Cottage became an increasingly popular tourist destination, where travelers could combine the modern advancements in train travel with the distinct pleasures of walking. As Olivia Murphy affirms, the late eighteenth-century "British transport revolution" made "non-pedestrian travel cheaper, quicker, and more widely available," which in turn "enabled walking to be seen as a pleasurable alternative to other modes of travel rather than as merely an arduous and hazardous necessity."[24] And, of course, the only way to get to Shottery from Stratford was on foot. As we shall see, part of the pleasure of walking this trek involved the opportunity to engage in imaginative reverie about Shakespeare's private life. The language travelers frequently used to describe the process of walking from Stratford to Shottery – wandering, strolling, roving – reveals the deliberate attempt to connect body and imagination with Shakespeare's life. In the words of one American traveler, "It had been one of my dreams to see Stratford. I had looked forward to strolling through the streets where Shakespeare passed his boyhood or wandering to Ann Hathaway's cottage."[25] If Shakespeare had married a neighbor girl from Henley Street in the heart of Stratford, linking her home to the fashion for perambulatory experiences would not have been possible.

Guidebooks and histories about Stratford continued to proliferate in the first half of the nineteenth century, and Anne Hathaway's Cottage became an increasingly important destination, largely because it offered a physical space where visitors could engage in imagining Shakespeare in scenes of courtship and romantic love set against a Warwickshire background, and one that resonated with walkable landscape sites of famous authors.[26] One of the first places that William Howitt visited on his 1840 trip to Stratford was Anne Hathaway's Cottage, about which he observed (with a nod to Dibdin's ballad), "not so many have visited, or known of, or inquired after the house where his modest, faithful, and affectionate wife, Ann Hathaway, she hath a way, was born, and lived, and became the wife of Shakespeare when he was nineteen, and she twenty-seven." Howitt promoted the Cottage as a site to visit because of its association with Shakespeare's "domestic peace with his true Ann Hathaway," the virtuous woman immortalized in Dibdin's verses. Stratford was Shakespeare's true home, where he "valued the enjoyments of domestic life," and with Anne, "in the depth of domestic existence [he] found his real happiness."[27] Because of Shottery's associations with Shakespeare's romantic life, Howitt confessed that "there was no spot connected with Shakspeare at Stratford that so strongly interested me as Shottery, the little rustic village where Ann Hathaway was born, and where Shakspeare wooed, and whence he married her." An undated engraving from the Folger Shakespeare Library (Figure 3.2) depicts this rustic, undeveloped space, with a traveler curiously pausing just outside the Cottage.

Howitt even imagines an elderly Shakespeare: "in his latter years, when he had renounced public life, and she was his 'all-the-world,'" and how "they might, led by the sweet recollections of the past, often stroll that way together, and perhaps visit some of their kindred under the same rustic

ANNE HATHAWAY'S COTTAGE — STRATFORD ON AVON

Figure 3.2. Anne Hathaway's Cottage, mid- to late nineteenth century. Image courtesy of the Folger Shakespeare Library.

roof." Howitt endows the Cottage with the natural inspiration for Shakespeare's plays: "I pleased myself with imagining the quiet happiness which he had enjoyed with his Ann Hathaway in this very spot, while these rural images and happy illustrations silently flowed into his mind from the things around him."[28] Howitt's observations reveal the suitability of the Cottage for bringing together a domestic Shakespeare with one rooted in the English countryside, as well as a walkable landscape that inspired narratives of romance and artistic stimulation from nature.

This connection is one that Howitt made on his own, but would be used by later members of the Hathaway family as part of a deliberate strategy. When Howitt visited the Cottage, he was left to wander through the space alone; he remarks that "there is a passage right through the house, with a very old high-backed bench of oak in it, said to have been there in Shakspeare's time," and "the whole of the interior is equally simple and rustic." He laments that "perhaps at the very moment I write these remarks this interesting dwelling may be destroyed, and all that I have been describing have given way to the ravages of modern change. The place is sold, and perhaps the cottage of Ann Hathaway is now no more."[29] As we shall see, the Cottage actually became much more aligned with Shakespeare, and subsequent visitors were treated to a carefully calculated presentation by the Hathaways.

In the summer of 1844, it took great effort for clergyman William Harness to locate Anne Hathaway's Cottage. While he was searching for the Cottage, he imagined "treading the very path to what was the house of the Hathaways which [Shakespeare] would have trod, as if I had seen him hurrying on before me, the limp in his gait become more conspicuous than it was in general from the rapid movement to which he was urged by his impatience to reach his love." Harness's emphasis on "treading the very path" that Shakespeare walked underlines the importance of walking as a cultural process that gave participants a first-hand experience.[30] Without the aid of a guidebook, Harness "walked round the village [of Shottery] to see if I could find out which was likely to be the house of the Hathaways – and after I had determined in my own mind which it must be, I enquired of a woman I saw at her cottage door, which it was? She told me I had passed it, and pointed out the one I had conjectured it to be."

Harness was one of the earliest tourists taken around the house by Hathaway family member Mary Baker, who encouraged him to imagine scenes with William and Anne by showing him the elaborate carved bed and the courting seat; it did not take much to convince him that "there is little doubt but Shakespeare and Ann Hathaway may often have sat on it together."[31] Even with no factual evidence that such a scene occurred, Harness was one of the many visitors eager to believe an imagined story about romantic love to bolster Shakespeare's growing position as "the great poet of heterosexual love."[32]

By the mid-nineteenth century, guidebooks of the area consistently included the Cottage. George May's 1847 *Illustrated Companion-Book to Stratford-upon-Avon* featured a section called "The Poet's Rural Haunts," where he described the Cottage as "among the peaceful and sequestered spots round Stratford," where the memory of a Shakespeare full of hope and potential is "cherished." May imagines the pathways from Stratford to Shottery, where "the poet and his future bride must have often strolled together, in the days when love was young, and hope was bright, and no cloud of disappointment yet loomed over them."[33] This nostalgic view of an unspoiled idyllic scene was only accessible by walking. In fact, an 1851 Stratford handbook specifically advocated walking as the best way to connect with Shakespeare: "These walks will ever derive their principal attraction for the thoughtful visitor from the conviction that they may each have been trodden by the feet of Shakspeare; that his eye must have rested on every hill and valley; that every turn of the classic river; every common flower that here takes root, was familiar to him."[34] As Harriet Beecher Stowe commented in her 1854 account of travel to Stratford, visitors could commune with Shakespeare's own time here, which "stands a little aloof from the bustle of modern progress," and is a part of the country "which is destined soon to pass away, under the restless regenerating force of modern progress."[35]

Travelers to Shottery continued to increase; by 1857, the *Hand Book for Visitors to Stratford-Upon-Avon* described the footpath to Shottery as a "well-frequented" point of access to a "scene of the youthful Shakespeare's love-suit" to the "rustic beauty" Anne Hathaway.[36] *Ward and Lock's Illustrated Guide to the Popular History of Leamington & Warwick, with Excursions to Kenilworth, Stratford-on-Avon* from 1888 reinforced the appeal of wandering on foot in search of Shakespeare: "Nothing can be more delightful than to wander from Henley Street, and to take the footpath which Shakespeare must so often have trodden when his heart was beating high with love and hope."[37]

The words "love" and "hope" recur in these accounts, suggesting that Anne Hathaway's Cottage stood in for much more than a picturesque site accessed by walking – it evoked a stage in Shakespeare's life before he became a playwright, a bucolic golden period of hopeful potential and youthful love, unspoiled by age and time. This is the "Shakespeare" poised to write the famous plays, without formal learning but nurtured by the Warwickshire countryside and by the woman who resided there, whom he sought by venturing deep into the country. Shakespeare's courtship of Anne Hathaway is thus a central myth in the conception of him as the quintessential English poet of nature and expert on love, and the physical space of the Cottage went a long way in promoting this idea.

In addition to the growing number of tourist guides, illustrations of Anne Hathaway's Cottage proliferated in the second half of the nineteenth century. In 1854, British painter Henry Wallis (best known for his painting *Chatterton*) included the Cottage in a series of paintings related to Shakespeare's life.[38] Charles Cattermole's (1832–1900) illustration *May Day Sports at Shottery – Shakespeare the Victor* (Figure 3.3, c. 1860) was one of thirteen illustrations commissioned by William Ryland for a lecture on Shakespeare's life.[39] Cattermole's depiction attempts to "match tourist expectations" by literally placing Shakespeare at Anne Hathaway's Cottage in an invented scene of courtship.[40]

In his 1890 work *Shakespeare's True Life*, part biography, part travel record, and part fiction, James Walter commissioned the well-known painter Gerald Moira to produce extensive pen and ink illustrations of Anne Hathaway's Cottage and of the Shottery area. Praised by reviewers for its "exquisite

Figure 3.3. Charles Cattermole, *May Day Sports at Shottery*.

illustrations," Walter's book includes a lengthy chapter on "Sweet Anne Hathaway," Shakespeare's "passionately-loved village belle." Walter provides a particularly evocative homecoming scene of Shakespeare returning to Stratford to see his wife and children, enjoying "sunset strolls across the daisied fields to the cottage of her childhood and of their first love and troth." Walter's effusive prose suggests that this emotionally charged version is Shakespeare's "True Life" of his title: "When roving with Anne in the fields around Shottery they would hear the ringing notes of the blackbird and thrush, and watch the skylark soaring aloft into the clear heaven above, pouring forth its notes in uncontrollable joy . . . As they returned homeward to the cottage, Anne's sweet home, what a paradise of delight was the quaint old garden, full of simple untrimmed beauty – warm, flowery, odorous – happy with the hum of bees in their diligence inspired of spring's first warmth." Gerald Moira's illustrations include numerous drawings of Anne Hathaway's Cottage, of "Old Cottages" in Shottery, and of the courting chair (Figure 3.4; see also Figures 2.2–2.3).

Walter recasts the Hathaway family home as Shakespeare's home, where he returns to recharge by communing with nature. In Walter's version, Shottery has become "a place for Shakespeare's lovers and none other." This contrived Cottage has a sacred aura that influenced the young poet, "surrounded by all that is suggestive of Arcadian times," with an orchard "where delicious fruit ripened in the early days of his romance." When offered the customary drink from the well just outside the Cottage, Walter summons the past and future together, imagining the "thousands" of pilgrims who have been there, the "army of devotees" yet to come, and the poet himself with his bride: "How many thousands have here slaked thirst, and how increasingly great will the army of devotees yearly become." He exclaims, "What a privilege to drink at the same fountain at which he drank from the hand of Sweet Anne!" There is no place in this account for the Anne who is an aggressive gold-digger, or the Anne whom Shakespeare sought to forget in his will. Readers of *Shakespeare's True Life* were presented with a subservient Anne who embodies the lush Warwickshire countryside, but who does not impede her husband's career: "Who does not, when in this quaintest of homes, picture Sweet Anne here alone sitting on the hereditary fire bench, dreaming of him, her intellectual superior, so far beyond her ken save in the utterances understood of all degrees."[41] James Walter's Anne is the passive inferior recipient of Shakespeare's affections, preserved amid the pastoral charm of the English countryside.

The appeal of access to Shakespeare's romantic past was widespread at the end of the nineteenth century, and others were inspired to document this

Figure 3.4. Illustration from James Walter, *Shakespeare's True Life*, 1890.

myth through illustrations and via the developing technology of photography. American dentist James Leon Williams spent four summers gathering the photographs for *The Home and Haunts of Shakespeare* (1892), lavishly illustrated with the "artful faking" of old scenes which offered a "magical link made by the photographs with this imagined past."[42] Williams took hundreds of photos in order to preserve the rural England of Shakespeare "for the benefit of Shakespeare lovers the world over,"[43] and especially for arm-chair travelers "who might never visit the country for themselves, and would have to enjoy it through imagination alone."[44] It is worth pointing out that Anne Hathaway's Cottage gift shop recently sold replicas of Williams's photos of the Cottage and surrounding Shottery countryside (Figure 3.5), underlining the long-term appeal of this timeless mythology.

Exactly a hundred years after Ireland's first illustration of the Shottery house, Mathilde Blind's 1895 collection of *Shakespeare Sonnets* exemplifies the full-blown commemorative potential of Anne Hathaway's Cottage to enshrine a story of Shakespeare's courtship. Blind describes the Cottage as "ivy-girt and crowned" with a "path down which our Shakespeare ran" to meet an Anne who "made all his mighty pulses throb and bound." As we shall see, the addition of a Shakespeare-centered narrative to the Hathaway family homestead "turned this plot to holy ground," in Blind's words, in order to satisfy the many devoted travelers seeking a physical experience of their imagined "Shakespeare."[45]

Transatlantic Tourism

James Leon Williams was part of an expanding transatlantic tourism that increased dramatically in the late nineteenth century; Christopher Endy estimates that between 1870 and 1885, the number of transatlantic travelers doubled.[46] According to Mark Rennella and Whitney Walton, the transatlantic voyage for these travelers served "as an initiation or transition into another world, both imaginative and physical."[47] As part of this trend, Americans in particular enthusiastically journeyed to Anne Hathaway's Cottage, inspired in part by the publicized accounts of ordinary citizens making their way to Shakespeare's domain.[48] In March of 1895, *The Ladies Home Journal*, published in Philadelphia, ran a feature story by editor William J. Rolfe, entitled "Mrs. Shakespeare: What We Really Know of Shakespeare's Wife." Rolfe's story included an illustration of Anne Hathaway's Cottage reproduced from James Walter's *Shakespeare's Home and Rural Life*, and one of Mrs. Baker in the kitchen of the Cottage, from Francis Millet's painting in James Leon

Figure 3.5. James Leon Williams, "At Shottery Brook," from *The Home and Haunts of Shakespeare*, 1892.

Williams's *The Home and Haunts of Shakespeare* (1892). Rolfe's piece disseminated interest in Anne to a broad general readership.

Other ordinary Americans increasingly publicized their accounts of travel to Stratford. *The Chautauquan*, a widely circulated monthly magazine designed for use in Chautauqua literary and scientific circles around the US, printed Minnesotan Samuel G. Smith's account of travels to Stratford in March of

1887. Smith detailed his second trip to Stratford (the first was in 1876), where he journeyed to Anne Hathaway's Cottage. Admiring the old building with a "front garden full of flowers and well-nigh smothered with shrubs and vines," Smith noted that "with all your imagination filled, you say, 'Yes, this is right.'"[49] In 1897, Margherita Arlina Hamm reported on her journey to Anne Hathaway's Cottage in *The American Shakespeare Magazine*, and she returned from Stratford with a photo of Mary Baker, which she presented to the Fortnightly Shakespeare Club of New York.[50]

Canadian schoolteacher Ada Pemberton even sketched Anne Hathaway's Cottage in 1897 when she traveled there in her group of 150 female teachers from Manitoba, noting that "the old well and the old woman [were] most interesting studies."[51] Renowned Belgian-American chemist Leo Baekeland took his own car and family on a transatlantic trip through Europe in 1905, including a stop at Shakespeare's birthplace and at Anne Hathaway's Cottage, where he noted "the numerous American names in the visitors' books," underlining the fact that "transatlantic travelers furnish the larger number of pilgrims to this shrine of early English literature."[52] Edward L. Wells, who ran a teacher's training school in Oregon, Illinois, wrote about his travels to Stratford in the monthly magazine for teachers, the *Illinois School Journal* of September, 1883. Wells details his trip to Shottery, where he walked "over the same path that Shakespeare walked to court Anne Hathaway." Wells was taken around the Cottage by "a fine old woman," who showed him the family Bible, courting settle, garden, well, and "told me stories of the olden time, and picked beside the cottage some lavender and a snowdrop for me to send to dear ones across the sea." Wells noted that Shottery was of interest for the Shakespeare connections, but added that "there is much to interest one in old English rural life."[53] As the next section will discuss, the "fine old woman" who escorted Edward L. Wells was a crucial component in the development of the Cottage, particularly for travelers from overseas in the decades before World War I.

Mary Baker: Charting the Legacy of the Cottage

The final evolution of Anne Hathaway's Cottage from an out-of-the-way locale that visitors had to track down, to a deliberately coordinated tourist experience that nurtured a nostalgic courtship myth, is largely due to one extraordinary individual. Mary Baker, a descendant of the Hathaway family, served as "a living link with the Stratford Bard," and set the agenda for the Cottage that remains in place today.[54] One notice of her death recounted that "in the minds of most visitors, Mrs. Baker's personality was indissolubly associated with the cottage. She was posed in it by photographers, painted in

Figure 3.6. Mary Baker with the Hathaway family Bible. Image courtesy of the Shakespeare Birthplace Trust.

it by artists, snap-shotted in it by amateurs, described in it by writers, seen in it by everyone. There can hardly be a town in the kingdom where hearts will not be touched by the news of her sad end."[55] Baker (pictured in Figure 3.6) was a central actor in the performance of Anne Hathaway's Cottage as a set piece of tourism. As Cecilia Morgan notes, "the discourses and practices of nineteenth-century tourism were dependent on local residents and workers in the tourist industry enacting particular categories and identities," and Baker fit this bill.[56]

Baker led tours of the Cottage for 70 years, until her death in 1899 as a result of slipping on the stone steps of the Cottage.[57] As part of her personal attention to each guest, Baker served tea, and until 1885 she admitted that "though she used to make a cup of tea for her visitors yet now there are so many, and she an old body, she couldn't be bothered wi' it."[58] She regularly handed out herbs and flowers from the Cottage's gardens to visitors, including sprigs of rosemary and daisies.[59]

Baker kept a visitor's book, where she recorded the reactions of famous guests when she gave her tours. Charles Dickens, for example, "took the visitor's book out into the garden and sat down on the stone by the well with the book on his knees while he wrote his name." Other famous visitors included Mark Lemon, the founding editor of *Punch*; the American General Ulysses S. Grant, who "asked a lot of questions"; US President James Garfield; Henry Wadsworth Longfellow; Mark Twain; Oliver Wendell Holmes; Edwin Booth; and actress Mary Anderson.[60]

Baker had a reputation as "quite a Shakespearean celebrity"; according to accounts at the end of her life, she "made the acquaintance of most of the eminent literary men and distinguished personages of the time" and will be missed by "American visitors in particular."[61] One American, Charles Warren Stoddard, remarked in 1874 that when he "stumble[d] upon the shrine for love," he was greeted by Baker "whose face was a kind of welcome," and he immediately felt "at once at home."[62] Stoddard wrote in January of 1874 to his friends in San Francisco, boasting that he was "not three feet from the very chimney in which Will Shakspeare used to make love to his Anne." Stoddard reveled in the immersive experiences at the Cottage, including dinner "cooked in the very spot where Shakespeare has many a time toasted his toes," with a "ham that was raised on the place and cured in this very chimney, and a pork-pie – a Shakspearean pork-pie you may call it – made in the house by a descendant of the Hathaways." To top off his experience, he flaunted, "To-night I am to sleep in Anne Hathaway's bed."[63]

Mary Baker's tours cleverly combined tales of William and Anne's courtship, physical mementos for pilgrims, and personal stories of her family's history and legacy. American critic William Winter praised Baker's domestic cordiality, noting her "custom to welcome, with homely hospitality, the wanderers, from all lands, seeking, – in a sympathy and reverence honorable to human nature, – the shrine of Shakespeare's love." Acting as priestess to this shrine, she guided tourists in their physical journeys and encouraged them to engage in imagined scenes of William and Anne's young love. Baker had a lasting effect on tourists like Winter, who described himself as a "wanderer who will never forget the farewell clasp of that kind woman's hand, and who has never parted with her gift of woodbine and roses from the porch of Anne Hathaway's cottage."[64]

Baker built a substantial audience for her stories among the growing number of visitors in search of romantic renderings of Shakespeare's life. According to one account, Baker had "a thorough knowledge of the value of Shakespeare commercially."[65] One American guest remarked that Baker's stories about Shakespeare courting Anne were "quite soothing and pleasant" and "seemed in accordance with the fitness of things."[66]

She was renowned for showing visitors "the ancient bedstead and furniture, the dresser and the wainscot, the settle and the fireplace that it is believed were so long and so pleasantly familiar to Shakespeare and his Anne."[67] As early as 1853, composer and musician James Bruton (1815–1867) ventured to the garden of the Cottage, where he penned a song immortalizing his experience. The thought of walking along the same road as Shakespeare gave him "such a wild thrill ... that shook to trembling all my frame." When Bruton arrived at the Cottage, he was shown Anne's bedroom, the carved bed, her linen, and the courting settle, as well as given a drink from the well outside. He imagines even nature contributing to the narrative of the Cottage; the oak trees "if they could speak, how they / Might tell what they'd heard Shakespeare say." He also sat on "the lovers stool," where he pictures "Anne and Willie sat, / In summer evenings, fair and cool." Bruton's description preserves this Shakespeare as a "fadeless youth" who is "the world's sweet William."[68]

The highlight of Mary Baker's tour was the courting settle, where she avowed that the courtship between Shakespeare and Anne Hathaway took place. This material object served as physical proof of the courtship, but it also allowed visitors to act out such a scene for themselves. Numerous visitors recount Baker's stories about this famous piece of furniture and remember her encouragement for them to engage in a romantic tableau. As one traveler remarked in 1900 about the settle, "Had I been able to give the old relic a tongue, what inspiring love tales it might have related, and no doubt it would have confided all in me, since I took so much interest in its once exalted station."[69] Baker even used illustrations of the courting settle to help visitors imagine the scene; according to one account, she invited a guest to sit on the settle and then showed them a picture of "this same courting-seat, with Shakespeare and Ann Hathaway as the lovers."[70] In his 1921 guidebook to the Cottage, custodian Frederick W. Bennett noted that the courting settle was "the most important piece of furniture in the house, as, had Shakespeare not come here on courting bent it would have remained just an old farm house instead of being of world-wide fame."[71]

The illustration *Shakespeare's Courtship*, c. 1860 by Thomas Brooks (1818–1891, Figure 3.7), likely sold to tourists in Stratford, was

Figure 3.7. Thomas Brooks, *Shakespeare's Courtship*, c. 1860. Image courtesy of the Folger Shakespeare Library.

ANNE HATHAWAY'S COTTAGE, SHOTTERY : GARDEN VIEW,
SHOWING THE OLD WELL

Figure 3.8. Postcard of the old well, Anne Hathaway's Cottage.

probably the picture that Baker showed to guests. Brooks immortalizes
William courting Anne inside the cottage, with a book on his knee,
suggesting that Anne was both the inspiration for, and the recipient of,
his poetry.[72]

Baker incorporated another immersive feature of the Hathaway homestead into her tours, through the old well (Figure 3.8). One visitor remembered in 1899 that Baker would "press new acquaintances to try the settle on
which Shakespeare did his wooing, and to derive inspiration from the well
from which he drank."[73] By sitting on the courting settle and drinking from
the well, visitors could enact a ritual of summoning the spirit of Shakespeare,
in scenes of romantic wooing. The courting settle also inspired artistic
renderings of this courtship, further inserting an imaginary Shakespeare
into the space of the Hathaway family home (Figure 3.7).

In addition to attracting visitors by promoting Anne Hathaway's Cottage as
the "shrine of Shakespeare's love," Baker was also determined to establish the
legitimacy of her family line through association with the Cottage, making sure
the Hathaway family held an indisputable claim over the physical space where
Shakespeare's courtship took place, and especially where he may have gleaned

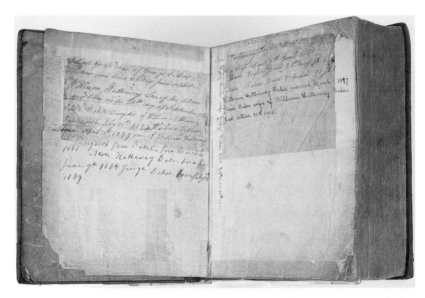

Figure 3.9. The Hathaway family Bible. Image courtesy of the Shakespeare Birthplace Trust.

inspiration for his literary works. Though Baker did accept tips for her tours, her motivations were not so much financial as they were part of a personal mission to secure her family's legacy as part of Shakespeare's amatory narrative.[74] Baker had the ancestry of the Hathaway family written in the fly-leaf of the family Bible, which she displayed for visitors (Figure 3.9).[75]

English preacher John C. M. Bellew in 1863 was impressed with the "length of time that we puzzled together in her kitchen over the old family Bible, until we got the Pedigree correct, as far as her knowledge went."[76] A later guest similarly testified in 1885 to the amount of personal attention Baker gave to each visitor in order to make sure the family legacy was clear: "I staid half an hour chatting with the contented old woman, who from long use is never at a loss to entertain visitors." Together they "looked over the family tree duly inscribed on the first leaf of the big family Bible" (Figure 3.9), which Baker's father had bound just before his marriage.[77]

Baker's ability to trace her lineage back through the Hathaway family to Anne gave her tours a sense of legitimacy and timelessness, suggesting to visitors that they were experiencing an authentic connection with Shakespeare through his wife's descendants. When James Walter visited in the 1880s, he reported that visitors could have an authentic experience in the Cottage "nearly in the same condition as when Shakespeare paid his love

Figure 3.10. Mary Baker at Anne Hathaway's Cottage, 1896. Image courtesy of the Folger Shakespeare Library.

visits, whilst the fact of its being still tenanted by a descendant of his wife's father helps wonderfully to realize to visitors its many charming and romantic associations."[78] While of course visitors could not actually encounter Anne there, they could commune with a member of her family and imagine a connection with Shakespeare himself.

Baker must have realized early on that her family home was perfectly poised to satisfy growing desires for a private emotional life connected to young love that might explain the genesis of Shakespeare's literary creations. American author Charles Warren Stoddard expressed just such a sentiment when he visited the Cottage in 1874 as part of his European tour as a journalist for the *San Francisco Chronicle*. When he entered the Hathaway home, he remarked that "here I put off the Old World and the New World, and went back into the past," and he felt "at the very threshold of his desires." He comments that "I had found the golden key to the mystery of a life that has ever seemed to me more like a fable than a reality." Stoddard was given special permission by Mary Baker to spend the night in the Cottage, and he remarked on his spiritual transformation as the night wore on: "I was taking on the spirit of the surroundings, and by degrees growing in grace." Baker served him dinner and tea, and together they smoked pipes after their meal. Stoddard's night was not without upheaval, though. He recorded that he was awakened in the middle of the night by a woman in white greeting her lover at her window, declaring "parting is such sweet sorrow." Stoddard was convinced that he had been visited by the ghosts of William and Anne, and attested that he had "come away with a firm belief in the identity of the bard and his bride, such as a visit to his birthplace and his sepulcher had failed to inspire me with."[79] For travelers like Stoddard, Anne Hathaway's Cottage revealed the "golden key" to Shakespeare's life: his love for his wife Anne. Other visitors noted the synergy between the Cottage and their desired "Shakespeares." One guest in 1888 remarked that at the Cottage, "all seem to be a part of Shakespeare's story."[80] By the end of the nineteenth century, the idea that William and Anne had a passionate courtship was part of the standard narrative for "Shakespeare's story," because it provided a private life for Shakespeare, offered an explanation for the genesis of his literary characters as creations rooted in his passion, and located his origins squarely within the heart of England.

Other travelers reported that they sought out Anne Hathaway's Cottage for qualities that Shakespeare's other surviving home, the Birthplace, could not provide. English missionary Elder C. G. Berry writes in 1900 that after visiting Shakespeare's birthplace, he embarked on the rustic journey to the Cottage:

> From Shakespeare's home we rambled through a few green fields and hedge-rows, following a narrow foot-path for a mile and a quarter, being slightly interrupted by having to climb over a stile that had been placed in the rustic fence for the sole benefit of the pedestrians, the terminus of which brought us to the Hathaway cottage, the sacred abode and birthplace of Ann Hathaway, where she resided when first her virtues and charms attracted the poet, notwithstanding she was eight years his senior. This little home is entirely enveloped in a complete net of running ivy that wends its way from the foundation to the edge of its thatched roof, and is thickly interlaced with the fragrant yellow-flowered jasmine, the evergreen rosemary, and plants of rue. Mrs. Mary Baker, a descendent of the Hathaways, devoted the principal part of her life from year to year receiving visitors to the cottage.

The "virtues and charms" of Anne, along with the overflowing natural bounty, provided a sensory experience where Shakespeare's amorous youth could be imagined. Like many guests before and after him, Berry was also shown the bed "where the lucky charmer slept during her earlier years, also the little Bible which records the date of her birth." On his way out, Berry was offered the customary "draft of clear water, drawn from the old well near by."[81] As numerous guests attest, the biographical story that the Cottage supplied was one of hope, potential, passion, and young love, eternally preserved, and accessible through physical experiences (walking, drinking from the well, sitting on the courting settle, etc.). This was unlike the experience proffered by the other two main tourist sites, the Birthplace and Holy Trinity Church. In fact, one visitor compared the Cottage to the Birthplace, reflecting that the Cottage "is even more antiquated in appearance" than the Birthplace, and "more obviously a relic of the distant past."[82]

In the last decade of the nineteenth century, the volume of tourists to the Cottage had increased substantially. By 1910, the number of visitors to the Cottage had tripled from the previous fifteen years.[83] Chicagoan Christian Tearle noted the "endless stream of excursionists" year-round; while the author and his companion were in the Cottage, two groups of tourists arrived, and they were stuck in the cramped conditions: "The new-comers were beginning to ascend the stairs and they surged up until both bedrooms were uncomfortably crowded. We were wedged against the wall of the larger room; so there was nothing for it but to stand still and watch the visitors."[84] Another visitor that year recorded a steady flow of pilgrims to the Cottage even at the end of the day: "On my way back through the fields, though the sunset colors were spreading, I met more tourists making for 'the cottage.'"[85] When the Cottage was sold to the Shakespeare Birthplace Trust in 1892, one writer announced that "the proper maintenance of the scene of Shakespeare's courting is thus assured."[86] The sentiment that the courtship narrative should be "maintained" speaks to the desires of visitors to enshrine this version of Shakespeare's life story, which the other tourist destinations (the Birthplace and Holy Trinity Church, for example) were unable to offer. As caretaker Mary Baker aged, guests became concerned about the future of the Cottage; James Walter fretted, "It is to be hoped that the cottage and orchard will ere long pass into the hands of the Shakespeare Trustees, to be preserved and cared for as the Henley Street Birthplace and New Place have already been."[87] Mary Baker remained as custodian even after the sale of the Cottage, negotiating a deal where she sold the Hathaway family furniture for £500 in exchange for living in the Cottage as custodian, rent-free, for a salary of £75 a year. Baker's son William was also allowed to live at the Cottage until his death, and after his mother died, he and his wife took over as guides. Baker's daughter-in-law Jane continued to cultivate the Cottage as a shrine to romantic love. One guest noted that Jane Baker "spared neither time nor pains in making us acquainted with events connected with the cottage and its many sacred relics."[88] A postcard of Anne Hathaway's Cottage sent to Ohio schoolteacher Olive Rush in 1902 (Figure 3.11), included the

Figure 3.11. Postcard of Anne Hathaway's Cottage, 1902.

note, "This is just the way it looks, and it was shown me by a descendent of the Hathaways."

Gradually, the Shakespeare Birthplace Trust began to standardize the tours and facilities at the Cottage, instituting a ticket system (Figure 3.12) and regulating the activities of tour guides. Frederick W. Bennett, previously a ticket taker at the Birthplace for five years, took over from the Bakers, and "built on the pattern of guiding handed on by Mrs. Baker and her son" until his retirement in 1944. Under Bennett, Baker's hand-picked mementos of flowers turned into more typical souvenirs, postcards, and guidebooks. Bennett even sold his own guidebook, along with postcards and other souvenirs, though he was soon reprimanded by the Trust for "unauthorized sales or publications."[89]

Even though it began to homogenize the tourist experience and to oversee the management of the Cottage, the Shakespeare Birthplace Trust still maintained the overall content put in place by Mary Baker: the emphasis on an amorous mythology, the investment in symbolic relics to underline and substantiate these myths, and the preservation of a pastoral rural Warwickshire setting. In one of their earliest initiatives, the Trust purchased land and estates surrounding the cottage (in the 1920s and 1930s), to "protect its setting."[90] In 1923–1924 the garden was remodeled by Ellen Willmott, described as "the greatest of all living women gardeners," supplemented by

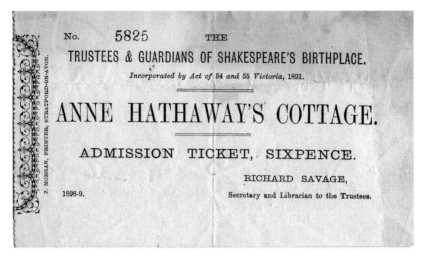

Figure 3.12. Admission ticket to Anne Hathaway's Cottage, 1898–1899. Image courtesy of the Shakespeare Birthplace Trust.

a donation from a New York patron.[91] According to Levi Fox, Willmott's flower beds were "essentially English in character, old-fashioned and suggestive of the countryside Shakespeare frequently referred to in his plays."[92] Willmott also helped develop an orchard to the west of the Cottage. In 1926, architect Guy Pemberton laid out the stone steps and paths as well as a timber and thatch tool shed.[93] Jackie Bennett observes that "the transformation of Anne Hathaway's Cottage encapsulates the rise of interest in cottage gardening and the way working plots gradually become more decorative."[94]

The garden at the Cottage has recently been renamed "Miss Willmott's garden" in honor of the famous gardener. The Trust maintained their investment in nearby land and properties, as a way of "safeguarding the unspoiled environment of Anne Hathaway's Cottage."[95] Shakespearian associations continue to be added; in 1977 the woodland along the banks of the Shottery Brook was renamed the Jubilee Walk in honor of Queen Elizabeth II.[96] In 1985, the Shakespeare Tree Garden was established, comprising trees and shrubs mentioned in Shakespeare's works.[97]

Mary Baker's tours were remarkably similar to the tourist experience at the Cottage today, and the fact that the narrative promoted by the Shakespeare Birthplace Trust has remained largely in line with what Baker initiated speaks to the longevity of this romantic myth. A recent brochure for the Cottage describes it as "the most romantic of Shakespeare's family homes where the young William Shakespeare courted his future wife."[98] In 2014, the "Love Struck Trail" ran from 14–23 February, where "Couples can follow the

Woodland Walk to find a selection of Shakespearian quotes, where one letter in each quote will be highlighted in a red heart for visitors to work out what romantic message the letters make. A special quiz will also be on offer where couples can search for a list of items in the Woodland Walk which includes a red rose. The trail finishes with the sweetheart tree which will feature red wooden hearts for people to write a message of love on."[99] Visitors are encouraged to visit the heart-shaped lavender maze, promoted as "the perfect place to declare your love or even propose to your loved one."[100] In 2016, an exhibit on "Tudor Courtship" invites visitors to take "a light-hearted look at the reality of finding a husband or wife in Tudor times" and to "find out how you might behave and the gifts you might give or receive in the process of finding your one true Tudor love!" This exhibit enriches "the story of the young Anne and William," which is "brought to life by our guides and volunteers throughout the cottage."[101] The longevity of Anne Hathaway's Cottage and the stability of the content of its tours suggests that it still holds a useful place in the array of Shakespeare tourist sites, namely for its unique ability to evoke myths of a romantic courtship set against an unchanging English landscape.

The World Wars and the Legacy of Anne Hathaway's Cottage

In large part because of the efforts of Mary Baker, by the end of the nineteenth century, the *space* of the Hathaway family farm was fully transformed into Anne Hathaway's Cottage, a *place* that commemorated a pastoral romantic Shakespeare deeply embedded in the "opening love" of youth and the "sights and sounds of country life," where visitors could go for a timeless dose of communion at the "shrine of love." As Tim Cresswell points out, "When humans invest meaning in a portion of space and then become attached to it in some way (naming is one such way) it becomes a place." The transformation of Anne Hathaway's Cottage is part of what Nicola J. Watson describes as a "biographically driven urge to imprint the virtual, readerly experience of Shakespeare onto topographical reality."[102]

In 1914, British historian and clergyman William H. Hutton (later Dean of Winchester Cathedral), in *Highways and Byways in Shakespeare's Country*, described what was by then a typical romantic view of Shakespeare through Anne Hathaway's Cottage. Hutton writes, "In the evening at sunset, in the hot summer afternoon when the sun shines on it, in the morning when the dew is still on the garden flowers, it has the same air of happy peace and brightness. The memory here of Stratford's great son is one wholly of happiness. You feel sure when you are here that the lovers were 'handfasted' in the true ancient form of betrothal, and knew it to be binding, long before they came together across the fields to Luddington Church."[103] During the two world wars, Anne Hathaway's Cottage became more than just a romantic tourist destination. The connotations of eternal happiness, ancient rituals, and the ghostly presence of William and Anne themselves took on additional significance in the coming years. The Cottage and its resonances were mobilized to support patriotic uses of Shakespeare, often conditioned by local economics, politics, and ideologies, as part of what Elizabeth K. Helsinger calls a "transformation of local rural places into English rural scenes."[104]

In the early decades of the twentieth century, Anne Hathaway's Cottage became a destination for international travelers, even in moments of global turmoil, as a testament to "the continuing existence of the past."[105] As early as 1907, the American Travel Club advertised tours from the States to England, including stops in both Stratford-upon-Avon and in Shottery.[106] One traveler from North Carolina made just such a journey, noting that the tour featured "the very bench . . . where Anne and William sat in the winter evenings when he came acourting," and that they were presented with flowers by a group of young girls after they finished touring the Cottage.[107] Likewise, Caroline French Benton, in *Women's Club Work and Programs, or First Aid to Club Women* (1913), recommended that her audience of American women embark on a tour of Shakespeare Country, and of the Shottery home of Anne Hathaway.[108] The University of California Extension Division also offered three-month educational tours, including stops in Stratford and Shottery.[109] One reader of a Lansing, Michigan educational journal reported in 1908 that on her journey from Michigan, she "had gone to Stratford to find Shakespeare" and instead in Shottery found "what Shakespeare found and loved, the undying essence of English life and art."[110] What this Michigan visitor called the "soul of England" and "the spell of the eternally feminine" would continue to attract pilgrims in the coming years, who sought access to young hopeful love set against the backdrop of undisturbed English countryside. William Salt Brassington, librarian of the Shakespeare Memorial Theatre, described the appeal of Stratford to Americans as its "quaint old-world appearance so dear to artists and antiquarians, so highly appreciated by American and Colonial visitors."[111] As Cecilia Morgan points out, such English landscapes and tourist sites "evoked an undifferentiated 'times past'" and "suggested that the English landscape might provide a refreshing antidote to modernity's frantic pace."[112] As the following section elucidates, the Cottage fulfilled this role.

The visitor's book to the Cottage, which began in 1912 and continued until after the end of World War II (the last entry is 1954), includes numerous international visitors from India, Northern Ireland, Jerusalem, Australia, and America. Alongside some of the more famous public figures, including early biographers Charlotte and Marie Stopes, Ellen Terry, George Bernard Shaw, Kenneth Clarke, William Poel, Ben Greet, Peggy O'Neill, Lilian Baylis, Stanley Lupino, Charlie Chaplin, Oliver Hardy, are some intriguing figures of greater political significance.

During World War I, several prominent national dignitaries spent time at Anne Hathaway's Cottage. Rennie MacInnes, the Anglican Bishop in Jerusalem, signed the guest book on 28 July 1915. He had been appointed Bishop of Jerusalem in 1914 but was prevented from going there due to the outbreak of the war.[113] Presumably he decided on a tour of the "country life" of England instead, including the "happy peace" of Anne Hathaway's Cottage.

In September of 1917, an entourage from Serbia also visited the Cottage, including Prince Alexis Karageorgevitch and his wife Princess Daria, originally from Cleveland, Ohio. Prince Alexis served as President of the Serbian Red Cross during World War I, but fled Serbia during the winter of 1915–1916. They spent part of the summer in Stratford, since a photo of them survives in Stratford, dated 31 July 1917. Neither MacInnes nor Karageorgevitch left personal records of their reactions to or motivations for visiting Anne Hathaway's Cottage, but, given their respective positions, these trips must have served as reprieves from the impending pressures of global turmoil, commemorating what Evelyn Waugh called "the dreaming ancestral beauty of the English country . . . something enduring and serene in a world that had lost its reason and would so stand when the chaos and confusion were forgotten."[114] The space that Mary Baker and the Hathaway family had carefully cultivated to evoke the permanence of young love amid the unspoiled countryside became a key symbolic sanctuary in the years ahead.

During World War II, Anne Hathaway's Cottage was adapted more extensively through a variety of venues to memorialize British wartime perseverance and "the peaceful sights and sounds of country life" associated with the Cottage at the end of the nineteenth century. This was part of the process that Elizabeth K. Helsinger describes, where "rural scenes are increasingly deployed as portable icons of England for those who have left home."[115] A series of wartime postcards (Figures 3.13–3.14) preserves and circulates these associations. The interior and exterior of Anne Hathaway's Cottage are featured on two of the cards, with the interior shot giving a

Figure 3.13. Postcard of Anne Hathaway's Cottage, c. 1940, exterior.

prominent place to the famous courting settle that had long been a symbol of romantic Shakespeare. The reverse sides feature Prime Minister Winston Churchill's inspirational words, "We shall never stop, never weary, never give in."[116] The postcards are undated, but Churchill's speech *Dieu Protége La France* was first broadcast on 21 October 1940.

The connotations of Anne Hathaway's Cottage as a sacred space that could sustain visitors with memories of their emotional investment were promoted widely. In a series of pamphlets put together for American servicemen by the British Council, Anne Hathaway's Cottage was included as one of the featured sites to visit during the war. Designed especially "to go easily into the pocket of a service jacket," these pamphlets gave brief historical information, suggestions about where to eat and sleep, and tips for local entertainment. The pamphlet about Stratford-upon-Avon describes it as a steadfast mecca of stability, reassuring readers that "in spite of the tremendous upheaval that is rocking the world at the present time Stratford-upon-Avon is still in the centre of England and maintaining its equilibrium." Anne Hathaway's Cottage is promoted as "a thatched house in a pretty setting" which includes of course "the oak settle on which the youthful William sat with Anne in courting days,"[117] reinforcing a version of youthful love, hope, and unspoiled countryside. Including in the list of items of interest to servicemen the courting settle, which had by now become a standard fixture of the Cottage, locates

Figure 3.14. Postcard of Anne Hathaway's Cottage, c. 1940, interior.

Shakespeare's romantic life (and by extension, Anne Hathaway) at the center of the "best" aspects of English culture and tradition. Visiting servicemen are reassured that "Stratford-upon-Avon stands for much that is characteristic in the English tradition and much that is best in the culture of English-speaking peoples everywhere." Many of the pamphlets had a larger secondary circulation when they were "posted as souvenirs to homes in the U.S.A. when they had served their purpose,"[118] which further secured the symbolic status of the Cottage as a representative of English culture and unchanging steadfast love.

An original photograph of Anne Hathaway's Cottage held by the Shakespeare Birthplace Trust (Figure 3.15) evokes a similar combination of pastoral country life amid global unrest. The notation on the back of the photograph reads "American Servicemen at AHC, c. 1945." Though the identity of the American servicemen is lost, we can surmise that they were probably part of what Simon Barker calls the "constant stream of military personnel" who were "established in the countryside around town" from Canada, the United States, and the other Allied nations.[119] The American Red Cross Service Club provided tours and even supplied bicycles for trips to enjoy the "charm" of "the Shakespeare countryside," much like the soldiers pictured in Figure 3.15.

Figure 3.15. American servicemen outside Anne Hathaway's Cottage. Image courtesy of the Shakespeare Birthplace Trust.

Attendance at Anne Hathaway's Cottage fell off dramatically with the start of the war in 1939, but around the time of this photo, military personnel were admitted for free, and attendance rose again. Visitors to the Birthplace Trust properties were scarce during the war years; Levi Fox reports that in 1940 only ten American visitors signed the guest book, but "in 1944, by which time American servicemen had arrived in this country to take part in the Normandy invasion, no fewer than 22,921 G.I.s, as they are called, visited the birthplace."[120] The account of one of the guides at the Cottage during the war years offers a window into how the Cottage fulfilled national and international needs. Emma Salmon remembered giving wounded World War II American servicemen a tour of the Cottage, and she recounts that a doctor regularly brought a coach of wounded US soldiers from a hospital in Birmingham for tours of the Cottage on Sunday afternoons.[121] Roma Innes, who lived at the Shottery Post Office during the war, similarly recalled that "the coach trade (round the Shakespeare area) really started with a doctor in Birmingham when there were some of the wounded soldiers in Birmingham" who "thought he'd like to bring them out to see Anne Hathaway's Cottage and he hired a coach."[122] Presumably the American doctor from Birmingham thought that wounded soldiers could benefit from being immersed in a space that evoked timeless romantic love inspired by a picturesque natural setting.

At least one description does survive about Anne Hathaway's Cottage's role in commemorating national identity during the war. American serviceman Eugene G. Schulz writes in his memoir about the typical associations American soldiers would have had about Anne Hathaway's Cottage. Schulz, who grew up on a farm in Wisconsin, was drafted in 1943 and was a typist in Patton's XX Corps, attached to Patton's Third Army. He describes his experience of touring the English countryside while stationed in Marlborough in 1944: "We really enjoyed walking along the lovely English roads and lanes that radiated out from our barracks ... These places were very charming with typical English cottages covered with thatched roofs and tiny front yards showing the early spring roses and other flowers ... I had seen pictures of scenes like this in geography books, and now it was a thrill to actually see these quaint English scenes with my own eyes." At one point, Schulz expresses the difficulty of remembering their reason for being there as opposed to enjoying the "peaceful sights" of the countryside: "We were in England for only one reason, to destroy the tyrant Adolf Hitler, who with his Wehrmacht was destroying the people and lands and cities of Europe ... It was time to get down to the business of war."[123]

Before leaving for the D-Day invasion, Schulz's group of ten American soldiers was given permission to do one last round of authorized sightseeing in early April of 1944. After traveling to Stonehenge and Avebury, they stopped in Stratford-upon-Avon. Schulz writes, "We walked on the streets of this small town, looking at the many sites relating to Shakespeare, including his home and Anne Hathaway's Cottage. There were no tourists, only soldiers, visiting here because all activities concerning this famous dramatist and poet were shut down for the duration of the war." Schulz recalled memorizing Portia's "Quality of Mercy" speech from his high school days, remarking on the euphoric feelings evoked by treading the same ground as William and Anne: "Wow! This day I had walked on hallowed ground where the author of this play had lived his life. I was on an emotional high during the ride back to camp as I stored these memories into the back of my brain."[124] Schulz's trip to Stratford was indeed a bucolic pause; General Patton arrived in early May to announce their role in his Third Army, in preparation for the D-Day invasion in June. They landed in Normandy and traveled across France, Germany, and Austria, later occupying Germany and liberating the Ohrdruf concentration camp. Schulz was awarded a Bronze Star for service, and made return pilgrimages to many of these sites again later in his life.

Anne Hathaway's Cottage was mobilized for a further global wartime use, to commemorate this version of youthful love, hope, and unspoiled countryside on one of the cover illustrations to the song *There'll Always be an England* (1939), (Figure 3.16). *There'll Always be an England* was the "first great hit song of the war," and its legacy extended past World War II; it was "one of the handful of wartime songs still remembered 50 years after the event."[125] The song posits a stable pastoral place that will always be there, "Tho' worlds may change and go awry."

> There'll always be an England—
> While there's a country lane;
> Wherever there's a cottage small
> Beside a field of grain.

While the song itself is a commentary on rural England in general, the cover illustration locates these values in Anne Hathaway's Cottage. Written by Ross Parker and Hugh Charles in 1939, the song sold over 200,000 copies within two months and "became the nation's rallying cry, uniting Britons as one in the fight against the Reich."[126] Linking Anne Hathaway's Cottage to this song further solidified the Cottage's role in commemorating British perseverance across the Atlantic, since the version of the song with Anne Hathaway's Cottage was sold only in the United States, Canada, and Newfoundland.[127] It is unclear why this version of the cover was confined to North America, but perhaps it related to the need to establish rapport with North Americans as allies during the war.

Global Anne Hathaway Cottages

In the twentieth century, the values and symbolic resonance of Anne Hathaway's Cottage – young love, hope, and the nurturing potential of the British countryside – were no longer confined to visitors who made the journey to the village of Shottery. Not content to bring home just a souvenir postcard, several visitors to the Cottage sought to export these associations to their homelands, resulting in the circulation of "Anne Hathaway Cottages" around the world. Some were galvanized by actual trips to the real space, and others were inspired by the mythical associations of romantic love, circulated

Figure 3.16. *There'll Always be an England*, by Hugh Charles and Ross Parker. Used with permission of Alfred Music.

since the time of Mary Baker. Outside of the UK, many of the Cottages have adapted the romantic, pastoral, and patriotic associations of the original place, spreading these various commemorative associations, and at times connecting Anne to a much larger symbolic landscape. Shakespeare gardens, often linked to Anne Hathaway's Cottage, were a further way to extend the feminine, domestic, and pastoral features, and also, as Nicola J. Watson notes, to "claim the Bard" in other spaces, notably in America, and "brin[g] Shakespeare home to somewhere he never knew."[128]

The replica of Anne Hathaway's Cottage in Wessington Springs, South Dakota can serve as a model for this global circulation. The cottage was built by faculty and students of Wessington Springs College in 1932 as a retirement home for Professor Clark Shay and his wife Emma, but was initially set up to commemorate her travel to England, quite a remarkable journey for a married woman traveling on her own in the 1920s. In 1926 at age 64, Emma Shay borrowed $1,000 in order to travel to England, entailing a train ride to Milwaukee, Chicago, Toronto, and Montreal, and eventually across the Atlantic by steamer to Liverpool. Shay traveled alone, and the trip took almost three months. Stratford was one of her first stops in June of 1926. After visiting the Birthplace, Holy Trinity Church, and the Memorial Theatre, she made her way to Anne Hathaway's Cottage. She was in search of a picture she had in her mind, and noted that "after many inquiries she found it, and it was just like the picture, with the thatched roof." She took a tour of the Cottage, making a special note about "the courting seat, where all love making was to be made in the presence of the father and mother."[129] Although she was not allowed to take a photograph inside, she did gather some grass, pansies and rosemary. In the process, she encountered the nurseryman, who expressed gratitude for the US visitors and told her "they did not know what they would do without the Americans coming to Stratford." American travel writer Elbert Hubbard likewise noted in 1928 that "ten thousand Americans visit Stratford every year, and all write descriptions of the place."[130] By this time, there was a mutually beneficial relationship between American tourists in particular, whose financial resources helped keep the tourist industry afloat; and the English sites that could supply visual evidence of the world imagined across the Atlantic. According to her memoir, for Emma Shay, it was "her dream of years gone by, to [visit] far away England," and Anne Hathaway's Cottage was a fundamental component of her trip.[131]

Shay's travels were so influential that she wanted to preserve her experience by recreating it back home. Of all the locales she visited in England, it was Anne Hathaway's Cottage that she chose to commemorate. In honor of Shakespeare's birthday in 1927, the Shays, students, and faculty began work on a recreated cottage garden in South Dakota. They finished the house in 1932, based on her postcard of the Shottery cottage, and it purports to be the only building in South Dakota with a thatched roof. It is significant that the Shays decided to build their own Anne Hathaway's Cottage as a monument to her Shakespeare journey rather than the Birthplace, which Shay also visited. This suggests that the associations she wanted to memorialize were linked to the "sweet communing" with the countryside and to the romantic pastoral Shakespeare associated with the Hathaway homestead, rather than with the family origins of the poet himself at the Birthplace. Shay's recreated garden is part of what Nicola J. Watson describes as "a sense that a love for Shakespeare could be appropriately described through plants and flowers," part of "how women individually and collectively appropriated Shakespeare to the domestic, amateur sphere."[132]

Shay's memorial to young romantic love continues to attract visitors to this rural corner of South Dakota. In 1989 the Shakespeare Garden Society of Wessington Springs was set up to take care of the cottage, in honor of the South Dakota state centennial. The Cottage now serves as one of several ethnic celebrations in South Dakota, featured in an article entitled "Celebrating our Ethnic Ways," alongside Czech and other heritages.[133] This South Dakota Hathaway Cottage also hosts marriages and May Day celebrations, further enshrining romantic myths about Shakespeare in upper Midwest America, and underlining Harald Hendrix's point that houses associated with writers "not only recall the poets and novelists who dwelt in them, but also the ideologies of those who turned them into memorial sites."[134]

Several North American bed and breakfasts commemorate and commodify this domestic version of Shakespeare. Anne Hathaway's Cottage Bed and Breakfast Inn in Staunton, Virginia features special "Elopement Packages" and offers to arrange an officiate, catering, and flowers for weddings.[135] The testimonies of the guests confirm their enjoyment of the commemorative practices associated with this space. One guest remarks, "the building itself is so authentic it was hard to believe I wasn't actually vacationing in Stratford-on-Avon."[136]

Anne Hathaway's Cottage in Green Lake, Wisconsin (Figure 3.17) serves a different and more personal commemorative purpose. This version was built in 1939 by Walter Smith and his wife Elsie, who was from England, and has been described as "independently wealthy and a woman of descreet [sic] taste."[137] When Elsie Smith sought to recreate an English space in the upper Midwest, she chose Anne Hathaway's Cottage. She spearheaded the construction of the house, hiring an English architect, insisting on a thatched roof, and importing furniture from England.[138] This Wisconsin Cottage commemorates English heritage, but omits any resonance of a romantic Shakespeare; one publicity blurb even describes the property as the "Anne Hathaway Cottage (inspired by the home of Anne Hathaway, mother of

Figure 3.17. Postcard of Anne Hathaway's Cottage, Green Lake, Wisconsin.

William Shakespeare, in Stratford Upon Avon in England)."[139] Clearly, every reproduction of Anne Hathaway's Cottage does not adhere to the same standards of authenticity.

One of the most intriguing Cottages is on the grounds of the Grove Park Inn in Asheville, North Carolina. This structure was built to the exact specifications of the Cottage in Shottery, but was constructed of local stone. The Cottage was completed in 1914, the year after the Grove Park Inn opened for business. Built by architect Fred Loring Seely, the Cottage probably owes its origins to the fact that Seely was "a great Anglophile" and "spent a great deal of his life in and out of England." Seely's uncle, Sir John Seely, was a British MP, served as Secretary of State for War during both world wars, and was a good friend of Winston Churchill.[140] Seely's choice of Anne Hathaway's Cottage as the property to represent his Anglophilia speaks to the Cottage's cachet as a heritage site.

As a component of the Grove Park Inn complex, this Hathaway Cottage was part of "the Finest Resort Hotel in the World," as its inaugural brochure proclaimed. Boasting that it was "built by hand in the old-fashioned way," the hotel provided guests with "rest and comfort and wholesomeness." Milk was produced by 200 registered Jersey cows from the estate of George

Vanderbilt; 400 of the rugs in the Inn were made at Aubusson, France; and bed linens were imported Oxford twill. There were "no radiators to be seen" and "no electric bulbs to be seen," and the 800 acres comprising the grounds offered "the finest combination of climate, of comfort and of happiness in surroundings that we believe has ever been made possible."[141]

One aspect of the "comfort and happiness" of guests was the absence of children, who were discouraged in the Inn. As a way to accommodate families, Seely built a series of cottages on the grounds of the Grove Park Inn, suitable for families. When he turned to constructing them, he also turned to the romantic and pastoral associations of Anne Hathaway, naming one of the cottages after Shakespeare's wife, and building it as close as possible to the dimensions of the original cottage. Built of stone native to the area, this three-bedroom structure is the only one of the three cottages that remains.

Anne Hathaway's Cottage in Asheville actually did provide a domestic space for the Philippine government during World War II, as part of the Grove Park Inn's transformation as a holding space for Axis diplomats and their families, who were kept in "complete luxury."[142] Manuel L. Quezon, President of the Philippines, stayed at the Cottage in the spring of 1944, where his government was headquartered for a month.[143] Unfortunately, Quezon and his staff did not record a response to the fact that the temporary wartime headquarters of their government replicated the family home of Shakespeare's wife across the Atlantic.

Before and after the war, this Hathaway Cottage continued to host US Presidents and other politicians. In April of 1947 General Dwight D. Eisenhower and his wife Mamie stayed at this Anne Hathaway's Cottage, as did President Herbert Hoover, former President and Chief Justice William Howard Taft, and President Franklin D. Roosevelt and his wife Eleanor.[144] The Grove Park Inn still commemorates the connection between Anne Hathaway and world politics, in the sign currently standing in front of the cottage (Figure 3.18), which memorializes both Anne Hathaway and English nostalgia alongside US history and global affairs. Although the Cottage was first known as the Hathaway Cottage, most recently it has been renamed the Presidential Cottage, and current signage simply refers to it as the generic "Cottage."

The romantic myths that Anne Hathaway's Cottage helped generate, perpetuate, and circulate are only possible because of the circumstances of history – the fact that Shakespeare married a woman from the outlying community of Shottery, and that her family home survived largely intact.[145] The longevity and embellishment of the Cottage have ensured that the Cottage remains the pre-eminent world-wide site of Shakespeare's

Figure 3.18. Sign at Anne Hathaway's Cottage, Asheville, North Carolina. Photo author's own.

courtship and the repository of myths of romantic love, one of the most popular and long-lived strands of memorialization of Shakespeare's wife. As part of the celebrations around the 400th anniversary of Shakespeare's death in 2016, the BBC filmed a short clip with actor Joseph Fiennes at Anne Hathaway's Cottage. As the camera pans over Fiennes entering the Cottage, he states, "Perhaps in this farmhouse they exchanged love tokens. Perhaps under these eaves they whispered their sweet nothings. And who knows – perhaps for Anne he began writing poetry."[146] In spite of some of the more unfavorable depictions of Anne that developed in the twentieth century (discussed in subsequent chapters), the survival of her family home has insured that the "Anne" of a romantic narrative remains viable and in circulation.

In his book on tourist travel, John Taylor remarks, "the journey to the heart of England, in search of Shakespeare, was always a journey towards loss and disappointment. For the visitor who saved Holy Trinity to the last, it ended in a graveyard."[147] Anne Hathaway's Cottage, however, offered a "Shakespeare" at odds with this – a Shakespeare fully alive, abounding with hope and potential, eternally preserved in the prime of his youth, engaged in a tender courtship with a native Warwickshire woman whom he sought across the florid countryside. The process of recreating an Anne Hathaway who can support this image of her husband has insured one version of her afterlife in connection with her family home, as the final three chapters of this book will show.

Coda

As part of the preparations for the Chicago World's Fair in 1893, British journalist William T. Stead wrote a Christmas novel, published in December of 1892. Designed to introduce British citizens to Chicago and to the features of the World's Fair, Stead's tale was also a love story. His plot concerns a party of British tourists traveling on the *Majestic* from Liverpool to Chicago, relating the experience of transatlantic travel and of life in Chicago. The love story features lead character Dr. Walter Wynne, who first encounters a "Shakespeare girl" named Rose, who lives in a cottage in the orchard behind Anne Hathaway's Cottage. The two fall in love at the Cottage, where they enjoy long walks through the countryside, amid "the first flush of springtime" when "the air was redolent with the fragrance and the music of Shakespeare's country."[148] Rose's father is a stonemason, and she spends her time reading Shakespeare and the Bible. As Dr. Wynne describes her, "her world was the realm which Shakespeare had peopled with the creation of his brain." The two are eventually separated on false premises, and both journey separately across the sea to Chicago. Rose's father is commissioned to build a replica of Anne Hathaway's Cottage in Chicago, which resembles the original "but for the warm sultry air, the great expanse of lake, and the strange and varied scene presented by the Exhibition, all blazing with electric light." As readers might expect, Dr. Wynne and Rose are reunited at the Chicago Cottage at the end of the novel. Stead's story is significant for his choice of Anne Hathaway's Cottage as a shorthand setting for a romantic plot. But this tale has further implications due to Stead's life story. In Stead's novel, the *Majestic* rescues passengers from a neighboring ship that struck an iceberg. Twenty years after Stead published his novel in *Review of Reviews*, he booked passage on the *Titanic*, at the invitation of President Taft. Stead reportedly aided women and children to lifeboats, and his body was never recovered. Because he wrote of a similar shipwreck in 1892, Stead and his story have added resonance. Stead circulates the association between Anne Hathaway's Cottage and romantic love to readers interested in the *Titanic*, thus reaching a wide audience beyond those interested in Shakespeare.

PART II
Imagining Anne

INTERLUDE: FACT AND FICTION

A NNE HATHAWAY WAS PART OF CRUCIAL FORMATIVE CHAPTERS in Shakespeare's life – his transition from teenager to parent, his Warwickshire life, and his final years at New Place. Yet few details survive about these consequential periods: how the Shakespeares met, what their relationship was like, or what circumstances led to her premarital pregnancy, just to name a few examples. Shakespeare spent part of his life in rented lodgings in London and there is no evidence that he returned to Stratford until the end of his life. In turn, there is no evidence that Anne ever set foot in London. Further, neither Shakespeare nor his wife left any documents in their own voices – no letters, diaries, or other first-person accounts of their lives. These gaps in the Shakespearian biographical record are extensive, resulting in what Roger Chartier calls a "tension which is intrinsic in all Shakespearean biography."[1]

For Anne Hathaway in particular, because such scarce records survive, every depiction of her, whether couched as a biography or as fiction, has to use fictional techniques to fill in the gaps in her life story. In other words, any version of Anne that departs from the basic skeletal biographical information, to create a narrative about her life, or especially to ascribe emotional or mental states to her or to Shakespeare, relies on fiction. Indeed, Ina Schabert has noted that fictional biography "is most successful with obscure lives, where lack of material reduces the factual portrait to a mere sketch or silhouette: figures of the remote past, lower-class heroes, artists about whose private lives little is known, and women."[2] Part I of this book has traced Anne Hathaway's evolution in Shakespeare's life story from a bare reference in Nicholas Rowe's 1709 biography to the occupant of a Cottage that has been exported worldwide. Part II of this book looks at how Anne has been imagined, in fictional and biographical works alike, from the eighteenth century to the present.

One of the central arguments of Part II is that the historical Anne Hathaway can never be retrieved or pinned down, and thus every narrative about "Anne" is a fictional account to some degree, developed in response to cultural, social, political, historical, or literary developments. The remainder of this book looks at these variant Annes across the past three centuries, in biography and fiction alike. I place these Annes side by side to allow them to resonate with each other and with their historical contexts, regardless of whether they are outwardly labeled "biography" or "fiction." The imaginary Annes covered in these final three chapters reveal an expansive, diverse, contradictory, and conflicted history, in relation to ideas about Shakespeare, women, sexuality, and creativity, often targeted at specific types of readers or audience members to whom Anne can appeal. Thus, at times, Anne seems to be constantly shapeshifting, with antithetical Annes existing in the same period, in biography and in fiction alike. Fittingly, James Shapiro observes that biographies tend to increase "when the portrait of the artist falls out of alignment with contemporary values and scholarship,"[3] and remaking Anne is often a way to keep remaking Shakespeare.

The Interplay between Biography and Fiction

Biography and fiction share common goals of explaining the mysteries of Shakespeare's life story – what Graham Holderness has described as "what biography really wants most of all to know, the interior life, the secrets of the private man: what he believed, how he felt, whom he loved."[4] To this end, biographers often veer into the territory of fiction by subjectively speculating about Shakespeare's emotional life and thoughts. John F. Keener has pointed out that one of the key markers of fictionalization is the use of "narrative descriptions of the internal states of human figures," especially "verbs of inner action."[5]

In describing the motivation behind his novel *My Name is Will: A Novel of Sex, Drugs, and Shakespeare* (2008), Jess Winfield espoused just such an aspiration, remarking that he "wanted to portray Shakespeare as a living, breathing, sensual, and all-too-human young man, rather than the pedestal-bound bust he's become in our cultural consciousness."[6] Novelist Bruce Duffy argues that this is the purview of a novel, to "get inside some human beings – into their world in a way that history or biography can't duplicate, or rather in a way that delivers a different kind of authority and a different kind of pleasure."[7] Biographers often share this objective. In the opening to his 2004 biography *Will in The World*, Stephen Greenblatt affirms that his intent is to "discover the actual person who wrote the most important body of imaginative literature of the last thousand years," and "to tread the shadowy paths that lead from the life he lived into the literature he created." Greenblatt justifies his journey down these "shadowy paths" by arguing that "to understand how Shakespeare used his imagination to transform his life into his art, it is important to use our own imagination."[8]

A number of critics have addressed this problematic border between biographical fact and fiction. Ina Schabert has argued that "both factual and fictional biographies thus are made up and in this sense are fictions." Schabert explains that there is no "clear dividing line between biography and the biographical novel," and conventional biographies are often "informed by personal and group prejudices, ideological assumptions and conventions of aesthetic patterning."[9] Likewise, Joanna Scott attests that "the territories of fiction and history are demarcated by a border that is jagged, maybe even porous in places."[10] Similarly, John F. Keener maintains that "the line between fictional and historical biographical narratives remains so intransigently difficult to define" due to "biography's formal interaction with both fictional and historical narrative modes," and "these problems are further exacerbated by the postmodern interrogation of historical truth, essentialist identity, and the relationship between the two."[11]

In Shakespeare studies, several scholars have observed that the form of biography entails a great deal of fiction in order to knit together the scraps of Shakespeare's life, or as Peter Holland succinctly puts it, "the inevitability of Shakespeare biography constitut[es] a space of fiction."[12] Graham Holderness, who has deliberately exploited the line between biographical fiction and non-fiction in *Nine Lives of William Shakespeare* (2011), remarks that "Shakespeare's various lives are multiple and discontinuous," and "every attempt to write a life for Shakespeare again embroiders fact and tradition into a speculative composition that is, at least partly, fictional."[13] "Shakespearean biography," adds William Leahy, is "characterized by the constant iteration of fictional forms."[14] Similarly, John Worthen remarks that "the narrative of a biography is in almost every case designed to conceal the different kinds of ignorance from which we suffer,"[15] and that ignorance is filled in with fiction.

The various Annes in biographies of Shakespeare traverse the fine line between fact and fiction. After all, speculating on the nature of Shakespeare's marriage, and the circumstances in which William met Anne, is germane to both biography and to fiction. In the end, there can often be little difference between a biographer molding an Anne to suit his or her narrative about Shakespeare, and a novelist crafting an Anne to fit a storyline.

These numerous Anne Hathaways keep alive a vivid variety of fantasies about Shakespeare as a lover, husband, father, and private man, filling in what Julia Reinhard Lupton describes as "the relative blankness of the biographical record around matters that intensely interest readers."[16] Since the "relative blankness" of the biographical record can only be filled in by fiction, this section of the book will suggest that since Anne's life has to be rounded out with fiction in the absence of new archival material, ostensibly biographical works that claim factual authority can often be just as subjective as overtly fictional works. In fact, fiction may have the better claim to represent the Anne that readers and audiences desire. As Russell Banks notes, "the novelist can humanize a historical figure by inhabiting the character in a way that a biographer and a historian can't."[17]

One of the challenges of Shakespearian biography is determining the relationship between Shakespeare's life and his literary works, "the central structural question for biographers."[18] Given the gaps in the Shakespearian archive, it is understandable that many biographies have turned to the literary works for substance. As William Leahy puts it, biography exists "as the richness of the works meets the poverty of the recorded life, where the complexity of the plays and poems meets the empty vessel that is the life of the author."[19] Likewise, biographies of authors "recognize[e] a yearning, a desire to bridge between works and life," observes Peter Holland, but "the chasm remains" with Shakespeare.[20] James Shapiro also criticizes the "circular and arbitrary" method of ransacking the works for "clues that can be read back" into Shakespeare's life story.[21] Yet conversely, Lois Potter contends that "to leave out the works is to make the life meaningless,"[22] and biographer Park Honan admits that his "understanding" of Shakespeare "was helped by research, but as much as anything else by his plays."[23] Paul Franssen describes this technique as "projecting an element from Shakespeare's work back onto his life and then treating this as the autobiographical source of inspiration."[24]

Further problematizing the use of Shakespeare's works to construct his life, Roger Chartier explains that beginning with Edmond Malone, the literary works were "conceived as original creations expressing the most intimate, the most personal feelings of the writer, linked to his or her most personal experiences." As Chartier puts it, both biographies and fictional works "build up a Shakespeare 'of the mind,'" and biographers who use the works to write the life are engaged in an "impossible challenge" to "reconstruct a past reality that cannot be caught." As a result, "biography becomes the self-portrait of the biographer, who projects onto Shakespeare's imaginary life his or her own obsessions or nostalgias."[25] As tempting as it might be to supplement Anne's life with components from Shakespeare's literary works, this process is of necessity selective and subjective. After all, it is impossible to know which female characters are more likely to have been inspired by Anne, if any were at all. Andrew Hadfield remarks that "there will always be a complicated and unsatisfactory link between the life and the writing, one that leaves matters open for speculation, informed, misinformed and deluded."[26] Augmenting Anne with material from Shakespeare's creative output has little basis in probability or likelihood, but nevertheless has continued to flourish as a biographical strategy.

Although Anne Hathaway has been the subject of imaginative texts since the late eighteenth century, several literary forms that are ideally suited for stories about Shakespeare's private life, and especially about the women connected to him, have continued to proliferate since the nineteenth century. Historical romance and biofiction in particular, inspired in part by the "postmodern blending of fact and fiction," have contributed to the growth of novels about Shakespeare's life.[27] Jerome De Groot suggests that the biographical novel is ideal for allowing authors to "rethink and revise accepted versions of the past" because it combines fact, fiction, history, and biography, and novelists often "create a fictional scene in order to express a subtextual biographical 'truth.'"[28] Similarly, Valentina Vannucci observes that biofiction "has the effect of dismantling in one fell swoop the canonical ideas of identity, historical identity and history, giving life to a contemporary hybrid that deconstructs, while pretending to revisit, the canonical historical novel."[29] The remainder of this book will show the subversive and destabilizing potential of these literary forms.

Building on the premise that any substantial representation of Anne is fictional by necessity, Chapters 4 and 5 take a roughly chronological structure to explore representative works about Anne Hathaway, in both biographies and in fictional works, allowing these stories to resonate within their historical moments. I have grouped similar works together to better identify patterns, even if strict chronology is interrupted briefly. Chapter 4 begins with the earliest accounts of Anne, through the 1940s. Chapter 5 opens with Anthony Burgess, who wrote both a biographical novel (1964) and a biography (1970), and whose version of Anne has had a far-reaching influence on later writers. Chapter 5 then examines a number of case studies where the seams of Anne's life story are apparent, looking at how and why she is constructed in the millennial cluster of scholarly and popular biographies and in fictional works. Chapter 6 centers on works (written largely by women) that co-opt Anne for women. Liberated from the constraints of historical fidelity and from the need to play a supporting role to Shakespeare,

many of these women-centered Annes are a refreshing, if unrealistic, change
from the confining narrow parameters of historical Annes.

The numerous Annes that emerge in the following chapters run the gamut
from the secret author of Shakespeare's plays, the lover of the Earl of Oxford,
the loyal wife minding the house while her husband worked, and the cast-off
oppressive spouse, gladly left behind in Stratford. Anne has also played
a number of roles in biographies of Shakespeare, from supportive wife to
"disastrous mistake," and the spectrum of biographical Annes bears
a surprising resemblance to the fictional Annes. Collectively, these Annes
speak to changing desires for variations in Shakespeare's life story.

Dark Ladies and Domestic Annes

From the earliest examples, Anne Hathaway has been difficult to fit into
accounts of Shakespeare's life, as part of the phenomenon Douglas Lanier has
described, where "Shakespeare the Author simply outstripped the known
facts of his mundane bourgeois life."[30] Recall David Garrick's inability to
reconcile the fact that Shakespeare married a local Warwickshire woman,
with the Shakespeare he sought to create in his 1769 Jubilee. Garrick
employed "Nature" and the Birthplace to stand in for Shakespeare's "personal story," and willfully excluded any mention of his wife. Eighteenth-
century editor Edmond Malone relied on Shakespeare's literary works and
on his will to concoct an unhappily married Shakespeare. Contemporary
biographers are not necessarily any more judicious in their treatment of
Anne.

As the domestic wife in Stratford, Anne has often been left out of
Shakespeare's life story because of her ordinariness. As Richard Holmes
points out, biography "has always been drawn towards the famous, the
glamorous, the notorious," and away from "the ordinary, the average, the
everyday lives that most of us lead and need to understand." He notes that
"where the mundane, in its richest sense, is central to a life – as in a happy
marriage, or a long and constant friendship – it is often peculiarly important,
both in its sources ... and in its narrative invention."[31] As part of
Shakespeare's everyday Stratford life, and by all accounts never anything
but an ordinary early modern woman, Anne has lacked the glamor, notori-
ety, and fame that Holmes links to biography. Works that endorse and
validate domestic life give Anne importance, but that rarely makes for
a good story or a compelling biography. Margreta de Grazia notes that
"there has always been some disappointment with what we know of
Shakespeare's life" because "it seems incommensurate with his plays and

poems," and in comparison, his life seems "quite ordinary and hardly inspiring."[32] Brian Cummings similarly observes that "whatever we find cannot live up to expectations" because "the life as we have it is insufficient to explain the genius of the writing."[33] If this is true for Shakespeare, it is even more so for Anne.

The relationship between Shakespeare's sexuality and his creative output is especially problematic for Anne, given the likely separation (part-time or full-time) between the Shakespeares during his most productive creative period. Numerous solutions have been put forth in both biographies and fiction to knit these pieces together, and Anne has even been replaced with substitute love interests, male and female, who could provide a London-based romance to inspire his works.[34] The search for alternative women has also been inspired by the long-standing desire to identify a Dark Lady behind Shakespeare's Sonnets, long considered "autobiographical statements" and "revelations of the life and mind of the greatest Englishman," according to Stuart Sillars.[35] Throughout the texts considered in the next three chapters, Anne Hathaway is often either willfully ignored, or placed in opposition to a more attractive, more sexualized, and less domestic woman. Clearly linked to the country, Anne is also part of the "uncultured and backwards" associations with Stratford, whereas rival lovers are usually associated with "sophisticated" London life.[36] As Paul Franssen points out, this is part of the "age-old ambivalence towards the countryside," where Shakespeare escapes to London "not just as a temporary place of refuge . . . but as his haven from Warwickshire backwardness."[37] Thus, the history of Anne's place in Shakespeare's life story is not a trajectory from a marginalized woman to a rehabilitated one, but rather is a repetitive and circular series of possible solutions to the same biographical problems, advanced by both biography and fiction.

Unsettling Biography

As the next three chapters will show, by offering alternative narratives to the stories told in biographies of Shakespeare, fiction challenges some of the hardened assumptions about Shakespeare's life, underlining the uncertainty of biographical narratives, and suggesting that there are other stories that may be equally "true." This process creates an interplay between ostensibly factual biographies and fiction, producing an array of life stories that exists on a continuum between fact and fiction, and inspiring questions about his life.

In a discussion of her novel *Mistress Shakespeare* (2009), which includes both Anne Hathaway and Anne Whateley, Karen Harper poses the question:

"What if Anne Whateley was really the love of his life, the dark lady of his sonnets, his inspiration and muse? What if you read their story, then decide for yourself?"[38] Readers of *Mistress Shakespeare* testify to just such a reaction: "I love the idea that Anne Whateley could have been Shakespeare's muse and that his great works were inspired by his unending love for her," wrote one fan, adding that "This book made me fall in love with Shakespeare all over again." Another reader recounts her satisfaction at discovering Shakespeare's works enmeshed with this fictional tale, confessing that "I found it terribly romantic when Will would whisper things to Anne like 'Parting is such sweet sorrow.'"[39]

Many of the fictional works about Shakespeare are championed by their authors as alternatives to formal biographies, and often include biographical material alongside the ostensibly fictional content.[40] The playtext of Vern Thiessen's *Shakespeare's Will* (2005), for example, includes a list of dates and life events, embedding the process of going from fact to fiction in the playtext itself. Thiessen even includes a version of Shakespeare's will as an appendix, admitting that he "played 'fast and loose' with the will and its meaning" and used it "as a springboard for my own imagination."[41] Likewise, Christopher Rush prompts readers to consider his novel *Will* (2008) as a faithful version of Shakespeare's life: "I have only very occasionally tweaked a date or a fact to suit the plot, apart from which I have stuck faithfully to the Shakespeare story in so far as it can ever be known."[42] Rush raises an important point about the function of biofiction. If Shakespeare's life story can never "be known," then biofiction and biography serve the same purpose of creating possible lives. Monica Latham points out that "the fundamental process at the heart of biofiction is manipulating the truth" because "absolutely objective historical truth does not exist."[43] As Jerome De Groot puts it, the "central paradox" of historical fiction is "the consciously false realist representation of something which can never be known."[44] In other words, if we can never know what Shakespeare's relationship with his wife was like, this uncertainty opens the door to multiple possibilities, any number of which might be "true."

Other authors have employed similar strategies to encourage their readers to engage in a back-and-forth between fiction and biography. Thomas Lennon, in his 1942 play *The Truth About Anne*, prefaces his work by defending Anne against biographers who have "damned" her. In the afterword to *My Name is Will: A Novel of Sex, Drugs, and Shakespeare* (2008), Jess Winfield discloses: "The events I've described as having taken place in 1582 are a pastiche of fact, legend, and surmise. My main goal was to tell a ripping yarn, but I also wanted, as much as possible, to make the Bard's story at least historically plausible in its larger points, and not contradict the historical record."[45] Robert Nye, in his afterword to *Mrs. Shakespeare: The Complete Works*, directs readers to Samuel Schoenbaum's *William Shakespeare: A Documentary Life* as "the best modern biography," noting that "none of my sources can be held responsible for the central imaginative thesis of my book: that Anne Hathaway might have been the Dark Lady of the *Sonnets*."[46]

Further justifications for considering biographies and fiction side by side come from readers, who frequently attest to the process of reading a work of fiction about Shakespeare's life, and then reading a biography, engaging in a back-and-forth interpretation between these texts. Fictional works about Shakespeare depend on readers having at least a minimal knowledge of the biography of Shakespeare. One reader of Arliss Ryan's novel *The Secret Confessions of Anne Shakespeare* (2010) reported that the novel "so intrigued me that I have gone on a sort of Shakespeare kick and purchased a 2 volume set of Shakespeare's entire works to peruse as well as a biography and another book based on the subject of Elizabethan theater." This reader confesses that it "feels strange to suddenly enjoy Shakespeare, when I didn't care for it at all in school, but that just goes to show that a really great novel such as this can change a mind and open a person to further reading."[47]

Why Anne Matters

The works under consideration in the second part of this book span well over two centuries, yet with few exceptions, these texts reveal a cyclical and recurring array of interests connected to Anne Hathaway. Anne Hathaway's Cottage regularly appears as a pastoral setting, and the tale of a faithful husband and his devoted wife likewise is a frequent motif. The idea of Anne Hathaway as an independent-minded woman reappears in the full range of texts as well, and even occurs in some of the relatively early works about her. So too, the idea of Anne as a "disastrous mistake," a cast-off wife whom Shakespeare sought to forget, dates from the late eighteenth century in Edmond Malone's interpretation of Shakespeare's will, but reappears regularly in fiction and biography alike. While few works construct a negative image of Shakespeare, likely so as not to alienate a potential audience seeking stories of Shakespeare's private life, some versions of Anne Hathaway do talk back to Shakespeare as a way to speak to women's concerns. These defiant "Annes" are often sexually independent – they take other lovers, including Shakespeare's brother Gilbert, who remained in Stratford his whole life; neighbor Hamnet Sadler; authorship rival the Earl of Oxford; and even fellow playwrights Christopher Marlowe and Ben Jonson. As Paul Franssen points out, works of fiction about Shakespeare "often reach bigger audiences" than scholarly biographies,[48] and though they may be outlandish at times, many of these novels and plays have a broader influence than do academic works.

This brief interlude has addressed many of the theoretical and methodological issues related to the interplay between Shakespeare biography and fiction. Though we can never attain the "real" Anne Hathaway, it is worth maintaining some degree of skepticism about the ways she is constructed, whether couched as fact or as fiction. Indeed, Lois Potter cautions that "fiction can easily become fact when it sounds poetically and imaginatively right," and can "sometimes turn up as fact in other writers."[49] The way Anne materializes in many of these works should underline the significance of the biographical choices at work. As Paula R. Backscheider puts it, from a feminist standpoint, biography entails a series of "choices and their implications,"[50] which for the stories of Shakespeare's wife have remained unexamined for too long.

4

"FIT TO MARRY"
Early Imaginary Annes

FROM THE START, THE BARE BONES OF ANNE'S SKELETAL LIFE have necessitated extra flesh. Anne's debut in Shakespeare's life story began with Nicholas Rowe's 1709 "Account," yet even this minimal reference to Anne includes the seeds for imaginative potential that would later be exploited in biography and in fiction alike. Readers may recall that Rowe did not even include Anne's first name, simply recording that "in order to settle in the World after a Family manner, [Shakespeare] thought fit to marry while he was yet very Young. His Wife was the Daughter of one *Hathaway*, said to have been a substantial Yeoman in the Neighbourhood of *Stratford*." Rowe's comment that Shakespeare "thought fit" to marry ascribes a deliberate agency to Shakespeare, an example of what John F. Keener identifies as one of the indications of fictionalization: "narrative descriptions of the internal states of human figures," especially "verbs of inner action."[1] In a mere two sentences, Rowe departs from the basic facts of Shakespeare's marriage, to suggest what Shakespeare's mental state was at the time of his nuptials: marriage was something Shakespeare *thought* he should do. Rowe rationalized his story of Shakespeare's life because it could help illuminate the works. "The knowledge of an Author may sometimes conduce to the better understanding of his Book," he noted.[2] The temptation to create a consciousness behind Shakespeare's works, and to connect his literary output with the story of his life, has bolstered both biographies and imaginative works, where his wife Anne often takes on a pivotal role.

Throughout this history, some authors have bypassed Anne, in favor of alternative love interests. In these "Anti-Anne" works, an alternate woman (or man) is posited as the lover of Shakespeare, the female muse, or the rival to Anne. Usually these candidates are urban women in London, they are not mothers, and they are involved in the literary scene in some way. These alternatives to Shakespeare's wife likely stem from several motivations. The idea that Shakespeare's literary output was influenced by his real life frequently involves a passionate erotic life, and a domestic, stay-at-home mother is rarely the most appealing literary muse. Second, a long-standing preference for city, urban, sophisticated life, over rural, provincial, and unschooled country life, was reflected in fictional works.[3] Since there is no evidence that Anne joined her husband in London, she either has to be transported to London for some period of time, or another lover has to be invented to stand in for her, in order to provide Shakespeare with an amatory life during the London period of his career. The more Shakespeare needs to be an urbane, sexually motivated, London-centered character, the less Anne figures in his life story.

Conversely, at times Anne even disappears completely from Shakespeare's life story. One of the earliest Shakespeare fictions, Alexandre Duval's popular and influential *Shakespeare Amoureux* (1804), "conveniently ignore[s]" Anne so that Shakespeare can pursue an actress unusually named Clarence.[4] Paul Franssen attributes Duval's omission of Anne to a "total lack of research," but audiences did not seem to mind, since Franssen notes that the play was "a great hit," and the role of Shakespeare became a "vehicle for star actors" across Europe and in America.[5] Likewise, in Charles A. Somerset's two-act play *Shakespeare's Early Days* (1829), a 21-year old Shakespeare is still living at home, and Anne Hathaway is curiously absent from the play. There is no mention of Shakespeare having married three years before the time of the play. Somerset instead focuses on the accusation of deer-stealing, with Queen Elizabeth crowning him "England's noblest bard" in the final scene. Somerset's play was performed at Covent Garden, with Charles Kemble in the lead role as Shakespeare.[6] As Peter Holland points out, "the search for a dramatically realized Shakespeare is also a quest for a normalized Shakespeare, caught, often, between duty to Anne and the children and the lure of fame and fortune in London." Holland notes that many of the dramas written about Shakespeare's life focus on his youth in Stratford, where he is not at work in the theatre, and is "the Shakespeare about to become Shakespeare, the man who will be Shakespeare but is not Shakespeare yet."[7] One of the most popular versions of this motif is to develop a love interest for Shakespeare related to the Dark Lady of the Sonnets, as in Clemence Dane's 1921 play *Will Shakespeare: An Invention in Four Acts.* Dane's play starred Claude Rains in a West End run, opposing a Dark

Lady in London with Anne Hathaway, who remained "waiting, endlessly waiting, for Shakespeare's return to Stratford." Dane's play was later broadcast by the BBC during World War II to boost morale, further circulating the depiction of Anne as a desperate wife.

This chapter examines representative Annes, from her earliest appearance in biographies of Shakespeare through World War II. The wide variety of Annes demonstrates her fluid position as a way to adjust Shakespeare according to fluctuating ideas about women, family, sexuality, and creativity. As this chapter will show, any work that extends beyond the bare facts of Anne's life, out of necessity has to involve fictional techniques. Numerous overt works of fiction, from novels to plays, create imaginary Annes, but so too do biographies that expand the basic skeletal details about her. The "real" Anne Hathaway can never be known, of course, but the diverse, contradictory, and often self-serving portrayals of her underline the premise of this book: that Anne's afterlife is fluid, flexible, and adaptable – thus, her longevity has been assured, regardless of historical fidelity.

Forgetting Anne: Edmond Malone

Nicholas Rowe's 1709 biography remained the standard until the end of the eighteenth century, when Edmond Malone sought to supplant Rowe by amassing copious amounts of material for his planned biography. Even after twenty years, he never completed his task, lamenting that writing a full biography of Shakespeare was "a formidable work, but if I can but live to finish it, I shall think nothing of the labour."[8] Nevertheless, Malone's depiction of Shakespeare's marital life is interwoven throughout his comments on Shakespeare's works, and his Anne has had a pervasive influence on her afterlife; as Lena Cowen Orlin puts it, Malone's version of Anne has been "stubbornly resistant to change."[9] James Shapiro observes that as late as 2004, Stephen Greenblatt's biography *Will in the World* returns to the "sour portrayal of married life" and "come[s] full circle, back to where Malone began."[10]

Using the age difference between the Shakespeares, the bequest of the "second best bed" in the will, and carefully culled literary works of Shakespeare, Malone embarked on the first extended fantasy of Anne as a disastrous mistake, a woman who made Shakespeare miserable in his married life, and who had no connection to his literary output. Such an interpretation, however, also required him to suppress key information about Anne, namely the epitaph on her grave. For Malone, the "second best bed" bequest in Shakespeare's will functioned as what Ina Schabert describes as "creative nuclei about which the accretion of an imagined, conscious and subconscious mental life" is constructed, and this component "functions as determinant for a whole chain of imagined inner and known outer events."[11] In other words, Malone imagines a scenario to explain Shakespeare's bequest to his wife, around which he builds an extended hypothetical narrative of marital unhappiness.

Taking his inspiration from William Oldys's note that Sonnet 93 ("So shall I live, supposing thou art true, / Like a deceived husband") was "addressed by Shakespeare to his *beautiful* wife on some suspicion of her infidelity," Malone develops an argument about Shakespeare's inner thoughts, and about the connection between his life and his writing, contending that "he appears to me to have written more immediately *from the heart* on the subject of jealousy, than on any other; and it is therefore not improbable he might have felt it."[12] Malone expands this allegation to the will, claiming that the bequest to Anne of the "second best bed" was due to Shakespeare's jealousy at her infidelities. "Jealousy is the principal hinge of *four* of his plays," he argues, and turning to lines from *Othello*, he contends that Shakespeare writes with "such exquisite feeling, as might lead us to suspect that the author, at some period of his life, had himself been *perplexed* with doubts, though not perhaps *in the extreme*." Malone moves from this hypothesis about Shakespeare's inner thoughts to a conviction about his emotional life, concluding that Shakespeare "might not have loved Anne, and perhaps she might not have deserved his affection."[13] In order to work, though, this argument requires a substantial infusion of fiction and a suppression of facts.

The age difference between the Shakespeares was further fodder for Malone's claim. Since Anne was older than Shakespeare, Malone contends, this "disproportion of age . . . seldom fails, at a subsequent period of life, to be productive of unhappiness."[14] Not content to simply relate the factual age difference, Malone concocts a story about Shakespeare's emotional state – the age difference made Shakespeare unhappy, and thus his marriage was a failure.

Malone's extreme stance on Shakespeare's marriage became a topic for dispute among his fellow editors, underlining the contested position that Anne would occupy in Shakespeare's life story. George Steevens attempted to discredit Malone by suggesting that the bequest of the bed was "a mark of peculiar tenderness," and that Malone's supposition of Shakespeare's jealousy was "fallacious."[15] Steevens even tried to dissuade Malone from "indulging in literary gossip," but to no avail.[16] Malone printed Steevens's cautionary note to him, adding an even more incendiary comment about Anne that readers may recognize from Chapter 2: "His wife had not wholly escaped his memory; he had forgot her, – he had recollected her, – but so recollected her, as more strongly to mark how little he esteemed her; he had already (as it is vulgarly expressed) cut her off, not indeed with a shilling, but with an old bed."[17] James Boswell also registered his discomfort at Malone's harsh view of Anne, noting that he "question[s] the truth of Mr. Malone's uncomfortable conjecture," adding that if jealousy had been Shakespeare's "motive for neglecting his wife in his will," he would not have "described it as he has uniformly done in his plays, as being causeless and unjust."[18]

Malone's denigration of Anne also depended on ignoring the epitaph on her grave, even though he knew of its content. His notes on the Stratford Parish Register, affixed to the posthumous Boswell–Malone 1821 edition, include the following account:

> This lady, who was the poet's widow, and whose maiden name was Anne Hathaway, died, as appears from her tomb-stone, at the age of 67, and consequently was near eight years older than her husband. The following is the inscription on her tombstone in the Church of Stratford:
> "Here lyeth interred the body of Anne, wife of William Shakespeare, who departed this life the 6th day of August 1623, being of the age of 67 years."
> After this inscription follow six Latin verses not worth preserving.[19]

Readers will recall from Chapter 1 that the Latin verses Malone dismisses as "not worth preserving" portray Anne as a devoted and devout mother, an image that does not fit with an Anne who was cut off with an old bed, the "'nightmare' narrative" of marriage, as described by Lena Cowen Orlin.[20] It is unclear what motivated Malone to undertake this campaign to denigrate Anne, though Michael Dobson attributes it to Malone's own unhappy personal life.[21] Regardless of his motives, Malone's misogynist claims have had a lasting influence. James Shapiro explains that Malone "introduced a new trend in Shakespearean biography: the infusion of autobiography, as writers projected onto Shakespeare their own personalities and prejudices."[22] We saw in Chapter 2 that Malone took William Henry Ireland to task for his forgeries, including his fictional love letter between William and Anne. Thus, his lengthy diatribe against Anne could also be a personal reaction against Ireland's fantasy. Whether motivated by personal or ideological agendas, Malone's desire to separate Shakespeare's literary life from his Stratford wife, and to relegate her to the category of a shrewish mistake, is a long-standing obsession, and as we shall see, has been regularly reinvigorated.

Reactions to Malone: Dyce, Knight, and Others

The fact that Malone formulated such an extreme version of the Shakespeare marriage, paradoxically may have provoked others to imagine Anne differently, and to substitute other fictions to fill in biographical gaps. Alexander Dyce's 1832 "Memoir of Shakespeare" espoused just such an opposing view: "It is indeed unlikely that a woman devoid of personal charms should have won the youthful affections of so imaginative a being as Shakespeare," he asserts, and that "it is unfair to conclude (as some biographers have done) from certain passages in his plays concerning marriage, that he afterwards repented of this connexion." Dyce highlights the tenuous nature of using the literary works as evidence, and contends that Shakespeare would not have associated with a woman unsuitable to his qualities. Dyce is unable to reconcile Shakespeare's London life with his Stratford wife, though, and he imagines that "when we find that during his almost constant residence in London, his wife remained at Stratford, and that he only remembers her slightly, and, as it were, casually in his will, we have some reason to suspect that their union was not productive of much domestic happiness."[23] Dyce's more measured and cautious biography "achieved extended exposure," notes Stuart Sillars, when it was reprinted in the 1868 Tauchnitz edition of Shakespeare's plays, and was "read by English émigrés in Europe." The 1857 version was "widely read until almost the end of the century,"[24] so the many readers of Dyce would recognize the instability inherent in this piece of Shakespeare's life story.

Charles Knight's popular biography of Shakespeare, included with his *Pictorial Edition* (1838–1843), offered yet another alternative to Malone's avowal of a loveless marriage. Knight countered that "it is too much to assume, as it has been assumed, that it was an unhappy influence. All that we really know of Shakspere's family life warrants the contrary supposition." Taking on Malone directly, Knight argues that "the marriage of Shakspere was one of affection" and that "there were no circumstances connected with it which indicate that it was either forced or clandestine, or urged on by an artful woman to cover her apprehended loss of character." Knight's interpretation, of course, is not supported by any additional facts, but as we shall see, his Anne was more in tune with the views of Anne by women of his day.

Like Malone, Knight also employs extensive fiction in his biography, imagining a picturesque wedding scene, where Shakespeare is "tall and finely formed, with a face radiant with intellect, and capable of expressing the most cheerful and most tender emotions," and Anne is "in the full beauty of womanhood, glowing with health and conscious happiness."[25] Knight's depiction of Anne is part of his larger aim, notes Stuart Sillars, to "subsume Shakespeare into early Victorian respectability, his home life first with parents and then with wife and children being presented as prosperous, comfortable, and conventional."[26] Knight's portrayal of the Shakespeare marriage, though more complimentary than Malone's, requires a similar amount of fictional input, but for a different outcome. Knight's version was circulated in several formats, reaching a variety of audiences in America and Britain, no doubt including some of the women I discuss in the next section.[27]

Likewise, Richard Grant White's 1865 *Memoirs of the Life of William Shakespeare* was widely read, especially in America. Contrary to Knight's version, White's Anne does not fare well: she is a predatory older woman, and White even goes so far as to wish Anne had died, rather than marry Shakespeare: "Should we not wish that one of them, even if it were he, had died before that ill-starred marriage?"[28] Already, by the mid-nineteenth century, conflicting constructions of Anne were in circulation, in response to ideas about the connection between Shakespeare's life and his literary works, the role of his family life in his biography, and the circumstances of his marriage.

Early Fictional Annes for Women

It is difficult to ascribe a direct cause and effect to various "Annes," but it is no accident that the increase in Shakespeare criticism with a focus on women, and the development of Anne Hathaway's Cottage as a tourist destination, coincided with the mid-nineteenth-century growth of fictional works about Anne. The many available editions of Shakespeare (162 between 1851 and 1860, according to Gary Taylor's count), helped to increase interest in the poet's life, and "encouraged added credibility to his construction as a domestic poet."[29] As this section will show, Anne became particularly important for creating a version of Shakespeare as a family man, married to a pious and devoted wife who supported him and provided an idealized domestic life. Several fictional works from both sides of the Atlantic, and frequently written by women, embellish Anne into a full-fledged literary character and a major figure in this version of Shakespeare's life story. In many of these works, Anne is the inspiration for her husband's literary works.[30] Even though Anne's importance was not guaranteed in biographies, in other literary forms she was given an increasingly crucial role.

An expanding body of criticism of Shakespeare *by* women increased enthusiasm *for* Shakespeare's women, both in the works and in his life. Anna Jameson's *Shakespeare's Heroines: Characteristics of Women, Moral, Poetical, and Historical* (1832; reprinted throughout the century), Mary Cowden Clarke's *The Girlhood of Shakespeare's Heroines* (1850–1852), Helena Faucit Martin's *On Some of Shakespeare's Female Characters* (1885), M. Leigh Elliott's *Shakespeare's Garden of Girls* (1885), and Agnes Mure MacKenzie's *Women in Shakespeare's Plays* (1924) represent this flourishing area of interest. Anna Jameson captured the view of many women when she noted that Shakespeare "looked upon women with the spirit of humanity, wisdom, and deep love," and "has done justice to their natural good tendencies and kindly sympathies."[31]

Mary Cowden Clarke, the first woman editor of Shakespeare, whose work was circulated in both England and America, was particularly influential in connecting Shakespeare with women. In her 1887 essay "Shakespeare as the Girl's Friend," she praised Shakespeare as "a valuable friend of woman-kind" with "keener insight than any other man-writer into womanly nature," who "depicted women with full appreciation of their highest qualities," and "vindicated their truest rights and celebrated their best virtues."[32] More to the point, in her 1860 edition of Shakespeare's works, Cowden Clarke directly attributed Shakespeare's sympathy for women to his relationship with his wife: "From the uniformly noble way in which Shakespeare drew the *wifely* character, we may feel certain of the esteem as well as affection with which his own wife inspired him; and the advantage in generosity which he has always assigned to women over men when drawing them in their mutual relations with regard to love, gives us excellent warrant for supposing that he had reason to know this truth respecting her sex from the mother of his children." Likewise, Shakespeare's marriage was "a signal proof of his poetic and ardent temperament," and Anne remained "the wife to whom he constantly returned amid the excitement of his metropolitan life."[33] In her biographical sketch of Shakespeare, Cowden Clarke offered more opposition to Malone by picturing the Shakespeares "strolling through the pleasant lanes of Shottery," where Will's "eye first encountered the sweet face and debonair figure of Anne Hathaway, then in the full bloom of womanhood, and of an age most likely to captivate the imagination of a lad-lover," who was "glowing with ideals of womanly perfection." The fact that Anne was older made her "something to worship, to idolize, to inspire him with all lofty aspirations, to emulate him to highest endeavor." To the young poet, Anne was "the breathing embodiment of all that his young poet-brain had conceived prophetically possible in a Helena, a Rosalind, and Imogen," providing the models for Shakespeare's literary women.[34] Cowden Clarke would not be the only woman to use Anne as a way to generate a woman-friendly version of Shakespeare.

A mere thirty-five years after Malone's infamous and long-lived "nightmare" Anne, Emma Severn offered an alternative fantasy of Anne in her three-volume work, designed primarily for women readers. Severn's brother was Dr. Joseph Severn, a physician who attended the poet John Keats, and who also edited the diary of John Ward, Vicar of Stratford in the seventeenth century. The author of *The Literary Gazette and Journal of the Belles Lettres, Arts, Sciences, etc.* (19 April 1845) reported that Emma Severn's brother's work on Shakespeare "may have turned her mind to the subject." One of the first extended fictional accounts of Anne, Severn's *Anne Hathaway, or Shakespeare in Love* (1845), features Shakespeare as a romantic hero who gets his literary inspiration from Anne Hathaway's Cottage.[35] Severn included a lengthy verbal tour of the cottage; as Nicola J. Watson notes, ten pages out of the first hundred were devoted to a lavish description of this courtship space.[36] Here, Anne is a saintly and moral influence over Shakespeare, who in turn worships her and has to compete with several rivals for her hand, including Sir Thomas Lucy and the poet Edmund Spenser. Anne and William are soul mates, and William even tells her "your songs and tales are ever braver than mine own." He feels "rapture" for her as well as "the reverential devotion of him who worships at holy shrine, or kneels before the feet of a living saint." At the end of volume one, Anne has been kidnaped, only to be saved in the second volume by Shakespeare in the role of a romantic hero. Her abduction inspires Shakespeare to confess: "Ann, for you, and for you alone, would I outface the whole universe, and dare as much, ay, more than man hath ever yet dared." Severn's Shakespeare unabashedly declares his allegiance to Anne: "'You inspire me!' said Shakespeare fervently. 'My life, my soul, how purely eloquent is the voiceless language of thought! – how sweet the dream of imagination! How exalted the hopes of love! Look thus upon me ever, and my fate shall be but one bright sun-lit path over a track of glory, beauty, and peace.'"[37] William's courtship of Anne allows him to demonstrate his heroic qualities, and his passion for this saintly woman explains the source of his literary works. Anne "inspires" him in a "voiceless language" of "rapture," awaiting an outlet in his dramatic works.

In Severn's story, passionate love for a virtuous woman – Shakespeare's
wife – provides a biographical explanation for his literary achievements and
a positive moral example. "Shakespeare's works contain a standard for
morals," wrote Mary Cowden Clarke in 1860, and a moral author needed
a moral life.[38] The dissonance between the Anne imagined by Malone and
Severn's Anne is emblematic of the contrasting Annes that would continue to
multiply in the following years.

The model of a devoted and faithful Anne is taken to the extreme in
The True Story of Mrs. Shakespeare's Life (1870), likely written by
American Harriet Beecher Stowe. In *The True Story*, originally published in London in the *Gentleman's Magazine*, Anne is "a gentle,
uncomplaining wife" who dwells "in retirement in the lonely country
house." Anne is so devoted to her famous husband that she is willing to
become an accomplice to his murdering deeds. Shakespeare's "dark and
guilty secret" is that he lures rival playwrights to his isolated
Warwickshire home, where he buries them under a mulberry tree to
do away with his competition. In this tale, Anne demonstrates the
"divine strength of love" and only reveals her husband's secret when
she is on her deathbed. As a steadfast and loyal wife, she is deemed "the
most remarkable woman the sixteenth century has produced." Stowe's
1870 story also underlines Anne's replacement of Mary Arden as the
paragon of female virtue. In her earlier work *Sunny Memories of Foreign
Lands* (1854), Stowe described Shakespeare's mother as the source of his
"deep heart-knowledge of pure womanhood." Anne, in Stowe's 1854
account, is "a mere rustic beauty, entirely incapable either of appreciat-
ing or adapting herself to that wide and wonderful mind in its full
development," a far cry from the divine, remarkable woman that she
becomes in Stowe's 1870 version.[39]

Back to the Archive: Halliwell-Phillipps

Later nineteenth-century biographers reflected the growing interest in
Anne Hathaway. James Orchard Halliwell-Phillipps (1820–1889),
described as "the greatest of the nineteenth-century biographers of
Shakespeare in the exacting tradition of factual research,"[40] was
a pioneering figure in assembling documentary evidence about Anne
and her family. In comparison to Charles Knight's 1843 biography, as
Stuart Sillars notes, Halliwell-Phillipps "reveals the two poles between
which almost every later Shakespeare biography has been constructed."
Knight wove his information into "a continuous, engaging narrative,

while Halliwell-Phillipps presented a multiplicity of documents not held together by an overarching narrative."[41] His reluctance to invent a story about Shakespeare's marriage resulted in a body of work that still serves as a standard scholarly reference, without the problematic fictionalizing that often taints biography.[42]

Halliwell-Phillipps approached Shakespeare's life story with what Samuel Schoenbaum describes as "passionate archaeological zeal," and "investigated every obscure nook of the poet's biography." His interest in the history of Shakespeare's wife may have stemmed from the fact that he married into the family of Sir Thomas Phillipps, who had discovered two crucial documents related to Anne: Shakespeare's marriage license bond (in 1836) and the will of Hathaway family shepherd Thomas Whittington (in 1837).[43]

In contrast to previous biographers, Halliwell-Phillipps vowed to "avoid the temptation of endeavouring to decipher [Shakespeare's] inner life and character through the media of his works." Shakespeare's biography, he noted, should be "studied in that truest spirit of criticism which deals with facts in preference to conjecture and sentiment."[44] Refusing to speculate about Shakespeare's private life, Halliwell-Phillipps instead focused on the history of the Hathaway family in depth, adding very little fiction. In fact, his initial intent was to publish factual discoveries in their fullest form on their own merit, but his publisher would only agree to it if they were in biographical form, i.e. held together with some sort of narrative. The subtitle to his *Life of William Shakespeare* trumpeted the fact that it included *Many Particulars Respecting the Poet and His Family Never before Published*, including the will of Anne's father, Richard Hathaway. In 1881 he published the *Outlines of the Life of Shakespeare*, which he continued to augment six times until 1887, when it reached nearly four times the length of the original version. Due to his methodology of relying on archival evidence and eschewing the literary works as evidence, Halliwell-Phillipps creates a Shakespeare whom Samuel Schoenbaum describes as "of the middle class imagination," in opposition to "the supreme being created by a century of bardolatry," and one whose goal was to accumulate income to "establish a family line."[45] This Anne and her family are crucial for anchoring this Shakespeare within a genealogical context and for rounding out his family life.

Domestic Annes

Other nineteenth-century writers continued to manipulate Anne to help create a Shakespeare who resonated with women and with domestic life, two concerns of a growing readership and tourist industry, as we saw in

Figure 4.1. "Shakespeare with his family, at Stratford, reciting the tragedy of *Hamlet*," c. 1869. Image courtesy of the Folger Shakespeare Library.

Chapter 3. The same year that Halliwell-Phillipps published his *Outlines of the Life of Shakespeare* (1881), Mary Elizabeth Braddon's novel *Asphodel* came out, set in Stratford, where one character remarks, "We may picture [Shakespeare] as a youth going across the fields to Shottery . . . yes, over the same meadows we tread this day: on the same ground, if not actually on the same grass."[46] This courtship model, also exploited by Anne Hathaway's Cottage, is one of the longest-lasting components of Anne's afterlife.

Other works around the fin de siècle promoted the image of Shakespeare as a family man, engaged in typical domestic scenes of the day with his wife and children around him. Thomas Bowdler's *The Family Shakespeare*, initially printed in 1818 but reprinted throughout the nineteenth century, circulated the idea of a domestic Shakespeare, where plays could be read aloud in the evenings. An engraving from the late nineteenth century (Figure 4.1) shows just such a family image, with William and Anne engrossed in conversation, presumably about the book in Shakespeare's hand, while his adoring children surround him. The family dog relaxes at Shakespeare's feet as his father reads and looks on in the background. This anonymous engraving locates Shakespeare at the heart of his family circle, in a harmonious image of domestic contentment far from the bustling

Figure 4.2. Illustration of Anne Hathaway from James Walter, *Shakespeare's True Life*, 1890.

London theatre environment. Julia Thomas notes that this engraving "is essentially a Victorian gathering in a Victorian parlor, with Shakespeare the Victorian patriarch reading aloud to his family." Shakespeare is "in every sense the family man, positioned within his Stratford home rather than a London playhouse."[47]

Like many of the evocative works inspired by Anne Hathaway's Cottage already discussed in Chapter 3, James Walter's appropriately titled 1890 work, *Shakespeare's True Life*, also creates an Anne Hathaway immersed in a Warwickshire setting. This "Sweet Anne" is a moral example for contemporary women, praised for her devotion to "domestic duties," as opposed to the irresponsible women who waste their time with "the piano and novel-reading." Similar to the Anne Hathaway of Mary Cowden Clarke, this Anne viewed her domestic responsibilities as "the duty of her life," providing Will with "a happy home" replete with meals "prepare[d] with her own hands," and nourishment "such as she knew would be best appreciated by her Will's palate after a day's hard brain work." Here, Anne "did not aspire to any of the learning of her Will, but she made amends through stores of domestic arts, soothing to the toil-worn and weary, and therefore so becoming to her sex."[48] In Walter's version, Anne is essential because her work in the Shakespeare family home supports the writing of the Shakespeare canon, his "day's hard brain work." English painter Gerald Moira's extensive illustrations (Figure 4.2) allow readers to easily imagine these household scenes.

Another domestic Anne appears in English children's author Emma Marshall's 1890 decorative book *Shakespeare and his Birthplace*, printed in both London and New York and lavishly illustrated. Marshall's Anne was so essential to Shakespeare that he worshiped at her feet as if "at the shrine of a saint," and she "knew more of William Shakespeare's inner life than anyone else."[49] Unlike the Anne that Malone created, whom Shakespeare wanted to forget, this Anne fueled his literary aspirations and encouraged his career, and he shared with her the "many desires stirring within him of which none but Anne Hathaway knew." Marshall gives her readers an intimate scenario of a nurturing Anne to a frustrated Shakespeare:

> We can imagine how, when the shadows were gathering over the fields, and one by one the stars came out in the deep-blue heaven above, while the daylight yet lingered in the west, and the old church-tower was clearly defined against the daffodil sky of the eventide, William Shakespeare would tell the story of his love, and Anne Hathaway would lend a willing ear to his passionate declaration, that if she would be his wife, all other longings would be set at rest, for she held his life and happiness in her hands.

As Marshall's readers no doubt knew, Anne married William, and Marshall imagines a later scene as Shakespeare is caught deer-stealing, where Anne commiserates with Shakespeare's mother Mary Arden: "We may imagine them mingling their tears as they talked of him, and yet, true-hearted women as they were, patient in the present, and hopeful for the future."[50] Here Anne remains a dutiful wife, offering "the sweets of domestic love" to her husband throughout his life. Marshall identifies a key component of Anne's afterlife that later writers would exploit and expand, namely her supposed knowledge of his "inner life."

Early North American Annes

The story of Shakespeare's life continued to be of interest to a growing general readership, especially in North America. The journal *Shakespeariana*, begun by the Shakespeare Society of New York and edited by Charlotte Endymion Porter, regularly featured articles and notes of biographical details, cruxes, and theories often related to Anne. The issue for 1886, for example, includes an announcement of the discovery by Rev. T. P. Wadley of Shakespeare's marriage license; a letter of inquiry from a "Shakespeare Student" about the Anne Hathaway/Anne Whateley enigma; a discussion of the theory of Anne's father Richard marrying a widow named Whateley from Temple Grafton; and a letter from the Vicar of Stratford on Shakespeare relics, including one at Anne Hathaway's Cottage.[51] Likewise, in 1891 *Shakespeariana* featured a critique of James Walter's *Shakespeare's True Life* by Mrs. C. H. Dall, with speculations on the parentage of Anne Hathaway; an account of a visit to Anne Hathaway's Cottage; a discussion of Richard Hathaway's will; and an article about the creation of the Shakespeare Birthplace Trust and their overseeing of Anne Hathaway's Cottage. In Canada, the journal *Canadian Monthly and National Review* for 1872 printed a dialog on Anne Hathaway by Daniel Wilson, Professor and later President of the University of Toronto, covering all of the major puzzles about her life, from her age to her bequest in Shakespeare's will, with reference to interpretations of Anne by critics including Edmond Malone and Charles Knight.[52] The fact that a more general readership was interested in and engaged with the mysteries related to Anne's life further underlines the key roles she could continue to play in various versions of Shakespeare's life story.

In the opening decades of the twentieth century, several American women writers took special interest in Anne, coinciding with the growth of interest by American women's clubs. Often lavishly illustrated, these works were designed for a female readership, and focused on Shakespeare's domestic and romantic life. Designed for young readers, Imogen Clark's novel *Will Shakespeare's Little Lad* (1897) revolves around Shakespeare's son Hamnet and was advertised as a way to involve the whole family in Shakespeare study, as part of the Scribner Series for Young People. The American weekly news magazine *The Chautauquan* promoted this use: "many of our readers who have young people about them may find it pleasant to guide their reading ... and so bring the householder into a sympathetic atmosphere."[53] American scholar and educator William James Rolfe recommended Clark's novel to his classes, and Clark's influence extended throughout the New York literary scene, in groups such as the Wednesday Afternoon Club and the Barnard Club, of which she was a member.

Fin de Siècle Contradictory Annes

The ebb and flow in depictions of Anne is evident in Sidney Lee's 1897 entry on Shakespeare in the *Dictionary of National Biography*, a widely read standard scholarly resource, not revised until Peter Holland's entry in 2004, over a hundred years later. In contrast to Knight, Dyce, and Halliwell-Phillipps, and to the growing body of women writers who celebrated Shakespeare, Lee returns to Malone's view and ascribes a negative interpretation to the

Shakespeare marriage. Lee imagines a scenario where "Anne Hathaway's seniority and the likelihood that the poet was forced into marrying her by her friends were not circumstances of happy augury," though he does admit that "it is dangerous to read into Shakespeare's dramatic utterances allusions to his personal experience." Nevertheless, Lee does not resist using selective evidence from the plays ("barren hate, sour-eyed disdain, and discord" from *The Tempest*) to argue that Shakespeare "bore his domestic ties with impatience."[54] In addition to the extensive readership of the *DNB*, Lee's description of the Shakespeare marriage was further disseminated in his 1898 book-length *A Life of William Shakespeare*, which also had a considerable distribution, reaching its fourth edition by 1899. It is impossible to gauge how many readers encountered Lee's version of Anne over the last century, but it must have been a substantial number, given the circulation of the *DNB*.

Danish critic Georg Brandes advanced an even more unfavorable view of Shakespeare's marriage in his widely read study, described by Tobias Döring and Ewan Fernie as "a highly influential biographical study that defined the dominant image of Shakespeare in the early twentieth century."[55] Asserting that it is unlikely that Shakespeare "left any great happiness behind him" in Stratford, Brandes argues that Anne "the peasant girl" could never "fill his life." Instead, he envisions Shakespeare living "the free Bohemian life of an actor and playwright," where "the woman's part in this life was not played by Anne Hathaway."[56] Brandes weaves this idea throughout his study of Shakespeare's plays, assuming with certainty that Shakespeare "must have felt his spirit light and free, not least, perhaps, because he had escaped from his home in Stratford." Lack of evidence of Shakespeare's marital state is no impediment, since Brandes argues that "ordinary knowledge of the world is sufficient to suggest that [Shakespeare's] association with a village girl eight years older than himself could not satisfy him or fill his life." Maintaining that "the study of his works confirms this conjecture," Brandes then cherry-picks examples from the plays to suit his argument that Shakespeare "regarded his marriage in the light of a youthful folly," and it was a point of "personal regret."[57] Originally published in 1895 in Denmark, Brandes's work was translated into English in 1898, printed in England and America, and was widely influential. Praised by Edmund Gosse as "the best popular or general portrait of Shakespeare yet given to a Continental audience," Brandes's study gained admirers including James Joyce, who would later create an Anne who was far more unfavorable than Brandes's.[58] A significant aspect of Brandes's work was his "belief that exceptional creations must derive from exceptional personalities and their extraordinary lives," so it is no surprise that the fictional "peasant girl" Anne Hathaway is cast off from this trajectory.[59]

Two biographies from 1901 display the often-striking disparity between the way Anne Hathaway's life story can be constructed, in the same time frame, cultural climate, and literary form, but for different ends. British suffragette Charlotte Carmichael Stopes vowed to avoid the "chaotic nonsense" of biographical speculation and boasted, "Perhaps never before has anyone attempted to write a life of the poet with so little allusion to his plays and poems." Proclaiming that "The time for romancing has gone by," she deduced that "nothing more can be done concerning the poet's life except through careful study and through patient research." The result of her methodology was her 1901 *Shakespeare's Family*. Compiled from her articles in the *Genealogical Magazine*, Stopes's work includes a substantial section on the Hathaways, and she is perhaps the first biographer to include the epitaph from Anne's grave in support of her account. Stopes recognized the contrasting versions of Anne in circulation, and observed that "many vials of wrath have been poured on the devoted head of Anne Hathaway by those who do not consider all sides of the question." She concluded that the Shakespeare marriage had elicited "much unnecessarily unfavourable comment."[60] Her reluctance to manufacture an Anne out of Shakespeare's works led to one of the most even-handed treatments of the poet's wife for its day.[61] Stopes signed the guest book at Anne Hathaway's Cottage for 1913, but this was likely not her first visit to the Hathaway home, given her interest in the family.

In spite of the resistance to using the works as evidence by biographers like Halliwell-Phillipps and Stopes, the appeal of filling in Shakespeare's private life with material from his works has proven to be irresistible for many biographers, and more often than not results in an unfavorable depiction of Anne. Such a methodology was the cornerstone of Edward Dowden's efforts around the fin de siècle. Dowden built on his 1875 work *Shakspere: A Critical Study of His Mind and Art*, the first study of Shakespeare's development as an artist through the chronology of his plays and his life experience. Dowden's work was wide-reaching. It went through fifteen editions during his lifetime; remained a standard source for Shakespeare's life for nearly a hundred years; was translated into German, Italian, French, and Russian; and was "the first complete work of Western Shakespeare scholarship to be translated into Japanese" in the 1890s.[62] In Dowden's later *Introduction to Shakespeare* (1901), he articulates his agenda about the Shakespeare marriage as a mistake from the start, a mismatch between an eighteen-year-old boy and an older woman, "of humbler rank than his own and probably

uneducated, [which] cannot be called prudent." Though his imagined scenario harks back to Malone's version, Dowden seems reluctant to cast the
Shakespeare marriage in a completely negative light, admitting that "we have
no evidence to prove that the union was unhappy," and that Shakespeare
must have "looked forward to returning to his native town, and living
henceforth by [Anne's] side." Dowden's Anne is not intelligent or refined
enough to hold Shakespeare's interest, though, and the poet thus must have
been "led astray by the intellectual fascination of a woman who possessed all
those qualities of brilliance and cultured grace which perhaps were lacking in
his wife." In due time, this Shakespeare realized his error and "returned to
the companion of his youth." Without prior knowledge that Dowden is
writing a critical study, not a novel, it would be impossible to discern from
this type of speculation.

Like later biographer Stephen Greenblatt, Dowden cannot imagine
a connection between the lowly Anne and William's artistry: "we cannot
suppose that the wife of his early choice, the daughter of a husbandman,
could have followed Shakespeare in his poetical mountings of mind or in his
profound dramatic studies of character." Dowden was hesitant to consign
Anne to a complete position of irrelevance, though, and gave her credit for
providing domestic tranquility to Shakespeare at the end of his life, where her
"homely goodness" could offer him comfort "in the common joys and
sorrows and daily tasks of household life."[63] Emblematic of Anne's contested
position in Shakespeare's life story, Dowden struggles between endorsing
Anne for her domestic qualities, or condemning her for her humble
background.

In 1905, the controversies over Shakespeare's marriage had garnered
enough attention for a book-length study. Joseph Gray's *Shakespeare's
Marriage, His Departure from Stratford and Other Incidents in His Life* sought to
correct "certain apparently erroneous impressions" about Shakespeare's
marriage license.[64] Covering such topics as the Anne Hathaway/Anne
Whateley crux, the marriage license location of Temple Grafton, and the
issue of parental consent, Gray also includes a chapter entitled "Facts and
Conjectures." He expresses his frustration with "the long series of adverse
comments upon Shakespeare and his wife," calling out John Aubrey,
Thomas de Quincey, Thomas Campbell, and Richard Grant White. Gray
takes these numerous biographers to task, urging them to have "a more
intimate acquaintance with the facts" and "a better knowledge and appreciation of modes of thought no longer in vogue." Gray is especially prescient in
remarking that "the objection to all of these surmises is not that they are
beyond belief or even improbable, but that there is no clear evidence upon

which any one of them can be substantiated" and that "an appearance of truth has been given to hypotheses which, owing to frequent repetition, are now often accepted as facts." The circumstances surrounding Shakespeare's marriage, he concludes, are "highly debatable," and the literary works can "tempt the biographer to set up a fictitious personality, a danger to which the widely different conceptions of Shakespeare evolved from the same sources bear witness." Gray disputes the idea that the sonnets are autobiographical, explaining that "in no circumstances was [Shakespeare] likely to have been tempted to reveal his inmost thoughts in the form of the fashionable sonnet for the entertainment of his literary acquaintances or of posterity."[65] Samuel Schoenbaum describes the strength of Gray's work as its "profoundly unexciting reading," which lessens the "drama and scandal" fellow biographers sought in Shakespeare's marriage.[66] Park Honan similarly calls Gray "a main source for moderate commentators,"[67] but moderation and banality do not offer much to animate biography.

Early Dissonant Annes

Three works from the early twentieth century by writers on both sides of the Atlantic illustrate the dissonant Annes that existed even in the earliest imaginative texts, and affirm that her place in Shakespeare's life story, whether as domestic helpmate or cast-off peasant girl, was far from stable. In the 1903 four-act play *The Favor of the Queen*, Roy Spann Sensabaugh (1880–1969), a twenty-two-year-old St. Louis-based printer, has Queen Elizabeth intervene in casting *Romeo and Juliet*, inadvertently selecting a woman dressed as a boy to play Juliet. Sensabaugh was one of the many "mythologizers [who] have loved to imagine Elizabeth attending a Shakespeare play at a playhouse, usually the Globe," according to Helen Hackett.[68] In the final act, Anne Hathaway makes a cameo appearance for a few brief lines, to facilitate Shakespeare's eventual return to Stratford. She complains about their separation and about his treatment of her, proclaiming, "I understand thee not. In the three weeks I spend with thee each year thou scarce doest notice me. 'T would seem thou didst belong to some far player world and gave it all thy sympathy." Anne provides Shakespeare with an opportunity to praise the rural life that nurtured his poetry, when he asks, "And still the Avon flows as when I bathed in it? The trees, the parks, are they all there?"[69] Sensabaugh's play premiered in May of 1903 at Ford's Opera House in Baltimore, starring DeWitt Jennings (who would later be featured in the 1935 film *Mutiny on the Bounty*) and Mrs. Percy Haswell, wife of Broadway actor-manager George Fawcett, and it won the annual play competition put on by Fawcett.[70] It is unclear why

Sensabaugh tried his hand at a work based on Shakespeare's life, but shortly after his play premiered, he boarded a ship from New York to England in June of 1904, likely to visit some of the Shakespeare-related sites.

A novel from about the same time, Clyde C. Westover's *The Romance of Gentle Will: A Hitherto Unpublished Chapter in the Story of the Love of the Immortal Bard* (1905), similarly connects Anne to Queen Elizabeth, but here Anne has a much larger role as the Queen's handmaiden. When Anne pleads for Shakespeare's life, Elizabeth rebukes her: "'Anne Hathaway, you impudent hussy!', fairly shrieked the angry Queen."[71] This Anne is a noble, strong-willed lady who saves Shakespeare's life and is rewarded with his love. Like Sensabaugh, Westover was also involved in the field of journalism, as secretary of the San Francisco Press Club. Both texts link Anne to Elizabeth as a way to give her a presence in London.

In the four-act play *William Shakespeare* (1907), dedicated to Herbert Beerbohm Tree, William Thomas Saward gives more attention to Anne Hathaway, making her a remarkably independent-minded woman. Michael Dobson notes that Saward based his play on Charles Somerset's *Shakespeare's Early Days* (1829), adding Shakespeare's "Romeo-like courtship of Anne" to Somerset's plot. Described by one character as the "Pride of Avon," this Anne tells a potential suitor that "she'll have the man she fancies, and not the man who fancies her."[72] Anne takes William as a secret lover, meeting outside the Cottage at night, and she is the inspiration for his youthful love poetry:

SHAKES: Hist, beauteous watcher of the starry night, 'Tis I, thy lover, Will, my beauteous Anne! My Lady Anne among the roses there.

ANNE: It is his voice prolongs the silent hour!

SHAKES: Sweet Mistress Anne!

Vowing her love to him, Anne exclaims, "For thou art Romeo, and I Juliet, / And I will love thee like the Capulet." He too confesses his devotion to her: "Thou has strengthened me / To battle on against the opposing tide," and he embarks on his journey to London "Armed with this angel's love." Shakespeare views his career as a conquest, and he vows, "I'll be thy true knight, Anne! Out in the wars! / And bring thee back a name worth all the going!" Saward explains Shakespeare's time in London by casting him as a hero, whose duty is to make his name as an author.

Saward only permits tepid critique of Shakespeare through a mother figure for Anne, who cautions her against the wiles of a strolling player

(Shakespeare), lamenting "the evils of a bad choice." A deceptive rival suitor to Anne tells her that Shakespeare has been unfaithful, which motivates her to travel to London to discover Shakespeare's "wild ways." Meanwhile, Shakespeare himself returns to Stratford to surprise Anne, and learns that she has been misled. He vows to hunt down the rival suitor and reclaim his honor with his wife, for whom he has "lived and waited."[73] By conquering the literary world of London and redeeming the honor of his wife, Shakespeare is venerated as a hero who triumphantly returns home.

At the end of the play, he is reconciled with his "honoured wife" and deemed by Queen Elizabeth as the "Immortal Bard" and "Our Shakespeare of the Universal mind!" In Saward's play, Anne and Stratford serve as Shakespeare's "sheltered haven of repose, / Whose fresh green bowers and folding valleys fair / Invite my wandering steps to turn once more, / Where all this strife comes not, nor pride, nor power." Saward's Anne is even endorsed by Queen Elizabeth, who hails her as a "jewel rare," a "Guardian of thy home, thy honoured wife." Here, Elizabeth I takes on the role described by Helen Hackett, to "presid[e] harmoniously over a nostalgically recalled 'merry England.'"[74] The Queen blesses their marriage, telling them "May all the years smile on your happiness, / Unto the end."[75] In Saward's play, the specter of an unfaithful and libertine Shakespeare is raised, only to be vindicated in the end. Anne is both a supporter of Shakespeare and an inspiration to him, rather than a neglected wife left behind in Stratford, and her perseverance, steadfastness, and domestic loyalty are endorsed by no higher authority than the Queen. It is likely that William Thomas Saward was the clergyman who composed the lyrics to the 1902 hymn *Almighty Father* for the coronation of Edward VII, with music by George C. Martin, organist of St. Paul's Cathedral, but there is no evidence that his play was ever performed.

These dissonant and contradictory Annes may reflect the contested position of women at the time, both in the United States and in Britain. Sensabaugh's 1903 play and Westover's 1905 novel appeared in America, in between the founding of the National American Woman Suffrage Association in 1890 and the 1911 National Association Opposed to Women's Suffrage. Likewise, Saward's 1907 play was printed in Britain not long after the founding of the Women's Social and Political Union in 1903. While none of the three writers mentions the larger political canvas, it would have been impossible to escape the resonance of these texts with contemporary women's issues.

Anne for American Women Readers

At a time when women's social and political roles were in flux, it is not surprising to see Anne take a larger role for women readers and writers. The popularity of American Shakespeare clubs named after Anne Hathaway indicates her continuing popularity with women. Anne Hathaway Shakespeare Clubs existed in Colorado Springs, Colorado (founded 1895); in Philadelphia, Pennsylvania (founded 1923); and in Concord, New Hampshire (founded 1894).[76] The Pasadena, California, Shakespeare Club, founded in the 1880s, even built a home for their club, modeled after Anne Hathaway's Cottage. Further, publications aimed at a general American readership, especially for women, promoted interest in Anne Hathaway, and many clubs included material on Anne during their programs. The Shakespeare Club of Marion, Iowa (founded 1909), for example, playfully discussed setting up an all-female "Anne Hathaway House" where they could live together and study.[77]

A cluster of American women writers in the first two decades of the twentieth century crafted extensive portrayals of Anne designed primarily for women readers, produced with generous illustrations and elaborate packaging appropriate for keepsake books. These Annes underline the desire for a version of Shakespeare with tangible and commodified evidence of a romantic marriage.

American schoolteacher Sara Hawks Sterling's lavishly illustrated novel *Shakespeare's Sweetheart* (1905) was targeted at this readership. Praised in the American journal *New Shakespeareana* as a "sumptuously decorated book" where "the diction is quaint, and the charm of the story fairly justifies its artistic setting," Sterling's novel had illustrations by Clara Elsene Peck (1883–1968), who was acclaimed for her specialty in depicting women and children (Figure 4.3).[78] Told from Anne's point of view, Sterling's novel was one of the first extended attempts to offer a woman's perspective on Shakespeare's romantic life, letting readers imagine what it would feel like to be on the receiving end of Shakespeare's passion. Paul Franssen underscores the fact that Sterling's novel also includes scenes of same-sex desire between Anne and the Dark Lady.[79] Sterling's early attempt to capture an insider's view of Shakespeare as a wooer also functioned as a souvenir for readers, its embellished florid packaging accentuating this meaning in a physical form. Sterling's novel calls to mind the Ireland forgeries, in its function as a material object that testifies to the romantic relationship between the Shakespeares. *Shakespeare's Sweetheart* reached beyond its initial American audience; Philadelphia publisher George W. Jacobs marketed

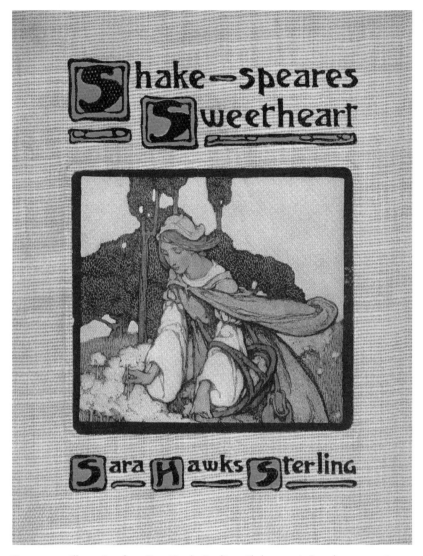

Figure 4.3.   Illustration from Sara Hawks Sterling, *Shake-speare's Sweetheart*, 1905. Image
courtesy of the Folger Shakespeare Library.

Sterling's work as a gift book, and it was printed in 1907 in London. Helen
Hackett explains that Sterling was able to steer "a middle course through the
turbulent gender politics of her day: Anne was no stay-at-home wife, but
neither was she a man-hating feminist, since she embarked upon travel and

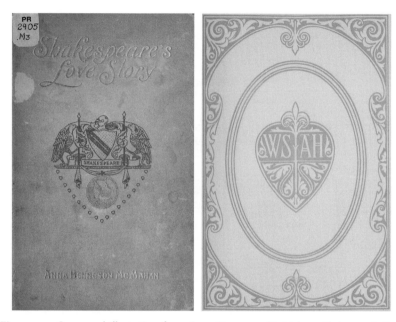

Figure 4.4. Cover and illustration from Anna Benneson McMahan, *Shakespeare's Love Story*, 1909.

adventure in the cause of love and marriage." Hackett observes that Sterling's Anne "succeeds in her bold and emancipated behavior because it is contained by the conventions of femininity and heterosexuality," while incorporating a cross-dressed heroine.[80] Sterling herself remained unmarried, and one wonders how much of the exploratory nature of her novel, packaged within a conventional feminine frame, was a way to use Anne to reflect her own life.

Another work by a female author designed for a female readership, American editor Anna Benneson McMahan's (1846–1919) *Shakespeare's Love Story, 1580–1609* (1909), caters to the same audience as Sterling's novel. The cover to McMahan's book (Figure 4.4) features a new heart-shaped coat of arms for Shakespeare, with a gold embossed illustration of Anne beneath it. This motif continues on the opening pages, with the initials WS and AH entwined in an Art Deco heart. The book itself is sumptuously illustrated, with twenty-six depictions of Warwickshire sites, designed for holiday book buyers, and advertised as having "a very pretty setting for the book. The illustrations are printed separately in tint on thin paper, and framed, as it were, in tinted borders."[81] McMahan was inspired by the tercentenary anniversary of the publication of Shakespeare's sonnets; she points out that she has placed the poems "between the lines of some of the pages that we know of Shakespeare's life." Her aim is for readers to "grant thereby that Shakespeare was not only the mightiest of poets, but the most devoted and inspired of lovers." McMahan's premise is that Shakespeare's sonnets were written to express his love for Anne, the "village maiden" who "only partly knows, what we now wholly grant, that never before has love found more glorious speech, never before has the great theme been set to lines which so run over with poetry and turn to music on the tongue." As the recipient of Shakespeare's sonnets, Anne is "supremely blessed among women" to be privy to Shakespeare's "inner life – a life of dreams and visions, both his own and other men's as he finds them in books." Like Petrarch's Laura, it is to Anne that William will "sing all the thoughts and feelings that fill his breast, and she will read and remember and rejoice." Shakespeare's sonnets even invade her domestic routines: "Spinning, weaving, baking, malting, brewing – each prosaic task is glorified by the little paper worn next her heart." In McMahan's story, this literate Anne is both Shakespeare's lover and his confidante; he "pours into sympathetic ears the story of his hopes, his fears, his discouragements, his ambitions." His love for Anne, located in the countryside, is his inspiration, and his memory of their love fuels his writing, "reviving scenes which now become vital in his life." His wedding to Anne is lauded by the community, and "many were the lads that day that envied Will Shakespeare his good fortune; none, looking upon the bonny pair, found aught for wonder or for blame in a marriage blessed by so much beauty, constancy, and romance." Anne is just as esteemed as a mother: "Anne Hathaway the maiden lost no charm as Anne Shakespeare the mother of the three little ones that came to bless the simple home." It is Anne's "womanly self-denial" that inspires Shakespeare to follow his dreams and leave for London, where he makes his fortune and dutifully sends money home to her.[82] McMahan's novel is unusual for linking Anne to the sonnets, a connection that, beginning with Malone, had usually been filled in with a Dark Lady.

Though McMahan is a bit cryptic about exactly what happens in Shakespeare's London life, she does say that he "meets court ladies, free of wit and sometimes of morals, and surrenders to their spell more than afterwards he is able to forgive himself," but returns to Stratford every year for "restoration and healing." Even with a temporary misstep in London, "at heart he was always true to love and home and family" and "is always looking forward to his own final return to the peaceful fireside" where his wife and children eagerly await him. McMahan's final defense of Anne proposes that Shakespeare's time in London did not mean he loved his wife any less. She

contends that "the man who created so many lovely and constant ladies –
Juliet, Rosalind, Desdemona, Imogen, and the rest" could not have had "a
wife of shrewish or jealous disposition." These characters, McMahan argues,
were created "in the likeness of the women he has known best," and
Shakespeare in his sonnets "was a lover speaking to his beloved," and there
we "may learn from them more of the man's real self than is anywhere else
possible."[83] McMahan's novel testifies to the enduring role for Anne in
narratives about Shakespeare as a family man, bolstered by the love of
a faithful Warwickshire woman who inspired and nurtured his works.

In the same year that McMahan's novel came out, Anna Morgan
(1851–1936) and Alice Ward Bailey's (b. 1857) play *The Great Experiment:
A Shakespearean Fantasy* (1909) was printed in Chicago. This collaborative
work centrally locates Anne in Shakespeare's literary works and in his
women, with a plot where Anne oversees Shakespeare's heroines. Anne
even complains about her afterlife, exclaiming, "no one argues if I did or
did not live, / Yet of my life make havoc as they will." In this version, she
functions as a surrogate for her husband, "Know it is Shakespeare's will that
here, to-day, / He shall be represented by Anne Hathaway." Shakespeare's
women (including Miranda, Lady Macbeth, Cleopatra, Gertrude, and
Ophelia) encourage Anne to tell her story, and she confesses, "I did fear
the power of [the Dark Lady], the unknown, unto whom my husband wrote,
and when I learned that he held her to be his dream wife, who did inspire his
thoughts – that I was but the drudge, the stay-at-home – bitter, indeed,
I grew of heart." [84] While no evidence survives that this play was ever
publicly performed, it is still notable that as early as 1909, American
women were crafting a play featuring an Anne who complains about her
afterlife, about her fears of a rival woman, and about the constraints of her
grim domestic life.

Another American work brought together Shakespeare's literary women
and his wife Anne. The popular one-act play written for the 1916
Tercentenary by Mabel M. Moran, of the Larchmont, New York, Garden
Club, entitled *The Shakespeare Garden Club: A Fantasy*, was set in Stratford-
upon-Avon, with Anne presiding over an imaginary women's garden club
comprising female characters from Shakespeare's plays. Here Shakespeare's
women (Lady Macbeth, Portia, Jessica, Titania, Ophelia, Mistress Ford, and
Juliet) plan a garden project to revive the landscape around the Avon River,
particularly with flowers that were beloved to Shakespeare.[85] At the end of
the play, Lady Macbeth delivers a "prophecy, that when our members have
died, and worms have eaten them and Master Shakespeare himself hath
become but ancient history – garden clubs in times to come will remember

fair Avon's shores made lovely by your sweet suggestions."[86] This project to honor Shakespeare combined wartime gardening, pastoral Englishness, and domesticity, centered around Anne Hathaway. Moran's play was advertised in *The National Plant, Flower and Fruit Guild Magazine* in 1919, and was later performed in 1920 in New York to raise funds for "shell-shocked soldiers" at the Danville Hospital and to reconstruct devastated gardens in St. Quentin, France. This society benefit had a cast of dozens of socialites from New York involved in the production, and the focus on Shakespeare's wife was a central part of the piece's success.[87] Another Tercentenary work, Leigh Mitchell Hodges's *The Bard At Home* (1916), was written for the Doylestown, Pennsylvania, Village Improvement Association's program "Afternoon with Shakespeare." In this brief skit, Shakespeare acknowledges that Anne would "rather have less home and more of a husband," but he tries to make up for his absence by buying her New Place.[88] As the title suggests, this commemorative piece highlights Shakespeare's domestic life, further circulating this version of Shakespeare for amateur performance.

Desecrating Anne: Frank Harris's "Jealous Scolding Shrew Wife"

The imaginative intensity of these late nineteenth- to early twentieth-century fictional accounts was matched in biographies of the same time period. Two twentieth-century biographers combined their interest in Shakespeare's life with their zeal for concocting lascivious stories about his personal life, producing some of most one-sided and bitter versions of Anne in the history of her afterlife. Determined to exploit the sensational potential in Shakespeare's life story, journalist and critic Frank Harris (1856–1931) used both Shakespeare's literary works and extensive fictional techniques in *The Man Shakespeare and His Tragic Life-Story* in 1909 (published in both Britain and in the United States, and translated into German).[89] The premise behind Harris's early work is that Shakespeare escaped an unhappy marriage by moving to London, where he indulged in a passionate affair with Mary Fitton, his Dark Lady. For Harris, Shakespeare was a man of "excessive sensuality" and "mad passion" that could only be assuaged by an extreme, libidinous lifestyle.[90] Such an emotionally charged Shakespeare required large-scale speculation to bolster this story.

Harris's follow-up to *The Man Shakespeare*, entitled *The Women of Shakespeare* (1911), fabricates a sensational emotional life for the Shakespeares, where William was "bruised and beaten in the sordid strife of wit by his wife and was forced to fly" to London, where he meets his mistress Mary Fitton. In this adverse tale, which Harris labels a "critical work," Anne becomes the "jealous scolding shrew wife, who was eight years his senior, overshadowed, as we shall see, all his early manhood, and left her bitter mark on most of his youthful work." As he argues in a lengthy chapter devoted to creating an Anne out of cherry-picking characters from the literary works, this "bitter nagging wife" is depicted as Adriana in *The Comedy of Errors*, as Katharina in *The Taming of the Shrew*, and as "the raging raving Constance of *King John*," with "her furious temper," a "jealous railing woman who made such an impression on young Shakespeare that he cannot but paint her and make her live for us by reason of his very hatred." Even at the end of his life, the "passions of lust and jealousy and rage had at length worn out Shakespeare's strength" and "he crept home to Stratford" to die, presumably in the company of his shrewish wife.[91]

Harris's heinous and loathsome Anne is finally "exorcised" from Shakespeare's life by Dark Lady Mary Fitton, who "changed the world for Shakespeare," inspiring him to create Juliet, Portia, Beatrice, and Rosalind, and who transformed him into "the greatest man who has left a record of himself." According to Harris, Fitton was the animating presence behind Shakespeare's great art: "The immortal significance of Shakespeare's life" and "the history of his soul" is "the story of his love for the imperious gipsy-wanton Mary Fitton." This Shakespeare was ignorant of life and love before Fitton, and even though he was married, he "knew little of life and less of women: through her he came to knowledge of both and to much self-knowledge," inspiring the "flame-like growth of Shakespeare's soul in the 'madding fever' of passion."[92]

In order to make his argument for "the conception of passion as a forcing-house of genius" for Shakespeare, which Harris contends he has "set forth here for the first time," he must jettison Shakespeare's wife as a shrew to the "lowest hell of jealousy, rage and humiliation."[93] Harris's work is significant for its fabrication of a strikingly disparaged Anne, couched within the confines of a "critical work," and not packaged as fiction. As Tobias Döring remarks, due to Harris's "extremely intimate interrelations between life and work, with special emphasis on Shakespeare's love life," he "gained remarkable prominence in popularizing neo-romantic Shakespeare myths."[94] The influence that Frank Harris's "Anne" had on later writers underlines the insidious nature of wildly fictional Annes, couched as critical doctrine. Harris commented that the story of Shakespeare's marriage "is in perfect consonance with Shakespeare's impulsive, sensual nature," since "hot, impatient, idle Will got Anne Hathaway into trouble, was forced to marry her, and at once came to regret." Harris's fantasy Shakespeare was "wooed by an older woman against [his] will" and was "probably

a little ashamed of being married to someone whom he could hardly introduce or avow."[95] Based on no factual evidence, Harris's Anne is a strident
and sordid portrait.

Harris's disturbing exploitation of Anne, exiling her to the "lowest hell of
jealousy, rage and humiliation" for being a "bitter nagging wife" with
a "furious temper" who provoked Shakespeare's "hatred," still stands as
one of the most vicious portrayals of her, made all the more stark by many
of the roughly contemporary works about Anne, especially among the
growing number of women readers. One wonders what these women readers made of a "critical work" entitled *The Women of Shakespeare* with such
a darkly misogynist concoction of a wife. Further, the travelers to Anne
Hathaway's Cottage (outlined in Chapter 3) around the time of Harris's
writing clearly sought a different Anne than the one Harris describes; no
visitors expressed a yearning to encounter the home of a "bitter nagging
wife."

More Shrewish Annes

The 1917 play *The Good Men Do: An Indecorous Epilogue* by Canadian Hubert
Osborne offers further evidence of popular interest in Shakespeare's real
women. Osborne's piece is based on an imaginary meeting between
a shrewish Anne Hathaway and an innocent rival Anne Whateley, which
begins on 23 April 1616, after Shakespeare has died. The two Annes are in
conflict, culminating in Whateley's denunciation of Hathaway for her treatment of Shakespeare: "You tricked him into marrying you knowing that he
did not love you. You made no home for him that loved the little niceties of
life, but made him live in squalor. You drove him from you by your nagging
tongue to taverns and low company. Your jealous tantrums made banishment a happy liberty!" Whateley continues to critique Hathaway for being
a bad wife and not supporting Shakespeare's artistry: "You were his wife.
You could have helped him much. Your love should have been the inspiration of his life and spurred him on to honorable fame. Instead, you drove him
to his worst and wrecked the promise of his youth. What he was you made
him. What sins are his, they are upon your head." When Hathaway threatens
to "tell his willfulness unto the world and let them know the kind of man he
was," her son-in-law John Hall reprimands her for airing the family's dirty
laundry: "You were his wife. What differences you had you should have hid
within the family walls and shown an outward sign of amity and love, not
airing your grievance to a tattling world and lain your children open to much
shame."[96] It is notable that in a piece entitled *The Good Men Do*, Shakespeare

does not even appear, and the purpose of the play is to vilify Anne Hathaway, through the castigations of a rival woman, for not supporting her husband.

Osborne was a theatre director in Chicago and on Broadway from 1906 to 1926, later a drama professor at Yale and at the Carnegie Institute of Technology, and the developer of a synthetic stage lighting system.[97] Osborne's play began as his student contribution to "The 47 Workshop," a playwriting course at Harvard, which involved audience feedback on the plays. *The Good Men Do* was printed in 1918 and continued on to Broadway, where it was performed 16 times in May of 1918. Osborne describes his play as "purely imaginary," but also "in strict accordance with the spirit of the times."[98] His censure of Anne on the basis of her lax approach to her wifely obligations was written in the period leading up to women's suffrage in America, and its correlation with "the spirit of the times" suggests that it resonated with debates about women's domestic roles and responsibilities, articulated through critique of Anne.

"A Boldfaced Stratford Wench": James Joyce's Anne

It is perhaps not surprising that one of the most highly imaginative works of the early twentieth century includes an abject Anne who is conscripted to serve a larger narrative purpose. Although Anne only appears in Book 9, the "Scylla and Charybdis" episode of James Joyce's modernist novel *Ulysses* (1918–1920), Joyce consolidates a number of unfavorable Annes, and his portrayal of what Cary DiPietro aptly calls "the nearly forgotten Anne Hathaway" has been especially influential on later writers.[99] Inspired by the Anne in Frank Harris's ostensibly "critical" study, Anne in *Ulysses* is "hot in the blood," "the ugliest doxy in all Warwickshire," and "a boldfaced Stratford wench who tumbles in a cornfield a lover younger than herself." Sexually aggressive, she "put the comether on him," Shakespeare "made a mistake," and he "got out of it as quickly and as best he could."[100] Joyce's Anne harks back to Harris's hellish "nightmare" Anne. In fact, readers of *Ulysses* are even directed to Harris's influence in the author notes to *Ulysses*: "Nor should we forget Mr Frank Harris," whose "articles on Shakespeare in the *Saturday Review* were surely brilliant."

The Anne that Joyce creates in *Ulysses* is a further distorted, sexualized, and decrepit creature, a haunting portrait of an elderly, haggard Anne even more lurid than in Harris's version: "And in New Place a slack dishonoured body that once was comely, once as sweet, as fresh as cinnamon, now her leaves falling, all, bare, frighted of the narrow grave and unforgiven."[101] According to Don Gifford, here Joyce relies on the work of Georg Brandes (discussed earlier in this chapter), who asserted that "His wife was extremely religious, as is often the case with women whose youthful conduct has not been too circumspect. When she captured her boy husband of eighteen, her blood was as warm as his, but now, on the eve of Shakespeare's return, she was vastly his superior in matters of religion."[102] Building on Harris's undesirable Anne, Joyce crafts an enduring and ominous image of a sexualized, spent, aggressive, and corrupt Anne, a pervasive portrayal that would have lasting effects.

Joycean Annes

These excessively derogatory Annes reverberated long after their initial debuts. British editor and essayist Charles Edward Lawrence (1870–1940) uses the age difference between the Shakespeares to imagine an older and unattractive Anne in his 1927 one-act play, *The Hour of Prospero*. The play opens with a scene in the garden of New Place, where Anne Hathaway is 54 but "looks ten years older." Her "expression is vacuous" and she sits with her eyes shut, "a picture of worn-out womanhood." Throughout the play she derides her husband for not staying in Stratford, and for writing poetry rather than becoming a Stratford alderman. "Who can want that poetry in a working-day world," she exclaims. Instead of becoming a leading citizen of Stratford, her husband "waste[d] his years over trash" writing poetry. She yearns for her home in Shottery, where William courted her, and complains that he left her "to wear out her heart, looking from the window at the cruel street; waiting, waiting, hoping, watching for year after year, as I did, working my fingers to the bone," while raising their children on her own. Throughout the play, Anne lapses into delusional muttering; as Shakespeare's brother Gilbert describes her, "Truly she has meant well and done bravely, spending her life in work."[103] She is often lethargic and comatose, but falls into Shakespeare's arms in the final tableau when she hears Prospero's speech from *The Tempest* (thus the title of the play), and recognizes the genius of a husband that she derided for most of the play. In Lawrence's work, Anne is given voice to lament about her situation as a single mother, but this "picture of worn-out womanhood" only serves to vindicate her husband's choice to leave her behind, when his artistic success outweighs her complaints in the end.

Anglo-Irish journalist John Brophy's novel *Gentleman of Stratford* (1939) also betrays the influence of Joyce's Anne. Brophy, who elsewhere wrote about his experiences in World War I, and offered a wartime bookreading series for the BBC during World War II,[104] creates an Anne who is "tireless in the hot response," prompting Shakespeare to complain that he is "kept like a stallion for a stud" and must take desperate measures to escape before he has "a family to be counted by the dozen."[105] Paul Franssen observes that Brophy's novel was influenced by George Bernard Shaw's image of Shakespeare as an "arrogant snobbish philanderer."[106] Brophy's Anne is part of the tradition of oversexualized women who only seek to hold Shakespeare back from his true promise.

The "Shakespeares" created by the critic Frank Harris, novelists James Joyce and John Brophy, and playwright Charles Lawrence all draw on the idea that a Stratford wife could not satisfy the sexual and creative needs of the poet. Beyond that, Anne is not just quickly dismissed (or even omitted) in these texts in order to focus on another love interest – she receives extended robust critique through elaborate fictional accounts of her appearance, sexual appetite, and physical decay. Lawrence's "picture of worn-out woman-hood"; Brophy's "tirelessly" sexual Anne; Joyce's "ugliest doxy in all Warwickshire" and "boldfaced Stratford wench"; and Harris's "jealous scolding shrew wife" who drove her husband to the "lowest hell of jealousy, rage and humiliation" are all Annes with long-lasting consequences for her afterlife. As late as 1941, for example, Frank Harris's *The Women of Shakespeare* was listed as recommended reading for a unit on "Women in Shakespeare's Life," designed for Shakespeare clubs, and Ton Hoenselaars has traced the influence of Harris's work on Anthony Burgess's 1964 *Nothing Like the Sun* and the 1999 film *Shakespeare in Love.*[107]

Virtuous Annes

In the 1930s and 1940s, another set of Annes contradicted the Joycean Annes, some based on archival and documentary interest, and others motivated by a desire to create a positive version of a wife who fostered her husband's creativity. When he turned his attention to Anne Hathaway, Reverend Edgar I. Fripp, who according to Samuel Schoenbaum "knew Warwickshire and its records better than anyone of his own day or since,"[108] invested in Anne as a way to anchor Shakespeare to Stratford. Fripp's commitment to Shakespeare's Stratford life is evident in his work on the Hathaway family, on the neighboring Quiney family, and on other relatives of Shakespeare. Later described by Ivor Brown as "a devoted encomiast of Anne's character as well as William's,"[109] Fripp's vision necessitated a sympathetic Anne, praised in his *Shakespeare, Man and Artist* (1938): "Godly, quiet, clinging, frail, is our thought of the great Poet's helpmate, pious like her daughter, silent like Virgilia ('my gracious silence'), wifely as his best-loved heroines are (Perdita and Imogen above the rest), delicate (the mother of only three children that lived, and only two who survived her), infirm in March of 1616 when he added to his will the affectionate little bequest of the 'second-best bed with its [sic] furniture', to ensure her possession of the fourposter and chamber which they had shared in New Place."[110] As Schoenbaum points out, Fripp "could never proceed beyond a romantic and uncritical love for his theme,"[111] and his Anne encapsulated this sentiment perfectly, encompassing Stratford, romance, and ordinary life.

Two fictional works from the 1930s and 1940s on either side of the Atlantic offer steadfast and loyal Annes who are rewarded for their virtue, similar to Fripp's biographical Anne. British writer Grace Carlton's (b. 1878) three-act play *The Wooing of Anne Hathaway* (1938) centers on Shakespeare's ability to satisfy a wife in Stratford while pursuing his career in London, contrasting the safe haven of domestic comfort in Stratford with the artistic world of London and all of its temptations. Carlton's play was first performed not long before Britain entered the war, at the Birmingham Repertory Company in November of 1938, directed by Herbert M. Prentice, and a radio version was recorded that same year for the BBC. Set entirely in Stratford, mainly at Anne Hathaway's Cottage, the play was performed for almost two weeks before the Christmas production of *The Swiss Family Robinson*. One contemporary described it as a play that "took on the air of an idyll of high romance, played in the homespun of old Stratford." This reviewer was amused "to find [Anne] emerging from rustic obscurity so adequately equipped to be the ideal helpmate of William Shakespeare, who came and went without question between the capital and the country." In Carlton's version, Shakespeare is "a sometimes fervent and always faithful husband," who preferred his quiet Stratford life to the bustle of London. Played by local actress Myrtle Richardson, Anne Hathaway was "endowed with a quiet charm and courage."[112] Interwar audiences responded positively to this story of Shakespeare "returning to the harbour of wife and home and ambition of re-building New Place in the end," with an Anne who "is not the shrew but the patient loyal wife," noted one reviewer.[113] Carlton's Anne is a faithful caregiver to her father and siblings, described by her brother as a woman with "patience for us all, enough and to spare." Shakespeare falls in love with her for her virtue, remarking, "I've won you, but the wooing of you will take long. Long years, it may be." This Shakespeare is conflicted between his duties to his family and his feelings of being "cooped up here, cabined and confined" in Stratford. When he is accused of treason, his problem is solved since he has no choice but to leave. He vows to return only when he is "worthy" of Anne's love.[114]

In a final scene, Carlton sets up a confrontation between Anne and rival London noblewoman Lady Carew. Anne is confident that in spite of his indiscretions, Shakespeare will return to her, "Because, when all's said and done, I'm his wife. Because I've seen him grow from lad to man and I've grown with him as a true wife should. Because I've borne his children." The faithful and loyal wife wins out in this version of the story, and triumphs over the rival London woman. Anne boasts that her position as "the stay-at-home wife" may be "dull and drab" in comparison to court women, but the pull of his Warwickshire roots is too strong for Shakespeare to resist: "It's here he's rooted and grounded, in Stratford, among his own people, and it is here and to me he will return." At the end of the play, Shakespeare buys New Place, where life with Anne will be "the haven of my desires, the harbour for my home-coming ships."[115]

Carlton uses Anne to validate the idea of a devoted faithful wife, whose endurance and patience prevail in the end, and who offers her husband a homecoming of domestic comfort. In the periodical *The Countrywoman*, one reviewer praised this Anne as "a woman capable of great suffering who stayed in the background of Shakespeare's life, giving him comfort and strength, until the last scene where she is made happy by the prospect of his coming back to Stratford for good."[116] This Anne was left behind to manage the household while her husband was away, and her perseverance and strength are rewarded at the end of the play when her husband returns to her. It is no accident that this play, written in between the two world wars, tackled a topic that must have been on the minds of many audience members.

A second play, written four years later than Carlton's, offers another vindication of Anne. *The Truth About Ann* (1942), penned by American screenwriter Thomas Lennon (1896–1963), was appropriately subtitled "Pavanne for a woman long dead and much maligned."[117] Lennon dedicates his play to his friend Albert Persoff, a Paramount Pictures executive, which suggests that Lennon was not the only one interested in redeeming Anne from unfair critique. In his Author's Note, Lennon offers an impassioned defense of Anne, against those who have "damned" her or "dismissed [her] brutally as an ignorant slattern, a vicious shrew, and a bawdy cheat," who "nagged" Shakespeare and "fed him the sour vitamins of misery."[118] Though he does not name names, Lennon clearly assumes his readership is familiar with debates about Anne.

Lennon creates an Anne who was a faithful woman "on Shakespeare's mental and spiritual level," and he denounces critics who "seek to exalt a great man by demeaning his wife." His play opens with Shakespeare writing a love scene in Stratford, with his wife and children around him, and later includes a remarkable scene of Anne whipping Sir Thomas Lucy so that Shakespeare can escape to London amid accusations of deer stealing. At the end of the play, Shakespeare asks his wife what she would like him to leave her in his will. When she chooses their marital bed, the "second-best bed," he notes presciently, "Anyone reading this undoubtedly will misconstrue it."[119] The Anne that Lennon fashions is a loyal wife who can physically defend her home against intruders, and is rewarded for her constancy and strength. Given the world events taking place while Lennon was writing his play, it is perhaps no surprise to see an "Anne" who could serve as a model to women of the day in her steadfastness. No information survives about performances of Lennon's play, but it was part of "The Living Drama Series," which made plays available for production, but also for a reading audience.

Hollywood screenwriter and Broadway producer N. Richard Nash's three-act play *Second Best Bed* opened on Broadway in July of 1946 for eight performances, starring American actress, novelist, and aviator (a friend of Amelia Earhart) Ruth Chatterton as Anne. In this plot, Anne is about to divorce Shakespeare (played by Chatterton's current husband Barry Thomson) and marry a local man named Poggs (played by Chatterton's first husband, Ralph Forbes, whom she divorced in 1932). Shakespeare, described by one reviewer as "a strutting, grandiloquent playboy on a three-day home-town leave," comes home to Stratford to save the day.[120] Added Elizabethan ballads for a rogue character were performed by folksinger Richard Dyer-Bennett, but despite the intrigue in the real-life romances of the cast, the play did not elicit much interest.

Biographies, critical works, and fiction alike provide an extensive array of Annes, inspired by her possible roles in Shakespeare's life and by her ability to represent a variety of positions for women. Domestic and moral Annes brought Shakespeare in line with late nineteenth-century ideas about women and domesticity. Dissonant Annes reflect changing views of women in the first few decades of the twentieth century, when women's suffrage was a fundamental issue on both sides of the Atlantic. Women especially latched on to Anne as a unique angle of access to Shakespeare, a way to bring him into alignment with their interests, and even to claim him as their own. This culminates at the end of the twentieth century, as Chapter 6 will show, when a critical mass of works by and for women gives a concentrated focus to Anne. Authors who locate the inspiration for Shakespeare's literary works in his sexuality rarely accommodate Anne into this vision, and this phenomenon of developing anti-Annes would continue

as well through the next century. All of these Annes, from the most complimentary to the most denigrating, whether in works outwardly labeled as
biographies, plays, or novels, are imaginary to some degree, relying on fiction
to round out the skeletal details of Anne's life. As the next two chapters will
show, the substantial body of imaginary Annes testifies both to the deficient
archive and to the insatiable desire to fill that absence.

5

DARK LADIES AND FAITHFUL WIVES
Post-World War II Imaginary Annes

W AS ANNE HATHAWAY A WOMAN WHO "FILLED [SHAKESPEARE] with revulsion" and "sour anger," as a 2004 best-selling biography of Shakespeare describes her, or could she have been the real author of Shakespeare's works, as a play published a year later (2005) imagines her? In the post-war period, imaginings of Anne Hathaway proliferated, in part due to the increased literary and critical interest in women, to the development of feminism, and to the upsurge in biography. New literary forms such as biofiction generated fresh interest in the marriage of fiction and biography, and a cluster of biographies around the millennium further underlines the enduring fascination with Shakespeare's life story. As Chapter 4 demonstrated, Shakespeare's wife has been constructed and reconstructed out of the same building blocks for nearly two centuries, in light of the absence of any new information about her. While the final chapter of this book looks at works about Anne designed specifically for women around the millennium, this chapter examines a number of Annes in the second half of the twentieth century, to question the role of fiction in biography and the influence of biography on fiction in these constructions.

Heralded by Jan Kott's seminal work *Shakespeare Our Contemporary* (1964), described by Andrew Hadfield as "the most influential critical work of the post-war period," the second half of the twentieth century includes an increase in works about Shakespeare for a popular audience, challenging what W. B. Worthen calls the "faultline between academic and popular Shakespeare."[1] The proliferation of biographies of Shakespeare, coupled with the dearth of new archival material, necessitated new narratives to tell Shakespeare's story – and thus, a greater variety of texts. Fiction helped to fill this void and bring Shakespeare's life story into the contemporary moment.

As Valentina Vannucci affirms, the form of biofiction was especially adept at offering "a rethinking of the past from a point of view in the present."[2] Likewise, Brian Cummings has argued that "The biography of Shakespeare explains not as much him as his relationship to us. This is one reason why fictions of the life of Shakespeare often outstrip biography."[3] As this chapter will demonstrate, in the second half of the twentieth century the separation between biography and fiction narrowed, with fiction often including brief biographies, and biographies engaging with greater degrees of fiction.

The "task of the responsible biographer," notes Samuel Schoenbaum, is to "clear away the cobwebs and sift, as disinterestedly as he may, the facts that chance and industry have brought to light."[4] The genre of biography presupposes that the biographer is not pursuing a personal fantasy at will, but rather is "disinterestedly" adhering to surviving facts. Michael Lackey refers to this as the "truth contract" between the biographer and the reader.[5] In light of the conflict between the "responsible biographer" and the desires of both writers and readers for a more intimate view of Shakespeare's life, stories about Shakespeare's private life have increased in literary forms that allow for more intimate, personal, and interior approaches to Shakespeare.

Variously termed "biographical novels," "historical fiction," "historical romance," and "biofiction," these forms are ideally suited for the mix of biography and fiction involved in crafting extended narratives about Shakespeare's private life. In 2009 Jerome de Groot observed that "the last few decades have seen an explosion in the sales and popularity of novels set in the past."[6] Similarly, Michael Lackey describes the biographical novel as "incredibly popular," beginning in the 1980s.[7] Biofiction is especially germane to stories that seek to update Shakespeare's life story, since it "uses the biographical subject in order to project" the writer's "own vision of life and the world," but it can also "enable[e] us to formulate new ways of thinking."[8]

In post-war works about Shakespeare's life, the gap in knowledge about Anne has been filled in to bolster ideological claims about women's place in marriage, about the connections between artistic genius and romantic life, about Shakespeare's views of women, and about the relationship between Shakespeare's works and his life. The many Annes discussed in this chapter support Douglas Lanier's argument that the "collective ideals, desire, and anxieties to which Shakespeare's life and his formidable poetic power have been made to give voice" are crucial for understanding the "shared fantasies" behind popular versions of Shakespeare.[9] Dark Ladies and other anti-Annes are especially prevalent in the later twentieth century, suggesting a correlation between the way Anne is fashioned (or omitted) and current ideas about women, sexuality, and marriage.[10]

It would be impractical (and quite ponderous) to discuss every work that includes an Anne in this period; readers are referred to the Appendix at the end of this book for a full list of texts. Instead, I look at representative texts, beginning with Anthony Burgess's novel and biography, examining biographical and fictional works in parallel. In the second part of this chapter, I take a closer look at how multiple biographies around the millennium (more than ten published in the last decade) have configured the same set of facts about Anne in vastly different ways. Using Stephen Greenblatt's best-selling *Will in the World* (2004) as a case study, I then look at how Anne is constructed in this blockbuster work designed to tell the story of Shakespeare's rise to fame, with an extensive circulation, written by one of the foremost Shakespeare scholars of the century. Ultimately, Anne's story is inseparable from that of her famous husband, but the politics of representing a one-sided version of this early modern woman in order to oblige her famous husband's story should give us pause.[11]

Anthony Burgess's "Groaning Old Crone"

The work of novelist and biographer Anthony Burgess makes a compelling case for the back-and-forth between biography and fiction. Burgess's novel *Nothing Like the Sun*, originally published in 1964, remains a perennially popular version of Shakespeare's private life, and has been reprinted nearly twenty times, most recently in 2013, and translated into Portuguese, Czech, and Swedish. *Nothing Like the Sun* carries on the tradition begun by Malone, expanded by Harris, and amplified by Joyce, of envisioning Anne as a sexually aggressive, repulsive, and predatory woman, who represents a rare mistake in Shakespeare's life. This Anne's voracious sexual appetite sours their relationship, forcing him into "bed-slavery," until finally "hatred rose in him like black vomit, seeing that she had turned him into a manner of a whoremaster." This Anne from "Shottery (Shittery)" gets her comeuppance when Shakespeare pays a surprise visit to Stratford and discovers her in bed with his brother Richard. Though Shakespeare himself has been cavorting with other women and men, Anne's sexual dalliance is couched as a disgusting scene, as she "wrapped her ageing treacherous bareness, bold as brass, into a night-gown," while Shakespeare felt "the cuckold's unspeakable satisfaction, the satisfaction of confirmation, the great rage which justifies murder and the firing of cities and makes a man rise into his whimpering strong citadel of self-pitying aloneness." Shakespeare's extra-marital dalliances catch up to him when he notices the growing sore of syphilis on his penis, but his sexual flings have inspired his plays and poetry, so his indiscretions are worth it in the end.

Anne is not given a redemptive turn at the end of the novel. She is not the loyal caregiver to whom he returns, but instead is "a groaning old crone [going] about her housewifely tasks, busying herself with the making of sick man's broth" who would "sit scratching her spent loins through her kirtle, mumbling her book."[12] As part of his extensive campaign to construct an Anne whose "aging treacherous bareness" impeded Shakespeare's career by pursuing her own carnality at the expense of satiating his libido, Burgess admitted that he created Anne as a "sexual monster" in order to produce a Shakespeare who was "very heavily seduced and, eventually, rendered sick . . . of the varied patterns of heterosexual lust."[13]

With the subtitle "A Story of Shakespeare's Love-life," *Nothing Like the Sun* portrays Shakespeare as a writer motivated by his sexual energy, an agenda that has no place for his wife. This Anne is an impediment to his writing, complaining that he has time for his poetry but no time for his wife "and her lawful pleasure." When he responds that "for one line of verse I would trade thirty such scolds as you," she insults his manhood, telling him that his "little thing is shrunken to a nib. Dip it in ink as a tool to write withal. I will go find me a man." According to one reviewer, Burgess "is making the case that Shakespeare's talent had its origin in his sexual drives and his topless towers of words were founded on his immense desire and will," as part of his "phallic power," so presumably, this adverse portrayal of Anne is justified because it explains the genesis of Shakespeare's literary works.[14] Shakespeare finds sexual satisfaction in another woman, a Dark Lady, who can satisfy his desires and inspire his poetry.[15] The cover to the 1965 US edition (Figure 5.1) depicts an oversized Shakespeare gazing pensively at an exotic naked woman. While it would be tempting to ascribe Burgess's Anne to a pre-feminist era and thus a product of its time, the novel's continued popularity suggests a more long-standing and disturbing appeal, beyond its immediate historical context.

As the author of the bestselling novel *A Clockwork Orange*, advertised on the cover, Burgess capitalized on his popularity as a novelist in order to attract a reading audience, and his fictional portrayal of Anne as a lusty, shrewish, "groaning old crone" has had a pervasive impact on her afterlife. Even though *Nothing Like the Sun* is clearly called a novel on the cover (as in Figure 5.1), it has been read as a truthful account and even described as a biography. Labelled by one critic as a "fictional Shakespeare-biography" and by another as "the only successful novel ever written about

Figure 5.1. Cover of Anthony Burgess, *Nothing Like the Sun*, 1965 US edition. Used with permission of W.W. Norton.

Shakespeare," Burgess's novel has had wide-ranging influence.[16] Aileen Pippett, in *The Saturday Review*, claims that, "If this is not truth it is as close to it as we are likely to get . . . the novelist is still the best witness to the reality behind the facts."[17] It should be obvious that Burgess's Anne is no more truthful than any number of Annes we have seen so far in this book, but the eagerness of readers and reviewers to embrace Burgess's Anne and his vision of a "reality behind the facts" is clear from the novel's many reprints.

Six years after publishing his novel, Burgess penned a biography of Shakespeare, which displays many of the same fictional techniques as his novel. The denunciation of Anne he contrived in *Nothing Like the Sun* reappears in his 1970 biography. This Shakespeare was "drawn to Anne by physical desire only," felt "disgust" at her, and "had to get away from Anne" and escape her "nagging him about his lack of ambition." In both texts, Burgess fantasizes about Shakespeare's feelings and emotions connected to women, and imagines scenarios to explain Shakespeare's erotically charged creativity. His biographical Shakespeare is infatuated with a Dark Lady and is unhappily married. The "copulation" between William and Anne was only "wanton fornication, doubtless perpetrated in a ryefield in high summer, and well-remembered in *As You Like It*." Using the two Annes named in the marriage documents, Burgess relies on what he admits are "the crude but convenient properties of the old women's-magazine morality-stories," that Shakespeare was "exercised by love for the one and lust for the other."[18]

Burgess's biography contains extensive speculation inspired by Anne's age, and it extends well beyond the boundaries of reason, such as imagining tense dinner conversations over Anne's age, for example. This biographical Anne was "already past the normal marrying age" and "must have started looking around fairly desperately for a husband." Imagining Anne's home life, Burgess maintains that "there may have been pointed remarks over the suppertable about her prolonged spinsterhood." Burgess continues his dia-tribe against Anne, presuming to know Shakespeare's mental state with conviction: "With bitter resignation," Shakespeare was "led to the slaughter, or the marriage bed" with Anne. Burgess admits the influence of Frank Harris when he contends that Will "entered on a forced marriage with a woman he did not really love," but he is nevertheless convinced that "the lovelessness of the marriage was one of his reasons for leaving Stratford and seeking a new life in London."[19] It also makes for a better story. If given an excerpt from Burgess's biography and one from his novel *Nothing Like the Sun*, it would be very difficult to tell the two apart. In fact, Stanley Wells describes Burgess's biography as a "biographical piece of fiction."[20]

Furthermore, Burgess's biography reveals the tensions inherent in the various ways Shakespeare's life can be written. Even though Burgess advances one of the most cynical portrayals of the Shakespeare marriage, he could not resist including a photo of the courting settle at Anne Hathaway's Cottage (discussed in Chapter 3), with the romantic caption, "On this settle at Hewland Farm, Shottery, the lovers Anne Hathaway and William Shakespeare sat and, despite its hardness, courted." Just below this illustration, with its caption of the Shakespeares as "lovers" who engaged in a courtship, Burgess offers a narrative of a crafty Anne who entrapped William, in contrast to the way he describes the marriage in the photo caption: "One way of finding a husband was to become impregnated by a man, who, having done the indecent thing, would then proceed, perhaps with threats in his ears or a gun in his back, to do the decent [thing]."[21] The Anne in Burgess's prose is certainly not the same Anne from the photograph of the settle, who is "courted" by Shakespeare as a "lover." The inconsistencies in Burgess's argument are thus betrayed by his desire to illustrate Shakespeare's courtship with a surviving material object, but the courting settle does not fit with the story of a Shakespeare who married Anne with "bitter resignation."

Burgess's treatment of Anne is all the more striking, given the developing critical climate for Shakespeare studies at the time. Published in 1970, his biography came out just before Juliet Dusinberre's landmark *Shakespeare and the Nature of Women* (1975), a work that has been called "the foundation of twentieth-century feminist Shakespeare criticism."[22] The field of biography also witnessed a new emphasis on women's stories around the same time; Linda Wagner-Martin notes that in the 1960s and 1970s, "readers developed a new consciousness about both the facts of women's lives and the many possible ways stories about those lives might be told." The result was that "women readers of women's biographies demanded different kinds of information," and correspondingly, "the role of the biographer changed dramatically."[23] While we might be tempted to dismiss Burgess's biography as a product of his time, like his novel, it has been frequently reprinted, as recently as 2013, and remains in print nearly 50 years after its composition.

Not all 1970s texts portrayed such a predatory, sexually decrepit, lusty Anne. Tim Kelly's *Second Best Bed* (1970), a short work designed for amateur performance, validates Hathaway as a stay-at-home mother whose sacrifices enabled the plays of Shakespeare to be written, and who is rewarded at the end of the play. In this brief skit designed for young girls, Anne discovers a love letter from Shakespeare after she has dutifully followed his posthumous instructions to cut open the mattress on the second-best bed. Inside she finds a pouch of jewels and a letter praising her for being a supportive wife. Shakespeare writes, "If you had not been so sympathetic all these years, if you had not sent me on to London when you did, I should very likely have ended a poor farmer and a poorer husband."[24] It is difficult to reconcile these contradictory 1970 Annes, one a biography for a popular readership, and one for young adult amateur theatre. Together they make the case for the long-standing dissonant narratives of a Shakespeare unhappily entrapped in a miserable marriage, and one who loves and rewards his loyal and supportive wife.

Popular Biographies

In the second half of the twentieth century, biographies of Shakespeare multiplied at an astonishing rate, written largely by academics, as part of what Samuel Schoenbaum calls "the great tide of popular biography."[25] Ivor Brown's extensive output of biographical works intended for a general readership can serve as a barometer for the critical climate of popular works about Shakespeare's life. Brown's *How Shakespeare Spent the Day* (1963) looks at the practical realities of Shakespeare's life in the theatre. Brown remarked that he was in search of "the man I want to find," and frustratedly lamented that "there is no end to the examination of his thinking, his personal philosophy, and his affairs of the heart."[26] Five years later, he published *The Women in Shakespeare's Life* (1968), written not for "Shakespearian specialists," but specifically for the women who "pass through the homes where Shakespeare's mother, wife, and daughters" lived. Brown's goal is to show Shakespeare as a "mortal family man as well as the Immortal Bard," in a work designed for "the general public," and dedicated to his own wife in honor of their journeys to Stratford.[27] Brown takes Frank Harris to task for his creation of an "irascible Anne Hathaway," and for playing the "customary game of Shakespearian biographers" by picking quotations to make his case. Instead, Brown contends that "the facts are stronger than the fancies," and that if Shakespeare's "marriage had been disastrous and bitterly regretted" he would not be "contented to end his life in the comfortable home which Harris took to be a shrew's nest."[28]

The work of prolific historian A. L. Rowse (1903–1997) was especially embraced in America, and he wrote two biographies of Shakespeare: *William Shakespeare: A Biography* in 1963 and *Shakespeare the Man* in 1973. His particular obsession was with identifying the Dark Lady of the sonnets, who he conjectured was Emilia Bassano-Lanier. Likely because of this interest in an alternative to Anne, the historical Anne does not fare well in

Rowse's biography. Rowse contends that the eight-year age difference between the Shakespeares was "a disparity more significant in those days when people aged earlier." In Rowse's account, "the adult Shakespeare had plenty of reason to regret his hasty and disadvantageous marriage" even though he was "a normal family man" with "characteristic good nature."[29] Here, Shakespeare comes off as a genial and savvy man who regretted his hasty marriage to Anne.

Rowse's biography was designed for a general readership, as numerous reviews attest. One blurb on the back cover from *The Library Journal* praised it as a book that will "delight general readers and scholars alike." The *Times Literary Supplement* also touted the book's appeal to a wide audience: "Tone and substance suggest that Dr. Rowse is casting his net to capture a . . . popular kind of readership." Rowse's status as "a bona fide scholar celebrity" who wrote "scores of essays, book reviews, travel articles and op-ed pieces for *The New York Times*" underlines the influence of his imagined Anne on a broad readership. Not everyone bought into Rowse's stories, however; one reviewer described Rowse as "not dissuaded by the lack of definitive evidence from proclaiming his conclusions as incontrovertible facts."[30]

Although his work was generally not designed for a broad non-specialist readership, Samuel Schoenbaum's magisterial contributions to Shakespeare studies also stem from this period. His *Shakespeare: A Documentary Life* (1975) and *Shakespeare's Lives* (1970) both advanced historical and archival knowledge, but equally important, underlined the constructed nature of "Shakespeare," and by extension, his wife, through explication of multiple possible lives.

The Dark Ladies of the 1960s–1980s

While biographies for a general reading audience proliferated, imaginative works about Shakespeare in the years from the 1960s to the 1980s were largely concerned with creating alternative love interests, mainly Dark Ladies. As Douglas Lanier points out, Shakespeare's "stature as a love poet" has provided inspiration for various Dark Ladies and their variations, who can serve as his "erotic muse."[31]

Conversely, Annes from this period are often lower-class, backward, lascivious, and out of touch with Shakespeare's artistic life. Edward Fisher's *Shakespeare & Son* (1962), for example, casts Anne Hathaway as a nanny in the Shakespeare household, who keeps an upper hand by bedding John Shakespeare before marrying his son. William Gibson's play *A Cry of Players*, first presented at the Berkshire Theatre Festival in Stockbridge,

Massachusetts in 1968, and then at Lincoln Center in November of that year, features a Stratford scene of rustic yokels, including a production note that the people in the play "have not yet discovered the fork, they live in filth, and wear rags not unlike those of, say, Appalachia." Here Anne embodies the backwards countryfolk, telling Will at one point, "Oh God, ye're a busy lad for doing nothing."[32] Will luckily escapes this stifling Stratford with a group of traveling players to fulfill his artistic destiny in London. Even with Anne Bancroft playing Anne opposite Frank Langella as Will, the play received lukewarm reviews; according to one critic, Anne's "aggressiveness has a peculiarly sour note about it, and her warmth is less a mellowing than an overripe fruit plopping open. Still she has a presence."[33] The dissonance between this unrefined Anne and her urbane husband was obvious in the dialog alone. Anne is similarly mundane and pedestrian in Eric Malpass's novel *Sweet Will* (1973), where she is left behind alone in Stratford. At least this Anne is literate, since she writes, "'Sweet Will, I am with childe, and very lonelie. Anne.'" Shakespeare feels guilty because she is "left to carry alone the fearful burden of love made flesh." Even so, Anne remains behind in Stratford, and Shakespeare "thought wistfully of the country peace, the slow country days; and of Anne, poor Anne, who wasn't having much of a life. Anne, who accepted her loneliness with such gentle resignation; even though for her the sun shone only when Will was there."[34] Other than her ability to read and write, this Anne offers little inspiration, and exists solely to mourn for her absent husband.

Anne is briefly mentioned in Native American playwright Laura Annawyn Shamas's play *The Other Shakespeare* (1981), with a plot mainly focused on Cassandra Shakespeare, a younger sister to Will, who also writes (inspired by Shakespeare's sister in Virginia Woolf's *A Room of One's Own*). John Shakespeare orders Will to marry Anne because she is pregnant, and she is an impediment to both Shakespeare's writing and to his sister's; Cassandra exclaims, "I cannot stay here any more! Your bride Anne will be here in the house. I shall barely be able to speak to you about poetry, or any questions of the heart!" Here Anne is a rival to Cassandra, and though she has no poetic talent, she surpasses Cassandra in domestic prowess. Casandra complains: "She will be liked better around the house than I, for her clever way with the stove or broom. She will begin to scold me for writing, saying that a young woman like myself will never catch a man. And I will reply, 'Aye! Who wants to catch a man, the way you enslaved my own brother!'" Cassandra helps Will escape from Stratford to "preserve [his] freedom."[35] Although Cassandra is not a love interest, she does stand in as a nonsexual female artistic muse and help-mate, leaving the mundane domestic tasks to the non-literary Anne.

The Annes discussed in this section are surprising, given the increased attention to women and feminism in Shakespeare studies at the time. Phyllis Rackin observes that the last thirty years of the twentieth century "witnessed an impressive and very influential body of scholarly work" on women and Shakespeare.[36] Valerie Traub similarly remarks that since 1980, the publication year of Carol Thomas Neely's *A Woman's Part: Feminist Criticism of Shakespeare*, "analyses of women and gender have represented one of the largest growth areas in Shakespeare studies."[37] Additionally, "feminism has permeated biography," noted Paula R. Backscheider.[38] Even with the growth of feminism and feminist work on Shakespeare, this was not necessarily an era of progressive Annes.

Anne as Erotic Muse

In one of the most enduring texts about Anne from the 1990s, Robert Nye uses Anne's own voice to boast about her ability to satisfy Shakespeare's sexual desire, inspire his literary works, and maintain her own independence. Nye's *Mrs. Shakespeare: The Complete Works* is presented as Anne's memoir after the death of her husband. This Shakespeare's literary canon is inspired by his libido, but here Anne is the one who satisfies him. Anne divulges "the biggest of Mr. Shakespere's little secrets," their "private playhouse" of the "second best bed" where their sexual fantasies fuel Shakespeare's imagination. Anne grudgingly accepts Shakespeare's infidelities, but when they discover their mutual enjoyment of sexual pleasures, she gains power over her husband. She writes that Shakespeare "had always been less than a man should be in the labours of love" and that she always had to do "the hard work" for him. Anne's degrading comments are part of what Sofía Muñoz-Valdivieso describes as "demystification of Shakespeare the man."[39] In a chapter called "The Acts," Anne details the role-playing that led to Shakespeare's creation of his characters, where he would pull the curtains around the ornamental bed and they would "act out his dreams." One night she was Miranda to his Caliban, who had "very beastly lusts." Another night she was the shrew and he was Petruchio, "whose pleasure it was to tame me of my shrewishness." She even dressed up as a man in a forest (Ganymede/Rosalind) while Shakespeare "became a country wench who fell in love" with her, à la Audrey. Other roles for Anne included Ophelia to his Hamlet, Desdemona to his Othello, and Juliet to his Romeo, where he "kissed his dead little Juliet and did that other thing to her." All of the role-playing culminated in sex, which led to the creation of his plays. Unsurprisingly, this Anne also served as the Dark Lady behind his sonnets. As his sexual muse,

Anne confesses that he "needed her" in order to fuel his creative power. She "was his Alpha and Omega, his beginning and his ending, his mother, his bride, and his layer-out. He was born at my hands. He came alive in my backside. Reader, he died in my arms."[40] The Anne that Nye creates is thus essential for Shakespeare's creative oeuvre, and she is empowered by her sexual expertise. The second-best bed that she inherits is of course the place where their sexual escapades fueled his imagination and allowed him to work out his plots.

Mrs. Shakespeare: The Complete Works was originally published in 1993, and has been reprinted regularly, most recently in 2007. Nye's novel has a global appeal and was translated into Russian in 2010; Portuguese in 2005; Hebrew in 2000; and German in 1999. Nye's novel was also adapted for the Brazilian stage in Portuguese in 2007 by Emilio Di Biasi, as *The Intimate Diaries of Madame Shakespeare*, and produced as a radio drama for the BBC in 2009 by Patrick Rayner. It has remained in print for at least 25 years, which suggests the appeal of this story that validates both marriage and women's sexual power.

It is worth pausing to compare Nye's novel to Anthony Burgess's *Nothing Like the Sun*, since both have remained in print and likely reach similar audiences. Both novelists locate the source of Shakespeare's artistic inspiration in his sex life, though Anne's role in this enterprise differs drastically between the two texts. In one, Anne is her husband's empowered partner, who enjoys a risqué sex life that fuels the creation of his plays and characters. In the other, Anne is a revoltingly voracious woman whose sexual advances elicit disgust from her husband. There is no direct evidence that the same audience read both novels, but the fact that both were frequently reprinted and translated in the same time frame suggests that they appealed to the same generation of readers, who endorsed both the story of a sexually empowered wife and a constraining stifling one. Emilio Di Biasi addresses this duality in *The Intimate Diaries of Madame Shakespeare* (2007), where Anne is played by two actresses, one who represents a "complacent and romantic" version, and the other who is a "hard, bitter but sharp and quick-witted woman." This combination suggests the vitality of texts that endorse and critique marriage through Shakespeare's wife, and underlines Anne's fluid role in bringing Shakespeare's life story into conversations about women.

The late 1990s also yielded one of the most successful anti-Anne texts, the 1999 Hollywood film *Shakespeare in Love*, featuring such A-list actors as Gwyneth Paltrow, Judi Dench, and Joseph Fiennes, with a screenplay by Marc Norman and Tom Stoppard. While Anne never actually appears in this work, it is worth considering her position in the plot, given its longevity as an enduring tale about Shakespeare's private life. Fiennes's Shakespeare gleans his artistic inspiration from his illicit liaison with noblewoman Viola de Lesseps, played by Paltrow. Described by one reviewer as "a romantic comedy that is genuinely romantic," in this film the fact that Shakespeare is a married man has little effect on the plot, and Anne only serves as an impediment to Shakespeare's true calling as a playwright, and to his pursuit of true love and sexual satisfaction.[41] Early on, Shakespeare meets with Dr. Moth to discuss his writer's block. When Moth prompts Shakespeare, "You have a wife, children …," Shakespeare dismisses his marriage as a youthful mistake:

WILL: I was a lad of eighteen, Ann Hathaway was a woman, half as old again.
DR. MOTH: A woman of property?
WILL (shrugs):   She had a cottage. One day, she was three month gone with child, so …
DR. MOTH: And your relations?
WILL: On my mother's side the Ardens …
DR. MOTH: No, your marriage bed.
WILL: Four years and a hundred miles away in Stratford. A cold bed too, since the twins were born. Banishment was a blessing.
DR. MOTH: So now you are free to love …
WILL: – yet cannot love nor write it.

Later in the film, Will gains his sexual satisfaction and his poetic ability from his lover Viola. At one point, he confesses that even though he is married, Viola is his true love: "My love is no lie. I have a wife, yes, and I cannot marry the daughter of Sir Robert de Lesseps. It needed no wife come from Stratford to tell you that. And yet you let me come to your bed." Stoppard and Norman meld together this fantasy of illicit love with the balcony scene in *Romeo and Juliet*, where "the words of the scene become Will's and Viola's."[42] Andrew Hadfield notes that *Shakespeare in Love* "reproduces a very familiar version of the Shakespeare story" where Shakespeare becomes "a normal bloke," though this courtship requires eliminating Anne from the story.[43] Readers may notice similarities with William T. Saward's 1907 play discussed earlier in Chapter 4, where William courts Anne in a version of the balcony scene from *Romeo and Juliet*. In the film produced nearly 100 years later, Anne has been replaced in this same scene by an upper-class fictional woman.

In the 2014 stage play, adapted by Lee Hall from Norman and Stoppard's film version, Anne is erased even further from this "stirring love story."[44] The play opens with a scene where Shakespeare tells Marlowe that he has "lost my gift . . . my quill is broken, my well is dry." When Marlowe asks how his "marital relations" are, Shakespeare replies, "As cold as her heart." In the film version, Shakespeare's "bed" is cold because of the birth of twins, but in the later stage play, it is Anne's "heart" that is cold. As in the earlier film, Shakespeare falls in love with Viola de Lesseps, who declares herself a woman who "will have poetry in my life. And adventure. And love. Love above all," unlike cold-hearted Anne. When Viola finds out that Will is married, he pleads, "I was only eighteen. My marriage is long dead and buried in Stratford. Everything I am is here in London. With you." Will admits that he "needs no wife from Stratford to tell you I could never marry the daughter of Robert de Lesseps." At the end of the play, Viola tells him, "I cannot be the woman who denies the whole world William Shakespeare."[45] Instead of Anne sacrificing her freedom and time to manage the household so that her husband can write, in the stage version of *Shakespeare in Love*, it is Shakespeare's clandestine lover who must facilitate his plays through her passionate inspiration.

The resolution of both the film and the play depends on the audience forgetting that Shakespeare is still married, and that he is technically an adulterer. Anne Hathaway uncomfortably stands in the way of an alternate love story, but Norman and Stoppard seem reluctant to omit her completely from their story, perhaps reflecting the assumed knowledge base of their audiences. The success of the film and stage play suggests that millennial audiences are willing to overlook an adulterous Shakespeare if it means that they can experience a love story that explains his creative process. This salacious tale of illicit love between a struggling playwright and a beautiful noblewoman promotes the idea that Anne was an impediment to Shakespeare's success, and that his artistic fruition was only possible if he abandoned his wife in favor of an urban, childless woman who can please him sexually but not tie him down with domestic responsibilities.

Anne's Revival

Anne has a more central role in Grace Tiffany's novel *Will* (2004), which reworks the relationship between the Shakespeares to mirror that of many modern couples – they face the challenges of a long-distance relationship, the difficulties of stay-at-home mothers and career fathers, the trials of extramarital affairs, and the struggles of keeping a marriage together at the end of their lives. Putting Will and Anne into scenarios that readers will recognize, and may have even experienced, makes Shakespeare not the poetic genius born of nature, but rather a flesh-and-blood man with a wife whose needs and desires can speak to those of her readers.

For this Anne, marriage to Shakespeare offered a ticket to a new life. She "found it hard to say him nay," and within a year she was saddled with the full weight of new motherhood: "the loud-lunged babe lay yelling in Anne's arms or in this spot or that of the cramped Henley Street home while its mother bustled about her new duties." A loud, crowded household is no climate for a writer, and Will decides it is best for him to leave Anne behind for London. Even when apart, the sexual chemistry remains between the Shakespeares; Will says he even "thought of Anne's body on the day he had left her." The long-distance relationship begins to falter, and Anne tries to convince Will that he can work from home, telling him, "thou couldst write plays here as well as there." Eventually the distance is too much for their relationship. After five years apart, "his love was stone cold." This self-sufficient Anne makes peace with her lot in life, and "began to plan her life without him. In her mind she made a bitter bargain. He would send her money and she would raise his children and never publicly shame him. He would do what he did in London, and she would do what she liked at home."[46]

Tiffany's Anne has no difficulty voicing her resentment at her husband's abandonment. She complains to daughter Judith: "Neglect is just what it spells! I have a husband's money instead of a husband . . . who hath betrayed and bewhored me and abandoned the three of you . . . ." Judith tries to pacify her mother by arguing that Shakespeare reflected Anne in his plays, which are full of "innocent, suffering *wives*." Both Anne and Will seek sexual satisfaction outside of their marriage, but also remain attracted to each other. Shakespeare struggles with his sexual identity, and thinks of Anne when he's trying to resist Henry Wriothesley. Back home in Stratford, the options for Anne are more limited. She has a disastrous tryst with Shakespeare's younger brother Gilbert; her "cheeks grew hot at the memory of the Christmas Night in Henley Street when, merry with wine and lonely for Will's body in bed beside her, she had gone in the dark to the room where Gilbert slept. Soused with ale, he had kissed and caressed her, then called her the name of a woman in the town." Though her rendezvous with Gilbert is unsuccessful, he protects her by buying up all of the copies of his brother's sonnets in hopes that Anne won't discover them, but he is too late. Anne is aghast at the public shame her husband caused to her family: "I care not what you do in your city," she tells her wayward husband, "But to shame me, and

Susanna, and Judith – ." At the end of the novel, despite her humiliation, this Anne comes to Shakespeare's rescue; she forgives him for his infidelities, and "In her arms he became human, and wept."[47] This final scene redeems Anne for her steadfastness, offering a sympathetic reading of a woman who sacrificed and suffered.

Responses from readers of Tiffany's *Will* call attention to the importance of biographical fiction for complicating the landscape of stories about Shakespeare's life. One reviewer appreciated the novel for showing "the raw human side" of Shakespeare.[48] Another reader described the novel as "a fictional biography of Shakespeare," praiseworthy for "filling in all the missing pieces – not the least of which is Shakespeare's point of view on things like his wife, his son's death, and his desire to act and write for the London stage."[49] While this reader recognized the "fictional" component, she also read it as a "biography." This melding of fiction with biography, not just in the texts themselves but in the expectations of readers, is characteristic of most latter twentieth-century works about Shakespeare's life.

One final example suggests the longevity of fictional Annes to address a variety of audience desires. Jude Morgan's *The Secret Life of William Shakespeare* (2012) traces Shakespeare's career through his fidelity to his wife; Will confesses that his greatest fear is "Anne thinking of him as faithless," and she provides both his inspiration and his stability. Before he leaves for London, he and Anne swear a blood oath on a pile of rocks, an image to which Will returns repeatedly as he faces temptations in London. He tells Anne, "*Your love, it made me*" and "I begin and end, with you." When Shakespeare feels distant from his wife, he loses his bearings: "Anne lay on the other side of the turning world – where he had placed her, or where she had placed herself, or where the great division had left them." In this version, Anne gives him strength, security, and confidence.

The parts of the novel set in London predictably provide sexual temptation for William, and his succumbing to another woman is his downfall, rather than his triumph. He refers to one of his affairs as "evil." Even after betraying Anne, he turns to her for understanding: "Anne who knew what life was like. Who knew that life was not ponds, but rivers . . . what Anne thought was important." Shakespeare's affair is his lowest point in the novel, not his moment of salvation, and Anne is his real inspiration and his true love.

This Shakespeare marriage is not perfect, and it offers readers an intimate look at their marital tensions. "I am full of rage and jealousy," Anne proclaims to Will, "and I want to – to do something, shake the world about me, and I cannot, I cannot even hate as I would wish, and that's because you made me, Will . . . I can forgive almost everything but that, for once you made me

I was yours, belonging to you, and that I cannot break." Their relationship is one of mutual dependence, not a one-sided mismatch, so Will too gets his chance to air his feelings: "But you made me . . . From the day we met at Shottery, that was the beginning of my creation. You made Will Shakespeare, Anne. And without you there wouldn't be a life, but the unformed shape of one, never to be."

Other characters reinforce the strong bond between the Shakespeares. Shakespeare's brother Edmund observes, "In you I've always seen what love can mean, and what things it can conjure from the coarse stuff of life . . . I'll never forget the knowing of you two, the sweetness there was, the showing how a life can be when truly lived, each in the other on this one earth." The novel ends with the reconciliation of the Shakespeares and the reaffirmation of their marital bond. Will "comes to her across the room, she comes motionless to him, waiting to enclose him, as lovers do, as people do, just that. They hold, kiss, thrust low despairing happy heads against each other's shoulders and ringing arms."[50]

Morgan's Anne is a steadfast inspiration and anchor, rather than a wife left behind in Stratford who hovers in the back of the story. Morgan's Shakespeare is a family man, grounded in love for his wife and children, rather than a womanizer. He uses Anne to craft a positive story about modern marriage, one of equality, mutual love, and co-dependence, where Shakespeare's infidelities are mistakes rather than triumphs, and where reconciliation with his wife is the goal of the novel.

Morgan's sympathetic view of Anne and his validation of her were praised by Gary Taylor as the "most engaging creation," and he describes Morgan's novel as "better written, and more interesting, than any scholarly biography."[51] The sentimental depiction of the Shakespeare marriage in *The Secret Life of William Shakespeare* (2012) offers a sharp contrast to that in the stage play of *Shakespeare in Love*, written two years later, where Anne is only referred to as the threatening wife left behind. *Shakespeare in Love* (2014), however, both the film and stage play, is by far the more popular version of Shakespeare's private life, and its monumental success in comparison to the relatively small circulation of Morgan's novel suggests that the story of Shakespeare as a devoted husband to a faithful wife holds less appeal for contemporary audiences than the illicit love affair that provides the inspiration in *Shakespeare in Love*.

Millennial Biographies

The numerous Shakespeare biographies in the decades around the millennium reflect the uncertainty about Anne's place in Shakespeare's life, about the nature of their relationship, about the reasons Shakespeare left Stratford for London, and about Shakespeare's feelings toward his wife. Gamaliel Bradford attributes the increase in biographies in the mid-twentieth century to "the desire to get out of ourselves and into the lives of others,"[52] and this may hold true for Shakespeare and for Anne as well. Barbara Everett remarked in 2007, "of Shakespearian biography in particular there has been a flood over the last few decades, good, bad and indifferent."[53] Similarly, Anne Barton noted in 2006 that biographies of Shakespeare are "alarmingly on the increase," and she counted at least one biography every year between 1996 and 2006.[54]

A brief survey of the major biographies here will allow for a more in-depth comparison later in this chapter. Park Honan's *Shakespeare: A Life* (1998) integrates Shakespeare's life with typical Elizabethan and Jacobean life, in an "endeavor to clothe the bare documentary fact in the flesh of an authentic Elizabethan milieu."[55] Avoiding the cradle-to-grave structure, Katherine Duncan-Jones's *Ungentle Shakespeare: Scenes from his Life* (2001), looks at key moments in Shakespeare's life around issues of "social class, sex and money."[56] Duncan-Jones uses this thematic approach to construct a Shakespeare who is a social climber and womanizer, a much coarser and less romanticized view of Shakespeare than many previous biographers espoused.

Biographies of Shakespeare aimed at a popular readership also multiplied in the latter decades of the twentieth century. Having written biographies of Princess Diana and Prince Charles, Anthony Holden turned to Shakespeare in 1997, crafting a biography designed for a broad readership (*William Shakespeare: The Man Behind the Genius*). Holden's biography featured Shakespeare as a "good-natured boozy heterosexual who had no time for academic pretensions."[57] Likewise, prolific biographer Peter Ackroyd, a "compulsive writer of lives," turned his attention to Shakespeare in *Shakespeare: The Biography* (2005), which relies heavily on the plays as evidence for the personality and life of the writer, claiming that Shakespeare put "a particle of himself in all of his characters."[58]

Stanley Wells has tackled Shakespeare's life story several times from a number of different angles, including *Shakespeare: A Dramatic Life* (1994, republished as *Shakespeare: A Life in Drama* in 1995); *Shakespeare for All Time* (2002); *Shakespeare and Co* (2006); and *Shakespeare, Sex, and Love* (2010). Throughout his work, Wells offers an even-handed appraisal of Shakespeare's wife, noting that "it would be nice to think that he had not left his wife to cope single handed with Susanna, Hamnet, and Judith during their early years, but there is no evidence either way," but concludes that "it is fruitless to enquire into the couple's relationship in their later years," and that, "a small family did not necessarily imply poor marital relations."[59] Similarly, in *Shakespeare, Sex, and Love*, he avoids using the literary works as evidence of the life because "it is ultimately impossible to sift the imagined from the real."[60]

One of the best-selling biographies of Shakespeare ever written is Stephen Greenblatt's *Will in the World: How Shakespeare Became Shakespeare* (2004), and his extensive imaginary Anne merits a fuller discussion later in this chapter. Two roughly contemporary biographies include an emphasis on Shakespeare's Warwickshire life, and by extension, assign greater importance to Anne: René Weis's *Shakespeare Revealed: A Biography* (2007), published in the United States as *Shakespeare Unbound: Decoding a Hidden Life*; and Jonathan Bate's *Soul of the Age* (2008). Using historical records from early modern women, Germaine Greer's *Shakespeare's Wife* (2007) seeks to fill in "the wife-shaped void in the biography" of Shakespeare, discussed at the end of this chapter. Greer's goal is to draw on archival research about women from Hathaway's day in order to suggest "other, more fruitful interpretations" instead of vilifying Anne, as do the many biographers she takes to task.[61] Deliberately departing from an ostensibly factual approach, Graham Holderness's *Nine Lives of William Shakespeare* (2011) re-tells Shakespeare's life story in nine different ways, each accompanied by a "metabiographical" piece exploring the life story through an imaginative work to "embrace freely the imaginative and fictional processes that are always at work" in biographies.[62] Lois Potter looks at Shakespeare's "imaginative life" and brings in other collaborators, both for linguistic influence and for actual co-authorship, in *The Life of William Shakespeare: A Critical Biography* (2012).

Many of these Anglophone biographies appeared in an unprecedented number of translations, increasing their influence and their domination of the narratives that are disseminated worldwide about Shakespeare's life. Even so, many non-Anglophone countries have produced their own biographies of Shakespeare, which were at times translated into yet other languages. In Spain, for instance, as Keith Gregor points out, "Shakespeare" was "not so much a body of works as a memorable character who also happened to be an author."[63] Spanish biographers of Shakespeare have been particularly interested in Shakespeare's married life. Alcalá Galiano interprets Shakespeare's marriage as a "life sentence," while Eduardo Juliá Martínez sees the Shakespeares as "the ideal married couple," with Anne Hathaway falling "down on her knees in front of an image of the Virgin Mary" and praying all night when Shakespeare leaves for London.[64] This admittedly brief summary hints at the potential for additional work on non-Anglophone biographies, situating them within their own cultural contexts and literary traditions.

Stephen Greenblatt's *Will in the World: How Shakespeare Became Shakespeare*

Looking at one biography in depth can elucidate the problematic nature when a work labeled as a biography substantially deviates into fiction. Stephen Greenblatt's *Will in the World: How Shakespeare Became Shakespeare* (2004) has been praised as "a beautifully assembled mosaic of Shakespeare's life, work, time, and place"; a "series of beautifully crafted episodes"; and a "magnificent digest of our knowledge," among other epithets.[65] The trajectory of artistic success, or "how Shakespeare became Shakespeare," provides a framework for this best-seller, which includes perhaps the most extended and influential derogatory account of Shakespeare's wife to date. This disturbing interpretation begs the question of why one of the most widely distributed biographies of Shakespeare includes one of the most negative portrayals of Anne Hathaway, in stark contrast to other contemporary narratives about her, both fictional and biographical.[66]

Throughout *Will in the World*, Greenblatt tells a story of Shakespeare as an artist trapped in a loveless marriage, miserably yoked to a woman who cannot share his art, from whom he must eventually escape to find love, success, and sexual satisfaction. In order to craft a convincing success story, he includes far-reaching conjecture about Shakespeare's mental state, motivations, and emotions, well beyond the bounds of reasonable biography, and eschewing what John F. Keener describes as the "calculated un-knowing" necessary for a responsible biographer.[67]

While Greenblatt admits that any biography of Shakespeare is an "exercise in speculation," he builds "an amazing success story" out of Shakespeare's life, without adding any new documentary discoveries or fresh pieces of evidence.[68] Often praised for its readability, *Will in the World* "tells a better story" than other Shakespeare biographies, though Gary Taylor observed in his review that "what matters is not the true story, but a good story."[69] The better the "story," the greater the narrative and use of fictional techniques to allow for unbridled speculation and for the creation of a full emotional register for Shakespeare, but one that cannot be entirely factual. And, Greenblatt's emphasis on "story," told through narrative, brings his biography more in line with fiction than with biography. In fact, Valentina Vannucci has criticized biographies for relying too much on "the inescapable filter of narrative, which organizes materials in a literary structure and imposes a meaning in order to make them understandable at all." The result, she argues, is that "the traditional distinction between true and false has been delegitimized."[70] Further, Bernard DeVoto goes so far as to argue that "literary people should not be permitted to write biography" because "the literary mind . . . selects vivid phrases of experience and coordinates them in such a manner that they give us the illusion of the whole."[71]

A brief summary of the "good story" Greenblatt tells about Anne will highlight the problematic overuse of fiction, and the resulting "delegitimization of true and false." Greenblatt headlines his discussion of Shakespeare's marriage with the foreboding chapter title "Wooing, Wedding, and Repenting," and constructs a narrative of a "disastrous mistake" that Shakespeare must abandon in order to attain his "amazing success story." A reluctant and unwilling Shakespeare was thus "dragged to the altar" and he viewed his wife with "distaste, and contempt." Indeed, in this saga, there was no courtship based on love, but instead just a "fumbling adolescent effort" resulting in the fateful conception of daughter Susanna and in much "repenting." Greenblatt extends his anti-Anne diatribe by suggesting that Anne "filled [Shakespeare] with revulsion," and that Shakespeare experienced the "misery of the neglected or abandoned spouse." This Shakespeare "made a disastrous mistake, when he was eighteen," and his imagination and experience of love "flourished outside of the marriage bond."[72] Greenblatt leaves little room in this tale for other possible interpretations of the Shakespeare marriage, and the Anne Hathaway sections have surprisingly little of the conditional language that permeates most other biographies.

A woman who could neither read nor write, this Anne had no connection with this Shakespeare, who as a result felt the "frustrated longing for spousal intimacy." As well as the separation inherent in a forced union between a poetic genius and an illiterate Midlands woman, religious differences divided the Shakespeares, who "almost certainly leaned toward Catholicism," and the Hathaways, who "almost certainly leaned in the opposite direction."[73]

The main flaw for the hero Shakespeare in this story is his return to Stratford, which does not allow for a full-scale obliteration of his loathsome mistake of a wife. Greenblatt addresses this by claiming that Shakespeare wanted to live near his daughter Susanna and her family, but not near his wife, for whom he felt only "sour anger." Indeed, this Shakespeare "could scarcely be expected to find comfort in the enduring bond with his wife," but instead harbored a "strange, ineradicable distaste for her that he felt deep within him." Greenblatt repudiates any possibility that Shakespeare may have had a joyful reunion with his wife in his last years of life, and even refuses to allow any sort of amiable alliance in their side-by-side burial: "So much for the dream of love. When Shakespeare lay dying, he tried to forget his wife and then remembered her with the second-best bed. And when he thought of the afterlife, the last thing he wanted was to be mingled with the woman he married."[74] Readers may recall the similarity with eighteenth-century editor Edmond Malone's diatribe against Anne (discussed earlier in Chapters 2 and 4), where he imagines Shakespeare's last days as an attempt to forget his wife and to "mark how little he esteemed her," and finally to "cut her off, not indeed with a shilling, but with an old bed." The resemblance between these two accounts of Shakespeare's deathbed castigation of his wife is surprising, especially given that they are over two hundred years apart.

The intensity with which Greenblatt denigrates Anne throughout his biography is striking. The usual linguistic turns common to biography ("may have," "it is likely that," "perhaps," etc.) are notably scarce. In summary, Greenblatt's Shakespeare was "dragged to the altar," Anne "filled him with revulsion" and an "ineradicable distaste," he knew the "misery of the neglected or abandoned spouse," his marriage was a "disastrous mistake," his love "flourished outside the marriage bond," and he felt "sour anger" toward his wife even in his last years of life. The result is a grim appropriation of Anne, designed to serve a disturbingly regressive agenda. As Andrew Hadfield has observed, Shakespeare's life has been constructed "in terms of who it was felt important that he should be rather than who he actually was or might have been."[75] Greenblatt's biography leaves no room for who Shakespeare "might have been," and he confidently pursues his one-sided narrative. Brian Cummings has described biography as "an exercise in wish fulfillment,"[76] and Gary Taylor contends that "Greenblatt has mined his own life to supply the emotional raw materials that energise this book," and notes that "what purports to be an image of Shakespeare is really an idealized image of the biographer himself."[77] There are pervasive ideological and political implications involved in constructing a Shakespeare who vehemently renounces his domestic life and feels only "sour anger" toward his wife throughout his life, without acknowledging other possible interpretations.

In light of the numerous possible ways to construct Anne Hathaway discussed so far in this book, one wonders why a contemporary biographer would choose such an extreme version. Readers will recall that according to John F. Keener, a basic indication of fictionalization is the use of "narrative descriptions of the internal states of human figures," especially "verbs of inner action."[78] Greenblatt's relentless construction of Anne requires fairly substantial fictional techniques to create Shakespeare's internal state – his "sour anger," his "distaste," his "revulsion" – are all hallmarks of a fictional account of Shakespeare's internal state. Perhaps it is fitting that Greenblatt's biography was inspired by the fictional film *Shakespeare in Love* (1999); he writes that "the idea of *Will in the World* originated years ago during conversations I had with Marc Norman, who was then in the early stages of writing a film script about Shakespeare's life."[79]

Given its extensive circulation and its vast readership, the version of Anne in *Will in the World* continues to be disseminated to an unprecedented number of readers around the world, including the legions of students who use the Norton Shakespeare and the companion biography.[80] Moreover, it has the largest global dominance of any biography to date. It was excerpted as "Shakespeare's Leap" in the *New York Times Magazine* in 2004, reprinted in Hebrew that same year; and has since been translated into Dutch, German, Japanese, Polish, and Portuguese. The global circulation of this work adds a further layer of influence well beyond the Anglophone world.

Greenblatt's intended audience is "the lay reader and nonacademic Shakespeare fan," in the estimation of *New York Times* reviewer Michiko Kakutani, and there is an alarming correlation between constructing a Shakespeare for a popular audience and offering a pejorative portrayal of Anne Hathaway.[81] John Simon points out the relationship between speculation and academic status, particularly "if a conjecture is developed in great detail and often enough repeated – and if the author is the Cogan University Professor of the Humanities at Harvard, as well as the editor of the *Norton Shakespeare* and the author of a number of books."[82]

Perhaps the million-dollar advance that Greenblatt reportedly received for the book necessitated "the greatest [story] of all time," as he promises in his preface, and thus the creation of "the Shakespeare of a celebrity booker for the Oprah Winfrey show,"[83] as Gary Taylor characterizes him. Perhaps the narrative of a genius husband trapped in an unhappy marriage is a way to increase the sensationalism of yet another Shakespeare biography. Indeed, more than one reviewer has suggested that financial gain may have been a motivating factor in the genesis of this biography. In his review in the *Guardian*, "Where there's a Will there's a payday," John Sutherland criticizes Greenblatt for writing "books which the hucksters in the book trade want rather than the books their discipline needs" and for accepting "the Mephistophelean invitation to write the great book about the great dramatist for a great sum."[84] The repercussions of associating financial success with the story of a maligned wife are disconcerting.

Will in the World suggests that one answer to the book's subtitle, "How Shakespeare Became Shakespeare," is that Shakespeare abandoned his mistake of a wife and rejected his domestic life. This argument is strikingly similar to regressive accounts of what one historian has termed the "stifling, oppressive, and old-fashioned domesticity" of the late nineteenth century, where anxieties about domesticity inspired "all-male fantasy worlds in which domesticity was a state and, often literally, a place from which to escape if full selfhood was to be realized."[85] Greenblatt's Shakespeare must escape Anne and her world of domesticity in order to achieve full artistic and personal satisfaction. Paula R. Backscheider has criticized just such a practice, noting that one effect of feminism on biography is to insure that "the importance of the private, domestic, or intimate sphere will be given attention."[86] This disturbing ideology, cloaked under the cover of a biography by one of the foremost scholars of the day, is promoted by multiple well-known reviewers on its dust jacket as a "landmark," a "tour de force" of "Elizabethan England bristling with authenticity," a "book for artists and ordinary people as well as scholars and students," and a work of "scholarship and sober good sense." Did not one of the four prominent reviewers notice the Anne produced as a by-product of this unsettling ideological portrayal of Shakespeare?[87]

Millennial Biographers and the Shakespeare Courtship and Marriage

Greenblatt formulated his story amid a cluster of Shakespeare biographies in the first decade of the twentieth century, all by major prominent Shakespeare scholars. Focusing on one topic – the Shakespeare courtship and marriage – can serve as a microcosm for how contemporary biographers have constructed an Anne in relation to the Shakespeare they envision in a succinct critical, cultural, and historical climate.[88] Since no new facts have come to light during the period of the biographies under consideration, they are presumably relying on the same set of facts about Anne, yet there is little agreement among biographers about even the central components of Shakespeare's life story.

This section looks at six biographies written within roughly ten years of each other: Park Honan's *Shakespeare: A Life* (1998), Katherine Duncan-Jones's *Ungentle Shakespeare: Scenes from his Life* (2001), Peter Ackroyd's *Shakespeare: The Biography* (2005), René Weis's *Shakespeare Revealed: A Biography* (2007), and Jonathan Bate's *Soul of the Age: A Biography of the Mind of William Shakespeare* (2008), with a brief detour to Germaine Greer's biography of Anne Hathaway, *Shakespeare's Wife* (2007). Readers will recall from Part I of this book that no information survives about how William and

Anne met, what they felt about each other, or what their marriage was like. Nevertheless, their courtship and marriage are crucial parts of Shakespeare's life story, and any extended biographical narrative needs to include some interpretation of the circumstances. Each of these biographers constructs a unique Anne, with a different story for the courtship and marriage, in spite of the fact that no new relevant historical evidence has come to light. As this section will show, Anne's uncertain position is a result of the biographer's personal agenda, methodology, employment of fiction, design of narrative, and selective use of literary works.

In his 1998 biography *Shakespeare: A Life*, Park Honan vows to avoid "[i]maginative reconstructions and elaborate psychological theories," focusing instead on illustrating "the complex evolution in Shakespeare's mind and being."[89] Yet, Shakespeare's "mind and being" can only be imaginatively reconstructed. The "evolution" that Honan charts is grounded in the Stratford components of Shakespeare's life, so it is no surprise that Honan wants to imagine a positive role for Anne. He titles his chapter "Love and Marriage," as opposed to Greenblatt's not-so-subtle choice of "Wooing, Wedding, and Repenting."

In this story of the Shakespeare courtship, "at no time, in his school years or later, had [Shakespeare] been a stranger at Anne's door," and the two families knew each other well. The Shakespeare family respected the Hathaways, and they found Anne's "age and practicality of benefit to their son," whose youth provided him with "small practical experience," compared to her "maturity of outlook." The death of her father and marriage of her brother may have inspired Anne "to take a lover," and Honan's terminology gives both agency and choice to Anne. Shakespeare was "evidently in love," and wanted to "arrange for his future as quickly as he could."[90]

Honan's Shakespeare is a responsible and loving husband, visiting his family regularly: "his investments and care to establish himself there, do not suggest he found Anne immaterial to his welfare." This Shakespeare "chose marriage, not that he was trapped." A playwriting career was the best way to support his family, but he also knew "the pain of separation for long periods from a substantial and consoling family," since his goal was to "serve his family best."[91] Honan's Shakespeare is both a successful artist and a responsible family man, whose career did not necessitate rejecting his Warwickshire domestic life or discarding his wife. In order to make this argument, Honan invents a suitable state of mind for Shakespeare and gives him a comfortable domestic life.

In *Ungentle Shakespeare: Scenes from his Life* (2001), published three years after Honan's biography, Katherine Duncan-Jones devises an Anne who is sexually independent but ultimately incapable of satisfying her soon-to-be-famous husband. In her quest to demote Shakespeare "from the lofty isolation to which he has been customarily elevated," Duncan-Jones works against the penchant to see Shakespeare as "liberal, unprejudiced, unselfish," or in other words, "nice." Hathaway is given a modicum of autonomy, described as a "free and independent" woman as a result of her father's death, "without much parental care or control."[92] Regrettably, Anne's independence is not an opportunity for maturity or agency, but instead for sexual looseness.

Duncan-Jones envisions the Shakespeare union as a "dalliance" arising from a "combination of boredom with the sexual curiosity natural to [Shakespeare's] years" and likely "his first experience of sex." In this story there is no courtship, per se; Duncan-Jones contends that Shakespeare suffered from "boredom" during an "agricultural lull," when "sexual relations began between the orphaned husbandman's daughter and the glover's eldest son." She also relies on the late summer to explain Shakespeare's surging hormones: "In the stickily hot August of 1582 Shakespeare was probably changing from boy into man, and experiencing the uncontrollable surges of testosterone accompanying that stage of development." This was not the consummation of a relationship born of long-familiar families; Shakespeare was simply "sowing wild oats," and his sexual dalliances showed "little or no thought to the lifelong problems he would reap." Given that there is no evidence to support this fictional account, Duncan-Jones admits that the Shakespeares' *could* be a "lovematch," but she nevertheless reverts to the "boredom" thesis of a Shakespeare "stuck in uncongenial employment with no prospects" who found "an outlet in sex." In the "ungentle" version, Anne is not the object of courtship, but instead serves as relief for the "boy" Shakespeare's surging sexual desire: "the boy was grateful to Anne for her compliance, and persuaded himself that he loved her."[93] In an interview with Arthur Maltby, Duncan-Jones elaborates on the summer sex scene she envisions for the Shakespeares:

> But as for the conception of Susanna, all I was doing was assuming a normal period of gestation, combining that with the known (young) age of the father, plus the climatic conditions and rural activities normal to the time of year when conception took place. I also start from the premise that making Anne Hathaway pregnant, given that she was not, economically or socially, a hugely desirable bride, and with John Shakespeare practically bankrupt, was not at all a prudent procedure. It seems to me reasonable to presume that the pregnancy was the outcome of impulse without foresight. This would also explain what appears to have been her husband's later

indifference to her ... [where] she was occasionally left short of money even around 1600 when her husband had become a very wealthy man.

Duncan-Jones adds a further defense, insisting that "As for overdoing the imaginative element: I was not writing a doctoral thesis, but a book that ... was aimed at a popular market, albeit grounded in traditional scholarship."[94] The story Duncan-Jones offers to this popular readership reduces the relationship to a "dalliance" arising from "boredom," resulting in a shotgun "compelled marriage" without a courtship. Presumably, then, once Shakespeare discovers his artistic calling and matures sexually, he has no need to sow his wild oats or bother having sex with a "spirited country girl" and can get on with his life.[95] This loveless marriage makes it easy to transport Shakespeare to his London playwriting career, since he is only leaving behind a woman whom he married out of duty due to the repercussions of his lust, not out of love or affection.

Turning from lusty motivations to business acumen, Peter Ackroyd, in *Shakespeare: The Biography* (2005) maintains that "far from being a *mésalliance* or forced marriage ... the partnership of William Shakespeare and Anne Hathaway could have been an eminently sensible arrangement." Inspired by Shakespeare's successful record as a savvy businessman, Ackroyd reads this back into the courtship, arguing that Shakespeare "may even have exercised a good deal of caution, or common sense, in his choice of lifelong partner. This was thoroughly in keeping with his practical and business-like approach to all of the affairs of the world."[96] Ackroyd's terms for the Shakespeare marriage are striking: this shrewdly intelligent Shakespeare would choose a "lifelong partner" and would not succumb to the "urges of testosterone" that characterize Duncan-Jones's Shakespeare, nor would Ackroyd's Shakespeare make the "disastrous mistake" of Greenblatt's hero.

There is no need for this Shakespeare to jettison his wife en route to London success, since she has been deliberately wooed as part of a planned partnership. Although this Shakespeare is lacking in romantic spontaneity, he is astute enough to troubleshoot the practical problems of wooing indoors at the Hathaway cottage, since its "timber construction" made it "a box of noise, so courtship would have been untenable as well as uncomfortable." Ackroyd's Shakespeare would be too clever to carry on a courtship in these conditions, since "from the upstairs bedchambers you can hear everything in the rooms below and, through the cracks in the floorboards, see everything as well."[97] Instead, this Shakespeare takes charge of the courtship, and relocates it to the full natural splendor of the Warwickshire countryside: he leverages his assets (a pastoral setting) to achieve his desired outcome (a lifelong partnership). A man of "judgement and intelligence," this savvy Shakespeare would not be so reckless as to copulate in a "stickily hot August" with "little or no thought to his future," as the Shakespeare of Duncan-Jones does.

Yet the problem still remains that Shakespeare was only eighteen when daughter Susanna's conception occurred. Ackroyd's solution is to suggest that the age difference between the Shakespeares could imply "sexual self-confidence on Shakespeare's part," rather than carelessness or imprudence, and to affirm that accounts of the Shakespeare courtship must do "justice to Shakespeare's judgment and intelligence which, even at the age of eighteen, might have been acute."[98] As part of Shakespeare's business strategy, Anne is a wise investment, and an accession that will pay off. While this Anne has little say in the courtship, at least she is a valuable asset and not an impulse purchase that Shakespeare regrets.

Two biographers have invested in Shakespeare's Stratford connections as a crucial part of his story, and thus have imagined a significant and influential role for Anne. In *Shakespeare Revealed* (2007), René Weis's account "begins and ends in a Midlands market town,"[99] so it is logical that he would find a way to give the Warwickshire components (including the Shakespeare marriage) a positive interpretation, rather than casting Stratford and Anne as something Shakespeare could not wait to escape on his journey to the metropolis of London in search of sexual and artistic satisfaction.

In order to defuse the "predatory older woman" myth, Weis suggests that the Shakespeares were closer in age. The only evidence for the 8-year gap between William and Anne is the inscription on her grave that states she was 67 when she died. Weis proposes that "the numbers 1 and 7 are easily confused in inscriptions," and 61 would be only a two-year age gap. Though Weis admits that it is impossible to know how William and Anne met, or how they "found the opportunity" to have sex, he uses Ophelia's lines ("Young men will do't if they come to't" and "Before you tumbled me, / You promised me to wed") to argue that in *Hamlet* Shakespeare was "recalling his own teenage sexual encounters," but in real life he "honour[ed] his commitment to Anne, and married her."[100]

By linking the Shakespeare and Hathaway families, Weis suggests that their relationship was a natural (albeit problematic) outgrowth of family connections. Proposing that Anne Hathaway's mother was a Whateley of Temple Grafton, Weis maintains that Anne was related to the Whateley family living in Stratford. Thus, Shakespeare's father's return to the town council in 1582 "just at the time when his son was having sex with Anne Hathaway" may have been due to a Verona-like feud with the neighboring Whateleys: "John Shakespeare's vote against Whateley [for mayor] appears to have been a hostile act, confirming that Anne was indeed related to this family, and that the two Henley Street clans had come to grief over the love affair between her and Will . . . John Shakespeare rejoined the council briefly and voted as he did to remind Whateley of his status before all assembled peers." Weis effectively turns William and Anne into Romeo and Juliet, and contends that they marry despite the tension between these "Henley Street clans." By extension, his relationship with Anne would have inspired Shakespeare to write *Romeo and Juliet*. Essentially, this is a marriage based on love, and one that inspired Shakespeare's literary works. "There is no reason to think that Shakespeare did not love Anne Hathaway," Weis writes, and he envisions them having "many intimate conversations. . . about the rearing of their children." Shakespeare's *The Comedy of Errors* and *Twelfth Night* reveal that he was "bewitched by his twins," and this happily married Shakespeare incorporated his domestic life into his art.[101]

Like René Weis's *Shakespeare Revealed*, Jonathan Bate's *Soul of the Age: A Biography of the Mind of William Shakespeare* (2009) emphasizes the Warwickshire components, due in part to his structural plan for the biography. To avoid a linear narrative (a "deadening march of chronological sequence," in his words), Bate conceives of Shakespeare's life as "cyclical, not sequential," since "the influence of our early childhood stays with us all our lives."[102] The Warwickshire pieces of the biography are thus given additional importance throughout the narrative, not just in chapters focusing on the 1580s and 1610s.

Bate suggests a clever way to solve the Anne Hathaway/Anne Whateley conundrum while empowering Anne at the same time. If Anne Hathaway married a Whateley in Temple Grafton, and then was widowed, this would give "young Will the opportunity to move in swiftly with the offer of sexual solace and the hope of a widow's ample marriage portion." This Anne is a desirable woman because of her financial security, not just as an outlet to satisfy teenage lust. "It is a biographical myth," Bate contends, "to suppose that Will was marched off to a shotgun wedding by friends of the Hathaways who were incensed at hearing that Miss Anne was in the family way."[103] Rather, this Anne remains an important part of William's life, and their union was equally desirable for both of them.

As we have seen, the practice of using Shakespeare's literary works to construct his life often yields disastrous results for Anne, depending on the female characters conscripted for her. Bate eschews this practice, noting that "it has too often been assumed that because Shakespeare wrote [*Shrew*], his wife must have been one." He offers instead another literary character as a model for Shakespeare the wooer – Bassanio from *The Merchant of Venice*, who is "clever but cold, an adventurer and a wordsmith who always looks after himself, a man on the lookout for a wealthy woman to help him out of a financial crisis and who has the good fortune to find one who is also beautiful, ultraintelligent, and attracted to him."[104] By extension, Anne is then Portia, a literate, witty, and intelligent counterpart to Bassanio, but as Bate readily admits, there is no evidence to support this connection. Even so, the imaginary narrative he suggests through the Portia–Bassanio relationship is strikingly more generous to Anne Hathaway than many other biographers have been.

Bate is one of the only biographers to offer multiple interpretations for the Shakespeare marriage: "a grand passion prematurely consummated" or "an arranged union between two families who knew each other well." Either option presumes a connection between the Shakespeares, either based on "passion" or on family. Like Ackroyd, Bate also uses Shakespeare's financial acumen as evidence for his mature attitude to love: "making enough money to keep the family going, and sustaining a marriage for well over thirty years" were "not the achievements of the romantic lover," but rather "manifestations of love."[105]

While some of these biographies construct stories that are more favorable to Anne, they are all imaginative in nature and they all tell different stories for different ends. Stanley Wells has described the task of the biographer as "trying to create a narrative out of those historical facts." Likewise, James Shapiro remarks that "the first decision every biographer must make is what kind of story to tell."[106] The variance in these stories should give readers pause, and should make us question the line between fiction and biography. As Dorrit Cohn notes, "the minds of imaginary figures can be known in ways that those of real persons cannot," and the correlation between biographical and fictional Annes and Williams underlines this premise.[107]

It seems fitting to end this chapter with Germaine Greer's biography *Shakespeare's Wife* (2007), since it serves as a bridge to the final chapter of this book, where texts about Anne Hathaway designed for a female audience get their due attention. Published in the same year as Weis's *Shakespeare Revealed*, Greer's *Shakespeare's Wife* is a substantial articulation of feminist concerns through Anne Hathaway. Both Greer's title and her introduction situate her biography within a larger context of women's issues, extending beyond a narrow reappraisal of an early modern woman from Stratford. Greer's choice of *Shakespeare's Wife* as her title underlines the significance of each of those terms – the cultural cachet and authoritative power associated with the name "Shakespeare" reveals her desire to chip away at the patriarchal authority represented by "Shakespeare." Greer deliberately uses honorific titles for Shakespeare, frequently referring to him as "the Bard" and "the Man of the Millennium," so that he represents the male sex in general as a sort of über male against whom she can argue, rather than an historical figure confined to his own time period. The "Wife" in Greer's title links Anne to a long history of silent "wives," and in the process redefines the possibilities for understanding the status of wives in the early modern period. As Greer puts it, "By doing the right thing, by remaining silent and invisible, Ann Shakespeare left a wife-shaped void in the biography of William Shakespeare, which later bardolaters filled up with their own speculations, most of which do neither them nor their hero any credit." Biographers of Shakespeare and misogynists (sometimes, as she points out, one and the same) have thus filled in this gap with material to suit a Shakespeare-centered narrative which often devalues Anne, in favor of an urban, sexually active Shakespeare.

To remedy this, though Greer locates her project in the genre of biography, she nevertheless regularly crosses the boundaries between biography and fiction. This Anne may have provided for her family through some sort of employment, and may have been financially self-sufficient, the equivalent of a working single mother, as in the following scene: "Ann Shakespeare could have been confident of her ability to support herself and her children," Greer writes, "but not if she had also to deal with a layabout husband good for nothing but spinning verses, who had the right to do as he pleased with any money she could earn." In Greer's narrative, Anne is a self-sufficient woman whose financial acumen may have led her to purchase New Place and even instigate the First Folio project, though Greer admits the improbability of this "absurd suggestion."[108] This account validates Anne's household industry, while making Shakespeare a "layabout husband" who does not produce anything of value and exploits the fruit of his wife's labor.

While many reviewers of Greer's work have appreciated her willingness to overturn every stone in Anne Hathaway's life, others have criticized her with an unusually vitriolic tone. Peter Conrad, for example, attacks Greer's wider agenda, calling her biography "reckless, baseless," "grim and gloating," a "war of attrition against the chromosome-deficient male sex" by a "spinster professor" with a "wild-eyed, foamy-lipped enthusiasm" who has a "sacred rage on behalf of her victimized sisters."[109] For Conrad, Greer's biography is not so much about redeeming the individual woman from Stratford as it is a war against men, with Shakespeare standing in for his sex. Greer's biography has provoked a great deal of hostility, even though her methodology differs little from other biographers who include substantial speculations – Burgess's uncomfortable dinner table discussions with spinster Anne; Greenblatt's "wooing, wedding, and repenting"; or Ackroyd's astute businessman poet, just to cite a few examples. As the next chapter will show, overtly fictional texts that tell a parallel (and at times a more blatantly revisionist) story have not received the same type of criticism, even though they have a similar goal of pushing the boundaries of believability for Shakespeare's wife.

Biography has been "carried to a wasteful and ridiculous excess," wrote James Orchard Halliwell-Phillipps in 1881, but he would have been shocked to discover the explosion of Shakespeare biographies yet to come.[110] While some might lament the flooded market of Shakespeare biography, the existence of multiple versions of Shakespeare's life helps to ensure that no single story remains unchallenged, and that the saga of Shakespeare's life is one of constant flux and change. As Graham Holderness puts it, "each act of biographical definition mediates fact and tradition through the labyrinthine web of speculation, and produces a new Shakespeare in every new iteration."[111] For Anne Hathaway, the unrest, instability, and mutability of the field of Shakespeare biography sustains interrogation of the contingent nature of well-worn platitudes and adages, and suggests that readers need to persist in their endless quest for the perfect "Shakespeare." The fictional works discussed in this chapter are equally vital for maintaining this crucial sense of inquiry, and the similarities between fictional components of works labeled "biographies," and overtly fictional works, reinforce the instability of Shakespeare's life story, and by extension, Anne's.

We have met many Annes over the course of this chapter, from the Anne who initiated the First Folio and ran her own brewing business at New Place (Germaine Greer's version) to the Anne who was a disastrous mistake and filled her husband with distaste and contempt (Stephen Greenblatt's Anne), to the "groaning old crone" of Anthony Burgess. Trapped in a supporting role to her famous husband, the sundry Annes covered in this chapter reveal the conflicting and contrasting ways that biographers have sought to make sense of this enigmatic woman, who was married to Shakespeare for over 30 years, and must have had *some* role in his life. Victorian poet Mathilde Blind described Anne Hathaway as "She, whose mortal lot / Was linked to an Immortal's unaware." The immortality of Anne Hathaway, this "shadowy figure in the corner of the great house in Stratford," will continue to flourish alongside interest in her husband's private life.[112] Reflecting on the enterprise of biography, Peter Holland remarks, "What we cannot do is stop ourselves writing and rewriting some version of the Shakespeare biography, addressing the impossible, enjoying the desire, never despairing, always hoping" while "always knowing that it is bound to fail."[113] So too, the quest to find a way to explain the role of Anne Hathaway in Shakespeare's life continues, targeted for an ever-growing female audience, while acknowledging the vexing, precarious, and indeterminate status of her afterlife. The next chapter features a number of works that attempt to meet this challenge.

6

MILLENNIAL ANNE HATHAWAYS AND WOMEN AUDIENCES

W OMEN HAVE HAD A LONG HISTORY OF ENGAGING WITH Shakespeare – sometimes enlisting him as a supporter and comrade, and other times reacting against him and talking back. In 1832, Anna Jameson remarked that Shakespeare "looked upon women with the spirit of humanity, wisdom, and deep love," and "has done justice to their natural good tendencies and kindly sympathies." Mary Cowden Clarke in 1887 also praised Shakespeare as "a valuable friend of woman-kind" with "keener insight than any other man-writer into womanly nature," who "depicted women with full appreciation of their highest qualities" and "vindicated their truest rights and celebrated their best virtues." As we saw earlier, Cowden Clarke specifically praised Shakespeare's adulation of wives, tracing his view of women to his relationship with his wife Anne: "From the uniformly noble way in which Shakespeare drew the *wifely* character, we may feel certain of the esteem as well as affection with which his own wife inspired him," and "he had reason to know this truth respecting her sex from the mother of his children."[1]

Looking back over the earlier part of this book, we can trace a substantial number of women readers, authors, critics, and travelers who have found a unique point of access to Shakespeare through Anne. This chapter considers the intersection of women's interest in Anne Hathaway with literary forms that allow for greater imaginative freedom, from millennial novels to young adult fiction to stage plays, where ideas about contemporary women's issues and concerns, both progressive and conservative, can be channeled through Anne (and in some cases, her alternate Anne Whateley).

As interest in Shakespeare's relationship to women has continued to increase – both about historical women and about women in his plays – so too have the depictions of Anne. The inner psychological life of Anne has also garnered attention from biographers and fiction writers alike, who have sought to explain Shakespeare's private life from Anne's point of view. Was she a devoted, eternally patient wife, waiting behind in Stratford for her husband to return? Did she have lovers of her own while her husband was away? What was it like to be married to William Shakespeare? What role did she have in Shakespeare's departure for London, and in his eventual return to Stratford? And what kind of marriage did the Shakespeares have, if they were separated between London and Stratford for most of their married life? As we have seen, a number of myths and fantasies have been created in imaginative works in order to explain, or even to avoid, these recurring biographical problems. Further, the identification of readers with Anne underscores the role she can play in adjusting Shakespeare's life story for contemporary women who seek intimate insight into his private experience.

With this growing focus on women and feminism, and on a wider context for the stories of great men, there has been a remarkable expansion of Annes in the later twentieth century, both in fictional forms and as part of Shakespeare's biography. Anne has also figured prominently in several niche markets, especially for women and young adult readers.[2] These various texts are designed to impart ideologies about gender, marriage, passion, sexuality, and female ambition through an often radically invented private life of the famous poet and his enigmatic wife. Unlike some of the other works in which Anne Hathaway appears – biographies of Shakespeare, for example – these works are not Shakespeare-centered, and their primary goal is to appeal to a female readership. Here, Anne can be expanded into a progressive, feminist, independent character, or she can take the form of a more moralistic, conservative woman. Either way, the point is to relate Shakespeare's life story through Anne, designed to meet the needs and desires of a contemporary female audience. Furthermore, socially networked readers can share their endorsements, critiques, and reactions to these works, extending their influence to a wide range of potential audiences.

The fact that any extended portrayal of Anne out of necessity must be fictional provides ample opportunities to remake her for women readers in search of works about historical women. As Monica Latham explains, "as historical figures become characters in a fictitious work, poetic license allows them to go off the beaten track and give the reader a different image of the subject from the one contained in the standard biographies."[3] Because Anne is yoked to the cultural authority of her famous husband, her story can legitimate and advocate for a number of issues related to women, authorized by a connection to Shakespeare. Geared to women and liberated from the constraints of tradition, historical fidelity, and allegiance to Shakespeare, the Annes in many of these works can offer refreshing fantastical solutions to the seemingly insoluble problems of Shakespeare's life story.

Anne Hathaway and Young Adult Readers

For a young adult female readership, Shakespeare's biography needs some adjustment.[4] After all, Shakespeare engaged in premarital sex with an older woman and left his wife with three young children at home.[5] The most common solution has been to focus on Anne Hathaway (and/or Anne Whateley), and center the story on the Shakespeares' courtship rather than on their subsequent married life. Such expansions require authors to take a great deal of liberty with the facts about Shakespeare's life, which likely would not be evident to a young adult readership. John Stephens points out that "the distinction between what is real and what is fictive is often difficult for young readers to make, so the authority with which the fictive events are invested by their interaction with actual events will be intensified."[6] It is probable that the intended readers of these novels would not know whether the expanded characters and plot are historically accurate or not, and these texts often involve a fairly radical reworking of historical reality, in favor of creating a story with a prominent, but not necessarily progressive, central female character.

Laurie Lawlor's *The Two Loves of Will Shakespeare* (2006) fabricates a romantic life for the Shakespeares to serve as a lesson in teenage unrequited love and unrestrained sexual activity. Building on the discrepancy between the two Annes in Shakespeare's marriage documents, Lawlor fashions a love triangle where Anne Hathaway bears the brunt of her premarital pregnancy and Anne Whateley becomes the love interest. Shakespeare escapes both to have his career. The cover of Lawlor's book (Figure 6.1) shows an obviously pregnant Anne Hathaway, an unrecognizable young Shakespeare, and a saintly Anne Whateley in the background. Caught between the two Annes, Shakespeare sees one as his moral salvation and the other as his sexual outlet. He falls in love at first sight with Anne Whateley when he presents the sonnets he has penned to her under his friend Richard's name, and he becomes her "project for salvation." A closet Catholic, she arranges for their secret marriage to take place. Anne Hathaway, meanwhile, is Shakespeare's "hell" and a punishment for his sins.[7] He first meets Hathaway when delivering gloves, and is surprised by her boldly suggestive behavior. They end up meeting clandestinely in the woods, where she comes prepared with a blanket and an herbal potion to ward off pregnancy. This medicine of course does not work,

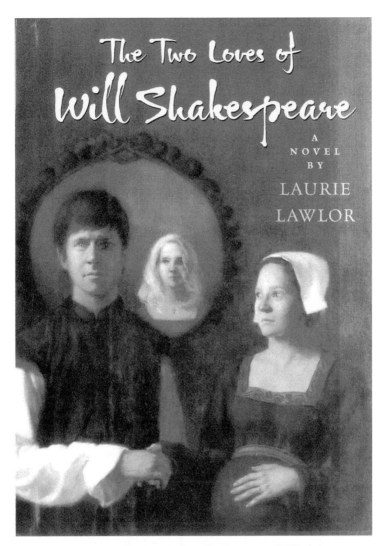

Figure 6.1   Cover of Laurie Lawlor, *The Two Loves of Will Shakespeare*.
Used with permission of Holiday House.

and Shakespeare is later approached by two bondsmen who drag him off to wed the pregnant Hathaway. Lawlor uses Hathaway to underline the dangers of premarital sex and to illustrate the folly of unplanned parenthood. Anne Whateley, on the other hand, remains the ideal model of chaste yet unattainable love; she falls in love with Shakespeare for his "sugar'd" sonnets, but Hathaway is attracted only to the sex.

The results of Shakespeare's sexual promiscuity are certainly not painted as an appealing picture in this novel for a teen audience: "He was supposed to be marrying Anne of Temple Grafton. He was supposed to be joining the theater company tomorrow at sunrise. He had a whole new life mapped out for himself, and now none of it was going to happen. His life was over . . . Suddenly he saw his whole life pass in front of his eyes. His brazen, too-loud wife shouting out of windows, cursing passersby. He'd be trapped with this woman of the enormous voice for eternity. A kind of hell, a punishment for all his past transgressions." The prospect of becoming a father with a shrewish wife is equally horrific to the teenage Shakespeare: "He hadn't even thought about the baby. The idea was horrifying and unreal at the same time. He knew nothing of babies except what he recalled about his disgusting brothers as toddlers."[8] Such sentiments would be appropriate in discussions of adolescent abstention; as Pat Pinsent affirms, novels for young adults are "likely to bear the cultural and political baggage of the periods in which the texts have been written."[9] Yet the Shakespeare courtship is not easily adaptable as a pro-marriage narrative of abstinence and chastity; the overall message of this novel is not to let domestic responsibilities stand in your way – that is, if you are a man. The pious Anne Whateley does not end up with Shakespeare, and he abandons the bad girl Anne Hathaway when he leaves to join a group of players in London.

Lawlor constructs a Shakespeare who is sexually promiscuous and unhappily married, yet able to elude his plight by writing. The novel ends before readers are given what would presumably be the next chapter, the story of Anne Hathaway the single mother living in the cramped Henley Street house with her in-laws, and William Shakespeare the adulterer enjoying his sexual and artistic freedom in London. In Lawlor's teen novel, Shakespeare is important not as the author of the plays and poems – in fact, the story ends before he becomes a playwright – but rather for the moral message about abstinence ("punishment for his transgressions") authorized through his life story. Both Annes have to be abandoned in order for Shakespeare to achieve literary greatness. In the moral world of this novel, Shakespeare wins because he attains his career, and Anne loses because she is shrewish, promiscuous, and controlling.

Carolyn Meyer's *Loving Will Shakespeare* (2006) imagines a strong-willed Anne, "a feisty young woman who is determined to live her own life in spite of societal confines," designed for young adult female readers who will "relate to Anne's rebellion against life's limitations." This independent-minded Anne "stops playing by the rules" in order to get the man she desires. Published the same year as Lawlor's novel, *Loving Will Shakespeare* opens with

Anne Hathaway first meeting Shakespeare when she is seven and he is an infant. Growing up in Stratford, she feels the confines of small-town life and yearns for her life to change, wondering who would be "*the right man*, the one who would someday soon change my life." She agrees to marry fellow townsman Henry Ingram, the choice of her stepmother, but feels trapped: "the door of my own cage had just snapped shut." Luckily, Shakespeare returns to Stratford just in time to rescue her from a doomed marriage, and fortunately he is attracted to her. Anne breaks off her engagement and begins her affair with Shakespeare. Readers are given scintillating details of what a romance with Shakespeare would resemble: "That was the first of many kisses, and I welcomed each one of them. From that moment on I wanted to spend every minute, every hour, every day with Will Shakespeare. I was in love, joyfully in love, and I believed he felt the same."[10]

Despite the appeal of being "joyfully in love" with Shakespeare, readers may notice the signs of an ill-fated marriage when they see the vastly different life goals of the Shakespeares: "Ofttimes we spoke of our dreams and private desires," exclaims Anne. "Mine were so common as to need no expression: a home, a loving husband, children. Will's were, to my way of thinking, far more fanciful," such as his desire to go to London and have a career as a playwright. Ignoring these warning signs, Anne follows her heart and makes the mistake of submitting to Shakespeare: "my love having weakened my resolve, I yielded to our shared passion. My virgin-knot was broken."[11]

At this point in the story, Meyer uses Anne's "mistake" as an opportunity to warn her readers about the dangers of premarital sex. Anne feels "remorse and despair" because "what had been done could not be undone, what was lost could never be restored," and she is "sick with shame." Even so, she cannot resist the sexual advances of Shakespeare, and admits that "I kissed him and he kissed me, and though I knew it was wrong and I would surely come to regret it, I yielded to our passion again, and more than once." Predictably, just a few pages later (in a chapter appropriately titled "Regret"), she learns she is pregnant. Shakespeare agrees to marry her, but their future is not the idealistic dream she had in mind: "For some time I had dreamed of a home of my own, and as the years passed I came to see it clearly: a simple croft with a fire blazing on the hearth, a snug loft for sleeping with my husband by my side and a babe in the cradle, a garth next to the cottage with a garden plot for herbs and vegetables . . . a bee-stall near a lavender field, mayhap even a rose-covered bower." Instead, his plan for them is to live with his family in the crowded house on Henley Street.

Adolescent readers are given a mixed message in this novel. On the one hand, married life and motherhood, even with Shakespeare, are not presented as desirable paths, yet Shakespeare's passion is irresistible, and Meyer does not want to condemn Shakespeare in her story. Her solution is to sidestep the issues connected with Shakespeare himself and instead focus on Anne's stepmother as the voice of morality. At one point she warns Anne to "heed my words: Will Shakespeare may be all that you say he is and more, but he is only eighteen years old and has many wild oats to sow before he takes a wife ... Do not deceive yourself: Will Shakespeare will not marry you."[12] When her stepmother discovers that Anne is pregnant, she is enraged that Anne has dishonored the family, though she is proven wrong when Will indeed marries Anne.

Once Anne is a married woman, all is well morally; she is content with motherhood and is overjoyed with her second pregnancy. Shakespeare, however, is "dissatisfied with his life." At the end of the story, Anne lets him leave for London to make his fortune, and their scene of separation is immortalized on the book's cover (Figure 6.2): "I watched with a breaking heart as Will started down the road toward London. He turned once and waved, and then he was gone. He did not look back." Meyer only leaves a few pages in the novel to wrap up the rest of the Shakespeares' life. In the final chapter, Anne's lost virginity and mismatched marriage seem worth it because her sacrifices made possible the development of Shakespeare the writer: "I recognized that my Will Shakespeare, the witty, lighthearted boy I had fallen in love with, had become William Shakespeare, the famous playwright." When he decides to return to Stratford at the end of his life, she is accommodating to her now-famous husband: "Let him come. I shall welcome him as I always have – with love and hope – for what may be the final chapter in our story."[13] Meyer reshapes Shakespeare's private life to authorize a warning against premarital sex and honey-tongued men, but in the end is unwilling to chastise the Shakespeare she creates. Her Anne is a forgiving character who seeks a "happy ending" with Shakespeare, no matter the personal cost, and the moral message is thus lost.

In these two novels designed for adolescent female readers, Anne Hathaway is expanded and updated to address issues of interest to this target audience: unrequited love, teenage pregnancy and motherhood, assertive and overbearing stepparents. Yet both of these novels run up against Anne's problematic status as a subject for contemporary young adult literature. In Lawlor's novel, Anne's sexuality is her downfall, and her story is manipulated to offer young adult readers a moral tale about promiscuity. Meyer's novel sets up Anne to be saved by "the right man" and she waits patiently for his return, just as she did in the many nineteenth-century texts discussed earlier in this book. Both of these young adult novels seek to tell a story about

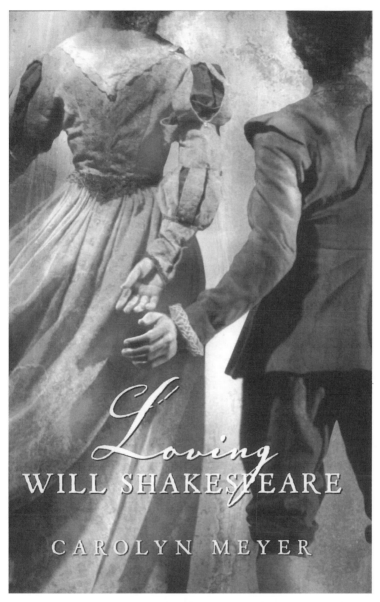

Figure 6.2 Cover of Carolyn Meyer, *Loving Will Shakespeare*.
Used with permission of Houghton Mifflin Harcourt.

Shakespeare through Anne's point of view, but cannot seem to find
a solution for her sexuality. Neither novel advocates premarital sex, even
with Shakespeare, which leaves very few options for a positive version of

Anne. While these two texts give a more prominent role to Anne, they are unable to offer a resolution to the story of Anne's youth.

Anne Hathaway and Women Readers

One of the fastest growing readerships for Shakespeare-related fiction is adult women, where, predictably, Anne is a central character. Using extensively rewritten and expanded versions of Anne's life, several authors create independent, literate, clever and resourceful women who substantially influenced the works of Shakespeare, albeit through artificial and unlikely (if not impossible) versions of Anne. These texts are part of the expanding field of "women-centered historical fiction" which "speak[s] directly to the female experience."[14] While some of these works extend past the bounds of believability, they still suggest possible alternatives to Shakespeare's life story, and in the process, destabilize hardened assumptions about Shakespearian biography. As fanciful as some of these stories may be, they can offer refreshing new alternatives to the well-worn narratives of the last few centuries.

Pamela Berkman's collection of short stories, *Her Infinite Variety* (2001), features an assortment of women, real and imaginary, including Ophelia, Juliet, Lady Macbeth, and Shakespeare's wife Anne, in order to address a variety of women's issues. The opening sentence of "In the Bed," Berkman's story about Anne, depicts a sexually aggressive and independent (but illiterate) Anne: "Anne Shakespeare, a swirl of rolling circles, bounced up and down atop her husband, driving him deeper and deeper inside her, the night before he left for London." His desire for her is almost enough to keep him in Stratford, as he tells her, "'You have killed me, Nan,' he said as she rolled off him and he lay immobile and watery. 'Now I cannot leave tomorrow. You have had your way after all.'" When in London, he remains true to Anne: "There were beautiful women in London, and he was finding how much he liked women, but it was her he wanted. Truly." When he returns to Stratford with a draft of *Romeo and Juliet*, Anne is perplexed, "looking at it by the candlelight, turning page after page, gazing at the magic markings she could not understand." Even after having three children, Anne is still attractive to Shakespeare; he confesses, "She was still so lovely. Her hair still thick and shining copper, her breasts and hips still so smooth and full, all the shapes still moving so elegantly together."[15] Presumably, Anne's sexual power outweighs her illiteracy, and their sexual chemistry keeps Shakespeare loyal to her.

Berkman remarked in an interview that she was inspired to write her stories in reaction to *Shakespeare in Love*, specifically to its brief rejection of

Anne. "I wanted to challenge the way his wife Anne is dismissed with a line or two in that screenplay and in most people's minds," she commented, and she wanted to address the "many misconceptions, beginning with the idea that she was an aging spinster he married for her property and because he got her pregnant."[16] Though Anne has a larger role in Berkman's story, in the end the source of her power is her sexuality and she remains illiterate.

Nevertheless, readers praise Berkman's story for its contemporary relevance. She "really helped me to imagine what Shakespeare might have been like as just a regular guy," wrote one reader, who adds that "he expresses many things you'd likely hear out of men today. I realize it's fiction, but it helped me to consider a side of Shakespeare I'd never really thought of before."[17] Historical novelist Susan Vreeland lauded Berkman for producing a "brave piece of work, to imagine Shakespeare's women," and for writing "a book to stimulate the imagination." Likewise, author Andrea Barrett gave similar acclamation: "These stories bring alive the women – both real and imagined – who delighted Shakespeare: and now delight us." It is worth pointing out that Berkman's text is not what most would call a feminist work – Anne is illiterate, and can only command Shakespeare's attention because she has maintained her svelte body after having three children. Even so, she clearly speaks to a contingent of readers who are invested in a woman's view of Shakespeare's life story.

Readers have attested to the influence of Berkman's work on their understanding of Shakespeare's biography. "A helpful note at the end sorts out some of the biographical sources and real people," attested one reader, which "made me look forward to reading a biography of Shakespeare that I just picked up in the fall."[18] In her author's note, Berkman herself affirms the influence of biography on her fiction, specifically praising Park Honan's *Shakespeare: A Life* because it "separates fact from legend and explores more fully than its predecessors the likely circumstances of Shakespeare's relationships with the women of his family and work."

Two later novels overtly marketed and designed for an adult female readership, Karen Harper's *Mistress Shakespeare* (2009) and Arliss Ryan's *The Secret Confessions of Anne Shakespeare* (2010), similarly update and rework Shakespeare's life story with a central female character, either Anne Hathaway or occasionally Anne Whateley. Harper promises that her readers will discover Anne Whateley's "intimate details of her daring life and her great love, William Shakespeare" along with the story of "two passionate souls whose union survives separation, betrayal, and the barbs of small-town gossips." Harper's other novels clearly position her work in the bodice-ripper/historical novel market designed for women, including *Mistress of Mourning*, about Elizabeth of

York and the early Tudors; *The Queen's Governess*, about women in the court of Henry VIII; and *The Irish Princess*, a Tudor-era novel about "the story of a daring woman whose will cannot be tamed."[19] In *Mistress Shakespeare*, Harper builds on the Anne Hathaway/Anne Whateley discrepancy in Shakespeare's marriage documents to feature the stories of two central female characters, and purports to tell "the real story of Shakespeare in love." Claiming that the two names actually signify two marriages, Harper constructs a story where Shakespeare secretly marries his childhood love Anne Whateley, who shares his love of theatre and accompanies him to London for his playwriting career. Whateley is the recipient of the "first best bed" which they shared at their London Blackfriars house. Hathaway, who Shakespeare marries when he learns she is pregnant, receives the "second best bed" and is excluded from inheriting his London property. By employing two Annes, Harper can still address women's concerns while giving Shakespeare a romantic life in London with a literate woman, unhindered by children and family responsibilities.

Harper structures the narrative from Whateley's point of view as a confession of her romantic relationship with Shakespeare, and includes the sort of love scene her target audience would expect. At one of their secret meetings, Shakespeare exclaims, "Anne Whateley, queen of my thoughts and, even after all this time, my heart." She responds, "I stared agape, with nothing else to say. He spoke so well, in such finely measured, moving tones and sweetly selected words. His presence emanated confidence and manliness. I studied his strong mouth, the slight stubble of the buckskin-hued beard that shadowed his chin. At the side of his strong brown throat a rapid pulse was beating – beating for me." Later she records that "our caresses and kisses flamed to passion. More than once we threw our garments aside and caution to the winds."[20]

Unfortunately, Whateley cannot exclusively enjoy the "manliness" of Shakespeare, because he is forced to marry the pregnant Anne Hathaway. Whateley feels "pent-up fury [pour] through me like the river torrents in rain-soaked spring" when she realizes that she has a rival, but reassures herself that her poetic connection with Shakespeare will trump Hathaway's position as the mother of his children: "But did Will trade couplets with her? Did she read to him and listen to his dreams in the depths of their bed?" Nevertheless, Whateley cannot escape being the other woman, and is rebuked by thirteen-year-old Susanna Shakespeare, who warns her, "I know about you, and I want you to stay away from my father."[21]

In Harper's story, Whateley is the heroine who gets the guy (Shakespeare) and triumphs over the other woman (Hathaway), who fails to support Shakespeare's career and instead stays home in Stratford to care for their children. Hathaway (the stay-at-home mom) thinks Shakespeare is "mad and selfish in general to want to write," whereas Whateley (the unfettered wife) clandestinely escapes with Shakespeare to London where he can abandon his family. Whateley confesses, "busy London seemed so far from little Stratford that it was easy to live in a world of our own. Discovery or shame seemed as distant as the Avon. Our love was heedless and headstrong, heightened by the aphrodisiac of the sales of Will's first two plays." Perhaps not surprisingly, the accusation of bigamy never enters the discussion in this novel, so as to maintain a desirable image of Shakespeare as a romantic love interest.

Instead, Harper creates a feminist character through Anne Whateley who can appeal to her target readership with her progressive ideas, but who also can snag one of the most desirable men in historical romance – Shakespeare. Whateley espouses her frustration with men and reveals her role model in Elizabeth I: "Men! We women sometimes arranged the world for them, and they only looked askance and cursed us too, thinking they had contrived their own good fortune. But this country had a female monarch, one who moved men about like chess pieces ... at least in how she handled men, I wanted to be just like her!"[22] Since the novel is narrated by Whateley, we hear little of Hathaway's view as the abandoned wife and mother, probably because this would cast too negative a light on Shakespeare himself, who presumably is part of the novel's draw for readers.

Readers of Harper's novel seem to have accepted her alternative history as an authentic version of Shakespeare's life, even though it is based on a single mention (likely a clerical error, as discussed in Chapter 1) of "Anne Whateley" in the marriage records. One reviewer adamantly notes, "I whole-heartedly believe that Anne Whateley and Will lived the life described and I have no doubt in my mind that she was a central part of who he was as a person as well as his stoic supporter through everything. As a matter of fact, I would find myself gravely disappointed if anything to the contrary was proven to be true!"[23] Other readers applaud Harper for combining faux Shakespeare biography and historical romance. Even though Harper's novel is a fairly extensive distortion of the facts, Margaret Ohnes, a reviewer for the website "Fresh Fiction ... For Today's Reader," calls it "a touching perspective of the life of William Shakespeare told by his soul mate and life-long love." Ohnes describes the novel as an "expertly researched" work that will provide readers with "a rare glimpse of real persons from history, turning their lives into narratives that will entertain and delight the most discriminating of readers."[24] In spite of its distance from the historical realities of Shakespeare's wife, Harper's novel clearly speaks to readers' desires for access to Shakespeare's private life through a female conduit.

Extensive online reviews, women's magazines, and book clubs have helped to promote Harper's novel to a wide female readership. *Mistress Shakespeare* was named one of the "Best 10 Summer Beach Reads" by *Woman's Day* magazine, where it is described as "an intoxicating, fictionalized memoir of Shakespeare in love" and "a romantic roller coaster rich with vivid details reminiscent of *Romeo and Juliet*," best read "while enjoying the sunshine."[25]

Harper's own aggressive positioning of her book for reading groups further encourages readers to identify personally with her story. On her author website, Harper offers her private email address for book club interviews, along with a list of reading group questions targeted at engaging an emotional reaction. One question asks readers to compare the world of the novel to their own "strictures on personal freedom." Another asks whether the conflicts and disagreements between Shakespeare and Anne Whateley weaken or strengthen their relationship, and if "In love, do opposites attract?" These questions encourage readers to engage personally with Shakespeare's life story. The blogger "Book-Club Queen" attests to such reading practices on her site: "There were times when I would get angry with Anne Whateley for continuing to hold her heart for Will only; however, those times were short-lived because I felt their love transcended all else. She really was his muse . . . [and] the root of his success." Clearly, part of the enjoyment of this text is that it provides opportunities for readers to imagine themselves as "Mistress Shakespeare," inspiring and copulating with the famous author. One book club member asks just such a question: "If you were Anne W, would you have been able to live as Shakespeare's mistress? Why or why not?"[26] The cover illustration to Harper's novel (see Figure 6.3), John William Waterhouse's well-known 1908 painting "The Soul of the Rose," suggests that the contents of the book will involve a sensual and romantic story of a woman, leaving readers free to imagine her male lover (Shakespeare). Regardless of historical plausibility, the plot of *Mistress Shakespeare* updates Shakespeare for a contemporary female audience by promoting the idea that women in Shakespeare's day faced the same challenges as today's women, and that historical difference is only a minor discrepancy.

A second novel in this same vein (and recommended by many of Harper's readers), Arliss Ryan's *The Secret Confessions of Anne Shakespeare* (2010), even more overtly targets a female reading audience, combining features of historical fiction, biofiction, and historical romance. Numerous online reviewers and bloggers recommend both books to their extensive audiences, suggesting that these works have widespread appeal. Karen Harper describes

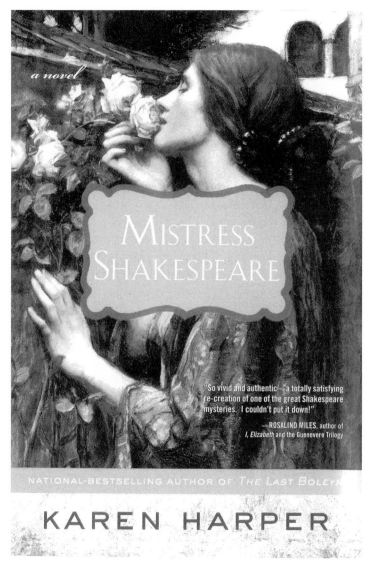

Figure 6.3 Cover of Karen Harper, *Mistress Shakespeare*.
Used with permission of Penguin Random House.

Ryan's novel as "sweeping and insightful, [as] tragic and comic as some of the bard's own plays," and a book that will "[shock] any modern day tell-all."[27] Readers get the next best thing to a Shakespeare play without having to read one, plus the salacious benefits of a modern confessional memoir. Anne

Hathaway, who "dared to be the equal of the Bard of Avon," begins the novel with her shocking deathbed revelation to granddaughter Elizabeth that "William Shakespeare of Stratford-upon-Avon did not write all the plays that appear in his name."[28] Told in Hathaway's own voice, the story relates Anne's refusal to be left behind in Stratford with her in-laws and children, and her subsequent journey from abandoned wife to successful ghostwriter of her husband's plays.

Ryan provides intimate details of the Shakespeares' early courtship, where Anne would "lie naked in our secret bower by Shottery Brook," while Shakespeare would "array long strands of my hair over me so that my breasts peeked through and the ends fringed above the patch of my soft woman's parts." Though Shakespeare is a good lover, he is a bad poet; he tries to write a sonnet to her, but she confesses, "This was not good poetry; believe me, I know. You have no idea how much bad poetry I was to endure until our future bard got the hang of it." Unlike other Annes we have encountered, who are illiterate and have no connection to Shakespeare's works, this Anne critiques Shakespeare's feeble attempts at romantic verse, preferring his love-making to his love poetry.

Ryan's Anne realizes that Shakespeare is not the ideal mate, and she thinks that she can do better: "He is pampered and pompous and overfond of himself. He is green and carries a headful of nonsense. Stay away, Anne, do you hear me? You must have a man who can give you a home and security, and you will bear him children and be his helpmate till death do you part. That is a woman's lot in the world. There is no way to escape it."[29] Anne knows that Shakespeare will not be a good provider, yet no woman (especially a reader of historical romance) could resist him. She faces a dilemma that readers may relate to, of sexual attraction versus domestic stability.

Ryan provides plenty of sex scenes for her target audience, mixing erotica with Shakespearian poetry. In one typical episode, Anne teases Shakespeare, promising to kiss him once he has taught her to read an entire sonnet on her own: "I pushed back his hands, and he pouted and obeyed, though heaven knows I was ready to unlace my bodice that very minute. I went to bed at night imagining his mouth upon mine, the heat of his panting on my neck." After another week of delay, "the tingling, the craving had almost reduced us to quivering jellyfish." Once she can read the last lines of the poem on her own, their passion is unleashed, and she gives in to his advances, in an exaggerated scene:

> I flung myself at his mouth, his lips, his tongue. I grappled my hands into his hair and clutched like a tiger. God help me, I was wanton! And

he returned my ardor not like a virgin boy, no, no, but as a lover who has conquered a thousand women, a man so sure of his power, he sweeps armies before him. Our tongues entwined, his hand plunged into my bodice and I could not get my clothes off fast enough. Naked, I ripped at him, still lean and with no more hair on his chest than a chicken plucked for the pot. We rolled and panted and coupled in the long grass; then we caught our breath and did it again. We ate of each other like famished beggars at a feast; our lust was a banquet ripe and overflowing. How is that for bad poetry?

Finally, at the height of their passion, she cries out with the memorable lines, "I love your sturdy lance … Oh, Will, shake me with your spear!"[30] Not long after the series of steamy encounters with Shakespeare the "plucked chicken," Anne the "wanton" becomes pregnant. They marry quickly and begin living with Shakespeare's family on Henley Street, where presumably the bodice-ripping episodes are curtailed.

While Ryan's sex scenes might seem overwrought, maudlin and gratuitous, they actually serve a number of purposes. As Maya Rodale observes, "Romance novels flip the script by focusing extensively on how it feels for the woman. In fact, the focus is on the pleasure a female feels, not just from her partner's touch but also from the entire experience with a lover."[31] Ryan is not the first writer to imagine sexual intimacy with Shakespeare. In Erica Jong's 1987 novel *Serenissima*, Hollywood actress Jessica Pruitt goes back in time to sleep with Shakespeare:

After all, who would dare describe love with the greatest poet the world has ever known, the poet who himself defined love? To detail organs, motions, sheets, wet spots, would be too gross, too literal, too finally deflating! It is quite one thing to imagine the poet of poets abed with his convent Juliet or his bisexual earl – but for a mere player like myself to go back in time, bed him, and then tell tales out of school? Fie on't! Was Will Shakespeare good in bed? Let the reader judge!

The consummation is successful, as the novel ends with "a bassinet trimmed with blue and silver ribbons, the baby, my little lion, cries."[32] Jillian Keenan's memoir *Sex with Shakespeare* (2016) takes this to the extreme, connecting her spanking fetish with Shakespeare's plays.

In addition to her erotic scenes with Shakespeare, Ryan incorporates other content to appeal to a female audience, including an extended scene of childbirth, a conflict between motherhood and career, a crisis for a woman whose once attractive appearance has waned with the birth of her children, and a dilemma for a woman who supports her husband yet receives no credit for her work. This Anne offers a grim view of the realities of motherhood in contrast to the sexual escapades of their courtship: "Those lusty afternoons with Will nine months before were hardly worth the price I was paying now." The early stages of motherhood are not glamorous either, even in the Shakespeare household. Anne relates, "As I looked around the room, my new daughter at my breast, no pretty sight greeted my eyes. The midwife's hair had come undone about her puffed face, and her arms were crusted with blood. Her body had lost all its bluster. My mother-in-law was a sick gray ghost propped on a chair. My daughter bawled at my breast, unhappy with the milkless fluid leaking from my nipple. I had no brain or body, only a numb wet ache as the afterbirth puddled out of me. I looked at the four of us, and I thought, God hates women."[33] The pain of childbirth and its exhausting messiness affect even the mother of Shakespeare's children, and readers are encouraged to identify with Anne's sympathetic tale of motherhood.

This Anne also struggles to balance her family life with her own pursuits. After the birth of the twins, she laments, "Good-bye, books. Farewell, evening lessons by the fire. Oh, both had been dwindling since Susanna anyway. What man has the inclination to recite verses when he has a wife and child – suddenly three children – to support? What woman has the leisure to absorb a bit of Latin after washing dirty linens all day?" Predictably, the Shakespeares' marriage begins to fall apart once their passion has disappeared and they have children. Anne regrets the loss of intellectual stimulation – books, lessons, Latin – in her life, and she mourns the decline of her appearance. "The lustrous fawn brown hair Will used to spread around me was dull and frayed," she relates, "My complexion was pallid, my mouth sagged. When I eased my shift off my shoulder to give the twins their suck, my collarbones jutted under my skin like the bony, folded wings of a bat. There was no poetry in my eyes, no music in my hips." When Shakespeare decides to leave his wife for London to begin his playwriting career, Anne must deal with being the wife of a career husband. She confesses, "Better to pretend I supported my husband's project than to concede I was a rejected wife."[34] "Damn him," she says, but soon picks herself up and plots her triumphant comeback. This Anne is an educated, literate, and determined woman, not content to waste away while her husband furthers his career.

At first, Anne has a brief intimate encounter with Shakespeare's brother Gilbert, but soon sneaks off to London, leaving her children behind with their grandparents. There she discovers that Shakespeare's career has foundered and that he has hidden his family life from his new friends: "With blinding clarity I grasped the situation. This last year Will had experienced a freedom not known since childhood. He had left both his personal mistakes – that would be me and the children – and his father's debts and disgrace behind him. He had shut his Stratford life away in a chest in the attic and meant never to unpack it again. Out of sight, out of mind, out of heart." Anne, being the feisty woman that she is in this story, fights back. Under disguise, she helps him with his playwriting career, enjoying her new-found freedom where "Will Shakespeare could no longer tell me what to think or feel."

Once she is part of the London theatre scene, Anne thrives on her independence. She takes rival playwrights as lovers, beginning with Christopher Marlowe, who trumps Shakespeare in bed and on stage:

> He kissed, he always kissed first, behind my ear and down my throat, into the hollow of my collarbone, like a key searching for its lock . . . I pounced on him and he pounced back, and with a tiger's passion we stripped each other, our mouths so hot and deep it seemed we would suck out our souls . . . Those who say Kit loved not women tell but half the story, for how else but with practice could he have gained such skill? He melted my bones, and God, what delight that man could inflict with his tongue . . . he locked his mouth and body into mine, and we rocked and surged and gave up our souls, a glistening couplet, a panting rhyme . . . It was never that good with you, Will. Never.[35]

After Anne describes this encounter in excruciating detail, she further vanquishes her husband by writing the play *Richard II* with Marlowe amid their lovemaking. Suffice it to say, Shakespeare is thoroughly outdone by his wife's artfulness, in bed and in writing.

Rival playwright Ben Jonson is a more subdued partner for Anne: "His kiss was soft, his beard fuzzy, his chest broad. When our lips parted, he looked at me in gratitude and wonder that I had not refused him. And now that rough, rude man became a shy lover, overwhelmed by good fortune. He held me so tenderly, murmured so fondly, I could scarcely have sworn it was the same man." The passionate Marlowe provided a "a breath-panting, bed-heaving affair – the kind every woman deserves at least once in her life," but Anne's romance with paunchy Ben Jonson was "almost a marriage. You would have thought on our evenings together we were an old domestic couple, mellowed by years of companionship . . . I pulled off Ben's shoes, took his left foot in my lap and began massaging the sole." Although there is no factual evidence that Anne Hathaway ever encountered Marlowe or Jonson, in this erotic fantasy she knows them more intimately than her husband does.

In addition to the salacious love scenes with rival playwrights, Ryan also reshapes Anne's story to address the work-life balance. Like many a working mother, when Anne returns home to Stratford to visit her children, all she can think about is the office – in this case, London and the world of the theatre. She has misgivings about abandoning her children, but in the end, puts her career first. As Anne finds success in playwriting, she is able to stand up to Shakespeare even more, telling him at one point to "Hire a laundress, eat your meals at the tavern, learn to use a dustpan."[36] Anne has overcome the pressures of motherhood to master her career, and even Shakespeare has to do his own housework in this novel.

Through Anne, Ryan also addresses the issue of women who let their husbands take credit for their work, the "behind every great man there's a woman" dictum. When *Richard III* is touted as Shakespeare's success, Anne says, "I bit my tongue and stifled the cry of injustice in my throat. It would not be the last time." Shakespeare's reaction to the success of her play *Romeo and Juliet* is even more disconcerting: "As he stood here, ashen, every instinct in his body fought to disbelieve what he held in his hands. To admit I could do this shook him to the core. It would have confounded every man and most women throughout Christendom. Women are inferior beings. They are incapable of writing plays, let alone an excellent one. And if an ordinary woman could do this, what did it say about him." Yet Anne lets Shakespeare take the credit: "*Romeo and Juliet* and every subsequent play went out the door with Will's name." Even Shakespeare's wife must sacrifice her labor to give him credit.

Setting a good example as a perfect woman who can have a full-time career writing the plays of "Shakespeare" and can take care of the house, this Anne even writes plays amid her household chores: "When a play was finished I often looked about our lodgings with a guilty uh-oh. Thick fuzz of dust on the mantel, smoke grime on the walls. Who stops to scrub the floor when your pen is calling? I would plunge in with the broom, bucket and goose-feather duster to set matters right." Moreover, this Anne is a consummate multitasker; while her family is moving into New Place, she begins to write *Hamlet* on the side as a way to overcome her child Hamnet's death, which she has missed because she was in London writing plays. The cover of the book (see Figure 6.4) shows a young Hathaway happily writing away in a domestic setting, presumably at her desk in New Place.

Like the other texts discussed in this chapter, Ryan's work takes great liberties with the possibilities of history in order to reshape Shakespeare's private life to appeal to contemporary women readers. In her Afterword, Ryan describes her goal as to let "Anne tell her side of the story" instead of

Figure 6.4 Cover of Arliss Ryan, *The Secret Confessions of Anne Shakespeare*. Used with permission of Penguin Random House.

deferring to the "experts [who] have no hesitation in making bold assumptions about her temperament, her appearance and her negative influence on the Bard." She admits that she has "taken a few minor liberties with history" in order to "tell a gripping story, and when faced with alternative scenarios I chose the one that best advanced my tale."[37] Even so, this fantasy version of Anne – author of Shakespeare's plays, lover of rival playwrights, successful "working mother" – disrupts narratives that consign her to a marginal role or that malign her as a shrewish, illiterate, nagging wife.

Numerous readers affirm Ryan's success at reforming Shakespeare's life story for modern women. Amy Lignor, reviewing the novel for www.featheredquill.com, describes it as "one woman's struggle to maintain her family ... [and] keep the love for her selfish husband."[38] Likewise, Sandra Worth, author of *The King's Daughter: A Novel of the First Tudor Queen* (2008), admires Hathaway as a woman "who shares, and helps shape, [Shakespeare's] dream." Ryan's novel resonates with readers who like to imagine that Shakespeare was influenced and perhaps even dominated by "a sensual, humorous, talented and daring woman,"[39] as one fan attested.

Comments from other readers reveal the porous boundaries between fiction and biography. Arleigh Johnson, on www.historical-fiction.com, attests that Ryan's novel motivated her to read a Shakespeare biography and buy a set of Shakespeare's works. Johnson treated this novel like a scholarly book; she reports that she "made myself read it slowly and take in every word, pausing to make notes and write down quotes as I went. It's that sort of book – Anne is so easy to identify with ... [I] copied quote after quote from this book."[40] Although Ryan does not promote the novel as a biography, some readers clearly read it as such. Susan Coventry, blogger and author of *The Queen's Daughter* (2010), notes her appreciation of this Anne as a critic of Shakespeare's plays: "Anne's drive-by analysis of each of the plays in the Shakespeare canon alone is worth the price of admission," she attests, concluding, "I fear I'll never quite look at Shakespeare in the same way."[41] While Ryan does not try to pass her novel off as a work of biography or of criticism, readers have appropriated it as both, despite its far-fetched plot. These reading practices fulfill the desires of readers for a significant female presence and influence in Shakespeare's life, and for an independent-minded woman who can commandeer the works of Shakespeare.

The comments of a blogger named "Holly" further testify to the appetite for an updated female connection to Shakespeare's world. She admires Anne as "a highly intelligent, strong voiced and conflicted woman whom you can totally relate to," who "feels guilt for choosing a life in London with Will over mothering her children back in Stratford." "Holly" is convinced in the end, though, admitting that "it becomes entirely plausible to see how Anne could have penned the famous works."[42] Other readers expressed their appreciation for Ryan's ability to modernize Shakespeare's private life to address contemporary debates about motherhood and career. "Kristen," who describes herself on her blog as "a voracious reader, fledgling runner, and full time kiddie chauffeur," admires Anne because she is "smart and resourceful, loyal and persevering. She could easily have been the playwright that we so revere today," writes "Kristen," and she notes her conviction that "even if Anne Hathaway didn't write Shakespeare's plays, I am quite certain that her fictional character here is a grand stand-in for some other real life woman."[43] Such responses work against depictions of Anne Hathaway as a minor figure in Shakespeare's life, a disastrous mistake, and a cast-off wife gleefully left behind in Stratford. These representative readers testify to the way biofiction can work in tandem with biography, by suggesting alternative stories and possibilities, and engaging in the "what if" of historical fiction.

Ryan deliberately promotes her novel as an alternative to traditional biographies, inviting readers to formulate their own opinions about Shakespeare's wife. She aggressively encourages this approach for book clubs, provides her email address and phone number on her website, and offers to chat with groups by speakerphone. Her group discussion questions incite readers to relate Anne and William's story to current debates among women: "In the end, do you feel Will and Anne had a successful marriage? A loving one?" And were Anne and Will "justified in abandoning their children even if it brought their family economic security and fame?" The question "How has the novel changed your view of Anne?" incites readers to use this fictional work to interpret the historical Anne Hathaway, and encourages them to view the novel alongside traditional biographies. We might recall the similarity with Germaine Greer's *Shakespeare's Wife* (2007), which begins Chapter 21 with the headnote, "in which the intrepid author makes the absurd suggestion" that Anne was involved in putting together the First Folio, an idea that Greer describes as "apparently too ridiculous to contemplate, which is why we shall now contemplate it." Whether Anne is imagined as the architect of the First Folio or the author of the plays, either option involves the same process of stretching Anne's story to the limits of possibility in order to recalibrate her conventional roles.

The Annes in these novels designed for women minimize the historical differences between contemporary and early modern women, bringing Anne into current debates about issues from premarital sex to stay-at-home mothers vs. career women. For an extensive female readership, Shakespeare's life story can speak to women's needs and desires, articulated through a version of his wife, and these works play a far more influential role in popular conceptions of Shakespeare's private life than do many traditional biographies and academic works.

Furthermore, online social networks like *Goodreads* provide platforms for readers of these novels to share book recommendations, criticism, and opinions with a broad audience. In her study of socially networked reading, Lisa Nakamura points out that *Goodreads* has more than six million users, and is linked to other social networks (Facebook, Twitter, Gmail), where reading recommendations are further circulated. The *Goodreads* platform invites readers to "comment, buy, blog, rant, and reply through a range of devices, networks, and services," creating a virtual "fan community" where "lively, provocative, and often surprisingly personal conversations" can occur, based on common reading practices. Nakamura notes that *Goodreads* "captures the value of our recommendations, social ties, affective networks, and collections of friends and books."[44] Specifically, *Goodreads* offers extensive evidence of how real readers interpret these texts about Anne, and this literary network circulates both comments and recommendations in an open access forum (linked to other vast social networks as well), broadening the potential audiences for these texts.

Numerous comments from readers reveal their ardent engagement with these various Annes in relation to contemporary mores and expectations for women, providing what Daniel Allington calls a "sense of a 'popular' aesthetic sensibility," where "books are valued for providing the reader with an entertaining reading experience with likeable characters and exciting events that relate to 'real' issues."[45] For example, one reader of Harper's *Mistress Shakespeare* criticized the novel because Anne "puts up with way too much rubbish from William Shakespeare to appeal to me . . . Maybe I wanted her to be more modern? This is probably unfair as Harper was staying true to women of the time but even in historicals, I'm used to reading heroines who give as good as they get."[46] Another reader chastised Harper's portrayal of Shakespeare for being "a selfish, jealous arsehole, who kept stringing our heroine Anne on for decades; never letting her go to get on with her life, but quite happy to have her running around after him, always on pause until he would next grace her with his presence, even though he was married to another woman and had several kids with her."[47] These comments on social networks encourage readers to participate in a conversation about Shakespeare's life as if he were a personal friend, and to play a part in critiquing, reviewing, and circulating the stories that should be told about him. One wonders how many networked readers, or potential readers, encountered the above description of Shakespeare as a "selfish, jealous arse-hole" and Anne as a "heroine," just to cite one example, and how this response may have affected their views of Shakespeare's life story.

These public reader responses also contribute to the subversive potential of the fictional works about Shakespeare's private life by engaging readers in the "what if" form of historical questioning, destabilizing prevailing narratives about Shakespeare's life, and encouraging communities of readers to rethink the certainty of various biographical premises. One reviewer of Arliss Ryan's *Secret Confessions* voiced just such a reaction to the alternative biography offered by this novel:

> But, what if they are all wrong? What if Anne wasn't a "homely, coarse, illiterate, immoral country wench," but, instead, half of a duo that aimed to be the foremost writer in the Elizabethan patriarchal England? What if she were truly the most gifted of playwrights but the gender laws and percep-tions of the times would never allow her work to see the light of day should she put her own name to her work. What if William Shakespeare was much more progressive than originally thought and was able to recognize a talent in the privacy of his own marriage bed what he could never admit publically?[48]

Imagining Anne as a co-author extends well beyond plausibility, but this version of her encourages readers to rethink the possibilities for Anne's life, and to share their reactions with others. Many of the testimonies from readers attest to their emotional engagement and personal investment in Shakespeare's life story. Through identification with Anne in particular, women readers can "talk back" to Shakespeare in a forum of shared reading interests. One reader of Harper's novel *Mistress Shakespeare* deems this Shakespeare as inadequate for the way he treats Anne, describing him as "not as brilliant as I wanted him to be. I know that he was just a man but I really wanted to see something special in him and I just didn't get it. He didn't seem different or even really quirky. Just another man unable to give the woman he loves what she wants." Another reader echoed this investment in Anne as a way to judge Shakespeare: "I really enjoyed getting to know Anne, and found that her personality really drew me in. She was a strong woman that used her mind to get what she wanted."[49]

Whether or not this Anne bears any resemblance to the historical Anne is irrelevant – readers are emboldened to pass judgment about Shakespeare's personal life based on a fictional account of his relationship with his wife. Socially networked communities of readers increase the circulation of these Annes, and of personal reactions to them, to a broad range of potential audiences.[50] Taken as a whole, the many fantasy Annes discussed in this chapter offer opportunities for women authors and readers to engage with Shakespeare's life story, rewrite it from a woman's view, and even invest in it as a statement about contemporary women's issues.

Embodying Anne Hathaway

As I have argued so far in this chapter, various Annes have often subsumed ideas about marriage, domestic responsibility and the workplace, part of the larger trend Jill L. Levenson identifies in stage adaptations since the 1960s, of politicizing Shakespeare "in response to pressing contemporary issues."[51] The final section of this chapter looks at three stage plays that update Anne as a figure of female empowerment by allowing her to voice ideas about independence, single motherhood, sexual freedom, unfaithful husbands, child care, women's education, and the power relations between husband and wife. Liberated from the framework of a novel, these stage Annes offer yet another way for audiences to engage with Anne's story through live performance.

In Avril Rowlands's play *Mrs. Shakespeare . . . The Poet's Wife* (2005), Anne is a work-at-home mother who manages her household and ghostwrites the plays of Shakespeare in her spare time. Likewise, Amy Freed's play *The Beard of Avon* (2001) depicts an independent-minded Anne who exacts revenge against her cheating husband (Shakespeare) by committing the ultimate act of Shakespearian adultery – copulating with author-rival the Earl of Oxford. Vern Thiessen's *Shakespeare's Will* (2005) casts Anne as the central character in what he describes as "the journey of a woman who faces adversity, rises above it, and ultimately re-kindles faith in herself." These roughly contemporary plays empower Anne as a modern woman of sexual desire, and endorse her domestic life. Shakespeare is critiqued for pursuing his own career without regard to the domestic costs of such an agenda, giving voice (literally) to many of the underlying tensions in feminist work on Shakespeare.

In *Shakespeare's Will* (2005), Canadian playwright Vern Thiessen constructs a lonely and neglected Anne, who survives as a single mother for nearly two decades. Thiessen conveys Anne's solitude by setting up his play as a monologue spoken by Anne as the sole character in the play (Figure 6.5), without a single appearance by Shakespeare (though he exists as a subject of her conversation). As Ann Wilson puts it, Thiessen constructs a "portrait of the playwright through the imagined memories and musings of his wife."[52] *Shakespeare's Will* recasts the poet's domestic life into a familiar narrative for

Figure 6.5 Cathy Fuller as Anne Hathaway in *Shakespeare's Will*, directed by Bain Boehlke, Jungle Theatre, Minneapolis, Minnesota. Photo copyright Michal Daniel.

a twenty-first century audience, a sort of inspirational "Chicken Soup for the Lonely Married Woman" based on the Shakespeare marriage.

In this play, despite her unfulfilling marriage, Anne is a self-sufficient and resourceful woman. Thiessen invents a relationship of mutual sexual gratification and companionship between the Shakespeares; they both confess to liking boys, and their secret shared desire bonds them throughout their separate lives:

> We make a vow:
> to wed yes
> but to live
> our own lives.
> To treat each other well
> but allow for our
> separate desires.

Rather than remain in Stratford as a passive neglected wife, Anne takes advantage of the freedom of her long-distance marriage and engages in an active extra-marital sex life: "I have only now discovered / being married / it is far more respectable to have many lovers."[53] Thiessen's Anne is not a lascivious and adulterous wife; her pursuit of sexual fulfillment is part of a mutual agenda that both partners attain independently.

This Anne makes sacrifices for her husband's career, adapting the Shakespeares into a familiar modern paradigm of working husband/stay-at-home-mother. At one point, William tells her, "You give me my work. / You give me my words. / You give me my life, Anne." Yet this is also the story of a woman who has failed in her domestic responsibilities, specifically in her duty to care for her children. During a time of plague, she takes the children to the sea, where their son Hamnet drowns when she looks away for a moment to swat a wasp. At the end of the play, Anne learns the contents of Shakespeare's will and interprets the infamous "second best bed" line as a punishment for her failings as a mother. She ends the play with a Malvolio-style curse to Shakespeare: "To hell. / To hell with your words,"[54] a resounding condemnation of his disregard for the sacrifices she has made for him, and of the tragic dénouement of her domestic life in comparison to his eternal fame. Shakespeare in this play is a vengeful husband who sets up a marriage of convenience so that he can pursue his artistic life, and the play gives voice to Anne's side of this story. Further, the printed version of the play includes biographical details that invite the audience to see the play as another version of Shakespeare's biography. *Shakespeare's Will* was commissioned by the Free Will Players and premiered at the Citadel Theatre in Edmonton, Alberta on 3 February 2005; since then, it has been performed widely around the world, notably at the Stratford Festival (Ontario) in 2007 and 2011; and elsewhere across the US, the UK, and New Zealand. The widespread success of *Shakespeare's Will* suggests the appeal of an inspirational story of a woman's struggle and triumph, even though it contains an unflattering rendering of Shakespeare as a self-interested husband who has little appreciation for the sacrifices his wife made to foster his career.

In a similar vein, Avril Rowlands's two-act play *Mrs. Shakespeare . . . The Poet's Wife* (2005) takes up the topics of career and motherhood by portraying Anne Hathaway as a full-time mother who writes the plays of "Shakespeare" on the side. Rowlands explicitly puts Anne at the center of the play, noting that "Anne definitely should remain on stage throughout. It is, after all, her production!" In this story, Anne was a writer before she married Shakespeare, and "tends the farm at Shottery, looks after her younger brothers and sisters and scribbles up in her room – a shocking thing for a woman!" This Anne even claims some of her husband's most famous lines: "I always was a writer . . . stories were there in my head . . . in the fields, in the forest, everywhere there were 'tongues in trees, books in the running brooks, sermons in stones and good in everything.'"[55] Here, the Warwickshire countryside has inspired Anne's poetic genius, and she only needs a venue for her artistic talents to flourish.

In Rowlands's account of the Shakespeares' domestic life, "Shakespeare" is merely a player whose nickname is "Wandering Willy" because his only interests are "star[ing] down at the rows of tightly-laced bosoms below, wondering which of them was softest to the touch and which you would fondle next." Their marriage is more a business partnership than a companionate relationship; when they meet, Anne tells him, "I think, Will lad, you and I can do business together." She supplies the plays to make his reputation on the London theatre scene, and marries him only because he can provide an outlet for her creative work.

In keeping with her revisionist agenda, Rowlands's Anne delivers polemical feminist statements about motherhood and the importance of her work (writing), effectively turning her into a modern work-at-home mother: "It is said that women are too weak to bear the pains of writing. But what is writing save giving birth, and in this alone we have the edge on men. I wrote when I should have been at my tasks . . . feeding the hens . . . mending the linen . . . busy about the stillroom . . . Like a thief I stole away and hid my scribblings–inside this very bed."[56] Here the second-best bed is a repository for Anne's literary achievements. As well as giving credit for the Shakespeare canon to his wife, Rowlands attributes to Anne several of the biographical stories about Shakespeare: she was inspired to write after seeing a group of touring players, for example, and she learns Latin and Greek at school. In this play, the material for rounding out a life of Anne Hathaway is appropriated from the biography of her husband, leaving him with a sketchy existence as a mediocre lusty player who has little literary talent and is dependent on his wife for his reputation as a playwright (and, in turn, his immortality).

Rowlands also incorporates issues of domestic responsibility by making Will the caregiver of their three young children while Anne works:

WILL (*Offstage*):   Anne? Anne? (*Enters.*) Anne, I'll not endure it!
ANNE: What?
WILL: Three babes and a wife who shuts herself in her room for hours on end! What kind of a wife is that?
ANNE: An obedient wife, Will, to have given her husband such fine proofs of her love.

Supporting an untalented aspiring playwright-husband, Anne spends her time in Stratford writing plays which her husband passes off as his own, even penning the sonnet "My Mistress' Eyes are Nothing Like the Sun" to her friend Alice. Anne is able to dominate her husband because she is the source of his oeuvre, and she does not hesitate to remind him of his inferior place. "The audience flock to see *my* plays, written, if they did but know it, by a woman's hand, created by a woman's brain," she chides him. "You are not the writer, Will. Never forget that. You are a player, playing a part of my devising, dancing to my tune!" Tellingly, his response to this tirade is "You unman me." Shakespeare must also take up his share of domestic duties so that his wife can work, i.e. write the plays to make his name. When Queen Elizabeth commands a play about Falstaff in love, Shakespeare begs his wife to compose a play so that he can maintain his reputation as a playwright. She orders him to "send the maids away. And take the children to Alice" so that she can write in peace. He keeps her glass of ale filled and her candle lit while she labors to write, a reversal of the traditional housewife who supplies her husband with necessary domestic comforts so that he can succeed in the workplace, and an inversion of the domestic Annes we saw in previous chapters.

Rowlands ends her play by rejecting some of the persistent myths about Anne Hathaway as a shrewish and illiterate woman; Anne declares, "I'm the greatest playwright that never was, but I'll be remembered as the shrew from Stratford who drove her genius husband away to fame and fortune. Anne Hathaway's name will never blaze like a comet to the stars. No. Yours will, even though you could never spell your name the same way twice."[57] Rowlands's version of Anne certainly extends beyond plausible belief, but her play is an obvious attempt to give meaning and significance to the domestic aspects of the Shakespeares' life by depicting Anne as a work-at-home mother and "unmanning" Shakespeare. In turn, by forcing Shakespeare to do his share of domestic labor and making Anne the source of their household income, Rowlands also validates gender equality in the household through an updated version of the Shakespeare marriage.

A third play about Shakespeare and his wife, Amy Freed's *The Beard of Avon* (2001), depicts an independent-minded Anne Hathaway who exacts revenge against her cheating husband (Shakespeare), amid a tale of Oxfordian authorship. Described in the cast list as "Lively, illiterate, promiscuous," Anne disguises herself as a prostitute and follows William to London so that she can torment him: "He knew me not as his wife, but thought me a wicked whore. He took me to his rooms, and we've scarcely been apart for a week. I've been just AWFUL to him. It's been WONDERFUL. Well, he himself hath taught me cruel inconstancy, since faithful kindness prompted him to flee." In the process, she discovers his seedy sex life, and they engage in "wild and stormy expanses of uncharted filth" involving whips and bondage. Freed does not employ the work-at-home or stay-at-home mother paradigms, but instead makes

Anne's story a tale of a woman's victory over her philandering husband. Readers may recall the earlier discussion of Nye's *Mrs. Shakespeare: The Complete Works* (1993), discussed in Chapter 5, where Anne's sexual acts inspire her husband's creativity. Here, Anne controls her own sexual behavior, and she uses it to vanquish her cheating husband.

Freed's Anne gets even with Shakespeare in a clever way, with the Earl of Oxford. When they first meet, Oxford describes her as a "hot bitch"; after discovering that she is Shakespeare's wife, Oxford is even more attracted to her: "I find my appetite revives! Honor then demands I do the job. Why, e'en now my friend doth feel the horns burst forth upon his brow and knows not why –." Anne returns to Stratford triumphant over her husband and sexually fulfilled from a "wicked and a sweet night" that "showed me what life might be, if only I had not been me." The Earl of Oxford procures both Shakespeare's identity and his wife, and in the process reveals Shakespeare as incompetent in bed and on paper.

In addition to the revenge that Anne Hathaway attains in this play, Freed also employs the Shakespeare marriage as a site of negotiation between the competing demands of the household and the workplace; William tells Anne, "You kill all that gives me pleasure . . . – You take from me all heart. And do deprive me of my necessary space!" She in turn accuses him, "You provide nothing and blame me for it!" Will warns her, "You have killed my soul already! . . . There is a great spirit in me that thou seekest to subdue – it will rebel." [58] In order for Shakespeare to attain his career goals, Anne must give him his "space," stop demanding that he "provide" for her, and become self-sufficient, both financially and sexually. Thus, in this play the creation of the Shakespeare canon is dependent on a wife who agrees to give her husband his freedom while she manages the household and attends to her own needs, and whose only recourse is to cuckold her husband. Though this Anne Hathaway obtains autonomy and sexual satisfaction, she must adhere (though not without a fight) to the domestic role of obedient wife whose submission facilitates her husband's achievements.

The Beard of Avon was commissioned by the South Coast Repertory in Costa Mesa, California, where it premiered in 2001. Since then, it has been performed in such venues as The Vortex in Austin, Texas; The Goodman Theatre in Chicago; City Theater Company in Delaware; The Rorschach Theatre in Washington, DC; Portland Center Stage in Oregon; and Off Broadway at the New York Theater Workshop. The play's popularity gives some indication of its appeal to present-day audiences, perhaps because of its engagement with contemporary gender politics in the household and its clever employment of the authorship question as a way to produce a sexually satisfied Anne Hathaway.

These stage versions of Anne Hathaway may be far removed from surviving facts about her, but like the other imaginative works discussed in this chapter, they work to destabilize biographical adages about Shakespeare by inviting audiences to imagine alternative scenarios for his private life and artistic influences. They also speak to the "what if" aspect of historical fiction – what if Anne Hathaway was not only literate, but was also a talented playwright? What if Shakespeare fell in love with a strong-willed, independent-minded woman, who influenced his creation of female characters? For women audiences in particular, these questions continue to animate their relationship with Shakespeare.

Taken as a whole, the representative novels and plays discussed in this chapter reflect a wide-ranging and diverse cast of Annes, with several conflicting versions of her available at any given historical moment. Recurring Annes include the faithful, loyal wife whose patience is rewarded, the shrewish woman who entrapped her famous husband and from whom he must escape, and the minor or absent figure in a story primarily about a rival Dark Lady or male lover. While on the one hand Anne can serve as a barometer for ideas about women, she also reveals the difficulty of placing her in Shakespeare's life story, and versions of Anne do not necessarily exist on a trajectory of female progress over time. These incompatible Annes hint at the instability of the historical Anne in Shakespeare's life story; at the long-standing role she has played in various writers' agendas about love, marriage, fidelity, and artistic inspiration; and at the eagerness for knowledge about her among diverse readerships.

The Annes covered in this chapter are crucial for sustaining questions about Shakespeare's life story and about his relationship with women, reflecting what Valerie Traub describes as "the ways Shakespeare continues to attract and frustrate" women. Indeed, engaging with Anne can offer what Traub calls "an opportunity to use some of the most complex literature of the past to reflect critically on the dilemmas and contradictions of our own time."[59] Socially networked readers, who share their emotional engagement, their critiques, and their recommendations, further extend the influence of these depictions of Anne to audiences beyond the initial circle of readers. Given the antithetical nature of this collective group of representative texts, the multiple versions of Annes reveal the instability of biographical information about her, as well as the manifold ways surviving facts about her can be interpreted.[60] In any given period, readers and audiences have had available a plethora of Annes – some are loyal wives, others are scorned spouses, but they all serve as reminders of how unstable biographical knowledge about Shakespeare is, how intense the desire has been for glimpses into the poet's private life in the last century, and how crucial Anne is for reshaping a life story that resonates with women's issues in various historical moments.

CONCLUSION

WHILE READING THE MANY TEXTS ABOUT ANNE HATHAWAY that underpin this book, I was struck by their consistent resistance to an orderly structure. Initially, I assumed that I would find a progression of texts that aligned with ideas about women, with criticism of Shakespeare, and with a general pattern of progress toward a more enlightened view of this woman whose life is inextricably bound with that of her famous husband. Instead, I encountered a frustratingly defiant range of works that, with a few exceptions, refused to fall into the organized sequence that I envisioned. I have come to realize that this disorder is crucial to the significance that Anne has had in Shakespeare's life story, and in his relationship with readers and audiences. Sometimes Annes correlate with what one would expect to find in a particular time and place, while others surprisingly depart from dominant cultural norms about gender, marriage, and women. Some of these texts offer an updated portrayal of Anne in line with current ideas about women, and others construct her in opposition to prevailing mores. For instance, the Anne in William T. Saward's 1907 play *William Shakespeare* autonomously vows to "have the man she fancies, and not the man who fancies her," while the Anne that Charles E. Lawrence creates in a play twenty years later (*The Hour of Prospero*, 1927) is a "picture of worn-out womanhood."

The diverse, contradictory, and irreconcilable Annes advance competing versions of Shakespeare's private life to audiences and readers, underlining the instability of knowledge about Shakespeare's wife, and about Shakespearian biography in general. These often-antithetical Annes maintain this tension among the irreconcilable elements of Shakespeare's life story, destabilizing set narratives and perpetuating the sense of mystery and the enigmas at the heart of Shakespeare's private life – in essence, fueling the continuation of her afterlife, and creating what John F. Keener calls

Figure 7.1. Elin Pritchard in *Hathaway – Eight Arias for a Bardic Life*, Helios Collective.
Photo courtesy of Ella Marchment.

a "cumulative cultural life story."[1] As this book goes to press, texts about
Anne continue to emerge, and to underline the central argument about Anne
Hathaway, that her story will continue to be rewritten and reinvented.

One such example is the operatic work *Hathaway – Eight Arias for a Bardic
Life*, put on by the London-based opera company Helios Collective, at the
Buxton International Festival, and the Copenhagen Opera Festival in summer 2016, commissioned for the 400th anniversary of Shakespeare's death.
This one-woman production weaves Shakespearian soprano arias from
Purcell, Gounod, Berlioz, and Verdi into a story told by Anne, a "plaria"
combining the form of a play with opera, written by Briar Kit Esme. Esme
comments that when he began the project, he was "looking for a grounded
story with a strong female character who can relate in a meaningful way to
a range of Shakespearean works, memes, and characters." He traveled to
Stratford for inspiration, and standing in front of Anne Hathaway's Cottage,
"in this moment, all the hours and days of research" coalesced around Anne
as the best way to celebrate Shakespeare.

The work was performed by soprano Elin Pritchard (Figure 7.1), who
describes this Anne as "a wonderful strong woman" who may have "had

more to do with William's work than we're aware of."[2] Drawing on Germaine Greer's biography *Shakespeare's Wife* (2007), along with a brief biography of Anne included in the script, Esme's goal is to "present Anne as far more than the wife of William Shakespeare," and he structures the work around eight acts, on topics such as Grief, Love, Adultery, Loss, Rejection, and Loyalty, all taking place immediately after Shakespeare's death in 1616. The script includes a note on production possibilities, to allow three interpretations: Anne relating the story of her life, aimed at "children or linear thinkers"; Anne as Shakespeare's muse, where she "fires his imagination and stirs the cauldron of his mind, but she is still essentially passive"; and Anne as "the real brains behind the works," where she is "very active, leading and guiding everything that Will does, or just using Will as a façade for her ideas and words."[3] Esme's options for interpretation underline the absence of one clearly defined interpretation of Anne, and highlight the need to adjust her for different audiences and ideological goals. Inspired by biography, by the possibilities for this woman so closely connected to Shakespeare, and by contemporary ideas about women, *Hathaway* embodies the fundamental arrangement of Anne's afterlife. In contrast, readers may recall the "Anne" that opened this book, from Bill Cain's 2014 play *Equivocation*, a work roughly contemporary to *Hathaway*, where Anne is derided as a lusty, predatory woman. These two works make the case for Anne's continued status as a contested space, where Shakespeare's relationship with women, both real and imagined, is articulated.

A third contemporary Anne lends yet another layer of complexity to her afterlife. The American television series on TNT entitled *Will* features a young, sexually promiscuous Shakespeare, described by *Entertainment Weekly* as "the young and sexy treatment that Shakespeare's origin story has been waiting for!"[4] Critic Marc Snetiker described Anne (performed by Deirdre Mullins) in the first episode: "in one nag [she] sets herself up as the single person in Shakespeare's life who doesn't immediately recognize his genius,"[5] and she is first seen crying amid the groundlings at the Globe Theatre. Shortly after the notice that this brief series had been canceled, Oscar-nominated actor Margot Robbie announced a new television series of retellings of Shakespeare's works from a female point of view, with an all-female creative team. It is unclear if Anne will have any role in these episodes, but the focus on retelling Shakespeare's plays for women resonates with interest in Anne.

One final example suggests future directions for the afterlife of Anne Hathaway. In March of 2010, the Shakespeare Birthplace Trust embarked

Figure 7.2. New Place display. Photo author's own.

on a re-excavation of New Place, Shakespeare's family home in Stratford-upon-Avon. Re-opened in the summer of 2016, New Place pays homage to Shakespeare's family life, described by Paul Edmondson as "his gentleman's family home."[6] In his "archaeological biography" of New Place, Edmondson has argued that "it was Anne who ran the household whether her husband was there or not, Anne who looked after the children, Anne who organized the work that took place on the site." As such, she has "emerged from centuries of silence" into the "lucrative, working-day world as manager of New Place" and is "now an important part of Shakespearian biography."[7] New Place should provide a second space for imagining Anne, in addition to Anne Hathaway's Cottage.

The re-presented New Place does not yet include a remounting of the actual space of the home. Instead, the Shakespeare Birthplace Trust has designed the space to urge visitors to imagine Shakespeare's final home, its occupants, and the literary works that were inspired and conceived in that space. The Shakespeare family, including Anne, is represented by a series of bodies in Tudor dress, with their heads replaced by digital displays that are largely blank slates (Figure 7.2). This book has demonstrated that those imaginary constructions can be some of the most compelling, enduring, and satisfying manifestations of Shakespeare's life, and are largely the only way that the life of Anne Hathaway *can* be created.

Yet behind all of the imagined, fictional, and fantasy "Annes," there is an actual historical woman, who outlived her famous husband by seven years, gave birth to his three children, and shared her life with him in some way. We will never know what the real Anne Hathaway was like, but the desire to know her shows no signs of ebbing. The year 2023 will mark the 400th anniversary of Anne Hathaway's death. By then, this book will be consigned to library and study shelves, but I hope it will have made a mark on the ways Anne can be imagined.

APPENDICES

Appendix I
Anne Hathaway in Biography and Fiction: A Timeline

Biographies and Biographical Criticism	Year	Fiction
	1804	Alexandre Duval, *Shakespeare Amoureux*
Edmond Malone, posthumous Boswell-Malone edition	1821	
	1829	Charles Somerset, *Shakespeare's Early Days*
Anna Jameson, *Shakespeare's Heroines: Characteristics of Women, Moral, Poetical, and Historical*	1832	
Alexander Dyce, "Memoir of Shakespeare"		
Charles Knight, *Pictorial Edition* (1838–1843)		
	1845	Emma Severn, *Anne Hathaway, or Shakespeare in Love*
Mary Cowden Clarke, *The Girlhood of Shakespeare's Heroines*	1850	
Richard Grant White, *Memoirs of the Life of William Shakespeare*	1865	
	1870	Harriet Beecher Stowe, *The True Story of Mrs. Shakespeare's Life*
Edward Dowden, *Shakspere: A Critical Study of his Mind and Art*	1875	
James Orchard Halliwell-Phillipps, *Outlines of the Life of Shakespeare*	1881	

Biographies and Biographical Criticism	Year	Fiction
Helena Faucit Martin, *On Some of Shakespeare's Female Characters*	1885	
M. Leigh Elliott, *Shakespeare's Garden of Girls*		
Mary Cowden Clarke, "Shakespeare as the Girl's Friend"	1887	
	1890	James Walter, *Shakespeare's True Life*
		Emma Marshall, *Shakespeare and his Birthplace*
Sidney Lee, entry on Shakespeare for the *DNB*	1897	Imogen Clark, *Shakespeare's Little Lad*
Sidney Lee, *A Life of William Shakespeare*	1898	
Georg Brandes, *William Shakespeare: A Critical Study*		
Charlotte Stopes, *Shakespeare's Family*	1901	
	1903	Roy Sensabaugh, *The Favor of the Queen*
Joseph William Gray, *Shakespeare's Marriage*	1905	Sara Hawks Sterling, *Shakespeare's Sweetheart*
		Clyde Westover, *The Romance of Gentle Will*
	1907	William T. Saward, *William Shakespeare*
Frank Harris, *The Man Shakespeare*	1909	Anna Benneson McMahan, *Shakespeare's Love Story*
		Anna Morgan and Alice Ward Bailey, *The Great Experiment: A Shakespearean Fantasy*
	1910	Hubert Osborne, *The Shakespeare Play*
Frank Harris, *The Women of Shakespeare*	1911	
	1913	Arthur Acheson, *Mistress Davenant: The Dark Lady of Shakespeare's Sonnets*
	1916	Leigh Mitchell Hodges, *The Bard at Home*
		Mabel Moran, *The Shakespeare Garden Club*
	1917	Hubert Osborne, *The Good Men Do*

Biographies and Biographical Criticism	Year	Fiction
	1918–1920	James Joyce, *Ulysses*
	1921	Clemence Dane, *Will Shakespeare*
Agnes Mure MacKenzie, *Women in Shakespeare's Plays*	1924	
	1927	C. E. Lawrence, *The Hour of Prospero*
E. K. Chambers, *William Shakespeare: A Study of Facts and Problems*	1930	
Edgar I. Fripp, *Shakespeare, Man and Artist*	1938	Grace Carlton, *The Wooing of Anne Hathaway*
William Ross, *The Story of Anne Whateley and William Shaxpere*	1939	
B. Roland Lewis, *Shakespeare Documents*	1940	
Hazelton Spencer, *The Art and Life of William Shakespeare*		
	1941	S. J. Simon and Caryl Brahms, *No Bed for Bacon*
	1942	Thomas Lennon, *The Truth about Ann*
	1946	N. Richard Nash, *Second Best Bed: A Comedy in Three Acts*
Charles Norman, *So Worthy a Friend: William Shakespeare*	1947	Ivor Brown, *William's Other Anne*
Leonard Dobbs, *Shakespeare Revealed*	1948	
Ivor Brown, *Shakespeare*	1949	
Marchette Chute, *Shakespeare of London*		
Frank Ernest Hill, *To Meet Will Shakespeare*		
Hesketh Pearson, *A Life of Shakespeare*		
	1950	W. J. Fraser Hutcheson, *Shakespeare's Other Anne*

Biographies and Biographical Criticism	Year	Fiction
Max Meredith Reese, *Shakespeare: His World and His Work*	1953	
F. E. Halliday, *Shakespeare: A Pictorial Biography*	1956	
F. E. Halliday, *Shakespeare in His Age*		
	1957	Rae Shirley, *Wife to Will Shakespeare*
Ivor Brown, *Shakespeare in his Time*	1960	
F. E. Halliday, *The Life of Shakespeare*	1961	
Hugh R. Williamson, *The Day Shakespeare Died*	1962	Edward Fisher, *Shakespeare and Son*
Ivor Brown, *How Shakespeare Spent the Day*	1963	Phyllis Bentley, *Shakespeare 400*
Peter Quennell, *Shakespeare: The Poet and his Background*		Cornel Adam Lengyel, *Will of Stratford*
A. L. Rowse, *William Shakespeare: A Biography*		
	1964	Anthony Burgess, *Nothing Like the Sun*
		John Garton, *Will Shakespeare, Gent*
		T. B. Morris, *Stratford Boy*
Ivor Brown, *The Women in Shakespeare's Life*	1968	William Gibson, *A Cry of Players*
Roland Mushat Frye, *Shakespeare's Life and Times: A Pictorial Record*		
Anthony Burgess, *Shakespeare*	1970	Tim J. Kelly, *Second Best Bed*
Samuel Schoenbaum, *Shakespeare's Lives*		
A. L. Rowse, *Shakespeare the Man*	1973	Eric Malpass, *Sweet Will*
Samuel Schoenbaum, *Shakespeare: A Documentary Life*	1975	
Juliet Dusinberre, *Shakespeare and the Nature of Women*		
Samuel Schoenbaum, *William Shakespeare: A Compact Documentary Life*	1977	Rosemary Sisson, *Will in Love*
Carol Thomas Neely, *A Woman's Part: Feminist Criticism of Shakespeare*	1980	

Biographies and Biographical Criticism	Year	Fiction
	1981	Laura Annawyn Shamas, *The Other Shakespeare*
	1983	Mollie Hardwick, *The Shakespeare Girl*
	1988	Pamela Melnikoff, *Plots and Players*
		Karen Sunde, *Dark Lady*
	1989	Faye Kellerman, *The Quality of Mercy*
	1993	Robert Nye, *Mrs. Shakespeare: The Complete Works*
Stanley Wells, *Shakespeare: A Dramatic Life*	1994	
	1995	Doris Gwaltney, *Shakespeare's Sister*
Anthony Holden, *William Shakespeare: The Man Behind the Genius*	1997	
Park Honan, *Shakespeare: A Life*	1998	Michael Baldwin, *Dark Lady*
		Judith Beard, *Romance of the Rose*
	1999	*Shakespeare in Love* (film)
Mita Scott Hedges, *The Second-best Bed: In Search of Anne Hathaway*	2000	Lynne Kositsky, *A Question of Will*
Katherine Duncan-Jones, *Ungentle Shakespeare*	2001	Amy Freed, *The Beard of Avon*
		Sarah A. Hoyt, *Ill Met by Moonlight*
		Pamela Berkman, *Her Infinite Variety*
Stanley Wells, *Shakespeare for All Time*	2003	
Stephen Greenblatt, *Will in the World*	2004	Grace Tiffany, *Will*
Peter Ackroyd, *Shakespeare: The Biography*	2005	Avril Rowlands, *Mrs. Shakespeare . . . the Poet's Wife*
		Graeme Johnstone, *The Playmakers*
		Audrey Peterson, *Murder in Stratford: As Told by Anne Hathaway Shakespeare*
		Vern Thiessen, *Shakespeare's Will*

Biographies and Biographical Criticism	Year	Fiction
	2006	Carolyn Meyer, *Loving Will Shakespeare*
		Laurie Lawlor, *The Two Loves of Will Shakespeare*
Rene Weis, *Shakespeare Revealed*	2007	
Germaine Greer, *Shakespeare's Wife*		
Jonathan Bate, *Soul of the Age*	2008	Christopher Rush, *Will: A Novel*
		Jess Winfield, *My Name is Will*
	2009	Karen Harper, *Mistress Shakespeare*
	2010	Arliss Ryan, *The Secret Confessions of Anne Shakespeare*
		Celia Rees, *The Fool's Girl*
Graham Holderness, *Nine Lives of William Shakespeare*	2011	
Lois Potter, *The Life of William Shakespeare*	2012	Jude Morgan, *The Secret Life of William Shakespeare*
		Aubrey Burl, *Shakespeare's Mistress: The Mystery of the Dark Lady Revealed*
		Alexa Schnee, *Shakespeare's Lady*
	2013	Victoria Lamb, *His Dark Lady*
	2014	Bill Cain, *Equivocation Shakespeare in Love* (play)
		Roy Chatfield, *The Other Shakespeare*
		Sally O'Reilly, *Dark Aemelia: A Novel of Shakespeare's Dark Lady*
	2015	Andrea Chapin, *The Tutor*
	2016	Briar Kit Esme, *Hathaway– Eight Arias for a Bardic Life* Mary Sharratt, *The Dark Lady's Mask*

Appendix II
Documents Related to Anne Hathaway

Document	Discovered by	Year	Present location
Epitaph on Anne's grave	William Dugdale (first transcriber)	1634	Holy Trinity Church, Stratford
Shakespeare's will	Joseph Greene	1747	National Archives, UK
Bartholomew Hathaway's will	Edmond Malone	c. 1790	Shakespeare Birthplace Trust
Burial notice of Anne Shakespeare, Parish Register of Holy Trinity Church	Edmond Malone	c. 1790	Shakespeare Birthplace Trust
Marriage license bond	Sir Thomas Phillipps	1836	Diocese of Worcester, UK
Thomas Whittington's will (Hathaway family shepherd)	Sir Thomas Phillipps	1837	Worcestershire Archive and Archaeology Service, Worcester, UK
Richard Hathaway's will	James Orchard Halliwell-Phillipps	1848	National Archives, UK
Bishop's registry entry for Shakespeare's marriage	Rev. T. P. Wadley	c. 1880	Diocese of Worcester, UK

NOTES

PREFACE

 1. Bill Cain, *Equivocation* (New York, NY: Dramatists Play Service, 2014), 23–24, 25, 33, 35.
 2. Charles Isherwood, "If He Can, Above All, to His Own Self Be True," *The New York Times*, 2 March 2010.
 3. Peter Marks, "A Lot to Ponder about Shakespeare through 'Equivocation,'" *The Washington Post*, 29 November 2011.
 4. Chris Jones, "Hard to Care about this Self-aware, Show-business Shakespeare," *Chicago Tribune*, 27 September 2012.
 5. Michael Lackey, *The American Biographical Novel* (New York, NY: Bloomsbury, 2016), 229.
 6. Alexa Alice Joubin and Elizabeth Rivlin, "Introduction," in *Shakespeare and the Ethics of Appropriation*, ed. Alexa Alice Joubin and Elizabeth Rivlin (New York, NY: Palgrave Macmillan, 2014), 3.
 7. Henry James, *The Birthplace,* in *Shakespeare in America: An Anthology from the Revolution to Now*, ed. James Shapiro (New York, NY: Penguin, 2013), 303.
 8. Brian Cummings, "Shakespeare, Biography, and Anti-Biography," Shakespeare's Birthday Lecture 2014, given at the Folger Shakespeare Library, 3 April 2014. Helen Deutsch's *Loving Dr. Johnson* (Chicago, IL: University of Chicago Press, 2005) and Claudia L. Johnson's *Jane Austen's Cults and Cultures* (Chicago, IL: University of Chicago Press, 2012) chronicle similar phenomena.
 9. James Orchard Halliwell-Phillipps, *Outlines of the Life of Shakespeare* (London: Longmans, Green, 1882), vi–vii.
10. "Shakespeare as a Man Among Men," *Harper's Monthly Magazine* 70 (March 1910), 489–490, 510.
11. *Wilhelm Meister's Apprenticeship*, Book III, Chapter IX.
12. *The Poetry Review*, vol. 29 (London: The Poetry Society, 1938), 425.
13. H. Snowden Ward and Catharine Weed Ward, *Shakespeare's Town and Times* (New York, NY: Truslove and Comba, 1896), 106.
14. This of course calls to mind the title of Jonathan Bate's biography, *Soul of the Age*, taken from Ben Jonson's elegy in the First Folio.
15. Thomas De Quincey, "Lake Reminiscences, No. 1," in *The Works of Thomas De Quincey*, ed. Grevel Lindop, vol. II; Articles from *Tait's Magazine* and *Blackwood's Magazine*, 1838–41, ed. Julian North (London: Pickering and Chatto, 2001), 61.

Quoted in Deidre Shauna Lynch, *Loving Literature: A Cultural History* (Chicago, IL: University of Chicago Press, 2015), 9.

16. "Bloke" is Andrew Hadfield's term. "William Shakespeare, My New Best Friend?," *Journal of Early Modern Studies* 5 (March 2016), 61.

17. Lynch, *Loving Literature*, 7.

18. Laurie Maguire, *Studying Shakespeare: A Guide to the Plays* (Malden, MA: Blackwell, 2004), 51, though this sentiment can be found in most studies of Shakespeare and marriage.

19. Andrew Hadfield, "Why Does Literary Biography Matter?," *Shakespeare Quarterly* 65.4 (2014), 377.

20. Carol Ann Duffy, "Anne Hathaway," *The World's Wife* (New York, NY: Faber and Faber, 1999), 30.

21. Hadfield, "Why Does Literary Biography Matter?," 375.

22. Gail Marshall, *Shakespeare and Victorian Women* (Cambridge: Cambridge University Press, 2009), 4, 9.

23. Germaine Greer, *Shakespeare's Wife* (London: Bloomsbury, 2007), 1.

24. Lena Cowen Orlin, "Shakespeare's Marriage," in Valerie Traub, ed., *The Oxford Handbook of Shakespeare and Embodiment: Gender, Sexuality, and Race* (Oxford: Oxford University Press, 2016), 39.

25. For other discussions of Shakespeare as a literary figure, see Annalisa Castaldo, "Fictions of Shakespeare and Literary Culture," in *Shakespeares After Shakespeare: An Encyclopedia of the Bard in Mass Media and Popular Culture*, ed. Richard Burt, 2 vols. (Westport, CT: Greenwood Press, 2007), 408–505; Paul J. C. M. Franssen, "The Life and Opinions of William Shakespeare, Gentleman: Biography between Fact and Fiction," in *Literature as History/History as Literature: Fact and Fiction in Medieval to Eighteenth-Century British Literature*, ed. Sonja Fielitz (Frankfurt: Peter Lang, 2007), 63–77; Douglas Lanier, *Shakespeare and Modern Popular Culture* (Oxford: Oxford University Press, 2002) and "Shakespeare™: Myth and Biographical Fiction," in *The Cambridge Companion to Shakespeare and Popular Culture*, ed. Robert Shaughnessy (Cambridge: Cambridge University Press, 2007); *The Author as Character: Representing Historical Writers in Western Literature*, ed. Paul Franssen and A. J. Hoenselaars (London: Associated University Presses, 1999); Maurice J. O'Sullivan, *Shakespeare's Other Lives: Fictional Depictions of the Bard* (Jefferson, NC: McFarland, 1997); and "Shakespeare's Other Lives," *Shakespeare Quarterly*, 38 (1987), 133–153.

26. Graham Holderness makes a similar argument in his discussion of Hamnet Shakespeare, where "diametrically opposed interpretations of the same data can co-exist without any recourse to definitive proof or conclusive argument." "His Son Hamnet Shakespeare," in *The Shakespeare Circle: An Alternative Biography*, ed. Paul Edmondson and Stanley Wells (Cambridge: Cambridge University Press, 2015), 104.

27. Joseph Howard, *The Life of Henry Ward Beecher* (Philadelphia, PA: Hubbard Brothers, 1887), 266.

28. Frank McGuinness, *Mutabilitie* (London: Faber and Faber, 1997), 93.

I   ORIGINS

1.   Samuel Schoenbaum, *William Shakespeare: A Documentary Life* (Oxford: Clarendon, 1975), 66. The Shakespeare Birthplace Trust, founded in 1847 with the purchase of Shakespeare's Birthplace, manages the Shakespeare properties in Stratford, including Anne Hathaway's Cottage.

2.   Kate Emery Pogue, *Shakespeare's Family* (Westport, CT: Praeger, 2008), 57; Mark Eccles, *Shakespeare in Warwickshire* (Madison, WI: University of Wisconsin Press, 1961), 67.

3.   C. J. Sisson, "Shakespeare's Friends: Hathaways and Burmans at Shottery," *Shakespeare Survey 12* (1959), 95–106. Richard Hathaway's wife Joan was buried as "Jone Gardner de Shottrey." Eccles, *Shakespeare in Warwickshire*, 69.

4.   Katherine West Scheil, "Hathaway Farm: Commemorating Warwickshire Will Between the Wars," *Shakespeare Survey 71* (2018), forthcoming.

5.   *A Brief Account of Stratford-Upon-Avon, With a Particular Description and Survey, of the Collegiate Church, the Mausoleum of Shakespeare, etc.* (Stratford: E. Walford, 1800), 55.

6.   Val Horsler, *Shakespeare's Church: A Parish for the World* (London: Third Millennium Publishing, 2010), 49.

7.   Sisson, "Shakespeare's Friends," 95, 100, 102.

8.   Pogue, *Shakespeare's Family*, 57. See also Richard Savage, *Minutes and Accounts of the Corporation of Stratford-Upon-Avon and Other Records, 1553–1620* (London: The Dugdale Society, 1924), 2:1–2. B. Roland Lewis notes that of the three Hathaway daughters mentioned in Richard's will, both Anne (who was twenty-five) and Catherine's (who was eighteen) bequests include the phrase "to be paide vnto her att the daye of her maryage," but Margaret, who was nine at the time, gets her bequest when she is "Seventeyne yeares." *The Shakespeare Documents*, 2 vols. (Stanford, CA: Stanford University Press, 1940), 1:157.

9.   Two children named Richard died in infancy. Anne had three sisters: Catherine, born 1563; Joan, born 1566 but only lived until 1572; and Margaret, born that same year (1572). Anne had four younger brothers who survived past infancy: Bartholomew (1554–1624); Thomas, born 1569; John, born 1575; and William, born 1578. Lewis, *Shakespeare Documents*, 1:158 and Germaine Greer, *Shakespeare's Wife* (London: Bloomsbury, 2007), 15–17.

10.   Greer suggests that Shakespeare's sister Joan may have been named after Joan Hathaway, and his brother Richard after Richard Hathaway. *Shakespeare's Wife*, 18, 42–57.

11.   Hewlands was divided into three dwellings by 1704, when a later Richard Hathaway owned it. Philip Styles, "The Borough of Stratford-Upon-Avon and the Parish of Alveston," in *Victoria County History of Warwickshire* (London: Oxford University Press, 1946), 3:17. For the history of Hewlands ownership in the Hathaway family, see Lewis, *Shakespeare Documents*, 1:158–159.

12.   Lewis, *Shakespeare Documents*, 1:156–157. Witnesses to Richard Hathaway's will include Richard Burman, John Richardson, and John Hemynge. Greer points out the possible connection with John Hemmings, who edited the Shakespeare First Folio. There was also a Richard Hathway [sic] who wrote plays for the Admiral's Men, but no link to Anne's family has been found. *Shakespeare's Wife*, 20–25.

13. Greer suggests that Bartholomew may have named his children after Anne Hathaway and Edmund Shakespeare. *Shakespeare's Wife*, 185.

14. Pogue, *Shakespeare's Family*, 120.

15. Edgar I. Fripp, *Shakespeare's Stratford* (London: Oxford University Press, 1928), 69n1.

16. Christopher Whitfield, "Four Town Clerks of Stratford on Avon, 1603–1625," *Notes and Queries* 11 (1964), 259. See also Philip Tennant, *The Civil War in Stratford-Upon-Avon: Conflict and Community in South Warwickshire, 1642–1646* (Gloucestershire: Alan Sutton, 1996), 160.

17. Greer, *Shakespeare's Wife*, 332. Anne's nephew John Hathaway was a churchwarden from 1622, and her nephew Richard Hathaway was an alderman from 1623. E. R. C. Brinkworth, *Shakespeare and the Bawdy Court of Stratford* (London: Phillimore, 1972), 23, 147.

18. Pogue's argument that there was an "estrangement" between Shakespeare and the Hathaways is not borne out by this evidence. *Shakespeare's Family*, 117.

19. James Orchard Halliwell-Phillipps, *Outlines of the Life of Shakespeare* (London: Longmans, 1887), 186.

20. Halliwell-Phillipps states that after Thomas Hathaway's death in 1654–1655, his widow Jane Hathaway was fined for "not repaireing the ground before her house in Chappell Street" in 1691. *An Historical Account of the New Place, Stratford-Upon-Avon* (London: J. E. Adlard, 1864), 81.

21. Halliwell-Phillipps, *Outlines*, 668–672.

22. Halliwell-Phillipps, *Outlines*, 693–694. Charlotte Carmichael Stopes points out that Elizabeth Hall's "preference for the Hathaway connections to those of the Shakespeare side" is notable in her will. Nash's will, particularly the attached codicil on the day of his death, gives £50 to his mother-in-law Susanna Hall as well as £50 to Elizabeth Hathaway, £50 to Thomas Hathaway, and £10 to Judith Hathaway. *Shakespeare's Family* (London: Elliot Stock, 1901), 89, 107; Lewis, *Shakespeare Documents*, 1:243; Edgar I. Fripp, *Shakespeare's Haunts* (London: Oxford University Press, 1929), 24–27.

23. Folger Shakespeare Library, ms. W.b.272.

24. Samuel Ireland, *Picturesque Views on the Upper, or Warwickshire Avon* (London: R. Faulder and T. Egerton, 1795), 206–209; Schoenbaum, *Documentary Life*, 61; Lewis, *Shakespeare Documents*, 1:119.

25. Julia Thomas, *Shakespeare's Shrine: The Bard's Birthplace and the Invention of Stratford-upon-Avon* (Philadelphia: University of Pennsylvania Press, 2012), 102.

26. Schoenbaum, *Documentary Life*, 69.

27. Greer, *Shakespeare's Wife*, 71–102.

28. Schoenbaum, *Documentary Life*, 71.

29. Schoenbaum, *Documentary Life*, 65. Sisson points out that Richard Burman, Fulk Sandells, Stephen Burman, and Roger Burman knew Shakespeare as well as Anne Hathaway and her father, and were all well placed in their village community. "Shakespeare's Friends," 103.

30. Robert Bearman, *Shakespeare in the Stratford Records* (Trowbridge, Wiltshire: Alan Sutton Publishing, 1994), 7–8.

31. Jeanne Jones, *Family Life in Shakespeare's England: Stratford-upon-Avon 1570–1630* (Phoenix Mill, Gloucester: Sutton Publishing, 1996), 97.

32. Around the same time he bought New Place, Shakespeare was contemplating a purchase of land in Shottery, which could have been connected with the Hathaway family. See the letter from Abraham Sturley to Richard Quiney, 24 January 1597–1598, printed in Halliwell-Phillipps, *Outlines*, 575–579; and Bearman, *Shakespeare in the Stratford Records*, 26.

33. Paul Edmondson, Kevin Colls, and William Mitchell, "Introduction: Finding Shakespeare's New Place," *Finding Shakespeare's New Place* (Manchester: Manchester University Press, 2016), 2.

34. "Shakespeare's Purchase of New Place," *Shakespeare Quarterly* 63.4 (2012), 485–486. Servants were also likely residents; in 1737, George Vertue sketched New Place "by memory," describing a "long gallery &c and for servants." Frank Simpson, "New Place: The Only Representation of Shakespeare's House from an Unpublished Manuscript," *Shakespeare Survey* 5 (1952), 56.

35. Bearman, *Shakespeare in the Stratford Records*, 39.

36. Robert Bearman, "Thomas Greene: Town Clerk and Shakespeare's Lodger," *Shakespeare Survey* 65 (2012), 290–305. Fripp argues that the Greenes lived in New Place from 1603–1611. *Shakespeare's Stratford*, 45, 58. See Tara Hamling, "His 'cousin': Thomas Greene," *The Shakespeare Circle: An Alternative Biography*, ed. Paul Edmondson and Stanley Wells (Cambridge: Cambridge University Press, 2015), 135–143.

37. Greer discusses widows in Stratford around the time of Shakespeare's death. *Shakespeare's Wife*, 336–337.

38. Vern Thiessen's play *Shakespeare's Will* (2005) imagines an antagonistic relationship between the two women, with Joan Hart eagerly and sinisterly anticipating Anne's reaction to Shakespeare's will, where Anne is punished for causing Hamnet's death due to her reputed negligence, but this is pure speculation.

39. Halliwell-Phillipps, *New Place*, 26.

40. In 1642, Thomas Nash refers to "my mother-in-law Mrs. Hall who lives with me" in New Place. Lewis, *Shakespeare Documents*, 2:583. See also Lewis, 1:245, for Susanna Hall living in New Place in 1648, the year before her death.

41. Joan Lane, *John Hall and his Patients: The Medical Practice of Shakespeare's Son-in-Law* (Stratford upon-Avon: The Shakespeare Birthplace Trust, 1996), xviii. Hall only described in his notes "cases of medical significance and almost exclusively those with a successful outcome" (xxi). Greg Wells similarly remarks, "We should not assume that the patients [Hall] recorded are typical of his practice as a whole." "His Son-in-Law John Hall," *The Shakespeare Circle*, 94.

42. Paul Edmondson "A Renaissance for New Place in Shakespearean Biography?," *Critical Survey* 25.1 (2013), 98.

43. Julian Bowsher and Pat Miller, *The Rose and the Globe: Playhouses of Shakespeare's Bankside, Southwark, Excavations 1988–91* (London: Museum of London Archaeology, 2009), 151.

44. Edmondson, *Finding Shakespeare's New Place*, 167.

45. Greer, *Shakespeare's Wife*, 160; Edmondson, *Finding Shakespeare's New Place*, 107. Lena Cowen Orlin's work on Elizabeth Quiney adds credence to Anne's financial independence. "Anne by Indirection," *Shakespeare Quarterly* 65.4 (2014), 421–454. See also Orlin's chapter "Shakespeare's Marriage," in *The Oxford Handbook of*

Shakespeare and Embodiment: Gender, Sexuality, and Race, ed. Valerie Traub (Oxford: Oxford University Press, 2016), 39–56.

46. Edmondson, *Finding Shakespeare's New Place*, 167.

47. Greer, *Shakespeare's Wife*, 175–177.

48. *Dig for Shakespeare: New Place, Season 3* (2011). Birmingham Archaeology.

49. See the bonds of indemnity (1603–1714) and the Hearth Tax Returns (1662–1663), cited in Styles, "The Borough of Stratford-Upon-Avon and the Parish of Alveston," 3:23.

50. Robert Bearman, "Shakespeare's Purchase of New Place," *Shakespeare Quarterly* 63.4 (2012), 482. Greer says that "Within months of acquiring New Place Shakespeare is listed as a holder of malt; the malt was almost certainly made by Ann or under her supervision. If she was making malt, she was probably also brewing ale, and raising pigs on the spent malt, curing her own bacon, and baking bread, for all these activities were interdependent" (217).

51. Paul Edmondson, "Shakespeare and New Place, 1597–1616, and later occupants to 1677," in *Finding Shakespeare's New Place*, 108.

52. Bearman, "Shakespeare's Purchase of New Place," 482. Lewis Theobald, in 1733, remarked that he had heard through Sir Hugh Clopton that Shakespeare "repair'd and remodell'd [New Place] to his own mind." Lewis, *Shakespeare Documents*, 1:240.

53. Lewis, *Shakespeare Documents*, 2:471.

54. Amanda Bevan, http://blog.nationalarchives.gov.uk/blog/shakespeares-will-new-interpretation/. See also Amanda Bevan and David Foster, "Shakespeare's Original Will: A Re-Reading, and a Reflection on Interdisciplinary Research Within Archives," *Archives* 51 (2016), 8–34.

55. Lewis, *Shakespeare Documents*, 2:471.

56. Ibid., 2:473.

57. Jones, *Family Life in Shakespeare's England*, 66.

58. Wells and Edmondson, *The Shakespeare Circle*, 157. See also Edmondson, *Finding Shakespeare's New Place*, 125.

59. Halliwell-Phillipps, *Outlines*, 2:244; Joyce Rogers, *The Second Best Bed: Shakespeare's Will in a New Light* (Westport, CT: Greenwood Press, 1993), 1; Stephen Greenblatt, *Will in the World: How Shakespeare became Shakespeare* (New York, NY: W. W. Norton, 2004), 146, 385. See also E. A. J. Honigmann, "Tiger Shakespeare and Gentle Shakespeare," *Modern Language Review* 107 (2012), 699–711.

60. See http://blog.nationalarchives.gov.uk/blog/shakespeares-will-new-interpretation/

61. Greer, *Shakespeare's Wife*, 315.

62. Halliwell-Phillipps, *Outlines*, 697–698.

63. Horsler, *Shakespeare's Church*, 114.

64. The curse on Shakespeare's grave is likely a reference to the charnel house that adjoined Holy Trinity Church at the time of Shakespeare's death, and to his reluctance to have his bones moved there at a later date.

65. Tom Reedy points out that Dugdale's transcriptions from Holy Trinity Church are dated 9 July 1634, though his inclusion of the 1635 death date for John Hall, for Thomas Nash in 1647, and for Susanna Hall in 1649 "confirm that the page is a later copy, not the original notes taken on-site, so obviously Dugdale visited the church or some other person supplied him with the information after that date." "William Dugdale on Shakespeare and His Monument," *Shakespeare Quarterly* 66.2 (2015),

194. See also "William Dugdale's Monumental Inaccuracies and Shakespeare's Stratford Monument," *Shakespeare Survey* 69 (2016), 380–393.

66.   The brass plaque itself dates from at least 1730. I am grateful to Robert Bearman for details on the history of the epitaph and its dating.

67.   Translation from Horsler, *Shakespeare's Church*, 123.

68.   Fripp, *Shakespeare's Stratford*, 59–60; Bearman, "Thomas Greene," 290–305.

69.   Phyllis Rackin, *Shakespeare and Women* (Oxford: Oxford University Press, 2005), 38.

70.   Marylynn Salmon, "The Cultural Significance of Breastfeeding and Infant Care in Early Modern England and America," *Journal of Social History* 28.2 (1994), 247–269, at 251. Salmon notes that for Puritans in particular, "breastfeeding represented God's gift of grace coming through his churches and ministers" (253). Wilson was "said to be a very good Scoler, and was the sonne of a very grave conformable doctor of divinity." Ann Hughes, "Religion and Society in Stratford Upon Avon, 1619–1638." *Midland History* 19 (1994), 69.

71.   Stopes, *Shakespeare's Warwickshire Contemporaries* (Stratford-upon-Avon: Shakespeare Head Press, 1907), 238.

72.   Hughes, "Religion and Society," 61.

73.   Lachlan MacKinnon, "His Daughter Susanna Hall," *The Shakespeare Circle*, 79.

2   FORGING THE SHAKESPEARE MARRIAGE

1.   Leonard Digges, "To the Memorie of the deceased Authour Maister W. Shakespeare," in *Mr. William Shakespeares Comedies, Histories, & Tragedies: Published according to the True Originall Copies*, ed. John Heminge and Henry Condell (London: Isaac Jaggard and Ed. Blount, 1623), B1r; *A Banquet of Jeasts; or Change of Cheare* (1632), jest 259. Both Edward Phillips's *Theatrum Poetarum* (1675) and William Winstanley's *The Lives of the Most Famous English Poets* (1687) mention the fact that Shakespeare was born in Stratford but provide no details about his family life. See also Paulina Kewes, "Shakespeare's Lives in Print, 1662–1821," in *Lives in Print: Biography and the Book Trade from the Middle Ages to the 21st Century*, ed. Robin Myers, Michael Harris, and Giles Mandelbrote (New Castle, DE: Oak Knoll Press, 2002), 55–82.

2.   Horsler, *Shakespeare's Church*, 27.

3.   Reedy, "William Dugdale on Shakespeare and His Monument," 188–196. Dugdale's ms. confirms the existence of the epigraph in 1634.

4.   In his 1656 *The Antiquities of Warwickshire*, William Dugdale reprints Anne's epitaph as one of four "Monumentall Inscriptions in the Quire," for the Shakespeare families. *The Antiquities of Warwickshire Illustrated* (London: Thomas Rarren, 1656), 518. E. A. J. Honigmann notes that John Weever transcribed Shakespeare's epitaph as early as 1626. Weever does not mention Anne Hathaway's grave, so it is unclear if her epitaph was there in 1626, three years after her death. *John Weever* (New York, NY: St. Martin's Press, 1987), 70. Thomas Fuller's *The History of the Worthies of England* (1662) overlooks Shakespeare's entire family.

5.   A Lieutenant Hammond in 1634 writes about visiting Holy Trinity to see "a neat Monument of that famous English Poet, Mr. William Shakespeere; who was borne here" but does not mention Anne's grave. Robert Dobyns, in 1673, copied Shakespeare's epitaph but ignored Anne's. E. K. Chambers, *William Shakespeare: A Study of Facts and Problems* (Oxford: Clarendon, 1930), 2:242–243, 250–251.

Likewise, in *An Account of the English Dramatick Poets* (1691), Gerard Langbaine describes Shakespeare's monument, reprinting the inscription on the monument as well as the epitaph on Shakespeare's grave. He notes that Shakespeare was "Buried in the Great Church in *Stratford* upon *Avon*, with his Wife and Daughter Susannah, the Wife of Mr. *John Hall*" (469), but neglected to include Anne Hathaway's name or the inscription on her grave.

6. As Alan Stewart puts it, "until Rowe cites the still unnamed daughter of Hathaway, this is Shakespeare without a wife." "The Undocumented Lives of William Shakespeare," in *The Oxford Handbook of Shakespeare and Embodiment: Gender, Sexuality, and Race*, ed. Valerie Traub (Oxford: Oxford University Press, 2016), 72.

7. Schoenbaum, *Documentary Life*, 205–206.

8. Schoenbaum points out that Manningham's story appears as early as *The Universal Magazine* of February 1785, but the Harleian manuscript at the British Museum was not discovered until around 1830 by John Payne Collier (*Shakespeare's Lives* [Oxford: Oxford University Press, 1991], 333–334). The fact that this early anecdote about a promiscuous Shakespeare circulated during his lifetime (and much later) complicates Margreta de Grazia's argument that anecdotes about Shakespeare record "the impression his works made after his death" and are "not about the man but about the writing that goes by the same name." "Shakespeare's Anecdotal Character," *Shakespeare Survey* 68 (2015), 14.

9. Kate Bennett, ed., *John Aubrey: Brief Lives* (Oxford: Oxford University Press, 2015), 2:1268.

10. Kate Bennett, "Shakespeare's Monument at Stratford: A New Seventeenth-Century Account," *Notes and Queries* 47.4 (December 2000), 464. Bennett notes that Aubrey's life of Shakespeare was "primarily written in 1680, [but] it incorporates material collected between 8 and 38 years earlier." *John Aubrey*, 2:1272. Aubrey clearly knew about Shakespeare's epitaph from Dugdale; a marginal note in his account says "V. his epitaph in Dugdales Warwickshire" (Chambers, *William Shakespeare*, 2:253).

11. Bennett, *John Aubrey*, 1:140.

12. See also Schoenbaum, *Shakespeare's Lives*, 101.

13. Wood would have had contact with Mrs. Davenant's family, and the Davenants lived in London near the Bankside theatre district. Mrs. Davenant's brothers worked with the Mountjoy family where Shakespeare rented lodgings, before the Davenants moved to Oxford around 1600 or 1601. Mary Edmond, *Rare Sir William Davenant* (Manchester: Manchester University Press, 1989), 14–16, 21.

14. Bennett, *John Aubrey*, 2:1268.

15. Bennett, "Shakespeare's Monument at Stratford," 464. Aubrey mentions Shakespeare's monument in his treatise *Chronologia Vestiaria*, written in the 1670s, but according to Bennett, his trip to Stratford was likely earlier. She indicates that Aubrey certainly was in Stratford in the fall of 1678 to see Shakespeare's monument in Holy Trinity (2:1270). Halliwell-Phillips dates Aubrey's visit to Stratford around 1662. *Outlines*, i, x.

16. Bennett, *John Aubrey*, 1:lxxviii.

17. Bennett, *John Aubrey*, 1:lxxviii; Chambers, *William Shakespeare*, 2:252–254; Schoenbaum, *Shakespeare's Lives*, 85. In another entry, Aubrey describes Shakespeare as "not a company keeper" and one who "wouldn't be debauched." Chambers, *William Shakespeare*, 2:252.

18. Anthony Wood, *Athenae Oxonienses*, ed. Philip Bliss, 4 vols. (London: F. C. and J. Rivington, 1813–1820), 3:803–804.

19. Gerard Langbaine, *The Lives and Characters of the English Dramatick Poets*, ed. Charles Gildon (London, 1691), 32. Thomas Hearne and Alexander Pope also repeat this story. See Schoenbaum, *Shakespeare's Lives*, 62–63. As E. K. Chambers points out, "provincial memories are long-lived," and "biographical tradition" is often underestimated. *William Shakespeare*, 2:238.

20. Giles Jacob, *The Poetical Register: or, the Lives and Characters of the English Dramatick Poets* (London, 1719), 58. Jacob reprints most of Rowe's biography, noting that Shakespeare "married the Daughter of Mr. *Hathaway*, a substantial Yeoman in the Neighbourhood of *Stratford*" (227).

21. Schoenbaum, *Documentary Life*, 165.

22. Bennett, *John Aubrey*, 2:1268.

23. Schoenbaum, *A Compact Documentary Life* (Oxford: Oxford University Press, 1977), 225–227.

24. Noted in Joseph William Gray, *Shakespeare's Marriage: His Departure from Stratford and Other Incidents in His Life* (London: Chapman and Hall, 1905), 186.

25. Joseph Spence, *Observations, Anecdotes, and Characters of Books and Men, Collected from Conversation*, ed. James M. Osborn (Oxford, 1966), 1:184.

26. William Chetwood, *A General History of the Stage* (1749), 21n.

27. Sir Walter Scott, *Woodstock* (London: Longman, Rees, Orme, Brown, and Green, 1826), 353. Michael Dobson, "Bowdler and Britannia: Shakespeare and the National Libido," *Shakespeare Survey* 46 (1993), 143. The anecdote about Shakespeare fathering Davenant also appears in the George Steevens and Samuel Johnson edition of Shakespeare in 1788.

28. H. P. Harman, "Shakespeare at Oxford," *Shakespeariana* (New York, NY: Leonard Scott, 1892), 115–116.

29. *Some Account of the Life of Mr. William Shakespear* (London, 1709), 20. Betterton probably traveled to Warwickshire around 1707–1708, according to David Roberts, *Thomas Betterton* (Cambridge: Cambridge University Press, 2010), 170–171. Edmond Malone stated that Rowe began "collecting materials" in 1708. *The Plays and Poems of Shakespeare*, ed. J. Boswell (London, 1821), 2:10.

30. Peter Martin, *Edmond Malone: Shakespearean Scholar* (Cambridge: Cambridge University Press, 1995), 125–130.

31. This is likely due to copyright, held by the Tonson family. See Adam G. Hooks, *Selling Shakespeare: Biography, Bibliography, and the Book Trade* (Cambridge: Cambridge University Press, 2016), 8.

32. Schoenbaum, *Shakespeare's Lives*, 91 and de Grazia, "Shakespeare's Anecdotal Character," 1.

33. Lewis Theobald, ed. *The Works of Shakespeare* (London: A. Bettesworth and C. Hitch, 1733), 1:vi.

34. The possible link between Anne Hathaway and Shakespeare's First Folio was followed up much later, in 2007, by Germaine Greer in *Shakespeare's Wife*, 345–355.

35. Simpson, "New Place," Plate II.

36. In depictions of the chancel of Holy Trinity Church, the brass plaque appears as early as 1828, in the painting "Sir Walter Scott's Visit to Shakespeare's Tomb," held by the Shakespeare Birthplace Trust. An early nineteenth-century watercolor (from before 1835) does not appear to have the brass plaque, but the 1836 plan of the chancel floor which recorded the inscriptions from the floor stones has a blank square where the plaque is now, as well as three rows of tiles between the graves of William and Anne. Horsler, *Shakespeare's Church*, 76, 81. By 1763, the author of *Biographia Britannica* (London, 1763) included a marginal note directing readers to "See her monument in the church of Stratford" (3628).

37. Nicola J. Watson, "Shakespeare on the Tourist Trail," *The Cambridge Companion to Shakespeare and Popular Culture* (Cambridge: Cambridge University Press, 2007), 205.

38. Ibid., 205.

39. Malone, *The Plays and Poems of Shakespeare*, 2:522.

40. John Hathaway was the owner until his death in 1746. Then the Cottage went to his sister Susanna and to his nephew John Hathaway Taylor and his son William Taylor, who died in 1846. His daughter was Mary Baker, wife of George Baker, and she died in 1899. Robert Bearman, "Anne Hathaway's Cottage," *The Oxford Companion to Shakespeare*, ed. Michael Dobson and Stanley Wells (Oxford University Press, 2001).

41. Christian Deelman, *The Great Shakespeare Jubilee* (New York: Viking Press, 1964), 105–107, 113.

42. Julia Thomas, *Shakespeare's Shrine: The Bard's Birthplace and the Invention of Stratford-upon-Avon* (Philadelphia: University of Pennsylvania Press, 2012), 16. The song composed in honor of the Birthplace praises the "enchanted ground" of Stratford where "Shakespeare walked and sung." Martha Winburn England, *Garrick and Stratford* (New York, NY: New York Public Library, 1962), 33.

43. England, *Garrick and Stratford*, 47, 25, 51–52.

44. Kate Rumbold, "Shakespeare and the Stratford Jubilee," *Shakespeare in the Eighteenth Century*, ed. Fiona Ritchie and Peter Sabor (Cambridge: Cambridge University Press, 2012), 256, 260, 262. See also Michael Dobson, *The Making of the National Poet* (Oxford: Oxford University Press, 1992).

45. *Shakespeare's Garland, Being a collection of new songs, ballads, roundelays, catches, glees, comic-serenatas, &c. performed at the Jubilee at Stratford upon Avon* (London: T. Becket, 1769), 14, 3.

46. England, *Garrick and Stratford*, 38; Dobson, "Bowdler and Britannia," 142.

47. Rumbold, "Shakespeare and the Stratford Jubilee," 261.

48. Michael Dobson, "A Boy from Stratford, 1769–1916: Shakespearean Biography and Romantic Nationalism," *On Life-Writing*, ed. Zachary Leader (Oxford: Oxford University Press, 2015), 33.

49. Rumbold, "Shakespeare and the Stratford Jubilee," 261, 254. David Garrick, *An Ode upon Dedicating a Building, and Erecting a Statue, to Shakespeare, at Stratford upon Avon* (London, 1769), 1.

50. *Boswell In Search of a Wife, 1766–1769*, ed. Frank Brady and Frederick A. Pottle (New York, NY: McGraw-Hill, 1959), 284.

51.	The gloves Garrick wore during the Jubilee were from John Ward, who claimed that they "were made me a present by a descendant of the family, when myself and company went over there from Warwick, in the year 1746, to perform the play of 'Othello.'" *The Private Correspondence of David Garrick*, 2 vols. (London: Henry Colburn and Richard Bentley, 1831), 1:352–353.

52.	Samuel Ireland, *Picturesque Views on the Upper, or Warwickshire Avon* (London: R. Faulder and T. Egerton, 1795), 206–209.

53.	Nathan Drake, *Shakspeare and His Times: Including the Biography of the Poet* (London: T. Cadell and W Davies, 1817), 1:60–61.

54.	Ibid., 1:63.

55.	William West, *The History, Topography, and Directory of Warwickshire* (Birmingham: R. Wrightson, 1830), 547.

56.	Charles Knight, *William Shakespeare, a Biography* (London: Routledge, 1843), 265.

57.	James Hain Friswell, *Life Portraits of William Shakspeare: A History of the Various Representations of the Poet, with an examination into their authenticity* (London: Sampson Low, Son, and Marston, 1864), 120–121.

58.	Vertue writes that the original will "may be Seen in Doctors Commons." Schoenbaum, *Documentary Life*, 242.

59.	Levi Fox, "An Early Copy of Shakespeare's Will," *Shakespeare Survey* 4 (1951), 69.

60.	Fox, "Early Copy," 73. Schoenbaum, *Documentary Life*, 242. This first transcript of the will was purchased by the Shakespeare Birthplace Trust in 1948 from Miss C. Hartwell Lucy. She had discovered it in the papers of her grandfather, Reverend Edmund Lane, also a rare book collector in Stratford. Fox notes that "how it came into Lane's possession is not known," nor is it clear for whom the copy was made and for what reason (69–70). Fox concludes that Greene was transcribing the Birthplace copy rather than the original will: "Greene copied from a copy and not from the original will" and failure to recognize this has led to Green being "credited with having discovered the will." (73).

61.	Both of Greene's transcriptions survive; the transcript Greene made for West is Lansdowne MS. 721, fol. 4 *et seq.* in the British Library. The other undated copy, previously owned by J. O. Halliwell-Phillipps, is at the Folger Shakespeare Library, item 114 in Halliwell-Phillipps's *Calendar of Shakespearean Rarities*. Stephen Nason, the vicar of Holy Trinity in 1769, had transcribed records of the Shakespeare family from the parish register to Garrick and to Joseph Greene. Greene forwarded them to James West, who then offered them to George Steevens, who printed them in his 1773 edition (with Samuel Johnson). Robert Bearman, *Shakespeare in the Stratford Records* (Gloucestershire: Alan Sutton, 1994), 11–12.

62.	Fox, "Early Copy," 72.

63.	Lewis Theobald, *The Works of Shakespeare . . . Collated with the Oldest Copies, and Corrected: With Notes, Explanatory, and Critical*, ed. Lewis Theobald, 8 vols. (London, 1752), 1:7.

64.	Schoenbaum, *Shakespeare's Lives*, 123, 126.

65.	Schoenbaum, *Shakespeare's Lives*, 120; Malone, *Supplement*, 1:654.

66.	*Biographia Britannica: or, the Lives of the most Eminent Persons who have Flourished in Great Britain and Ireland*, volume 6 (London: J. Walthoe, 1763), 3637.

67.	Schoenbaum, *Shakespeare's Lives*, 93, 119–120.

68. *Prolegomena to The Dramatick Writings of Will. Shakspere*, vol. 2, ed. Samuel Johnson and George Steevens. (London: John Bell, 1788), 2:487. Steevens reprints the bequest to Anne Hathaway as the "brown best bed" but notes that it was an interlineated line (2:519).

69. Jeffrey Kahan, *Reforging Shakespeare: The Story of a Theatrical Scandal* (Bethlehem, PA: Lehigh University Press, 1998), 9.

70. Paul Franssen, *Shakespeare's Literary Lives: The Author as Character in Fiction and Film* (Cambridge: Cambridge University Press, 2016), 38.

71. Roger Pringle, "Stratford-upon-Avon's First Guide-books," *Warwickshire History* 16.2 (Winter 2014–2015), 72.

72. James Orchard Halliwell-Phillipps, *Original Collections on Shakespeare and Stratford-on-Avon, by John Jordan the Stratford Poet . . . About the year 1780* (London: Thomas Richards, 1864), 59.

73. Schoenbaum, *Shakespeare's Lives*, 131, 133.

74. Ellen MacKay, "Acting Historical with Shakespeare, or, William-Henry Ireland's Oaken Chest," *Shakespeare Survey* 67 (2014), 208.

75. Robert Bell Wheler, *A Guide to Stratford-upon-Avon* (Stratford: J. Ward, 1814), 143.

76. Kahan, *Reforging Shakespeare*, 41.

77. W. T. Moncrieff, *Excursion to Warwick* (Leamington: Elliston, 1824), 44–45.

78. Doug Stewart, *The Boy Who Would be Shakespeare: A Tale of Forgery and Folly* (Cambridge, MA: Da Capo Press, 2010), 124–125.

79. Schoenbaum, *Shakespeare's Lives*, 150.

80. Stewart, *The Boy Who Would be Shakespeare*, 111.

81. Jonathan Bate, "Faking It: Shakespeare and the 1790s," in *Literature and Censorship*, ed. Nigel Smith (Woodbridge, Suffolk: D. S. Brewer, 1993), 69.

82. Samuel Ireland, *Miscellaneous Papers* (London: Cooper and Graham, 1796).

83. Subscribers included Richard Brinsley Sheridan, Edmund Burke, Robert Southey, and Charles Macklin. Stewart, *The Boy Who Would be Shakespeare*, 101, 202–203. See also Jack Lynch, *Deception and Detection in Eighteenth-Century Britain* (Aldershot, Hampshire: Ashgate, 2008), 84–85.

84. Schoenbaum, *Shakespeare's Lives*, 170.

85. James Shapiro, *Contested Will: Who Wrote Shakespeare?* (New York, NY: Simon and Schuster, 2010), 27.

86. Stewart, *The Boy Who Would be Shakespeare*, 202–203.

87. According to Dibdin's great grandson Edward Rimbault Dibdin, "it is not improbable that the poem may have been written as far back as 1769, when Dibdin produced a large amount of work for Garrick's Jubilee," though there is no record of the song being performed in Stratford that year. Edward Rimbault Dibdin, "Anne Hathaway," *Notes and Queries*, 7th series (29 May 1886), 434.

88. Sidney Lee, *A Life of William Shakespeare* (London: Macmillan, 1916), 26.

89. *The Professional Life of Mr. Dibdin* (London, 1803), 4:30–32.

90. *Dibdin's Songs* (London: G. H. Davidson, 1848), 2:127.

91. Dibdin, "Anne Hathaway," 434.

92. Kate Louise Roberts, *Hoyt's New Cyclopedia of Practical Quotations* (New York, NY: Funk and Wagnalls, 1923), 888.

93. Fiona Ritchie, *Women and Shakespeare in the Eighteenth Century* (Cambridge: Cambridge University Press, 2014), 82.

94. David Ellis, *The Truth about William Shakespeare: Fact, Fiction and Modern Biographies* (Edinburgh: Edinburgh University Press, 2012), 48.

95. Kate Rumbold, "Shakespeare Anthologized," in *The Edinburgh Companion to Shakespeare and the Arts*, ed. Mark Thornton Burnett, Adrian Streete, and Ramona Wray (Edinburgh: Edinburgh University Press, 2011), 88.

96. Rumbold, "Shakespeare Anthologized," 101.

97. Thomas, *Shakespeare's Shrine* 35.

98. MacKay, "Acting Historical with Shakespeare," 214.

99. F. W. Fairholt, *The Home of Shakspere: Illustrated and Described* (New York, NY: Williams Brothers, 1848), 57. See also Edmondson, *Finding Shakespeare's New Place*, 170–172.

100. Gail Marshall, *Shakespeare and Victorian Women* (Cambridge: Cambridge University Press, 2009), 38.

101. Mary Cowden Clarke, "Shakespeare as the Girl's Friend," *Shakespeariana* 4 (1887), 355–356. Some of the more intense manifestations of women's identification with Shakespeare are the women who "forsook the usual limits of literary tourism" and moved to Stratford to invest "in the town as a form of living memorial" to Shakespeare. Marshall, *Shakespeare and Victorian Women*, 129.

102. Jonathan Bate, *Soul of the Age: A Biography of the Mind of William Shakespeare* (New York, NY: Random House, 2009), 28.

3   THE LEGACY OF ANNE HATHAWAY'S COTTAGE

1. *The Official Programme of The Tercentenary Festival of the Birth of Shakespeare, To be held at Stratford-upon-Avon, commencing on Saturday, April 23, 1864* (London: Cassell, Petter, and Galpin, 1864), 29–30.

2. James Walter, *Shakespeare's True Life* (London: Longmans, Green, and Co., 1890), 123.

3. "Anne Hathaway's Cottage." *All the Year Round* (30 April 1892), 420.

4. See Alison Booth, *Homes and Haunts: Touring Writers' Shrines and Countries* (Oxford: Oxford University Press, 2016).

5. Nicola J. Watson, *The Literary Tourist: Readers and Places in Romantic and Victorian Britain* (Basingstoke: Palgrave Macmillan, 2006), 58.

6. Harald Hendrix, "Writers' Houses as Media of Expression and Remembrance: From Self-Fashioning to Cultural Memory," in *Writers' Houses and the Making of Memory*, ed. Harald Hendrix (London: Routledge, 2008), 6.

7. For the history of ownership and additions to the property, see Robert Bearman, "Anne Hathaway's Cottage," *The Oxford Companion to Shakespeare*, ed. Michael Dobson, Stanley Wells, Will Sharpe, and Erin Sullivan (Oxford: Oxford University Press, 2015).

8. http://list.historicengland.org.uk/resultsingle.aspx?uid=1298551

9. As Graham Holderness has pointed out, Stratford "was renamed after the literary reputation from which its existence has become inseparable: 'Stratford' had become 'Shakespear's Stratford.'" The guidebook entitled *The Shakespeare Myth* was republished in 1912 under the new title *Shakespeare-land*. "Stratford

Revisited," in Martin Procházka, Andreas Hoefele, Hanna Scolnicov, and Michael Dobson, eds., *Renaissance Shakespeare/Shakespeare Renaissances: Proceedings of the Ninth World Shakespeare Congress* (Newark, DE: University of Delaware Press, 2014), 367.

10. Barbara Hodgdon, *The Shakespeare Trade: Performances and Appropriations* (Philadelphia, PA: University of Pennsylvania Press, 1998), 203.

11. William Henry Ireland, *The Confessions of William Henry Ireland* (1895). Mary Hornby, tenant of the Birthplace in 1793, reportedly kept a letter from Shakespeare to his wife as well as his wife's shoe. W.T. Moncrieff, *Excursion to Stratford upon Avon* (Leamington: Elliston, 1824), 15–16 and Henry C. Shelley, *Shakespeare and Stratford* (London: Simpkin, Marshall Hamilton, Kent, 1913), 151.

12. Nicola J. Watson, "Shakespeare on the Tourist Trail," in *The Cambridge Companion to Shakespeare and Popular Culture*, ed. Robert Shaughnessy (Cambridge: Cambridge University Press, 2007), 212.

13. Booth, *Homes and Haunts*, 6.

14. "A Summer School in Europe," *Moderator-Topics* 28.32 (April 1908), 631.

15. Cecilia Morgan, *"A Happy Holiday": English Canadians and Transatlantic Tourism, 1870-1930* (Toronto, Ont.: University of Toronto Press, 2008), 15.

16. William Winter, *Shakespeare's England, Illustrated edition* (New York, NY, and London: Macmillan, 1892), 1, 3.

17. Ibid., 138.

18. Winter, *Shakespeare's England*, 4–5. Winter's work was reprinted in both Britain and America numerous times with illustrations added in 1892. He details the publication history in the preface to the 1892 edition.

19. Winter, *Shakespeare's England*, 142.

20. Roger Pringle, "Stratford-upon-Avon's First Guide-books," *Warwickshire History* 162 (Winter 2014–2015), 72.

21. Aaron Santesso, "The Birth of the Birthplace: Bread Street and Literary Tourism before Stratford," *ELH* 71.2 (Summer, 2004), 378.

22. *History and Antiquities of Stratford-Upon-Avon* (Stratford-upon-Avon: J. Ward, 1806).

23. Washington Irving, *The Sketch Book of Geoffrey Crayon, Gent* (New York, NY: Putnam, 1820); Nathan Drake, *Shakespeare and His Times: Including the Biography of the Poet* (London: T. Cadell and W. Davies, 1817), 61. Balz Engler discusses Stratford as a "place of pilgrimage" in the nineteenth century in "Stratford and the Canonization of Shakespeare," *European Journal of English Studies* 1.3 (1997), 354–366.

24. Olivia Murphy, "Jane Austen's 'Excellent Walker': Pride, Prejudice, and Pedestrianism," *Eighteenth-Century Fiction* 26.1 (2013), 124.

25. "A Summer School in Europe," *Moderator-Topics* 28.32 (April 1908), 631.

26. See Watson, *The Literary Tourist*, 87.

27. William Howitt, *Visits to Remarkable Places: Old Halls, Battle-Fields, and Scenes Illustrative of Striking Passages in English History and Poetry* (London: Longman, Brown, Green, 1840), 84, 87.

28. Ibid., 91, 92, 96.

29. Ibid., 97.

30. Anne D. Wallace, *Walking, Literature, and English Culture: The Origins and Uses of Peripatetic in the Nineteenth Century* (Oxford: Clarendon, 1993). Walking in

Shakespeare's footsteps is still popular, notably in Dominic Dromgoole's memoir about walking from Stratford to London, *Will and Me: How Shakespeare Took Over My Life* (2006).

31. "Stratford-Upon-Avon a Hundred Years Ago: Extracts from the Travel Diary of the Reverend William Harness," *Shakespeare Survey* 14 (1961), 111–112.

32. David Ellis, *That Man Shakespeare: Icon of Modern Culture* (Robertsbridge: Helm Information, 2005), 183.

33. George May, *Illustrated Companion-Book to Stratford-upon-Avon* (Evesham, 1847), 50–55.

34. *The Hand Book for Visitors to Stratford-upon-Avon* (Stratford-upon-Avon: F. & E. Ward, 1851), 40.

35. Wallace, *Walking, Literature, and English Culture*, 7–8, 13–14; Harriet Beecher Stowe, *Sunny Memories of Foreign Lands* (London: Sampson Low, Son and Co., 1854), 1:76.

36. *Hand Book for Visitors to Stratford-Upon-Avon* (Stratford-upon-Avon: Edward Adams, 1857), 35.

37. *Ward and Lock's Illustrated Guide to the Popular History of Leamington & Warwick, with Excursions to Kenilworth, Stratford-on-Avon* (Leamington: Thomas Simmons, 1888), 76.

38. Richard D. Altick notes that Henry Wallis's painting of Anne Hathaway's Cottage was not exhibited at the Royal Academy, but was shown in 1854 at the British Institution. *Paintings from Books: Art and Literature in Britain, 1760–1900* (Columbus, OH: Ohio State University, 1985), 147–148.

39. Helen Hackett, *Shakespeare and Elizabeth: The Meeting of Two Myths* (Princeton, NJ: Princeton University Press, 2009), 83.

40. Watson, "Shakespeare on the Tourist Trail," 213–214.

41. Walter, *Shakespeare's True Life*, 101, 106–107, 102, 103–104.

42. Simon Pugh, *Reading Landscape: Country, City, Capital* (Manchester: Manchester University Press, 1990), 192.

43. George Wood Clapp, *The Life and Work of James Leon Williams* (New York, NY: The Dental Digest, 1925), 250.

44. John Taylor, *A Dream of England: Landscape, Photography, and the Tourist's Imagination* (Manchester: Manchester University Press, 1994), 69.

45. As Gail Marshall has pointed out, Blind's poems are a "vicarious romantic memory" about a Shakespeare who is "embedded fundamentally in the land in which he was born." Gail Marshall, "Women Re-Read Shakespeare Country," in *Literary Tourism and Nineteenth-Century Culture*. Ed. Nicola J. Watson (Basingstoke: Palgrave Macmillan, 2009), 96–97.

46. Christopher Endy, "Travel and World Power: Americans in Europe, 1890–1917," *Diplomatic History* 22.4 (1998), 567.

47. Mark Rennella and Whitney Walton, "Planned Serendipity: American Travelers and the Transatlantic Voyage in the Nineteenth and Twentieth Centuries," *Journal of Social History* 38.2 (2004), 377.

48. North American travelers to Stratford were part of the larger phenomenon of increasing travel to Europe in the second half of the nineteenth century. See Endy, "Travel and World Power," 565–594.

49. Samuel G. Smith, "A Shakespearean Adventure," *The Chautauquan* 7 (March 1887), 358. En route back to Stratford, Smith encountered a clergyman who accosted him, "You are an American. You are interested in Shakspere. You have visited Anne Hathaway's cottage."

50. "The Fortnightly Shakespeare Club," *The American Shakespeare Magazine* 3 (January 1897), 26.

51. Cited in Morgan, *"A Happy Holiday,"* 95. Newton MacTavish describes the "trip of a lifetime" for the 150 women teachers, including a stop at Anne Hathaway's Cottage, where they enjoyed the "humble domicile and four-poster bed." "Manitoba Teachers Abroad," *Canadian Magazine* 36 (November 1910), 25–33.

52. Leo H. Baekeland, "A Family Motor Tour Through Europe," *The Horseless Age* 19 (1907), 508.

53. Edward L. Wells, "Stratford on Avon," *Illinois School Journal* 3.5 (September 1883), 113. The journal was published monthly for school teachers and administrators from 1881–1889.

54. *Country Life Illustrated*, 30 September 1899, 391. Baker's mother, Mary Taylor, was the daughter of William Taylor, son of John Hathaway Taylor, son of William Taylor and Susan Hathaway.

55. *Stratford-upon-Avon Herald*, 29 September 1899.

56. Morgan, *"A Happy Holiday,"* 16.

57. *The Brighton Herald* 30 September 1899 reports that a week before her death, "the poor old lady, who had reached the great age of eighty-seven, slipped from a stone step in the cottage, and fractured one of her thighs."

58. E. Poingdestre, "A Summer Day at Stratford-on-Avon," *Frank Leslie's Popular Monthly* 20 (July–December 1885), 415.

59. William Winter, *The Stage Life of Mary Anderson* (New York: George J. Coombes, 1886), 79; Poingdestre, "A Summer Day," 415; *Stratford-upon-Avon Herald*, 29 September 1899. The resemblance to Ophelia handing out flowers in *Hamlet* is likely deliberate.

60. "Pilgrims to the Shrine of Shakespeare: A Chat with Mrs. Hathaway Baker," *The Woman's Signal* (24 January 1895), 50.

61. Christian Tearle, *Rambles with an American* (London: Mills & Boon, 1910), 85; *The Brighton Herald* 30 September 1899; *Country Life Illustrated*, 30 September 1899, 391.

62. Charles Warren Stoddard, "The Shottery Tryst," *The Overland Monthly* 12.5 (May 1874), 406. Stoddard's essay was reprinted in his *Exits and Entrances: A Book of Essays and Sketches* (Boston, MA: Lothrop Publishing, 1903) and excerpted in James Walter's *Shakespeare's True Life* (1890), though Walter attributes the piece to William Winter. Part of Stoddard's essay on Shottery (retitled "Anne Hathaway's Cottage") was included in *The New Century Catholic Series: The Fifth Reader* (New York, NY: Benziger Brothers, 1905), designed for students and "drawn largely from the writings of Catholics of recognized standing in the world of letters" (5). Thus, Stoddard's piece reached a wide audience of all ages.

63. Charles Warren Stoddard, "Anne Hathaway's Cottage," *The Overland Monthly* 12 (March 1874), 285.

64. William Winter, *Shakespeare's England* (New York, NY: Moffat, Yard and Company, 1910), 156–157.

65.   *Stratford-upon-Avon Herald*, 29 September 1899.
66.   Tearle, *Rambles with an American*, 85.
67.   *Stratford-upon-Avon Herald*, 29 September 1899.
68.   *A Handbook for Visitors to Stratford-upon-Avon* (Stratford: E. Adams, 1872), 41–42.
69.   Elder C. G. Berry, "Stratford-on-Avon," *Improvement Era* 3.9 (July 1900), 689–690.
70.   "Pilgrims to the Shrine of Shakespeare," 50.
71.   Frederick W. Bennett, *Anne Hathaway's Cottage: Its History, Contents and Traditions* (n.p., 1921), 25.
72.   Thomas, *Shakespeare's Shrine*, 26. Brooks's illustration was later used in Walter Hutchinson's *Story of the British Nation* in 1923.
73.   *Stratford-upon-Avon Herald*, 29 September 1899.
74.   Charles Warren Stoddard remarked that "many a liberal sixpence is dropped into the hand of the good woman by pilgrims from the very ends of the earth." "The Shottery Tryst," 408. When the Shakespeare Birthplace Trust took over in 1892, they enforced a rule of no gratuities for the staff. Levi Fox, *The Shakespeare Birthplace Trust: A Personal Memoir* (Norwich: Jarrold Publishing, 1997), 43.
75.   *The Brighton Herald* 30 September 1899.
76.   John Chippendall Montesquieu Bellew, *Shakespeare's Home at New Place, Stratford-upon-Avon* (London: Virtue Brothers, 1863), 375.
77.   Poingdestre, "A Summer Day," 415.
78.   Walter, *Shakespeare's True Life*, 108.
79.   Stoddard, "The Shottery Tryst," 406, 407, 410.
80.   "What is Known about Shakespeare," *Frank Leslie's Popular Monthly* 27.4 (October 1888), 427.
81.   Berry, "Stratford-on-Avon," 689–690.
82.   *Harper's New Monthly Magazine* 58 (May 1879), 874.
83.   Fox, *The Shakespeare Birthplace Trust*, 45.
84.   Tearle, *Rambles with an American*, 81, 83–84.
85.   Poingdestre, "A Summer Day," 415.
86.   "Ann Hathaway's Cottage," *The Illustrated American* (10 September 1892), 162.
87.   Walter, *Shakespeare's True Life*, 104.
88.   American drama critic William Winter similarly records that Mary Baker "continues to reside in the Hathaway house and to show the wainscot, the great timbers, the antique bedstead, the dresser, the settle, and the fire-place with which it is believed that Shakespeare and his Anne were long and happily familiar." *Old Shrines and Ivy* (New York, NY: Macmillan, 1894), 43. Jane Baker died in 1901, and her two daughters joined their father as custodians until his retirement in 1910. Fox, *The Shakespeare Birthplace Trust*, 43.
89.   A Mrs. Hopkins sold postcards in the garden during the summer, and beginning in 1927, a room at the Cottage was dedicated as the "postcard shop," which remained in use until 1993. Fox, *The Shakespeare Birthplace Trust*, 45, 62.
90.   http://list.historicengland.org.uk/resultsingle.aspx?uid=1298551
91.   Jane Brown, "Miss Willmott's Ghost," *The Independent* 11 September 1999; Jackie Bennett, *Shakespeare's Gardens* (London: Frances Lincoln, 2016), 99.
92.   Fox, *The Shakespeare Birthplace Trust*, 60.

93. http://list.historicengland.org.uk/resultsingle.aspx?uid=1001184, accessed 25 May 2015.

94. Bennett, *Shakespeare's Gardens*, 90.

95. Fox, *The Shakespeare Birthplace Trust*, 60. It is worth pointing to the controversy over the Shakespeare Birthplace Trust's sale of land near Anne Hathaway's Cottage in 2015.

96. www.parksandgardens.org/places-and-people/site/101?preview=1

97. http://list.historicengland.org.uk/resultsingle.aspx?uid=1298551

98. "Welcome to Anne Hathaway's Cottage & Gardens," Shakespeare Birthplace Trust Brochure, 2014.

99. www.shakespeare.org.uk/about-us/press-information/news/perform-romeo-and-juliet.html

100. www.shakespeare.org.uk/visit-the-houses/anne-hathaways-cottage-amp-gardens/beautiful-cottage-gardens.html

101. www.shakespeare.org.uk/visit-the-houses/anne-hathaways-cottage-amp-gardens/beautiful-cottage-gardens.html

102. Tim Cresswell, *Place: A Short Introduction* (Malden, MA: Blackwell, 2004), 10; Watson, "Shakespeare on the Tourist Trail," 200.

103. William H. Hutton, *Highways and Byways in Shakespeare's Country* (London: Macmillan, 1914), 230.

104. Elizabeth K. Helsinger, *Rural Scenes and National Representation: Britain, 1815–1850* (Princeton, NJ: Princeton University Press, 1997), 7.

105. Taylor, *A Dream of England*, 79. This view is evident in W. Jerome Harrison's *Shakespear-Land* (1907).

106. Tours were advertised in the monthly magazine *Education* 27.7 (March 1907), 446.

107. M. S. Williard, *Letters from a Tar Heel Traveler in Mediterranean Countries* (Oxford: Oxford Orphan Asylum, 1907), 117.

108. Caroline French Benton, *Women's Club Work and Programs, or First Aid to Club Women* (Boston: Dana Estes Publishers, 1913), 91–92.

109. *The Spokesman* (November 1922), 101–103.

110. "A Summer School in Europe," *Moderator-Topics* 28.32 (April 1908), 630–631.

111. William Salt Brassington, "Notes on the Old Houses in Stratford-upon-Avon," Birmingham and Midland Institute, Birmingham Archaeological Society, Transactions, Excursions, and Reports for 1898, 33.

112. Morgan, *"A Happy Holiday,"* 81.

113. Lester Pittman, "The Formation of the Episcopal Diocese of Jerusalem 1841–1948: Anglican, Indigenous and Ecumenical," in *Patterns of the Past, Prospects for the Future: The Christian Heritage in the Holy Land*, ed. Thomas Hummel, Kevork Hintlian, and Ulf Carmesund (London: Melisende, 1999), 98.

114. Evelyn Waugh, *Decline and Fall* (London: Chapman and Hall, 1928), 148.

115. Helsinger, *Rural Scenes*, 7.

116. Other postcards in the series featured Shakespeare's Birthplace and the Shakespeare Memorial Theatre.

117. "Stratford-upon-Avon," vol. 4 (London: Spottiswoode, Ballantyne, & Co., 1943–44), 11.

118. *British Council Series of Informative Pamphlets for United States Armed Forces in the United Kingdom*, "Introduction."

119. Simon Barker, "Shakespeare, Stratford, and the Second World War," *Shakespeare and the Second World War: Memory, Culture, Identity*, ed. Irena R. Makaryk and Marissa McHugh (Toronto, Ont.: University of Toronto Press, 2012), 206. Fox, *The Shakespeare Birthplace Trust*, 59. See also Nicholas Fogg, *Stratford: A Town at War, 1914–1945* (Gloucester: Sutton Publishing, 2008), 114–116.

120. Fox, *The Shakespeare Birthplace Trust*, 49.

121. Stratford Society and Shakespeare Birthplace Trust Oral History Project, Interview on 29 November 1990 with Emma Salmon. Salmon began as a guide in 1941, the year her son was shot down.

122. Roma Innes, "Shottery Post Office in Wartime," WW2 People's War Oral History project, 18 April 2005.

123. Eugene G. Schulz, *The Ghost in General Patton's Third Army: The Memoirs of Eugene G. Schulz during his Service in the United States Army in World War II* (Xlibris, 2013), 72, 76, 74.

124. Schulz, *The Ghost in General Patton's Third Army*, 79–80.

125. John Baxendale, "'You and I: All of Us Ordinary People': Renegotiating 'Britishness' in Wartime," in *"Millions Like Us"?: British Culture in the Second World War*, ed. Nick Hayes and Jeff Hill (Liverpool: Liverpool University Press, 1999), 295. Baxendale points out that the song's lyrics "aspire to a timeless and high-minded sense of nationhood" (296).

126. Steven Seidenberg, Maurice Sellar, and Lou Jones, *You Must Remember This: Songs at the Heart of the War* (London: Boxtree, 1995), 28–29.

127. This version was published by Gordon V. Thompson in Toronto. The version published in London featured British sailors from the song's premiere in the 1939 film *Discoveries* instead of Anne Hathaway's Cottage.

128. Nicola J. Watson, "Gardening with Shakespeare," in Clara Calvo and Coppélia Kahn, *Celebrating Shakespeare: Commemoration and Cultural Memory* (Cambridge: Cambridge University Press, 2015), 318–319, 329.

129. Shay's memoir was written by Grace Abrahamson, based on Shay's journal. See *Mrs. Shay Did It!* (Wessington Springs, SD: A. L. Webb, 1976), 30.

130. Abrahamson, *Mrs. Shay Did It*, 31. Elbert Hubbard, *Good Men and Great. Little Journeys to the Homes of the Great*. Vol. 1. (Cleveland, OH: World, 1928), 312.

131. Abrahamson, *Mrs. Shay Did It*, 1.

132. Watson, "Gardening with Shakespeare," 304–305.

133. John Andrews, "Celebrating our Ethnic Ways," *South Dakota Magazine* (May/June 2009): 49–54.

134. Hendrix, "Writers' Houses as Media of Expression and Remembrance," 5.

135. Other Anne Hathaway Cottage bed and breakfasts include Ashland, Oregon and Perth, Australia.

136. www.anne-hathaways-cottage.com/

137. www.sunrisepm.com/rentalAHC_23/rental23.html

138. Kathleen Kleinpaste, *Just do it Jessie's Way!: A Story of a Parcel of Land on the Shores of Green Lake, Wisconsin* (K. Kleinpaste, 2003), 124–125, 105.

139.   http://estatesoflawsonia.com/about-the-estates.html

140.   Fred L. Seely Oral History, D. H. Ramsey Library, Special Collections, University of North Carolina at Asheville. Interview on 23 June 1983.

141.   Brochure prepared by the Grove Park Inn, 1913. Biltmore Industries Archive, *The Biltmore Industries Collection (1901–1980)*, D. H. Ramsey Library, Special Collections, University of North Carolina at Asheville.

142.   Beginning in April 1942 through June of that year, the Grove Park Inn hosted Italian, Bulgarian, and Hungarian diplomats, including "their families, servants, pets and private possessions," as well as diplomats from Mexico, Cuba, El Salvador, and Japan. By July of 1944 the Inn was leased by the U.S. Army as a place of rest for returning combat veterans until September of 1945. See Richard E. Osborne, *World War II Sites in the United States: A Tour Guide & Directory* (Indianapolis, IN: Riebel-Roque Publishing, 1996), 180–181. The Fred L. Seely Oral History describes the prisoners as living in "complete luxury."

143.   Bruce E. Johnson, *Built for the Ages: A History of the Grove Park Inn* (Asheville, NC: Grove Park Inn and Country Club, 1991), 72.

144.   Ibid., 75.

145.   The recent clamor over the housing development planned for the area around Anne Hathaway's Cottage is a case in point. "The local MP, Nadhim Zahawi, went further, warning MPs during a debate on the decision that the future of a house that had survived 'the English Reformation, the English Civil War and even 13 years of Labour' may now have been jeopardised by the 'careless stroke of a planning inspector's pen.'" *The Daily Mail*, 8 November 2012.

146.   www.bbc.co.uk/events/ehw2mb/live/c96v4f

147.   Taylor, *A Dream of England*, 64.

148.   William Thomas Stead, *From the Old World to the New; Or, a Christmas Story of the Chicago Exhibition* (London: Horace Marshall and Sons, 1892), 8, 9, 121.

INTERLUDE: FACT AND FICTION

1.   Roger Chartier, "Everything and Nothing: The Many Lives of William Shakespeare," *Journal of Early Modern Studies* 5 (2016), 17.

2.   Ina Schabert, "Fictional Biography, Factual Biography, and their Contaminants," *Biography* 5.1 (1982), 13.

3.   Paul Edmondson, "Writing and Re-Writing Shakespeare's Life: A Roundtable Discussion with Margreta de Grazia, Katherine Scheil, James Shapiro, and Stanley Wells," *Shakespeare Survey* 70 (2017), 63.

4.   Holderness, *Nine Lives of William Shakespeare* (London: Continuum, 2011), 3.

5.   John F. Keener, *Biography and the Postmodern Historical Novel* (Lewiston, NY: Mellen Press, 2001), 172–173. Keener derives these categories from Kate Hamburger's *The Logic of Literature* (Bloomington, IN: Indiana University Press, 1973).

6.   Jess Winfield, *My Name is Will: A Novel of Sex, Drugs, and Shakespeare* (New York, NY: Twelve, 2008), 289.

7.   Bruce Duffy, "In the Fog of the Biographical Novel's History," in *Truthful Fictions: Conversations with American Biographical Novelists*, ed. Michael Lackey (New York, NY: Bloomsbury, 2014), 113.

8. Greenblatt, *Will in the World*, 12, 14.
9. Schabert, "Fictional Biography," 1–2, 7.
10. Joanna Scott, "On Hoaxes, Humbugs, and Fictional Portraiture," *a/b:Auto/Biography Studies* 31.1 (2016), 30.
11. Keener, *Biography and the Postmodern Novel*, 162.
12. Peter Holland, "Shakespeare and Biography," in *Shakespeare in Our Time: A Shakespeare Association of America Collection* (London: Bloomsbury, 2016), 250. See also David Ellis's *That Man Shakespeare: Icon of Modern Culture* (2006). Lois Potter descries the divide between fiction and biography as a question of "how much imagination a book can contain and still be taken seriously as a biography." "Having our Will: Imagination in Recent Shakespeare Biographies." *Shakespeare Survey* 58 (2005), 1.
13. Holderness, *Nine Lives of William Shakespeare*, 18–19.
14. William Leahy, "'The Dreamscape of Nostalgia': Shakespearean Biography: Too Much Information (but not about Shakespeare)," *Journal of Early Modern Studies* 5 (2016), 41.
15. John Worthen, "The Necessary Ignorance of a Biographer," in *The Art of Literary Biography*, ed. John Batchelor (Oxford: Clarendon Press, 1995), 227.
16. Julia Reinhard Lupton, "Birth Places: Shakespeare's Beliefs / Believing in Shakespeare," *Shakespeare Quarterly* 65.4 (2014), 404.
17. Russell Banks, "The Truth Contract in the Biographical Novel," in *Truthful Fictions*, 48. Exhaustive surveys of Shakespeare biographies can be found elsewhere, such as David Bevington's *Shakespeare and Biography* (Oxford: Oxford University Press, 2010); David Ellis's *The Truth about William Shakespeare: Fact, Fiction, and Modern Biographies* (Edinburgh: Edinburgh University Press, 2012); and Arthur Maltby's *Shakespeare as a Challenge for Literary Biography: A History of Biographies of Shakespeare Since 1898* (Lewiston, NY: Mellen Press, 2009).
18. Katherine West Scheil and Graham Holderness, "Introduction: Shakespeare and the 'Personal Story,'" *Critical Survey* 21.3 (2009), 5.
19. Leahy, "'The Dreamscape of Nostalgia,'" 40.
20. Holland, "Shakespeare and Biography," 248.
21. James Shapiro, "Toward a New Biography of Shakespeare," *Shakespeare Survey* 58 (2005), 9.
22. Potter, "Having our Will," 2.
23. Park Honan, "To Change the Picture of Shakespeare Biography," *Critical Survey* 21.3 (2009), 106.
24. Franssen, *Shakespeare's Literary Lives*, 83. Adam G. Hooks notes that "the underlying motivation of Shakespearean biography is to understand the connections between the life and the works." *Selling Shakespeare: Biography, Bibliography, and the Book Trade* (Cambridge: Cambridge University Press, 2016), 3.
25. Chartier, "Everything and Nothing," 23–24.
26. Andrew Hadfield, "William Shakespeare, My New Best Friend?" *Journal of Early Modern Studies* 5 (2016), 55.
27. Lackey, *Truthful Fictions*, 1–2.
28. Jerome De Groot, *The Historical Novel* (London: Routledge, 2009), 1. Lackey is drawing on Linda Hutcheon's work in *A Poetics of Postmodernism* (1988), 13; Lackey, *Truthful Fictions*, 17.

29. Valentina Vannucci, "The Canon and Biofiction: The Subjects of History and New Literary Worlds," in *Biographical Fiction: A Reader*, ed. Michael Lackey (New York, NY: Bloomsbury, 2017), 380.

30. Douglas Lanier, "Shakespeare™: Myth and Biographical Fiction," in *The Cambridge Companion to Shakespeare and Popular Culture*, ed. Robert Shaughnessy (Cambridge: Cambridge University Press, 2007), 100.

31. Richard Holmes, "Biography: Inventing the Truth," in Batchelor, *The Art of Literary Biography*, 18–19.

32. Edmondson, "Writing and Re-Writing Shakespeare's Life," 67.

33. Brian Cummings, "Shakespeare, Biography, and Anti-Biography," Shakespeare's Birthday Lecture 2014, Folger Shakespeare Library, 3 April 2014.

34. Extensive fictional works explore the mystery of a Dark Lady, including Karen Sunde's play *Dark Lady* (1988), Michael Baldwin's novel *Dark Lady* (1998), Meredith Whitford's *Shakespeare's Will* (2010), Alexa Schnee's *Shakespeare's Lady* (2012), Victoria Lamb's *His Dark Lady* (2013), Grace Tiffany's *Paint: A Novel of Shakespeare's Dark Lady* (2013), Sally O'Reilly's *Dark Aemilia* (2014), Andrea Chapin's *The Tutor* (2015), and Mary Sharratt's *The Dark Lady's Mask* (2016). Critical works have also sought the identity of a Dark Lady behind the Sonnets. Aubrey Burl, in *Shakespeare's Mistress* (2012), contends that it was Aline Florio, the Italian wife of John Florio. Duncan Salkeld's *Shakespeare Among the Courtesans: Prostitution, Literature and Drama 1500–1650* (2012) identifies her as Lucy Negro, a prostitute in Clerkenwell. Simon Andrew Stirling even argues that Jane Davenant, mother of William Davenant, was the Dark Lady. *Shakespeare's Bastard: The Life of Sir William Davenant* (Stroud, Gloucestershire: The History Press, 2016), 235. A board game called Black Sonata challenges players to identify Shakespeare's Dark Lady.

35. Stuart Sillars, *Shakespeare and the Victorians* (Oxford: Oxford University Press, 2013), 133.

36. Franssen, *Shakespeare's Literary Lives*, 77.

37. Ibid., 103.

38. www.karenharperauthor.com/mistress_shakespeare.html

39. www.goodreads.com/book/show/3864007-mistress-shakespeare

40. Lois Potter points out that in many of these biographical novels, "fact is carefully distinguished from invention in the notes, though readers can skip them if they prefer fiction." "Biography vs. Novel," in *Shakespeare in our Time*, 259.

41. Thiessen, *Shakespeare's Will*, 74. In Thiessen's version of the will, the "second best bed" line is not printed as an interlineation, but instead as a line of its own, in all capital letters. Even though Thiessen includes the factual content of the will, he distorts it in his presentation on the page.

42. Christopher Rush, *Will: A Novel* (Woodstock, NY: Overlook Press, 2007), iv. In his acknowledgments, Rush also cites most of the major Shakespeare biographers: Schoenbaum, Wells, Levi, Ackroyd, Honan, Greenblatt, and Bate.

43. Monica Latham, "'Serv[ing] under two masters': Virginia Woolf's Afterlives in Contemporary Biofictions," *a/b: Auto/Biography Studies* 27.2 (2012), 373.

44. De Groot, *The Historical Novel*, 113.

45. Winfield, *My Name is Will*, 287.
46. Nye, *Mrs. Shakespeare*, 215–216.
47. http://historical-fiction.com/review-the-secret-confessions-of-anne-shake speare/
48. Franssen, *Shakespeare's Literary Lives*, 5.
49. Potter, "Biography vs. Novel," 259.
50. Paula R. Backscheider, *Reflections on Biography* (Oxford: Oxford University Press, 1999), 128.

4 "FIT TO MARRY"

1. Keener, *Biography and the Postmodern Historical Novel*, 172–173.
2. Nicholas Rowe, *Some Account of the Life, etc. of Mr. William Shakespear, in The Works of Mr. William Shakespear*, ed. Nicholas Rowe, 6 vols. (London: Jacob Tonson, 1709), 1:ii.
3. Franssen, *Shakespeare's Literary Lives*, 77.
4. Peter Holland, "Dramatizing the Dramatist," *Shakespeare Survey* 58 (2005), 139.
5. Franssen, *Shakespeare's Literary Lives*, 38, 42–43.
6. Charles A. Somerset, *Shakespeare's Early Days: A Drama in Two Acts* (London: T. H. Lacy, 1829), 48. See Holland, "Dramatizing the Dramatist," 142, for plays similar to Somerset's. Robert Folkstone Williams (1810–1870) was one of many who took on the topic of Shakespeare's youth, in his 3-volume novel, *Shakespeare and his Friends or, "The golden age" of Merry England* (1838), translated into German in 1839, followed with another 3-volume study, *The Youth of Shakespeare* (1839).
7. Holland, "Dramatizing the Dramatist," 143–144.
8. Schoenbaum, *Shakespeare's Lives*, 240. Before he died in 1812, Malone asked James Boswell to complete his edition, which appeared in 1821, with a partial biography of Shakespeare (only up to his appearance in London) comprising the second volume.
9. Orlin, "Shakespeare's Marriage," 39.
10. James Shapiro, *Contested Will: Who Wrote Shakespeare?* (New York, NY: Simon and Schuster, 2010), 265.
11. Schabert, "Fictional Biography," 12.
12. Edmond Malone, *Supplement to the Edition of Shakspeare's Plays Published in 1778 by Samuel Johnson and George Steevens*, 2 vols. (London, 1780), 1:653–657. Lena Cowen Orlin notes that "Oldys's notes descended to George Steevens, from Steevens to Edmond Malone, and as quoted by Malone in 1790, entered the critical mainstream." "Shakespeare's Marriage," 39.
13. Malone, *Supplement to the Edition of Shakspeare's Plays*, 1:654. Margreta de Grazia notes that Malone was the first to "[cast] Shakespeare as the subject of his own writing, reflecting on his own psychological condition as an engaged poet who observed himself." *Shakespeare Verbatim: The Reproduction of Authenticity and the 1790 Apparatus* (Oxford: Clarendon, 1991), 159.
14. *The Plays and Poems of William Shakespeare*, ed. Edmond Malone (London: F.C. and J. Rivington, 1821), 2:112.
15. Malone, *Supplement to the Edition of Shakspeare's Plays*, 1:655–656.

16.   Peter Martin, *Edmond Malone, Shakespearean Scholar: A Literary Biography* (Cambridge: Cambridge University Press, 1993), 50.

17.   Malone, *Supplement*, 1: 657.

18.   Boswell's note is in the third Variorum edition. *The Plays and Poems of William Shakespeare, with the Corrections and Illustrations of Various Commentators: Comprehending A Life of the Poet, and An Enlarged History of the Stage, by the Late Edmond Malone* (London, 1821), 20:309.

19.   *The Plays and Poems of William Shakespeare*, 2:616.

20.   Orlin, "Shakespeare's Marriage," 40.

21.   Michael Dobson, "Dwarf-Basher." Rev. of *Edmond Malone, Shakespearean Scholar: A Literary Biography*, by Peter Martin. *London Review of Books* 17.11 (1995): 12–13.

22.   James Shapiro, "Unravelling Shakespeare's Life," in *On Life-Writing*, ed. Zachary Leader (Oxford: Oxford University Press, 2015), 13.

23.   Alexander Dyce, "Memoir of Shakespeare," in *The Poems of Shakespeare* (London: W. Pickering, 1832), xi.

24.   Stuart Sillars, *Shakespeare and the Victorians* (Oxford: Oxford University Press, 2013), 144.

25.   Charles Knight, *William Shakspere; a Biography* (London: William Clowes and Sons, 1843), 268–270.

26.   Sillars, *Shakespeare and the Victorians*, 142.

27.   Thomas, *Shakespeare's Shrine*, 157; Andrew Murphy, *Shakespeare in Print* (Cambridge: Cambridge University Press, 2003), 181.

28.   Richard Grant White, *Memoirs of the Life of William Shakespeare* (Boston: Little, Brown and Company, 1865), 53.

29.   Gary Taylor, *Reinventing Shakespeare: A Cultural History from the Restoration to the Present* (Oxford: Oxford University Press, 1991), 184; Thomas, *Shakespeare's Shrine*, 157.

30.   See Potter, "Having our Will," 8.

31.   Anna Jameson, *Shakespeare's Heroines: Characteristics of Women, Moral, Poetical and Historical* (London: Saunders and Otley, 1832), 1:iii.

32.   "Shakespeare as the Girl's Friend," in *Shakespeariana* 4 (1887), 355–356; originally published in *The Girl's Own Paper* (London, June 1887).

33.   Mary Cowden Clarke, ed., *Shakespeare's Works, Edited, with a Scrupulous Revision of the Text* (New York, NY, and London, 1860), ix–x.

34.   Mary Cowden Clarke, "A Biographical Sketch of William Shakespeare," in *The Complete Works of William Shakespeare, from the Text of Johnson, Steevens, and Reed* (Edinburgh, 1864), lv.

35.   Severn's work was listed as one of the 10,000 circulating books in the *Catalogue of Books Belonging to the Library of the British Factory, St. Petersburg* (Leipzig: B. Tauchnitz, 1869), and also in the *Catalogue of the Liverpool Free Public Library* (Liverpool: George McCorquodale, 1855).

36.   Watson, "Shakespeare on the Tourist Trail," 211.

37.   Emma Severn, *Anne Hathaway, or Shakespeare in Love*, 3 vols. (London: R. Bentley, 1845), 1:8, 1:7, 1:242, 1:36, 2:135.

38.   Cowden Clarke, ed., *Shakespeare's Works*, vi.

39.   Stowe, *Sunny Memories of Foreign Lands*, 1:203, 212.

40. Schoenbaum, *Shakespeare's Lives*, 407.

41. Sillars, *Shakespeare and the Victorians*, 143.

42. Schabert, "Fictional Biography," 1–16.

43. Schoenbaum, *Shakespeare's Lives*, 397, 404.

44. Halliwell-Phillipps, *Outlines of the Life of Shakespeare*, vii.

45. Schoenbaum, *Shakespeare's Lives*, 415.

46. Mary Elizabeth Braddon, *Asphodel* (London, 1881), 41–42.

47. Thomas, *Shakespeare's Shrine*, 158.

48. Walter, *Shakespeare's True Life*, 107.

49. Emma Marshall, *Shakespeare and his Birthplace* (London: E. Nister; New York, NY: E. P. Dutton, 1890), 17.

50. Marshall, *Shakespeare and his Birthplace*, 19–20.

51. *Shakespeariana* 3 (1886), 375, 434.

52. Daniel Wilson, "Anne Hathaway: A Dialogue," *Canadian Monthly and National Review* 1 (1872), 19–26.

53. *The Chautauquan* 44 (1906), 121.

54. Sidney Lee, "Shakespeare, William (1564–1616)," in *The Dictionary of National Biography*, ed. Sidney Lee, vol. 17 (London: Smith, Elder, & Co., 1897), 1290.

55. Tobias Döring and Ewan Fernie, "Introduction: Something Rich and Strange," in *Thomas Mann and Shakespeare: Something Rich and Strange* (London: Bloomsbury, 2015), 15.

56. Georg Brandes, *William Shakespeare: A Critical Study* (London: Heinemann, 1898), 1:15.

57. Brandes, *William Shakespeare*, 1:42–43.

58. Niels Bugge Hansen, "Observations on Georg Brandes's Contribution to the Study of Shakespeare," in *Shakespeare and Scandinavia: A Collection of Nordic Studies*, ed. Gunnar Sorelius (Newark, NJ: University of Delaware Press, 2002), 165.

59. Döring and Fernie, "Introduction: Something Rich and Strange," 15.

60. Charlotte Carmichael Stopes, *Shakespeare's Family: Being a Record of the Ancestors and Descendants of William Shakespeare* (London: Elliot Stock, 1901), v, 62.

61. In her later work *Shakespeare's Warwickshire Contemporaries* (Stratford-upon-Avon: Shakespeare Head Press, 1907), Stopes does speculate about Anne: "Anne Hathaway was of an extremely delicate constitution. I always imagine she looked young for her years, and Shakespeare old for his; that she was fair and clinging and dependent; he, bold and masterful; and so the difference in age passed unnoticed" (182).

62. Daniel Gallimore, "Tsubouchi Shoyo and the Myth of Shakespeare Translation in Modern Japan," in *Translating Others*, ed. Theo Hermans (New York, NY: Routledge, 2012), 485.

63. Edward Dowden, *Introduction to Shakespeare* (New York, NY: Charles Scribner's Sons, 1901), 9–10.

64. Joseph William Gray, *Shakespeare's Marriage, His Departure from Stratford and other Incidents in His Life* (London: Chapman and Hall, 1905), v. Appleton Morgan, President of the Shakespeare Society of New York, also took on the topic of Shakespeare's marriage in *Mrs. Shakespeare's Second Marriage* (New York, NY: The Shakespeare Society of New York, 1925).

65. Gray, *Shakespeare's Marriage*, 4, 5, 8, 138, 139.

66. Schoenbaum, *Shakespeare's Lives*, 475.

67. Park Honan, *Shakespeare: A Life* (Oxford: Oxford University Press, 1998), 83.

68. Hackett, *Shakespeare and Elizabeth*, 10.

69. Roy Spann Sensabaugh, *The Favor of the Queen: A Play in Four Acts* (Birmingham, AL: n.p., 1929), 110, 111.

70. "The Favor of the Queen," *The New York Times* 12 May 1903; "News and Notes," *The American Printer* (1903), 285.

71. Clyde C. Westover, *The Romance of Gentle Will: A Hitherto Unpublished Chapter in the Story of the Love of the Immortal Bard* (New York, NY: Neale Publishing, 1905), 20.

72. William T. Saward, *William Shakespeare* (London: Elkin Mathews, 1907), 10. Michael Dobson, "Shakespeare as a Literary Character," *The Oxford Companion to Shakespeare*, ed. Stanley Wells and Erin Sullivan (Oxford: Oxford University Press, 2015), 494.

73. Saward, *William Shakespeare*, 29, 35–38, 64, 77, 86, 85.

74. Hackett, *Shakespeare and Elizabeth*, 18.

75. Saward, *William Shakespeare*, 100, 118, 119, 120.

76. See Katherine West Scheil, *She Hath Been Reading: Women and Shakespeare Clubs in America* (Ithaca, NY: Cornell University Press, 2012).

77. Minutes from 15 May 1925. https://uiowa.edu/shakespeareiniowa/article/shakespeare-and-women.

78. Peck also illustrated Sterling's *A Lady of King Arthur's Court; being a Romance of the Holy Grail* (1907).

79. Franssen, *Shakespeare's Literary Lives*, 117.

80. Hackett, *Shakespeare and Elizabeth*, 192–194.

81. Marianne Moore, *The Dial* (1 December 1909), 466.

82. Anna Benneson McMahan, *Shakespeare's Love Story, 1580–1609* (Chicago, IL: A. C. McClurg, 1909), 14, 19, 21, 28, 33, 39, 46, 55, 61, 62.

83. Ibid., 75, 78, 83, 84.

84. Anna Morgan and Alice Ward Bailey, *The Great Experiment: A Shakespearean Fantasy* (Chicago, IL: R. F. Seymour, 1909), 6, 22.

85. Mabel M. Moran, *The Shakespeare Garden Club: A Fantasy* (New York, 1919). See Nicola J. Watson's discussion of Moran's play in connection to Shakespeare gardens, in "Gardening with Shakespeare," 320.

86. Moran, *The Shakespeare Garden Club*, 9.

87. "Society Acts for the Shell-Shocked," *The New York Times* 13 March 1920.

88. Leigh Mitchell Hodges, *The Bard at Home* (n.p., 1916).

89. Ton Hoenselaars points out that *The Man Shakespeare and His Tragic Life-Story* appeared in the 1890s as newspaper articles. "Frank Harris, Bardolatry and Wagnerism," in *Metamorphosing Shakespeare: Mutual Illuminations of the Arts*, ed. Patricia Kennan and Mariangela Tempera (Bologna: Clueb, 2004), 173.

90. Frank Harris, *The Man Shakespeare and His Tragic Life-Story* (New York: Mitchell Kennerley, 1909), 391.

91.   Frank Harris, *The Women of Shakespeare* (London: Methuen, 1911), x–xi, 22, 266.
92.   Ibid., xiii.
93.   Ibid., xiii.
94.   Tobias Döring, "A Note on Mann's Shakespeare," in *Thomas Mann and Shakespeare: Something Rich and Strange*, 16.
95.   Harris, *The Man Shakespeare*, 358–359, 368.
96.   Hubert Osborne, *The Good Men Do: An Indecorous Epilogue*, in *Plays of the 47 Workshop* (New York, NY: Brentanos, 1918), 52–53, 55.
97.   Information on Osborne is taken from www.canadianshakespeares.ca.
98.   The typescript is cited at www.canadianshakespeares.ca/a_goodmen.cfm.
99.   Cary DiPietro, *Shakespeare and Modernism* (Cambridge: Cambridge University Press, 2006), 81.
100.   James Joyce, *Ulysses*, ed. Hans Walter Gabler (New York, NY: Vintage Books, 1986), 166, 156–157.
101.   Ibid., 159.
102.   Brandes is quoted in Don Gifford, *Ulysses Annotated: Notes for James Joyce's* Ulysses (Berkeley, CA: University of California Press, 1988), 216.
103.   Charles Edward Lawrence, *The Hour of Prospero* (London: Gowans and Gray, 1927), 7, 9, 12, 15, 28.
104.   Robert L. Calder, *Beware the British Serpent: The Role of Writers in British Propaganda in the United States, 1939–1945* (Montreal: McGill-Queens Press, 2004), 230.
105.   John Brophy, *Gentleman of Stratford* (New York: Harper, 1939), 55–56.
106.   Franssen, *Shakespeare's Literary Lives*, 136.
107.   E. H. Butler, "Shakespeare Through the Imaginative Writers," *The English Journal* 30.9 (1941), 749–753. Hoenselaars, "Frank Harris, Bardolatry and Wagnerism," 167.
108.   Schoenbaum, *Shakespeare's Lives*, 499.
109.   Ivor Brown, *The Women in Shakespeare's Life* (London: The Bodley Head, 1968), 53.
110.   Edgar I. Fripp, *Shakespeare, Man and Artist* (London 1938), 1:186.
111.   Schoenbaum, *Shakespeare's Lives*, 502.
112.   Thomas C. Kemp, *Birmingham Repertory Theatre: The Playhouse and the Man* (Birmingham: Cornish Brothers, 1948), 91.
113.   *The Poetry Review* 29 (London: The Poetry Society, 1938), 425.
114.   Grace Carlton, *The Wooing of Anne Hathaway* (London: The Mitre Press, 1938), 12, 44, 83.
115.   Ibid., 119–120, 123.
116.   *The Countrywoman* 5.56 (October 1938), 14.
117.   Thomas Lennon, *The Truth About Ann* (New York, NY: John Day, 1942), title page.
118.   Ibid., vii.
119.   Ibid., ix, 130.
120.   *The Billboard* (15 June 1946), 53.

5 DARK LADIES AND FAITHFUL WIVES

1. Andrew Hadfield, "William Shakespeare, My New Best Friend?" *Journal of Early Modern Studies* 5 (2016), 56; W. B. Worthen, "Jan Kott, Shakespeare our Contemporary," *Modern Theatre* 25.2 (2010), 91.

2. Valentina Vannucci, "The Canon and Biofiction: The Subjects of History and New Literary Worlds," in *Biographical Fiction: A Reader*, ed. Michael Lackey (New York, NY: Bloomsbury, 2017), 388.

3. Brian Cummings, "Last Words: The Biographemes of Shakespeare," *Shakespeare Quarterly* 65.4 (2014), 486.

4. Schoenbaum, *Documentary Life*, 75–76.

5. Lackey, *Truthful Fictions*, 43–44.

6. De Groot, *The Historical Novel*, 1.

7. Lackey, *Truthful Fictions*, 1–2.

8. The form of biofiction, which Lackey defines as "literature that names its protagonist after an actual biographical figure," has become "a dominant literary form" since the 1980s. Michael Lackey, "Locating and Defining the Bio in Biofiction," *a/b: Auto/Biography Studies* 31.1 (2016), 3, 7; "The Futures of Biofiction Studies," *a/b: Auto/Biography Studies* 32.2 (2017), 343–344.

9. Douglas Lanier, *Shakespeare and Modern Popular Culture* (Oxford: Oxford University Press, 2002), 141–142.

10. Estimates on the declining marriage rate vary, but one typical estimate is that 82 percent of women were married in 1950, compared to 62 percent in 2000. Jeremy Greenwood and Nezih Guner, "Marriage and Divorce since World War II: Analyzing the Role of Technological Progress on the Formation of Households," *NBER Macroeconomics Annual* 2008 (23), 231.

11. As Paula R. Backscheider has observed, "reviewers now castigate biographers for writing as if in men's lives it is still acceptable to cast others completely in shadows in order to reinforce the subject's individualism." *Reflections on Biography*, 157.

12. Anthony Burgess, *Nothing Like the Sun: A Story of Shakespeare's Love Life* (New York, NY: W.W. Norton, 1964), 42–43, 30, 191, 31.

13. Anthony Burgess, "Genesis and Headache," in *Afterwords*, ed. Thomas McCormack (New York, NY: Harper and Row, 1969), 36.

14. Peter Buitenhuis, "A Lusty Man was Will," *The New York Times* 13 September 1964. Cary DiPietro traces the longer history of associating Shakespeare's sex life with his writing. See *Shakespeare and Modernism*, especially 43–82.

15. Burgess of course was not the first writer to fantasize about a mysterious Dark Lady. Frank Harris's 1910 unperformed play *Shakespeare and his Love* involves Shakespeare in a love triangle with Mary Fitton (the supposed Dark Lady) and William Herbert. George Bernard Shaw's play *The Dark Lady of the Sonnets* (1910; 1914) also involves Fitton.

16. Paul Franssen, "The Bard, The Bible, and the Desert Island," in *The Author as Character: Representing Historical Writers in Western Literature*, ed. Paul Franssen and A. J. Hoenselaars (London: Associated University Presses, 1999), 107; Harold Bloom, *The Western Canon: The Books and School of the Ages* (New York: Harcourt, Brace, and Company, 1994), 386.

17. Aileen Pippett, "The Sonneteer Was Not All Talk," *The Saturday Review* (17 October 1964), 38.

18. Anthony Burgess, *Shakespeare* (London: Jonathan Cape, 1970), 67, 56, 57.

19. Ibid., 57–58, 60.

20. Edmondson, "Writing and Re-Writing Shakespeare's Life," 59.

21. Burgess, *Shakespeare*, 58.

22. Phyllis Rackin, *Shakespeare and Women* (Oxford: Oxford University Press, 2005), 138.

23. Linda Wagner-Martin, *Telling Women's Lives: The New Biography* (New Brunswick, NJ: Rutgers University Press, 1994), 4.

24. Tim Kelly, *Second Best Bed: A Romantic Speculation in One Act for Eight Girls* (New York, NY, 1970), 15.

25. Schoenbaum, *Shakespeare's Lives*, 550.

26. Ivor Brown, *How Shakespeare Spent the Day* (New York, NY; Hill and Wang, 1963), 7, 10.

27. Ivor Brown, *The Women in Shakespeare's Life* (London: The Bodley Head, 1968), 10–11.

28. Brown, *The Women in Shakespeare's Life*, 77. Earlier in his career, Brown authored a play entitled *William's Other Anne* (1937), where he advanced his argument that Anne Whateley was the Dark Lady of the Sonnets and was Shakespeare's real love. Brown's play was broadcast as late as 1953 on the BBC, with Irene Worth as Anne and John Gregson as Shakespeare.

29. A. L. Rowse, *Shakespeare the Man* (New York, NY: St. Martin's Press, 1973; 1988), 31–32.

30. Robert McG. Thomas, Jr., "A. L. Rowse, Masterly Shakespeare Scholar, Dies at 93," *The New York Times* 6 October 1997.

31. Lanier, "Shakespeare™: Myth and Biographical Fiction," 102.

32. William Gibson, *A Cry of Players: A Play* (New York: Dramatists Play Service, 1969), 7, 15.

33. John Simon, "A Spear Reshaken," *New York Magazine* (2 December 1968), 55.

34. Eric Malpass, *Sweet Will* (London: Macmillan, 1973), 85, 87, 250.

35. Laura Annawyn Shamas, *The Other Shakespeare* (Woodstock, IL: Dramatic Publishing, 1981), 36, 23.

36. Rackin, *Shakespeare and Women*, 1.

37. Valerie Traub, "Introduction: Feminist Shakespeare Studies," in *The Oxford Handbook of Shakespeare and Embodiment: Gender, Sexuality, and Race*, ed. Valerie Traub (Oxford: Oxford University Press, 2016), 8.

38. Backscheider, *Reflections on Biography*, 128.

39. See Sofía Muñoz Valdivieso, "Postmodern Recreations of the Renaissance: Robert Nye's fictional biographies of William Shakespeare," *SEDERI* 15 (2005), 43.

40. Robert Nye, *Mrs. Shakespeare: The Complete Works* (New York: Arcade, 1993), 68, 149, 184, 186, 208.

41. Jeremy Paxman, "Stop Whingeing about Shakespeare in Love," *The Telegraph* 23 January 1999.

42. Marc Norman and Tom Stoppard, *Shakespeare in Love: A Screenplay* (New York, NY: Hyperion, 1998), 11–12, 112, 116. It has often been pointed out that the 1941

comic play *No Bed for Bacon*, by Caryl Brahms and S. J. Simon, is a precursor to Norman and Stoppard's play, with its focus on a cross-dressing woman in the theatre.

43. Andrew Hadfield, "William Shakespeare, My New Best Friend?" *Journal of Early Modern Studies* 5 (2016), 61.

44. Charles Spencer, "Shakespeare in Love, review," *The Telegraph* 23 July 2014.

45. Lee Hall, *Shakespeare in Love*, based on the screenplay by Marc Norman and Tom Stoppard (London: Faber and Faber, 2014), 3–4, 13, 73, 77, 97.

46. Grace Tiffany, *Will: A Novel* (New York: Turnaround, 2005), 23, 47 119, 164.

47. Grace Tiffany, *Will: A Novel*, 379, 237, 360, 403.

48. www.goodreads.com/book/show/1111242.Will

49. http://bardfilm.blogspot.com/2014/03/book-note-grace-tiffanys-will-novel.html

50. Jude Morgan, *The Secret Life of William Shakespeare* (London: Headline, 2012), 114, 111, 318, 357, 383, 388, 387, 390. Jude Morgan is the pseudonym for Peterborough, UK writer Tim Wilson, who specializes in historical romances and also writes under the name Hannah March.

51. Gary Taylor, "The Secret Life of William Shakespeare," by Jude Morgan, *The Washington Post* 3 April 2014.

52. Gamaliel Bradford, *Biography and the Human Heart* (Boston, MA: Houghton Mifflin, 1932), 3.

53. Barbara Everett, "Read him, therefore," *Times Literary Supplement* 17 August 2007.

54. Anne Barton, "The One and Only," *The New York Review of Books* 11 May 2006. Both Barton and Everett do not account for biographies by Greer, Bate, Weis, Holderness, and Potter.

55. Maltby, *Shakespeare as a Challenge for Literary Biography*, 150.

56. Katherine Duncan-Jones, *Ungentle Shakespeare: Scenes from his Life* (London: Arden, 2001), xi.

57. Hadfield, "William Shakespeare, My New Best Friend?" 56.

58. Peter Ackryod, *Shakespeare: The Biography* (London: Anchor Books, 2005), 261. Maltby, *Shakespeare as a Challenge for Literary Biography*, 162.

59. Stanley Wells, *Shakespeare for All Time* (Oxford: Oxford University Press, 2003), 27, 44.

60. Stanley Wells, *Shakespeare, Sex, and Love* (Oxford: Oxford University Press, 2012), 85.

61. Greer, *Shakespeare's Wife*, 4, 9.

62. Holderness, *Nine Lives of William Shakespeare*, 19, 17.

63. Keith Gregor, *Shakespeare in the Spanish Theatre: 1772 to the Present* (London: Continuum, 2010), 162.

64. Clara Calvo, "Shakespeare and Spain in 1916: Shakespearean Biography and Spanish Neutrality in the Great War," in *Shakespeare and Spain*, ed. Jose Manuel Gonzalez and Holger Michael Klein (Lewiston, NY: Edwin Mellen Press, 2002), 67–68.

65. Laura Shapiro, "Greer Tames the Shrew," *Slate* 31 March 2008; Lois Potter, review in *Shakespeare Quarterly*, 56 (2005), 374; Colin MacCabe, "The Bard as a Chat-Show Celeb," *The Independent* 5 November 2004. Of course, *Will in the*

World has received its fair share of critiques, most notably Alastair Fowler's review in the *Times Literary Supplement*, 20 February 2005.

66. In *Shakespeare's Wife*, Germaine Greer takes Greenblatt to task for this representation.

67. Keener, *Biography and the Postmodern Novel*, 172–173.

68. Greenblatt, *Will in the World*, 18, 12.

69. Gary Taylor, "Stephen, Will and Gary Too," *The Guardian*, 9 October 2004.

70. Vannucci, "The Canon and Biofiction," 384.

71. Bernard DeVoto, "The Skeptical Biographer," *Harper's Magazine* (January 1933), 181–192.

72. Greenblatt, *Will in the World*, 140, 12, 124, 123, 120, 129, 130, 140, 143.

73. Ibid., 129, 118.

74. Ibid., 387, 361, 145, 147.

75. Hadfield, "William Shakespeare, My New Best Friend?" 55.

76. Cummings, "Last Words: The Biographemes of Shakespeare," 488.

77. Taylor, "Stephen, Will and Gary Too."

78. Keener, *Biography and the Postmodern Novel*, 172–173.

79. Greenblatt, *Will in the World*, 15–16.

80. M. G. Aune, "Crossing the Border: Shakespeare Biography, Academic Celebrity, and the Reception of *Will in the World*." *Borrowers and Lenders* 2.2 (Fall/Winter 2006). Aune's article also provides extensive details of the marketing, sales, and critical reception of Greenblatt's book. On a number of occasions, Greenblatt has remarked that he intended to reach the general public as well as an academic audience. See for example his interview with Sara F. Gold in *Publishers Weekly*, 19 July 2004.

81. Michiko Kakutani, "Shakespeare Attracts a New Pursuer," *New York Times* 1 October 2004.

82. John Simon, "Bardolatry Made Easy." *New Criterion* April 2005.

83. Taylor, "Stephen, Will and Gary Too."

84. Taylor, "Stephen, Will and Gary Too." Oprah Winfrey reference is from Colin MacCabe's review, *The Independent*, 5 November 2004. John Sutherland, *The Guardian* 16 February 2005.

85. Judy Giles, *Parlour and Suburb: Domestic Identities, Class, Femininity, and Modernity* (Oxford: Oxford University Press, 2004), 3, 13.

86. Backscheider, *Reflections on Biography*, 153.

87. The reviews quoted on the dust jacket are by Robert Pinsky, Tina Packer, Natalie Zemon Davis, and Simon Russell Beale.

88. See also David Bevington's discussion of biographers and the Shakespeare marriage in *Shakespeare and Biography*, 35–39 and 146–150.

89. Park Honan, *Shakespeare: A Life* (Oxford: Oxford University Press, 1999), ix, xi, xii.

90. Ibid., 74, 80–82.

91. Ibid., 87, 91.

92. Duncan-Jones, *Ungentle Shakespeare*, x, 17.

93. Ibid., 17–18.

94. Maltby, *Shakespeare as a Challenge for Literary Biography*, 227–228.

95. Duncan-Jones, *Ungentle Shakespeare*, 17–19.

96. Ackroyd, *Shakespeare: The Biography*, 88.

97. Ibid., 91.

98. Ibid., 88.

99. René Weis, *Shakespeare Revealed: A Biography* (London: John Murray, 2007), 3, 4–5.

100. Ibid., 51–52.

101. Ibid., 57, 60, 67.

102. Bate, *Soul of the Age*, xviii.

103. Ibid., 152.

104. Ibid., 152–153.

105. Ibid., 153, 161.

106. Edmondson, "Writing and Re-Writing Shakespeare's Life," 59, 62.

107. Dorrit Cohn, "Signposts of Fictionality: A Narratological Perspective." *Poetics Today* 11, no. 4 (1990), 785.

108. Greer, *Shakespeare's Wife*, 4, 162, 221, 344–346.

109. Peter Conrad, "Dr. Greer on the Warpath," *The Observer*, 2 September 2007. Other reviews have praised Greer's work; René Weis says "she dares to think the unthinkable and sometimes it works well" and the book "does a huge favour to its subject as wife and woman." *The Independent* 7 September 2007. Jonathan Bate commends the book as "a marvelous imagining of the life of Shakespeare's wife and a devastating exposure of the misogyny of the male biographers who have disparaged her." *The Telegraph* 7 August 2007. Duncan Wu similarly applauds Greer's work as "a corrective to the fantasies of her predecessors." Duncan Wu, "On Mrs. Shakespeare's Kitchen Table." *The Telegraph* 1 September 2007. Katie Roiphe criticizes Greer for romanticizing female independence but concludes that "Greer's speculations are, for the most part, surprisingly responsible." Katie Roiphe, "Reclaiming the Shrew." *The New York Times* 27 April 2008. Stanley Wells praises Greer's biography for opening up "new perspectives" and "offering alternative hypotheses to many of the all-too-easy assumptions about Shakespeare's wife and his relationship to her." Stanley Wells, "Mistress Shakespeare." *The New York Review of Books* 55.6 (17 April 2008).

110. Halliwell-Phillipps, *Outlines of the Life of Shakespeare* (London: 1881), v.

111. Holderness, *Nine Lives of William Shakespeare*, 21.

112. Mathilde Blind, "Anne Hathaway." *The Poetical Works of Mathilde Blind*, ed. Arthur Symons (London: T. F. Unwin, 1900), 439–440. The "shadowy figure" phrase is from Katie Roiphe, "Reclaiming the Shrew."

113. Holland, "Shakespeare and Biography," 252.

6 MILLENNIAL ANNE HATHAWAYS AND WOMEN AUDIENCES

1. Anna Jameson, *Shakespeare's Heroines: Characteristics of Women, Moral, Poetical, and Historical* (London: Saunders and Otley, 1832), 1:liii; Mary Cowden Clarke, "Shakespeare as the Girl's Friend," *Shakespeariana* 4 (1887), 355.

2. Many of these texts accord with Douglas Lanier's survey of biographical fiction, where Shakespeare is a "romantic hero" and Anne is a "surrogate for the reader" and a representative of "rural provinciality." "Shakespeare™: Myth and Biographical Fiction," 102.

3. Monica Latham, "'Serv[ing] under two masters': Virginia Woolf's Afterlives in Contemporary Biofictions," *a/b: Auto/Biography Studies* 27.2 (2012), 354.

4. See Fiona M. Collins and Judith Graham, "The Twentieth Century: Giving Everybody a History," in *Historical Fiction for Children: Capturing the Past*, ed. Fiona M. Collins and Judith Graham (London: David Fulton, 2001), 10–22, at 15. Pat Pinsent, "'Not for an Age but for all time': The Depiction of Shakespeare in a Selection of Children's Fiction," *New Review of Children's Literature and Librarianship* 10.2 (2004), 118.

5. Douglas Lanier notes that "typically children's narratives present Shakespeare as a substitute father or mentor for the young protagonist, who is often orphaned or alone and taken in by the bard and his stage compatriots." "Shakespeare™: Myth and Biographical Fiction," 105.

6. John Stephens, *Language and Ideology in Children's Fiction* (Harlow: Longman, 1992), 209. Trevor John remarks that "By supplying the details of time and place, a children's historical novel can take children back into the past and make it a living reality in their minds in a way few information or textbooks can or even attempt to do." "Children's Historical Fiction and a Sense of the Past," in *The Children's Bookroom: Reading and the Use of Books*, ed. Dorothy Atkinson (Stoke-on-Trent: Trentham Books, 1989), 101–102. Although Suzanne Rahn has argued that the historical novel "preserves the past, by bringing it to life through the imagination of a child" (16), these texts seem more interested in updating the past to reflect present concerns of adolescent readers. See "An Evolving Past: The Story of Historical Fiction and Nonfiction for Children," *The Lion and the Unicorn* 15.1 (1991), 1–26.

7. Laurie Lawlor, *The Two Loves of Will Shakespeare* (New York: Holiday House, 2006), 170, 240.

8. Ibid., 235, 240, 238.

9. Pinsent, "'Not for an Age but for all time," 117. According to Perry Nodelman, "children's literature exists as a way for adults to influence children for the children's good" and "is primarily a didactic literature." *The Hidden Adult: Defining Children's Literature* (Baltimore, MD: Johns Hopkins University Press, 2008), 157.

10. Carolyn Meyer, *Loving Will Shakespeare* (Orlando: Harcourt, 2006), 83, 183, 216.

11. Ibid., 218, 220.

12. Ibid., 220, 222, 239–240, 217.

13. Ibid., 150, 254, 262.

14. Martha Tuck Rozett, *Constructing a World: Shakespeare's England and the New Historical Fiction* (Albany, NY: State University of New York Press, 2003), 107.

15. Pamela Berkman, *Her Infinite Variety: Stories of Shakespeare and the Women He Loved* (New York, NY: Simon and Schuster, 2001), 22, 23, 30, 32, 34.

16. http://marymackey.com/shakespeare-in-historical-fiction/

17. www.goodreads.com/book/show/1675779.Her_Infinite_Variety
18. www.librarything.com/work/259326/reviews/28311936
19. www.karenharperauthor.com/index.html
20. Karen Harper, *Mistress Shakespeare* (New York: Penguin, 2009), 60, 62.
21. Ibid., 81, 112, 279.
22. Ibid., 158, 191, 248.
23. www.book-club-queen.com/mistress-shakespeare.html
24. http://freshfiction.com/review.php?id=22755
25. www.womansday.com/life/entertainment/mistress-shakespeare-by-karen-harper #slide-4
26. www.book-club-queen.com/mistress-shakespeare.html
27. www.arlissryan.com/books/reviews-of-the-secret-confessions-of-anne-shakespeare/
28. Arliss Ryan, *The Secret Confessions of Anne Shakespeare* (New York: Penguin, 2010), 8.
29. Ibid., 9, 32, 33.
30. Ibid., 36–39.
31. Maya Rodale, *Dangerous Books for Girls: The Bad Reputation of Romance Novels Explained* (New York, NY: Maya Rodale, 2015), 110.
32. Erica Jong, *Serenissima* (New York, NY: Dell, 1987), 295–296, 381. "Shakespeare as lover" is one of Douglas Lanier's "interlocking mythic narratives" for Shakespeare biography. *Shakespeare and Modern Popular Culture*, 150. As Graham Holderness has pointed out, "the erotic adventures of Shakespeare 'in love' [is] something we literally know nothing whatsoever about." *Nine Lives of William Shakespeare*, 96. See especially Holderness's chapter "Shakespeare in Love: 'Husband I come'" (96–105).
33. Ryan, *Secret Confessions*, 48–49.
34. Ibid., 53–54, 56, 64.
35. Ibid., 104, 107, 169–171.
36. Ibid., 361, 364, 206.
37. Ibid., 228, 232, 313, 464.
38. www.featheredquill.com/reviews/biographies/ryan.shtml
39. www.arlissryan.com/books/reviews-of-the-secret-confessions-of-anne-shakespeare/. This phrase is from Jeane Westin, author of *The Virgin's Daughters*.
40. http://historical-fiction.com/?tag=arliss-ryan
41. http://susancoventry.blogspot.com/2011/05/escape-to-past-with-secret-confessions .html
42. http://bippityboppitybook.blogspot.com/2010/11/review-secret-confessions-of-anne.html
43. http://booknaround.blogspot.com/search?q=arliss+ryan
44. Lisa Nakamura, "'Words with Friends': Socially Networked Reading on Goodreads." *PMLA* 128.1 (2013), 239–242.
45. Daniel Allington, "'Power to the reader' or 'degradation of literary taste'? Professional Critics and Amazon customers as reviewers of *The Inheritance of Loss*," *Language and Literature* 25.3 (2016), 258.
46. www.goodreads.com/book/show/3864007-mistress-shakespeare
47. www. thelifephotographic.com/?Mistress-Shakespeare–A-Novel.pdf

48. www.goodreads.com/book/show/7098379-the-secret-confessions-of-anne-shakespeare
49. www.goodreads.com/book/show/3864007-mistress-shakespeare
50. See Ann Steiner, "Private Criticism in the Public Sphere: Personal Writing on Literature in Readers' Reviews on Amazon," *Particip@tions* 5.2 (2008).
51. Jill L. Levenson, "Shakespeare in Drama since 1990: Vanishing Act," *Shakespeare Survey* 58 (2005), 149.
52. Ann Wilson, "Waves and Wills: Vern Thiessen's *Shakespeare's Will*." *Borrowers and Lenders* 3 (Fall/Winter 2007). Wilson argues that Thiessen's play "speaks to contemporary Canada and the shifts in understanding around marriage," and that "another indication of *Shakespeare's Will*'s Canadianness is Thiessen's refusal to create a portrait of the Bard and so, his refusal to give Shakespeare 'center stage,'" though I think this is a bit narrow, given the similar concerns of other plays about domestic Shakespeare. Other playwrights have employed this same dramatic structure. Roy Chatfield's 2014 play *The Other Shakespeare* is based on the same premise – a monologue for Anne, allowing her to say what she really thinks. Appropriately, Chatfield's play was performed at Anne Hathaway's Cottage. Another play that same year, Ian Wild's *Mrs. Shakespeare* (2014), is a one-woman show that imagines Shakespeare reincarnated as a modern woman in a psychiatric ward.
53. Vern Thiessen, *Shakespeare's Will* (Toronto: Playwrights Canada Press, 2005), 12, 35.
54. Ibid., 43, 72.
55. Avril Rowlands, *Mrs. Shakespeare … The Poet's Wife* (Malvern, PA: J. Garnet Miller, 2005), 7, 11, 18.
56. Ibid., 10, 14, 20–21.
57. Ibid., 16–17, 50, 44, 58.
58. Amy Freed, *The Beard of Avon* (New York: Samuel French, 2004), 50, 52, 56, 62, 15.
59. Valerie Traub, "Introduction: Feminist Shakespeare Studies," in *The Oxford Handbook of Shakespeare and Embodiment*, 28–29.
60. Readers are encouraged to consult the Appendix to this book for additional texts.

CONCLUSION

1. Keener, *Biography and the Postmodern Historical Novel*, 1–2.
2. https://buxtonfestivalblog.wordpress.com/2016/07/19/guest-blog-elin-pritchard-on-hathaway/
3. Briar Kit Esme, *Hathaway: Eight Arias for a Bardic Life* (Houghton and Farnham, 2016). The Kindle version of Esme's work, from which I quote, is unpaginated.
4. http://ew.com/tv/2017/01/30/tnt-young-shakespeare-will-teaser-trailer/
5. http://ew.com/recap/will-series-premiere/
6. Edmondson, *Finding Shakespeare's New Place*, xvii, 2.
7. Ibid., 107.

BIBLIOGRAPHY

Abrahamson, G. *Mrs. Shay Did It!* Wessington Springs, SD: A.L. Webb, 1976.

Ackroyd, P. *Shakespeare: The Biography.* New York, NY: Nan A. Talese, Doubleday, 2005.

Allington, D. "'Power to the reader' or 'degradation of literary taste'? Professional Critics and Amazon Customers as Reviewers of The Inheritance of Loss," *Language and Literature* 25.3 (2016), 254–278.

Altick, R. D. *Paintings from Books: Art and Literature in Britain, 1760–1900.* Columbus, OH: Ohio State University, 1985.

Andrews, J. "Celebrating our Ethnic Ways," *South Dakota Magazine* (May/June 2009), 49–54.

"Ann Hathaway's Cottage," *The Illustrated American* (10 September 1892), 162.

"Anne Hathaway's Cottage," *All the Year Round* (30 April 1892), 420.

Aune, M. G. "Crossing the Border: Shakespeare Biography, Academic Celebrity, and the Reception of *Will in the World*," *Borrowers and Lenders* 2.2 (Fall/Winter 2006).

Backscheider, P. R. *Reflections on Biography.* Oxford: Oxford University Press, 1999.

Baekeland, L. H. "A Family Motor Tour through Europe," *The Horseless Age* 19 (1907), 508.

Barton, A. "The One and Only," *The New York Review of Books*, 11 May 2006.

Batchelor, J., ed. *The Art of Literary Biography.* Oxford: Oxford Clarendon Press, 1995.

Bate, J. *Soul of the Age: A Biography of the Mind of William Shakespeare.* London: Viking, 2008; New York, NY: Random House, 2009.

"Faking It: Shakespeare and the 1790s," in *Literature and Censorship*, ed. Nigel Smith. Woodbridge, Suffolk: D.S. Brewer, 1993.

Bearman, R. "Anne Hathaway's Cottage," in *The Oxford Companion to Shakespeare*, ed. Michael Dobson, Stanley Wells, Will Sharpe, and Erin Sullivan. Oxford: Oxford University Press, 2015.

"Shakespeare's Purchase of New Place," *Shakespeare Quarterly* 63.4 (2012a), 465–486.

"Thomas Greene: Town Clerk and Shakespeare's Lodger," *Shakespeare Survey* 65 (2012b), 290–305.

Shakespeare in the Stratford Records. Trowbridge, Wiltshire: Alan Sutton Publishing, 1994.

Bellew, J. C. M. *Shakespeare's Home at New Place, Stratford-upon-Avon.* London: Virtue Brothers, 1863.

Bennett, F. W. *Anne Hathaway's Cottage: Its History, Contents and Traditions*, n.p., 1921.

Bennett, J. *Shakespeare's Gardens.* London: Frances Lincoln, 2016.

Bennett, K., ed. *John Aubrey: Brief Lives.* Oxford: Oxford University Press, 2015.

"Shakespeare's Monument at Stratford: A New Seventeenth-Century Account," *Notes and Queries* 47.4 (December 2000), 464.

Benton, C. F. *Woman's Club Work and Programs, or First Aid to Club Women.* Boston, MA: Dana Estes Publishers, 1913.

Berkman, P. *Her Infinite Variety: Stories of Shakespeare and the Women He Loved.* New York, NY: Simon and Schuster, 2001.

Berry, Elder C. G. "Stratford-on-Avon," *Improvement Era* 3.9 (July 1900), 689–690.

Bevan, A. http://blog.nationalarchives.gov.uk/blog/shakespeares-will-new-interpretation/.

Bevan, A. and D. Foster. "Shakespeare's Original Will: A Re-Reading, and a Reflection on Interdisciplinary Research within Archives," *Archives* 51 (2016), 8–34.

Bevington, D. *Shakespeare and Biography.* Oxford: Oxford University Press, 2010.

Biographia Britannica: or, the Lives of the most Eminent Persons who have Flourished in Great Britain and Ireland. London: J. Walthoe, 1763.

Blind, M. *The Poetical Works of Mathilde Blind,* ed. Arthur Symons. London, 1900.

Booth, A. *Homes and Haunts: Touring Writers' Shrines and Countries.* Oxford: Oxford University Press, 2016.

Bowsher, J. and P. Miller. *The Rose and the Globe: Playhouses of Shakespeare's Bankside, Southwark, Excavations 1988–91.* London: Museum of London Archaeology, 2009.

Bradford, G. *Biography and the Human Heart.* Boston, MA: Houghton Mifflin, 1932.

Brady, F. and F. A. Pottle, eds. *Boswell in Search of a Wife, 1766–1769.* New York, NY: McGraw-Hill, 1959.

Brandes, G. *William Shakespeare: A Critical Study.* London: Heinemann, 1898.

Brassington, W. S. "Notes on the Old Houses in Stratford-upon-Avon," Birmingham and Midland Institute, Birmingham Archaeological Society, Transactions, Excursions, and Reports for 1898.

Brinkworth, E. R. C. *Shakespeare and the Bawdy Court of Stratford.* London: Phillimore, 1972.

Brophy, J. *Gentleman of Stratford.* New York, NY: Harper, 1939.

Brown, I. "Miss Willmott's Ghost," *The Independent,* 11 September 1999.

The Women in Shakespeare's Life. London: The Bodley Head, 1968.

How Shakespeare Spent the Day. New York, NY: Hill and Wang, 1963.

Burgess, A. *Shakespeare.* London: Jonathan Cape, 1970.

Nothing Like the Sun: A Story of Shakespeare's Love Life. New York: W.W. Norton, 1964.

"Genesis and Headache," in *Afterwords,* ed. Thomas McCormack. New York, NY: Harper and Row, 1969.

Burt, R., ed. *Shakespeares After Shakespeare: An Encyclopedia of the Bard in Mass Media and Popular Culture,* 2 vols. Westport, CT: Greenwood Press, 2007.

Butler, E. H. "Shakespeare Through the Imaginative Writers," *The English Journal* 30.9 (1941), 749–753.

Cain, B. *Equivocation.* New York, NY: Dramatists Play Service, 2014.

Callaghan, D. and S. Gossett, ed. *Shakespeare in our Time: A Shakespeare Association of America Collection.* London: Bloomsbury, 2016.

Calvo, C. and C. Kahn, *Celebrating Shakespeare: Commemoration and Cultural Memory.* Cambridge: Cambridge University Press, 2015.

Carlton, G. *The Wooing of Anne Hathaway.* London: The Mitre Press, 1938.

Chambers, E. K. *William Shakespeare: A Study of Facts and Problems.* Oxford: Clarendon, 1930.

Chartier, R. "Everything and Nothing: The Many Lives of William Shakespeare," *Journal of Early Modern Studies* 5 (2016), 17–26.

Chetwood, W. *A General History of the Stage*. London, 1749.

Clapp, G. W. *The Life and Work of James Leon Williams*. New York, NY: The Dental Digest, 1925.

Cohn, D. "Signposts of Fictionality: A Narratological Perspective," *Poetics Today* 11. 4 (1990), 775–804.

Collins, F. M. and J. Graham. "The Twentieth Century: Giving Everybody a History," in *Historical Fiction for Children: Capturing the Past*, ed. F. M. Collins and J. Graham. London: David Fulton, 2001, 10–22.

Conrad, P. "Dr. Greer on the Warpath," *The Observer*, 2 September 2007.

Cowden Clarke, M. "Shakespeare as the Girl's Friend," in *Shakespeariana* 4 (1887), 355–356.

"A Biographical Sketch of William Shakespeare," in *The Complete Works of William Shakespeare, from the Text of Johnson, Steevens, and Reed*. Edinburgh, 1864.

Cowden Clarke, M. ed., *Shakespeare's Works, Edited, with a Scrupulous Revision of the Text*. New York, NY, and London, 1860.

Creswell, T. *Place: A Short Introduction*. Malden, MA: Blackwell, 2004.

Cummings, B. "Last Words: The Biographemes of Shakespeare," *Shakespeare Quarterly* 65.4 (2014), 482–490.

"Shakespeare, Biography, and Anti-Biography," Shakespeare's Birthday Lecture 2014, given at the Folger Shakespeare Library, 3 April 2014.

Deelman, C. *The Great Shakespeare Jubilee*. New York, NY: Viking Press, 1964.

de Grazia, M. "Shakespeare's Anecdotal Character," *Shakespeare Survey* 68 (2015), 1–14.

Shakespeare Verbatim: The Reproduction of Authenticity and the 1790 Apparatus. Oxford: Clarendon, 1991.

de Groot, J. *The Historical Novel*. London: Routledge, 2009.

DiPietro, C. *Shakespeare and Modernism*. Cambridge: Cambridge University Press, 2006.

Deutsch, H. *Loving Dr. Johnson*. Chicago, IL: University of Chicago Press, 2005.

DeVoto, B. "The Skeptical Biographer," *Harper's Magazine* (January 1933), 181–192.

Dibdin, E. R. "Anne Hathaway," *Notes and Queries*, 7th series, (29 May 1886), 434.

Dobson, M. "Shakespeare as a Literary Character," in *The Oxford Companion to Shakespeare*, ed. Stanley Wells and Erin Sullivan. Oxford: Oxford University Press, 2015.

"'Dwarf-Basher.' Rev. of *Edmond Malone, Shakespearean Scholar: A Literary Biography*, by Peter Martin," *London Review of Books* 17.11 (1995), 12–13.

"Bowdler and Britannia: Shakespeare and the National Libido," *Shakespeare Survey* 46 (1993), 137–144.

The Making of the National Poet. Oxford: Oxford University Press, 1992.

Döring, T. and E. Fernie, "Introduction: Something Rich and Strange," in *Thomas Mann and Shakespeare: Something Rich and Strange*. London: Bloomsbury, 2015.

Dowden, E. *Introduction to Shakespeare*. New York, NY: Charles Scribner's Sons, 1901.

Drake, N. *Shakespeare and His Times: Including the Biography of the Poet*. London: T. Cadell and W. Davies, 1817.

Duffy, C. A. *The World's Wife*. New York, NY: Faber and Faber, 1999.

Dugdale, W. *The Antiquities of Warwickshire Illustrated*. London: Thomas Rarren, 1656.

Duncan-Jones, K. *Ungentle Shakespeare: Scenes from his Life*. London: Arden, 2001.

Dyce, A. "Memoir of Shakespeare," in *The Poems of Shakespeare*. London: W. Pickering, 1832.

Eccles, M. *Shakespeare in Warwickshire*. Madison, WI: University of Wisconsin Press, 1961.

Edmond, M. *Rare Sir William Davenant*. Manchester: Manchester University Press, 1989.

Edmondson, P. "Writing and Re-Writing Shakespeare's Life: A Roundtable Discussion with Margreta de Grazia, Katherine Scheil, James Shapiro, and Stanley Wells," *Shakespeare Survey* 70 (2017), 58–66.

"A Renaissance for New Place in Shakespearean Biography?" *Critical Survey* 25.1 (2013), 90–98.

Edmondson, P., K. Colls, and W. Mitchell, *Finding Shakespeare's New Place: An Archaeological Biography*. Manchester: Manchester University Press, 2016.

Edmondson, P. and S. Wells, eds. *The Shakespeare Circle*. Cambridge: Cambridge University Press, 2015.

Ellis, D. *The Truth about William Shakespeare: Fact, Fiction and Modern Biographies*. Edinburgh: Edinburgh University Press, 2012.

That Man Shakespeare: Icon of Modern Culture. Robertsbridge: Helm Information, 2005.

Endy, C. "Travel and World Power: Americans in Europe, 1890–1917," *Diplomatic History* 22.4 (1998), 565–594.

England, M. W. *Garrick and Stratford*. New York, NY: New York Public Library, 1962.

Engler, B. "Stratford and the Canonization of Shakespeare," *European Journal of English Studies* 1.3 (1997), 354–366.

Everett, B. "Read him, therefore," *Times Literary Supplement* 17 August 2007.

Fairholt, F. W. *The Home of Shakspere: Illustrated and Described*. New York, NY: Williams Brothers, 1848.

Fielitz, S., ed. *Literature as History/History as Literature: Fact and Fiction in Medieval to Eighteenth-Century British Literature*. Frankfurt: Peter Lang, 2007.

Fogg, N. *Stratford: A Town at War, 1914–1945*. Gloucester: Sutton Publishing, 2008.

"The Fortnightly Shakespeare Club," *The American Shakespeare Magazine* 3 (January 1897), 26.

Fox, L. "An Early Copy of Shakespeare's Will," *Shakespeare Survey* 4 (1951), 69–77.

The Shakespeare Birthplace Trust: A Personal Memoir. Norwich: Jarrold Publishing, 1997.

Franssen, P. *Shakespeare's Literary Lives: The Author as Character in Fiction and Film*. Cambridge: Cambridge University Press, 2016.

Franssen, P. and A. J. Hoenselaars, eds. *The Author as Character: Representing Historical Writers in Western Literature*. London: Associated University Presses, 1999.

Freed, A. *The Beard of Avon*. New York, NY: Samuel French, 2004.

Fripp, E. I. *Shakespeare, Man and Artist*. London: Oxford University Press, 1938.

Shakespeare's Haunts. London: Oxford University Press, 1929.

Shakespeare's Stratford. London: Oxford University Press, 1928.

Friswell, J. H. *Life Portraits of William Shakspeare: A History of the Various Representations of the Poet, with an examination into their authenticity*. London: Sampson Low, Son, and Marston, 1864.

Garrick, D. *The Private Correspondence of David Garrick*, 2 vols. London: Henry Colburn and Richard Bentley, 1831.

An Ode upon Dedicating a Building, and Erecting a Statue, to Shakespeare, at Stratford upon Avon. London, 1769.

Gibson, W. *A Cry of Players: A Play.* New York, NY: Dramatists Play Service, 1969.

Gifford, D. *Ulysses Annotated: Notes for James Joyce's Ulysses.* Berkeley, CA: University of California Press, 1988.

Giles, J. *Parlour and Suburb: Domestic Identities, Class, Femininity, and Modernity.* Oxford: Oxford University Press, 2004.

Gonzalez, J. M. and H. Klein, eds. *Shakespeare and Spain.* Lewiston, NY: Edwin Mellen Press, 2002.

Gray, J. W. *Shakespeare's Marriage: His Departure from Stratford and Other Incidents in His Life.* London: Chapman and Hall, 1905.

Greenblatt, S. *Will in the World: How Shakespeare became Shakespeare.* New York, NY: W.W. Norton, 2004.

Greer, G. *Shakespeare's Wife.* London: Bloomsbury, 2007.

Gregor, K. *Shakespeare in the Spanish Theatre: 1772 to the Present.* London: Continuum, 2010.

Hackett, H. *Shakespeare and Elizabeth: The Meeting of Two Myths.* Princeton, NJ: Princeton University Press, 2009.

Hadfield, A. "William Shakespeare, My New Best Friend?" *Journal of Early Modern Studies* 5 (2016), 53–68.

"Why Does Literary Biography Matter?" *Shakespeare Quarterly* 65.4 (2014), 371–378.

Hall, L. *Shakespeare in Love.* London: Faber and Faber, 2014.

Halliwell-Phillipps, J. O. *Outlines of the Life of Shakespeare.* London: Longmans, 1887.

Original Collections on Shakespeare and Stratford-on-Avon, by John Jordan the Stratford Poet . . . About the year 1780. London: Thomas Richards, 1864.

An Historical Account of the New Place, Stratford-Upon-Avon. London: J. E. Adlard, 1864.

Handbook for Visitors to Stratford-upon-Avon. Stratford-upon-Avon: F. & E. Ward, 1851.

Harman, H. P. "Shakespeare at Oxford," *Shakespeariana* (1892), 115–116.

Harper, K. *Mistress Shakespeare.* New York, NY: Penguin, 2009.

Harper's New Monthly Magazine 58 (May 1879), 874.

Harris, F. *The Women of Shakespeare.* London: Methuen, 1911.

The Man Shakespeare and his Tragic Life Story. New York, NY: Mitchell Kennerley, 1909.

Hayes, N. and J. Hill, eds. *"Millions Like Us"?: British Culture in the Second World War.* Liverpool: Liverpool University Press, 1999.

Helsinger, E. K. *Rural Scenes and National Representation: Britain, 1815–1850.* Princeton, NJ: Princeton University Press, 1997.

Hodgdon, B. *The Shakespeare Trade: Performances and Appropriations.* Philadelphia: University of Pennsylvania Press, 1998.

Hoenselaars, T. "Frank Harris, Bardolatry and Wagnerism," in *Metamorphosing Shakespeare: Mutual Illuminations of the Arts*, ed. Patricia Kennan and Mariangela Tempera. Bologna: Clueb, 2004.

Holderness, G. "Stratford Revisited," in Martin Prochàzka, ed., *Renaissance Shakespeare/Shakespeare Renaissances.* Dover, DE: University of Delaware Press, 2013.

Nine Lives of William Shakespeare. London: Continuum, 2011.

Honan, P. "To Change the Picture of Shakespeare Biography," *Critical Survey* 21.3 (2009), 103–106.

Shakespeare: A Life. Oxford: Oxford University Press, 1999.

Honigmann, E. A. J. "Tiger Shakespeare and Gentle Shakespeare," *Modern Language Review* 107 (2012), 699–711.

John Weever. New York, NY: St. Martin's Press, 1987.

Hooks, A. G. *Selling Shakespeare: Biography, Bibliography, and the Book Trade.* Cambridge: Cambridge University Press, 2016.

Horsler, V. *Shakespeare's Church: A Parish for the World.* London: Third Millennium, 2010.

Howard, J. *The Life of Henry Ward Beecher.* Philadelphia, PA: Hubbard Brothers, 1887.

Howitt, W. *Visits to Remarkable Places: Old Halls, Battle-Fields, and Scenes Illustrative of Striking Passages in English History and Poetry.* London: Longman, Brown, Green, 1840.

Hubbard, E. *Good Men and Great. Little Journeys to the Homes of the Great.* Cleveland, OH: World, 1928.

Hughes, A. "Religion and Society in Stratford Upon Avon, 1619–1638," *Midland History* 19 (1994), 58–85.

Hutton, W. H. *Highways and Byways in Shakespeare's Country.* London: Macmillan, 1914.

Innes, R. "Shottery Post Office in Wartime," WW2 People's War Oral History project, 18 April 2005.

Ireland, S. *Miscellaneous Papers.* London: Cooper and Graham, 1796.

Picturesque Views on the Upper, or Warwickshire Avon. London: R. Faulder and T. Egerton, 1795.

Irving, W. *The Sketch Book of Geoffrey Crayon, Gent.* New York, NY: Putnam, 1820.

Isherwood, C. "If He Can, Above All, to His Own Self Be True," *The New York Times,* 2 March 2010.

Jacob, G. *The Poetical Register: or, the Lives and Characters of the English Dramatick Poets.* London, 1719.

James, H. "The Birthplace," in *Shakespeare in America: An Anthology from the Revolution to Now,* ed. James Shapiro. New York, NY: Penguin, 2013.

Jameson, A. *Shakespeare's Heroines: Characteristics of Women, Moral, Poetical and Historical.* London: Saunders and Otley, 1832.

Johnson, C. L. *Jane Austen's Cults and Cultures.* Chicago, IL: University of Chicago Press, 2012.

Jones, C. "Hard to Care about this Self-aware, Show-business Shakespeare," *Chicago Tribune* 27 September 2012.

Jones, J. *Family Life in Shakespeare's England: Stratford-upon-Avon 1570–1630.* Phoenix Mill, Gloucester: Sutton Publishing, 1996.

Jong, E. *Serenissima.* New York, NY: Dell, 1987.

Joubin, A. A. and E. Rivlin, eds. *Shakespeare and the Ethics of Appropriation.* New York, NY: Palgrave Macmillan, 2014.

Kahan, J. *Reforging Shakespeare: The Story of a Theatrical Scandal.* Bethlehem, PA: Lehigh University Press, 1998.

Kakutani, M. "Shakespeare Attracts a New Pursuer," *New York Times* 1 October 2004.

Keener, J. F. *Biography and the Postmodern Historical Novel.* Lewiston, NY: Edwin Mellen Press, 2001.

Kelly, T. *Second Best Bed: A Romantic Speculation in One Act for Eight Girls.* New York, NY: 1970.

Kemp, T. C. *Birmingham Repertory Theatre: The Playhouse and the Man*. Birmingham: Cornish Brothers, 1948.

Kennan, P. and M. Tempera, eds. *Metamorphosing Shakespeare: Mutual Illuminations of the Arts*. Bologna: Clueb, 2004.

Kleinpaste, K. *Just do it Jessie's Way!: A Story of a Parcel of Land on the Shores of Green Lake, Wisconsin*. K. Kleinpaste, 2003.

Knight, C. *William Shakspere; a Biography*. London: William Clowes and Sons, 1843.

Lackey, M. "The Futures of Biofiction Studies," *a/b: Auto/Biography Studies* 32.2 (2017), 343–346.

The American Biographical Novel. New York, NY: Bloomsbury, 2016.

"Locating and Defining the Bio in Biofiction," *a/b: Auto/Biography Studies* 31.1 (2016), 3–10.

Lackey, M., ed. *Truthful Fictions: Conversations with American Biographical Novelists*. New York, NY: Bloomsbury, 2014.

Lane, J. *John Hall and his Patients: The Medical Practice of Shakespeare's Son-in-Law*. Stratford upon-Avon: The Shakespeare Birthplace Trust, 1996.

Langbaine, G. *The Lives and Characters of the English Dramatick Poets*, ed. Charles Gildon. London, 1698.

An Account of the English Dramatick Poets. London, 1691.

Lanier, D. *Shakespeare and Modern Popular Culture*. Oxford: Oxford University Press, 2002.

Latham, M. "'Serv[ing] under two masters': Virginia Woolf's Afterlives in Contemporary Biofictions," *a/b: Auto/Biography Studies* 27.2 (2012), 354–373.

Lawlor, L. *The Two Loves of Will Shakespeare*. New York, NY: Holiday House, 2006.

Lawrence, C. E. *The Hour of Prospero*. London: Gowans and Gray, 1927.

Leader, Z., ed. *On Life-Writing*. Oxford: Oxford University Press, 2015.

Leahy, W. "'The Dreamscape of Nostalgia': Shakespearean Biography: Too Much Information (but not about Shakespeare)," *Journal of Early Modren Studies* 5 (2016), 31–52.

Lee, S. *A Life of William Shakespeare*. London: Macmillan, 1916.

"Shakespeare, William (1564–1616)," in *The Dictionary of National Biography*, ed. Sidney Lee, vol. 17. London: Smith, Elder, & Co, 1897.

Lennon, T. *The Truth About Ann*. New York, NY: John Day, 1942.

Levenson, J. L. "Shakespeare in Drama since 1990: Vanishing Act," *Shakespeare Survey* 58 (2005), 148–159.

Lewis, B. R. *The Shakespeare Documents*, 2 vols. Stanford, CA: Stanford University Press, 1940.

Lupton, J. R. "Birth Places: Shakespeare's Beliefs / Believing in Shakespeare," *Shakespeare Quarterly* 65.4 (2014), 399–420.

Lynch, D. S. *Loving Literature: A Cultural History*. Chicago, IL, and London: University of Chicago Press, 2015.

Lynch, J. *Deception and Detection in Eighteenth-Century Britain*. Aldershot, Hampshire: Ashgate, 2008.

MacCabe, C. "The Bard as a chat-show celeb," *The Independent* 5 November 2004.

MacKay, E. "Acting Historical with Shakespeare, or, William–Henry Ireland's Oaken Chest," *Shakespeare Survey* 67 (2014), 202–220.

Maguire, L. *Studying Shakespeare: A Guide to the Plays*. Malden, MA: Blackwell, 2004.

Makaryk, I. R. and M. McHugh, eds. *Shakespeare and the Second World War: Memory, Culture, Identity.* Toronto, Ont.: University of Toronto Press, 2012.

Malone, E. *The Plays and Poems of Shakespeare,* ed. J. Boswell. London, 1821.

Supplement to the Edition of Shakespeare's Plays published in 1778 by Samuel Johnson and George Steevens. London, 1780.

Malpass, E. *Sweet Will.* London: Macmillan, 1973.

Maltby, A. *Shakespeare as a Challenge for Literary Biography: A History of Biographies of Shakespeare Since 1898.* Lewiston, NY: Edwin Mellen Press, 2009.

"Manitoba Teachers Abroad," *Canadian Magazine* 36 (November 1910), 25–33.

Marks, P. "A lot to ponder about Shakespeare through 'Equivocation,'" *The Washington Post* 29 November 2011.

Marshall, E. *Shakespeare and his Birthplace.* London: E. Nister; New York, NY: E. P. Dutton, 1890.

Marshall, G. *Shakespeare and Victorian Women.* Cambridge: Cambridge University Press, 2009.

Martin, P. *Edmond Malone, Shakespearean Scholar: A Literary Biography.* Cambridge: Cambridge University Press, 1993.

May, G. *Illustrated Companion-Book to Stratford-upon-Avon.* Evesham, 1847.

McGuinness, F. *Mutabilitie.* London: Faber and Faber, 1997.

McMahan, A. B. *Shakespeare's Love Story, 1580–1609.* Chicago, IL: A. C. McClurg, 1909.

Meyer, C. *Loving Will Shakespeare.* Orlando, FL: Harcourt, 2006.

Mitchell Hodges, L. *The Bard at Home.* n.p., 1916.

Moncrieff, W. T. *Excursion to Stratford upon Avon.* Leamington: Elliston, 1824.

Excursion to Warwick. Leamington: Elliston, 1824.

Moore, M. *The Dial.* 1 December 1909.

Moran, M. M. *The Shakespeare Garden Club: A Fantasy.* New York, NY, 1919.

Morgan, A. and A. W. Bailey. *The Great Experiment: A Shakespearean Fantasy.* Chicago, IL: R. F. Seymour, 1909.

Morgan, A. *Mrs. Shakespeare's Second Marriage.* New York, NY: The Shakespeare Society of New York, 1925.

Morgan, J. *The Secret Life of William Shakespeare.* London: Headline, 2012.

Morgan, C. *"A Happy Holiday": English Canadians and Transatlantic Tourism, 1870–1930.* Toronto, Ont.: University of Toronto Press, 2008.

Morgan, J. *The Secret Life of William Shakespeare.* London: Headline, 2012.

Murphy, A. *Shakespeare in Print.* Cambridge: Cambridge University Press, 2003.

Murphy, O. "Jane Austen's 'Excellent Walker': Pride, Prejudice, and Pedestrianism," *Eighteenth-Century Fiction* 26.1 (2013), 121–142.

Myers, R., M. Harris, and G. Mandelbrote, eds. *Lives in Print: Biography and the Book Trade from the Middle Ages to the 21st Century.* New Castle, DE: Oak Knoll Press, 2002.

Nakamura, L. "'Words with Friends': Socially Networked Reading on Goodreads," *PMLA* 128.1 (2013), 238–243.

Nicoll, A. "Stratford-Upon-Avon a Hundred Years Ago: Extracts from the Travel Diary of the Reverend William Harness," *Shakespeare Survey* 14 (1961), 110–115.

Nodelman, P. *The Hidden Adult: Defining Children's Literature.* Baltimore, MD: Johns Hopkins University Press, 2008.

Norman, M. and T. Stoppard, *Shakespeare in Love: A Screenplay.* New York, NY: Hyperion, 1998.

Nye, R. *Mrs. Shakespeare: The Complete Works.* New York, NY: Arcade, 1993.

The Official Programme of The Tercentenary Festival of the Birth of Shakespeare, To be held at Stratford-upon-Avon, commencing on Saturday, April 23, 1864. London: Cassell, Petter, and Galpin, 1864.

Orlin, L. C. "Anne by Indirection," *Shakespeare Quarterly* 65.4 (2014), 421–454.

Osborne, H. *The Good Men Do: An Indecorous Epilogue, in Plays of the 47 Workshop.* New York, NY: Brentanos, 1918.

Osborne, R. E. *World War II Sites in the United States: A Tour Guide & Directory.* Indianapolis, IN: Riebel-Roque Publishing, 1996.

O'Sullivan, M. J. *Shakespeare's Other Lives: Fictional Depictions of the Bard.* Jefferson, NC: McFarland, 1997.

Paxman, J. "Stop Whingeing about Shakespeare in Love," *The Telegraph* 23 January 1999.

"Pilgrims to the Shrine of Shakespeare: A Chat with Mrs. Hathaway Baker," *The Woman's Signal* (24 January 1895), 50.

Pinsent, P. "'Not for an Age but for all time': The Depiction of Shakespeare in a Selection of Children's Fiction," *New Review of Children's Literature and Librarianship* 10.2 (2004), 115–126.

Pippett, A. "The Sonneteer Was Not All Talk," *The Saturday Review* (17 October 1964), 38.

Pogue, K. E. *Shakespeare's Family.* Westport, CT: Praeger, 2008.

Poingdestre, E. "A Summer Day at Stratford-on-Avon," *Frank Leslie's Popular Monthly* 20 (July–December 1885), 415.

Potter, L. *The Life of William Shakespeare: A Critical Biography.* Chichester: Wiley-Blackwell, 2012.

"Having our Will: Imagination in Recent Shakespeare Biographies," *Shakespeare Survey* 58 (2005), 1–8.

Pringle, R. "Stratford-upon-Avon's First Guide-books," *Warwickshire History* 162 (Winter 2014–15), 72–85.

Procházka, M., A. Hoefele, H. Scolnicov, and M. Dobson, eds. *Renaissance Shakespeare/ Shakespeare Renaissances: Proceedings of the Ninth World Shakespeare Congress.* Newark, DE: University of Delaware Press, 2014.

The Professional Life of Mr. Dibdin. London, 1803.

Pugh, S. *Reading Landscape: Country, City, Capital.* Manchester: Manchester University Press, 1990, 192.

Rackin, P. *Shakespeare and Women.* Oxford: Oxford University Press, 2005.

Rahn, S. "An Evolving Past: The Story of Historical Fiction and Nonfiction for Children," *The Lion and the Unicorn* 15.1 (1991), 1–26.

Reedy, T. "William Dugdale's Monumental Inaccuracies and Shakespeare's Stratford Monument," *Shakespeare Survey* 69 (2016), 380–393.

"William Dugdale on Shakespeare and His Monument," *Shakespeare Quarterly* 66.2: (2015), 188–196.

Rennella, M. and W. Walton. "Planned Serendipity: American Travelers and the Transatlantic Voyage in the Nineteenth and Twentieth Centuries," *Journal of Social History* 38.2 (2004), 365–383.

Ritchie, F. *Women and Shakespeare in the Eighteenth Century.* Cambridge: Cambridge University Press, 2014.

Ritchie, F. and P. Sabor, eds. *Shakespeare in the Eighteenth Century.* Cambridge: Cambridge University Press, 2012.

Roberts, D. *Thomas Betterton.* Cambridge: Cambridge University Press, 2010.

Rodale, M. *Dangerous Books for Girls: The Bad Reputation of Romance Novels Explained.* Maya Rodale, 2015.

Rogers, J. *The Second Best Bed: Shakespeare's Will in a New Light.* Westport, CT: Greenwood Press, 1993.

Roiphe, K. "Reclaiming the Shrew," *The New York Times* 27 April 2008.

Rowe, N. *Some Account of the Life, etc. of Mr. William Shakespear, in The Works of Mr. William Shakespear,* ed. Nicholas Rowe, 6 vols. London: Jacob Tonson, 1709.

Rowlands, A. *Mrs. Shakespeare . . . The Poet's Wife.* Malvern, PA: J. Garnet Miller, 2005.

Rowse, A. L. *Shakespeare the Man.* New York, NY: St. Martin's Press, 1973; 1988.

Rozett, M. T. *Constructing a World: Shakespeare's England and the New Historical Fiction.* Albany, NY: State University of New York Press, 2003.

Rush, C. *Will: A Novel.* Woodstock, NY: Overlook Press, 2007.

Ryan, A. *The Secret Confessions of Anne Shakespeare.* New York, NY: Penguin, 2010.

Salmon, M. "The Cultural Significance of Breastfeeding and Infant Care in Early Modern England and America," *Journal of Social History* 28.2 (1994), 247–269.

Santesso, A. "The Birth of the Birthplace: Bread Street and Literary Tourism before Stratford," *ELH* 71.2 (Summer, 2004), 377–403.

Savage, R. *Minutes and Accounts of the Corporation of Stratford-Upon-Avon and Other Records, 1553–1620.* London: The Dugdale Society, 1924.

Saward, W. T. *William Shakespeare.* London: Elkin Mathews, 1907.

Schabert, I. "Fictional Biography, Factual Biography, and their Contaminations," *Biography* 5.1 (1982), 1–16.

Scheil, K. W. "Hathaway Farm: Commemorating Warwickshire Will Between the Wars," *Shakespeare Survey* 71 (2018), forthcoming.

    She Hath Been Reading: Women and Shakespeare Clubs in America. Ithaca, NY: Cornell University Press, 2012.

Scheil, K. and G. Holderness. "Introduction: Shakespeare and the 'Personal Story,'" *Critical Survey* 21.3 (2009), 1–5.

Schoenbaum, S. *Shakespeare's Lives.* Oxford: Oxford University Press, 1991.

    William Shakespeare: A Compact Documentary Life. Oxford: Oxford University Press, 1977.

    William Shakespeare: A Documentary Life. Oxford: Clarendon, 1975.

Schulz, E. G. *The Ghost in General Patton's Third Army: The Memoirs of Eugene G. Schulz during his Service in the United States Army in World War II.* Xlibris, 2013.

Scott, J. "On Hoaxes, Humbugs, and Fictional Portraiture," *a/b: Auto/Biography Studies* 31.1 (2016), 27–32.

Scott, Sir W. *Woodstock.* London: Longman, Rees, Orme, Brown, and Green, 1826.

Seidenberg, S., M. Sellar, and L. Jones. *You Must Remember This: Songs at the Heart of the War*. London: Boxtree, 1995.

Severn, E. *Anne Hathaway, or Shakespeare in Love*. 3 vols. London: R. Bentley, 1845.

Shakespeare's Garland, Being a collection of new songs, ballads, roundelays, catches, glees, comic-serenatas, &c. performed at the Jubilee at Stratford upon Avon. London: T. Becket, 1769.

Shamas, L. A. *The Other Shakespeare*. Woodstock, IL: Dramatic Publishing, 1981.

Shapiro, J. *Contested Will: Who Wrote Shakespeare?* New York, NY: Simon and Schuster, 2010.

"Toward a New Biography of Shakespeare," *Shakespeare Survey* 58 (2005), 9–14.

Shapiro, L. "Greer Tames the Shrew," *Slate* 31 March 2008.

Shaughnessy, R., ed. *The Cambridge Companion to Shakespeare and Popular Culture*. Cambridge: Cambridge University Press, 2007.

Shelley, H. C. *Shakespeare and Stratford*. London: Simpkin, Marshall Hamilton, Kent, 1913.

Sillars, S. *Shakespeare and the Victorians*. Oxford: Oxford University Press, 2013.

Simon, J. "Bardolatry Made Easy," *New Criterion* April 2005.

"A Spear Reshaken," *New York Magazine* (2 December 1968), 55.

Simpson, F. "New Place: The Only Representation of Shakespeare's House from an Unpublished Manuscript," *Shakespeare Survey* 5 (1952), 55–57.

Sisson, C. J. "Shakespeare's Friends: Hathaways and Burmans at Shottery," *Shakespeare Survey* 12 (1959), 95–106.

Smith, S. G. "A Shakespearean Adventure," *The Chautauquan* 7 (March 1887), 358.

"Society Acts for the Shell-Shocked," *The New York Times* 13 March 1920.

Somerset, C. A. *Shakespeare's Early Days: A Drama in Two Acts*. London: T. H. Lacy, 1829.

Sorelius, G., ed. *Shakespeare and Scandinavia: A Collection of Nordic Studies*. Newark, DE: University of Delaware Press, 2002.

Spence, J. *Observations, Anecdotes, and Characters of Books and Men, Collected from Conversation*, ed. J. M. Osborn. Oxford: Oxford University Press, 1966.

Spencer, C. "Shakespeare in Love, review," *The Telegraph* 23 July 2014.

The Spokesman (November 1922), 101–103.

Steiner, A. "Private Criticism in the Public Sphere: Personal Writing on Literature in Readers' Reviews on Amazon," *Particip@tions* 5.2 (2008).

Stephens, J. *Language and Ideology in Children's Fiction*. Harlow: Longman, 1992.

Stewart, D. *The Boy Who Would be Shakespeare: A Tale of Forgery and Folly*. Cambridge, MA: Da Capo Press, 2010.

Stirling, S. A. *Shakespeare's Bastard: The Life of Sir William Davenant*. Stroud, Gloucestershire: The History Press, 2016.

Stoddard, C. W. "The Shottery Tryst," *The Overland Monthly* 12.5 (May 1874), 406–410.

Stopes, C. C. *Shakespeare's Warwickshire Contemporaries*. Stratford-upon-Avon: Shakespeare Head Press, 1907.

Shakespeare's Family: Being a Record of the Ancestors and Descendants of William Shakespeare. London: Elliot Stock, 1901.

Stowe, H. B. *Sunny Memories of Foreign Lands*. London: Sampson Low, Son and Co., 1854.

Styles, P. "The Borough of Stratford-Upon-Avon and the Parish of Alveston," in *Victoria County History of Warwickshire*. London: Oxford University Press, 1946.

"A Summer School in Europe," *Moderator-Topics* 28.32 (April 1908), 630–631.

Taylor, G. *Reinventing Shakespeare: A Cultural History from the Restoration to the Present.* Oxford: Oxford University Press, 1991.

"The Secret Life of William Shakespeare," by Jude Morgan, *The Washington Post* 3 April 2014.

"Stephen, Will and Gary Too," *The Guardian* 9 October 2004.

Taylor, J. *A Dream of England: Landscape, Photography, and the Tourist's Imagination.* Manchester: Manchester University Press, 1994.

Tearle, C. *Rambles with an American.* London: Mills & Boon, 1910.

Tennant, P. *The Civil War in Stratford-Upon-Avon: Conflict and Community in South Warwickshire, 1642–1646.* Gloucestershire: Alan Sutton, 1996.

Theobald, L. *The Works of Shakespeare . . . Collated with the Oldest Copies, and Corrected: With Notes, Explanatory, and Critical,* ed. Lewis Theobald, 8 vols. London, 1752.

Thiessen, V. *Shakespeare's Will.* Toronto, Ont.: Playwrights Canada Press, 2005.

Thomas, J. *Shakespeare's Shrine: The Bard's Birthplace and the Invention of Stratford-upon-Avon.* Philadelphia, PA: University of Pennsylvania Press, 2012.

Thomas, R. McG., Jr. "A. L. Rowse, Masterly Shakespeare Scholar, Dies at 93," *The New York Times* 6 October 1997.

Tiffany, G. *Will: A Novel.* New York, NY: Turnaround, 2005.

Traub, V., ed. *The Oxford Handbook of Shakespeare and Embodiment: Gender, Sexuality, and Race.* Oxford: Oxford University Press, 2016.

Valdivieso, S. M. "Postmodern Recreations of the Renaissance: Robert Nye's fictional biographies of William Shakespeare," *SEDERI* 15 (2005), 43–62.

Vickers, B. *William Shakespeare: The Critical Heritage.* London: Routledge, 1979.

Wagner-Martin, L. *Telling Women's Lives: The New Biography.* New Brunswick, NJ: Rutgers University Press, 1994.

Wallace, A. D. *Walking, Literature, and English Culture: The Origins and Uses of Peripatetic in the Nineteenth Century.* Oxford: Clarendon, 1993.

Wallace, C. W. "Shakespeare as a man Among Men," *Harper's Monthly Magazine* 70 (March 1910), 489–510.

Walter, J. *Shakespeare's True Life.* London: James Walter, 1890.

Ward and Lock's Illustrated Guide to the Popular History of Leamington & Warwick, with Excursions to Kenilworth, Stratford-on-Avon. Leamington: Thomas Simmons, 1888.

Ward, H. S. and C. W. Ward. *Shakespeare's Town and Times.* New York, NY: Truslove and Comba, 1896.

Watson, N. J., ed. *Literary Tourism and Nineteenth-Century Culture.* Basingstoke: Palgrave Macmillan, 2009.

The Literary Tourist: Readers and Places in Romantic and Victorian Britain. Basingstoke and New York, NY: Palgrave Macmillan, 2006.

Weis, R. *Shakespeare Revealed: A Biography.* London: John Murray, 2007.

Wells, E. L. "Stratford on Avon," *Illinois School Journal* 3.5 (September 1883), 113.

Wells, S. *Shakespeare, Sex, and Love.* Oxford: Oxford University Press, 2012.

"Mistress Shakespeare." *The New York Review of Books* 55.6 (17 April 2008).

Shakespeare for All Time. Oxford: Oxford University Press, 2003.

West, W. *The History, Topography, and Directory of Warwickshire.* Birmingham: R. Wrightson, 1830.

Westover, C. C. *The Romance of Gentle Will: A Hitherto Unpublished Chapter in the Story of the Love of the Immortal Bard.* New York, NY: Neale Publishing, 1905.

Wheler, R. B. *A Guide to Stratford-upon-Avon*. Stratford: J. Ward, 1814.

History and Antiquities of Stratford-Upon-Avon. Stratford-upon-Avon: J. Ward, 1806.

White, R. G. *Memoirs of the Life of William Shakespeare*. Boston, MA: Little, Brown and Co., 1865.

Whitfield, C. "Four Town Clerks of Stratford on Avon, 1603–1625," *Notes and Queries* 11 (1964), 251–261.

Williard, M. S. *Letters from a Tar Heel Traveler in Mediterranean Countries*. Oxford: Oxford Orphan Asylum, 1907.

Wilson, A. "Waves and Wills: Vern Thiessen's *Shakespeare's Will*," *Borrowers and Lenders* 3 (Fall/Winter 2007).

Wilson, D. "Anne Hathaway: A Dialogue," *Canadian Monthly and National Review* 1 (1872), 19–26.

Winfield, J. *My Name is Will: A Novel of Sex, Drugs, and Shakespeare*. New York, NY: Twelve, 2008.

Winter, W. *Shakespeare's England, Illustrated edition*. New York, NY: Moffat, Yard and Company, 1910.

Old Shrines and Ivy. New York, NY: Macmillan, 1894.

The Stage Life of Mary Anderson. New York, NY: George J. Coombes, 1886.

Wood, A. *Athenae Oxonienses*, ed. Philip Bliss, 4 vols. London: F. C. and J. Rivington, 1813–1820.

Worthen, W. B. "Jan Kott, Shakespeare our Contemporary," *Modern Theatre* 25.2 (2010), 91.

Wu, D. "On Mrs. Shakespeare's Kitchen Table," *The Telegraph* 1 September 2007.

Web Resources

http://bardfilm.blogspot.com/2014/03/book-note-grace-tiffanys-will-novel.html

http://bippityboppitybook.blogspot.com/2010/11/review-secret-confessions-of-anne.html

http://booknaround.blogspot.com/search?q=arliss+ryan.

http://freshfiction.com/review.php?id=22755

http://historical-fiction.com/?tag=arliss-ryan

http://historical-fiction.com/review-the-secret-confessions-of-anne-shakespeare/

http://list.historicengland.org.uk/resultsingle.aspx?uid=1001184

http://list.historicengland.org.uk/resultsingle.aspx?uid=1298551

http://marymackey.com/shakespeare-in-historical-fiction/

http://susancoventry.blogspot.com/2011/05/escape-to-past-with-secret-confessions.html

https://uiowa.edu/shakespeareiniowa/article/shakespeare-and-women

www.anne-hathaways-cottage.com/

www.arlissryan.com/books/reviews-of-the-secret-confessions-of-anne-shakespeare/

www.bbc.co.uk/events/ehw2mb/live/c96v4 f

www.book-club-queen.com/mistress-shakespeare.html

www.canadianshakespeares.ca.

www.canadianshakespeares.ca/a_goodmen.cfm

www.featheredquill.com/reviews/biographies/ryan.shtml

www.goodreads.com/book/show/1111242.Will

www.goodreads.com/book/show/1675779.Her_Infinite_Variety
www.goodreads.com/book/show/22571611-the-tuto
www.goodreads.com/book/show/3864007-mistress-shakespeare
www.goodreads.com/book/show/7098379-the-secret-confessions-of-anne-shakespeare
www.karenharperauthor.com/index.html
www.karenharperauthor.com/mistress_shakespeare.html
www.librarything.com/work/259326/reviews/28311936
www.memoriesfrombooks.com/2015/02/the-tutor.html
www.parksandgardens.org/places-and-people/site/101?preview=1
www.shakespeare.org.uk/about-us/press-information/news/perform-romeo-and-juliet.html
www.shakespeare.org.uk/visit-the-houses/anne-hathaways-cottage-amp-gardens/beautiful-cottage-gardens.html
www.sunrisepm.com/rentalAHC_23/rental23.html
www.thelifephotographic.com/?Mistress-Shakespeare–A-Novel.pdf
www.womansday.com/life/entertainment/mistress-shakespeare-by-karen-harper#slide-4

INDEX